karajan

NOTES ON A CAREER

NOTES ON A CAREER

karajan

ROBERT C. BACHMANN

TRANSLATED BY SHAUN WHITESIDE

WITH AN AFTERWORD BY MICHAEL TANNER

 QUARTET BOOKS

Published in Great Britain by Quartet Books Limited 1990
A member of the Namara Group
27/29 Goodge Street, London W1P 1FD

British Library Cataloguing in Publication Data
Bachmann, Robert C. *1944–*
    Karajan : notes on a career.
    1. Music. Conducting. Karajan, Herbert von, 1908–
    I. Title   II. Karajan. *English*
    784.2092
                 ISBN 0–7043–2754–6

Phototypeset by Input Typesetting Ltd, London
Printed and bound in Great Britain by
BPCC Hazell Books
Aylesbury, Bucks, England
Member of BPCC Ltd.

Contents

Acknowledgements

I should like to thank everyone who has contributed to the success of this book. I am especially grateful to Frau Elisabeth Prachensky, psychologist, Basle, for her shrewd advice and valuable suggestions and for looking through the manuscript; Frau Lovice Ullein Reviczky, Zurich, and all the others, too numerous to mention, who lent me inspiration; and Dr Josef Augstein, solicitor, Hanover, for his legal advice.

Introduction

Maestro assoluto, Meister aller Klassen, Generalissimo, Europe's leading conductor, Pontifex Maximus of music theatre, seducer, magician, wonder, riddle, myth – such and similar terms were used by advertisers, critics and music promoters to describe a phenomenon, a musical figure of the century who provoked violent dissent and hysterical enthusiasm to the same degree: Herbert von Karajan. Between these two poles of rejection and approval this conductor, always controversial, had a career unparalleled in the history of the performing artist, one so extraordinary as to explode traditional standards. Never in the history of music has any performing artist enjoyed the omnipotence granted to Herbert von Karajan.

No conductor has ever soared to greater heights of glory, fame and public attention. Karajan consorted with the world's most powerful men as if he were among their number, and imperiously set himself at their head even where he seemed to be out of his own domain. But where that domain is domination *per se*, it is not exclusively restricted to the field of art.

This most prominent of European conductors held more positions of power than any of his predecessors or contemporaries. He sought to become extraordinary, and he achieved his aim: at its greatest point, his empire reached from Vienna via Berlin, Salzburg and Milan to London. In 1967, in Salzburg, he finally founded a one-man festival combining opera and concerts, the Easter Festival, leading to impressive artistic and culturally political achievements. In the artistic sphere, combining the roles of conductor, director and manager in one, he most significantly

1

staged Richard Wagner's music dramas in a presentation appropriate to the monumental dimensions of the stage in the Großes Festspielhaus, and brought the interpretation of Wagner from an undifferentiated and bombastic sound to a transparent and pared-down rendering. And, in terms of cultural politics, he was the first to recognize the necessity of the media in art.

Karajan was the incarnation a new type of interpreter, whose artistic world recognized the media of modern technology as a self-evident necessity. He had a greater influence than any other single figure on the transmission and communication of music. The gramophone records and the music films which he directed himself have made his style of interpretation ubiquitous. His intensive work in recording studios, on records and films, was emphatically future-oriented, aimed as it was at exploitation through mass media such as video cassettes, video discs and worldwide television, media whose full scope will be revealed only over the decades to come. It is beyond question that the mass-production of banks of sound and images was not aimed solely at the present day, but also at the future. Karajan worked towards total, permanent musical communication after his death; the 'democratization' of the enjoyment of art by means of the mass media.

The epitome of what a conductor can achieve in terms of fame and popularity, Karajan set his goals higher than any other conductors before or since: along with his many-faceted artistic activity he devoted himself to the care of coming generations as well as researching into the physical and psychological processes involved in playing and listening to music. The Herbert von Karajan Foundation, which he founded in 1968, assumed the task of carrying out basic research in the fields of music therapy and musical reception, in a research institute for experimental musical psychology established for that purpose at the Psychological Institute of Salzburg University. The foundation also holds competitions for young conductors and youth orchestras and singing seminars in collaboration with famous singing teachers. In setting up an orchestral academy with the Berlin Philharmonic Orchestra, Karajan also sought to provide more focused training and encouragement for the younger generation of qualified musicians than that propagated at the established conservatoires and music colleges.

If the musician Karajan proved to be a pioneer in these fields, as an interpreter he was the custodian of a great musical tradition. As the artistic archetype of a highly technologized century, he declared his devotion, in a world in which beauty has grown rare, to the ideal of aesthetic beauty through harmony. This artistic declaration of faith probably also helps to explain Karajan's rather regressive repertoire, which often took notice of contemporary music only when it had already proven its quality elsewhere. The conductor's *ius primae noctis*, the right to the first performance, the first contact with a work – often amounting to a rape of that work – was something that he exploited very seldom. That may also be due to the fact that contemporary music did not provide him with the range of works necessary to nourish his delight in the sublime beauty of sound and his artistic cult of the sensualism of sound. Indisputably, his repertoire, which resembled a tour through the museum of Western music covering a very limited period of time, showed a tendency towards petrification, a regression, in fact, into antiquarianism.

In building up what is described as his musical empire, Karajan was spared nothing, mistakes and failures included. He worked his way up from the bottom rung of the conducting ladder, as general factotum, coach and *répétiteur* – doggedly at first, and subsequently relying on good fortune of various kinds. He worked for his fame with tenacity, quiet fanaticism, calculation, intense ambition and unflagging industry. A superior craftsmanship, a fanatical devotion to work and the urge for perfection were at the root of his successes. As a paragon of strong will and a high level of achievement and energy, he showed singular persistence, even monomaniac tenacity, in the organization of his career, which he shaped according to the standards of his personal curriculum vitae and an ideology of absolute will.

Karajan made the principle 'power through achievement' the theme of his life. His underlying drive was the desire for masculinity, and he orchestrated his world in terms of this desire. The urge constantly to remain on top, to be at the forefront, to be the first, the best or the greatest seems always to have been a compulsion, and it was an urge expressed in a rigorous demand for achievement.

Another thing manifested in his art was his innate penchant for luxury, to satisfy which the very best was only just good enough. This went hand in hand with a need constantly to portray himself in the best possible light, which found expression just as much in his artistic as in his private life. It has therefore not always been easy to determine whether Karajan, the master of the pose that has now come to seem entirely natural, was portraying himself as he wished to be seen, or whether he was presenting himself as he thought people might like to see him. Never before in musical history has the concept of an 'image' been introduced into musical life and exploited for commercial ends with such grandeur, ambition and tenacity.

In a letter to the former General Director of the Metropolitan Opera, New York, Sir Rudolf Bing, he once confessed that 'regardless of when and where I am conducting, my attitude to my work is always based on the standard of a festival *en permanence*'.[1] For decades what Karajan offered us was the festival of self-dramatization taken to its highest level. Addicted to the exhilaration of greatness through music, he lived entirely within music, and, cut off from reality, he made excursions from music into life. Herbert von Karajan's solo attempt, intoxicated with music, to accomplish the perilous journey towards the realization of his artistic visions was inseparable from the aspect of power. Admittedly this power was not only rooted in a kind of power-thinking; it was also, to a considerable extent, based on organization.

'True efficiency can only come about through precise organization,' said Karajan, who, as a big businessman in the field of music could finally call upon a perfectly organized apparatus which gave him the freedom to fulfil his aspirations as an artist. The magic of his charisma and his superior ability also created a myth that was felt far beyond Karajan's actual sphere of influence, in areas in which art music is seen as the luxury of an élite. His name is world-famous. Today Karajan is a concept even to people who have never heard a symphonic concert. But they are precisely the ones whom he wished to lead to music through his intense efforts towards the mass communication of it.

The fascination that he exuded in turn reflected back on him, making him the epitome of the musical star. Probably no interpreter of our time featured in so many headlines, not all of which were directly related to his artistic activity. This may be due to the fact that Karajan approached everything he set out to do with a demand for thoroughness. He was a perfectionist in everything that interested him, as a pilot just as much as a sailor. The epitome of suppleness and an insatiable urge for activity, there was something almost timeless about him, something eternally young, even boyish, like the type of the *puer aeternus*, the apparently precocious, eternal adolescent, who never fully develops, and who loses himself in the quest for his own identity.

Like no other, he managed to sustain his image as a constant sensation. Karajan's performances in the world's concert halls and

4

opera houses were always programmed sensations. They bore the mark of consecrating festivals, of seductive manifestations from which no one was able or willing to escape. Conducting virtuoso, festival entrepreneur, maestro and manager, Karajan, flattered and celebrated by the business clan that made up the festival audience, enjoyed his fame to the full. Blue-eyed and blue-blooded, the Messiah of beautiful sound, he conducted his way into the annals of musical history.

Musical history, note. Not world history, where a type of Karajan's mould, with his urge for achievement and his will to power, could take a leading role given the right circumstances. No – Karajan was a protagonist, a player and a pioneer, taking the lead among showmen and actors, in the resonant realm of music, which he exploited and commanded both artistically and commercially, at least within the limits of performed music. But Karajan would not have been the person he was if he had not also wished to control the writing of musical history – at least as far as it concerned his own life, which was, to a large extent, the history of his career. For anyone driven by a personal urge for power, anyone who, in his febrile and consuming hunger for power, calculatedly treated himself and his audience not with sobriety but with rapture, suggestion and intoxication, would have wanted to make substantial corrections to this biography where it does not conform in every respect to the demands of the 'image'.

What then comes into play is what I would call the principle of the 'facticide': the principle of suppression, dissimulation, distortion, displacement, the obliteration and attempted erasure of facts, data, events. A facticide is a fact withheld, crippled, mutilated, murdered until it becomes a lie. It is an irrevocable fact, not undone, yet apparently undone and revoked by means of falsification, omission, silence, misrepresentation and mutilation. A facticide is a murdered event. It is a case of invention erasing facts so as to take their place, so that factual events relinquish their status as reality, becoming fictional.

In the literature on Karajan, which has so far taken the form of various astounding and laboured excursions into fact-blurring, obeisance has been done to this principle. Here the biographer becomes a hagiographer, the author of legends of the saints – and no reasonable person would seriously contend that Karajan is numbered among the saints. But the maestro's bright-eyed heralds, with Ernst Haeusserman at their head, followed by Karl Löbl, Paul Robinson and Jacques Lorcey, are bold and brazen enough to try and have us believe this. Perhaps these authors, who for a long time led the field in the shaping of the Karajan legend, have, in their credulous innocence and ardent sympathy, simply swallowed whole the fairytale told them by Karajan, the phoney king. It is possible that each has simply copied the others without ever doubting what they had borrowed, all of which had been presented as truth. Neither is it unthinkable that Karajan served them all up the same stories – we have just as much reason to believe this. With a peculiar sense for spotting weakness, inferiority and susceptibility, Karajan was constantly in search of mouthpieces who soaked up untruths, kitsch and gossip like blotting-paper. With wearying consistency these ingenuous authors' books are primarily litanies of admiration, exoneration and beautification, designed to preserve the purity of the exalted wonder. But it would be a bad thing if these books were to form the image that Karajan's admirers have of him.

Karajan, great in many ways – and it was not a mere fantasy on his part, he really was great – was also a great storyteller. Over the years he honed and polished his fairytales, giving them the sheen of truth. But what is true in the life of an actor who immerses himself so totally in his roles that he can no longer tell truth from fantasy? And how could he do so, when the role he played had replaced an absent substance? Karajan presented his biographers with the entire gamut of problems that the writing of lives can involve. Within the very question of whether a person can be grasped from the facts of his life, in the case of a personality of Karajan's type, there lies the seed of failure. Even if able to check certain facts in Karajan's life, how is the biographer to distinguish between facts and illusions, between truth and fiction in the face of the readily ascertainable, sad and tragic fact that actors live with lies as though they were the truth? If Karajan spoke of his past at particular moments of his life, he was not, to put it politely, overly scrupulous with the truth. For Karajan, truth was what people ought to believe, and he made them believe what they ought to believe: the alternatives to reality that he himself had developed.

A life lived with a false truth is usually not the worst kind there is, and a truth changed to a falsehood often reveals more truth content than a truth that has not been lovingly beautified. For the very process of straightening, altering or retouching biographical facts and events can at the same time reveal what is concealed behind the apparent truth of factuality. But in order to understand this, what is needed from the start is a critical, unprejudiced and

6

independent observer, carefully examining and weighing up his material.

This noble and admittedly rigorous set of demands can certainly not be applied to the quadriga of Karajan's court reporters thus far – Haeusserman, Löbl, Robinson and Lorcey. This four-in-hand, apparently led by the supreme master on the long rein of his phoney truths, belongs in the stable of the apologists, whose dung, rich in the stuff of fairytales, can fertilize nothing but books like *Das Wunder Karajan* by the Viennese 'cultural reporter' Karl Löbl, or the 'portrait of a personality', presented as a diagnosis of Karajan by the director and conductor Ernst Haeusserman. These two authors demonstrate beyond all doubt the limitations of the traditional ways of considering and dealing with biographical material. Their books are a trove of 'interesting' details, prefabricated in Karajan's public-relations word-factories, and released to the public as 'authentic' – and, taken all together, they produce the false picture that Karajan sought to disseminate.

The process is in many respects like a puzzle made of nothing but individual parts from various different jigsaws which, with a degree of care, can be combined into a seeming whole. But it remains a meaningless game, since the puzzle does not, in the end, produce a picture. The montage of biographical fragments, invented details and distorted facts does not produce a conclusive whole. In any case it is an insult to the reader, who is misled by synthetic facts presented as truth.

Haeusserman's *summum opus* is, aside from the incorrect representation of important biographical facts about Karajan, also enriched with remarkable psychoanalytic insights; the kind that might be heard in any Viennese café, or whose equal might be found in the better sort of kitchen, when the servants had made an observation about the psychological determinants of their master's moods; insights of the kind that are these days tossed about at every 'sophisticated' cocktail party, when the representatives of some smart clique or other fall to analysing whichever celebrity happens, as the result of some fatuous fashion, to be considered 'in' at the time.

In Haeusserman's book, then, we read about enlightening matters such as the 'total Karajan complex', 'the quality complex', 'compensation' and 'over-compensation', of 'internal hypochondria' and 'pseudo-hypochondria', of the 'double-entry psyche' and 'inherited negativism', as well as all kinds of speculative stuff about 'the trauma of fear' – which soon really will become a trauma for many of us.[2]

7

Paul Robinson's 'critical evaluation' of Karajan goes a long way down the same track of pseudo-critical parroting and literary apocrypha. Like all the books so far published on the subject of Karajan, this one casts a clear light on the emotional background of its author's need to idealize the object of his investigation. But luckily we have learned, in the meantime, that the way a biography is written is dependent on its author's own biography. But only strong, independent characters, who love the mountain air (because they need it) should busy themselves with this theme, so difficult because it is so complex. For the labyrinth of Karajan's twists and turns can only be puzzled out – if indeed it ever can be – by the detached observer, equipped, as it were, with the searching eye of the eagle circling on high. Things do not become clearer the closer one gets to them.

So what, if anything, do such books prove? They show us that vulgar psychological gossip can quite emphatically not be used to illuminate and explain the specific qualities of the creative person's character and the vicissitudes of his life story. This kind of 'diagnostics' cuts its own throat. It no more deserves to be taken seriously than the argument on which it is based; it is too paltry. Quite in accordance with Karajan's own strategy, books of this kind try to establish and anchor in the consciousness of the musical public an image of the great master that will entice it far from the actual course of his career. For all the crassness of this arrangement, however, they repeatedly succeed in duping other authors of works written to Karajan's greater glory: thus Helena Matheopoulos, in her work *Maestro*, also fell for that Karajan 'facticide' designed to obscure his role in the Third Reich.[3]

One of the foundations of the legend is stubbornness, and the other a fear of the truth. It may be that the portrayal of Karajan as a saint will never hold sway entirely, because certain major decisions in his life showed him to be vulnerable. The writing of legends is also the last thing that Karajan would have wished. He deserves better. For this reason we must continue to protect him from himself and the idolatry of his credulous, ingenuous and portentous literary clique.

This book seeks to provide that kind of protection, and to counteract the formation of the legend. Which brings us to the question of how the author of this book won his contract. A question which, more than any others, those readers who have been misled by the literature on Karajan have a right to see answered. In the end, some demands will be placed on them: they will be asked to rethink certain things, to free themselves from beloved half-truths, to renounce all the lovely stories and fairytales about Herbert von Karajan, who became a myth *en route* to the domination of the world's music.

The story of my relationship with Karajan goes back to the early sixties. It is one of the foundations on which this book has been written. But this is not the place to describe it, and in any case it is not of general interest. A few details should suffice. For what is required is a general account of the reasons behind this book and the reasons why it is as it is: the reader has a right to know how this book came about, particularly the processes and circumstances which led to its present form, which are inseparable from the man Karajan and which, I believe, might shed some light on the structure of his personality.

I met Herbert von Karajan while studying music in Berlin. From 1963, when Karajan and the Berlin Philharmonic Orchestra moved into the new Philharmonie in October of that year, Karajan gave me the opportunity to be present, watching, and learning as well, as he worked in the recording studio and the concert hall. In this way I was able to follow large amounts of his artistic work from close to, as well as the structure of what was to mark the consolidation of his musical power, the Easter Festivals with all their media connections. I was present at his first television experiments with the station *Freies Berlin*, on which *Till Eulenspiegel's lustige Streiche* by Richard Strauss was broadcast on an experimental basis. I also witnessed the first music films, brilliantly and powerfully made, which, in collaboration with the French film director Henri Clouzot, peaked in an exemplary filmic treatment of Beethoven's Fifth Symphony.

I was present at many recording sessions which made interpretational history: first, when I was still a young student, in the Jesus-Christus-Kirche in Dahlem, where the recordings had to be interrupted every time a Pan Am Clipper from Tempelhof Airport left the divided city for the West. Then, later, when the Dahlem church could no longer fulfil the demands (never fully satisfied) that Karajan was making in his recordings, in the new Philharmonie, whose acoustics had been optimized in the meantime.

When, at the beginning of the seventies, I had conceived a project to write a book of portraits of prominent interpreters, it was obvious that Herbert von Karajan should be one of those included. This led to a series of detailed conversations with Karajan. Extracts from them were finally published in the volume that appeared under the title *Große Interpreten im Gespräch*. Despite the quiet irony and polite criticism that accompanies the chapter

9

concerning him, Karajan seemed taken with the essay (which, with hindsight, requires a number of corrections). At least he wrote, in April 1977: 'I have read with great interest not only the chapter about myself, but also the others. I feel we ought to talk about it.'[4]

The following autumn, at the Lucerne International Music Festival, he told me his plan for a general biography, and offered me this thankless yet attractive task. It all seemed very enticing, in fact. The most important and indispensable premise was the fact that the impulse and the offer should have come from Karajan himself. I genuinely believed that this included Karajan's readiness to contribute all he could to the demanding project. The publishing house had also already been decided. We all reached a prompt agreement. Broad outlines and concepts were drawn up, and were agreed by all parties concerned, Karajan and the publishing house, with which he had a friendly involvement. We enthusiastically set to work, at least on the research. And then came the rude awakening.

What soon transpired was that Karajan had entirely different ideas from my own about our collaboration on this book. Ideas entirely the opposite of mine. What he clearly wanted was a biography as he imagined it, a collection, more or less, of all the biographical 'material' in book form, designed to polish and maintain his image, with all kinds of lovely stories such as those unquestioningly presented to us by the publicity departments of record companies.

In the spring of 1978, in Salzburg, I was confronted with the astonishing fact that I was by no means the only author collecting material for Karajan's biography with his permission. Karajan (or was it the publisher?) had clandestinely set several bloodhounds on the spoors that he had left, all of which led to him. Strange to say, our paths crossed. We got in each other's way. We held one another up and lured interviewees away from each other, a situation that was impossible because it was uncreative. One biographer was leaving as the next turned up. Throughout this time Karajan kept himself busy with his biographers and journalists, since the journals and magazines which are a window on the world for many people were celebrating, with all due dignity, the seventieth birthday of the supreme master.

Returning home in his Falcon-10 jet from Paris to Switzerland, Karajan set me off in Zurich in order to pick up, without a moment's delay, the journalist Rolf R. Bigler, whom he flew on to St Moritz where they were to sit down for a series in a glossy magazine which was later, in extended and completed form, to appear as a book. Fate, as we now know, had other ideas. In Salzburg, where we met in a wrangle over the master, I asked Bigler whether this wasn't all rather too much for him, knowing about the great amount of writing he was up to. I mentioned overwork. He continued to dismiss the idea. Four weeks later he was dead.

Another intended Karajan biographer, William Bender from New York, went livid with shock when I explained to him, in the Großes Festspielhaus where we were both waiting for the boss for the same reason, that he was far from being alone in his work on Karajan. Never before have I seen a person lose composure so quickly. The bucolic red of his contented face abruptly switched to the corpse-like pallor of a sweat-pearled skin, the complexion of those fighting against death. When Bender's long-awaited book had still not been delivered at the end of 1981, Karajan voiced his suspicion to me that certain circles had put pressure on Bender not to write the book. It was otherwise unimaginable that someone would promise a book and fail to deliver it.

Well, if Karajan can't do something, other people can't be expected to do it either. What about this idea: Bender refused, because he saw himself as having been swindled and cheated? That probably comes closer to the mark than the far-fetched suspicion of some mysterious outside pressure. If pressure there was, then it came from Karajan himself. In his dealings with me at least he repeatedly resorted to his method – sometimes subtle, sometimes quite open – of 'withdrawing love'. When this happened he would suddenly disappear, he had no time, he forbade me access to rehearsals (despite prior arrangement) and frankly declared that he would end the relationship for ever when he saw that I wasn't dancing to his tune. But Karajan, as I see it, always kept things that way. If someone failed to sense what Karajan wanted and respond accordingly, Karajan was wounded. This is the behaviour of people with arrested development. In a conversation in December 1981 it took this form: 'Then you must do what you want. But in that case we shall cease to have anything to do with one another.' And in response to my objection, he held the knife to my chest: 'I'm not holding a knife to your chest, but in that case the matter will simply be closed. Go ahead and write whatever you want regardless!'

That at least is correct. And that is how things went over the last few years. There was a great deal of correspondence which included Karajan's sudden attempt to influence the manuscript through his lawyers. For they were the ones who did the talking at that time. Well, the difficulties have been swept aside, and we can now comfortably cast our eyes over the correspondence that occurred between myself and Karajan at that time.

The letter reproduced below in full goes back, among other things, to an event that happened in Berlin at the beginning of December 1979. I had travelled from the USA to be present at the recording sessions of Richard Wagner's stage consecration play, *Parsifal*. When I arrived in Berlin I was to a certain extent stonewalled: Karajan was sulking, and refused to allow me to observe the recording session. With a bad conscience, and in order to calm me down, so to speak, he then exonerated himself, quite in the spirit of the stick-and-carrot 'pedagogical method' that was so characteristic of him, with an invitation to the concert and the rehearsal that preceded it. He stood in the way of the actual purpose of my visit. Trivial, one might object, momentary ill-feeling, temporary touchiness; no point going on about it. Actually it wouldn't be worth mentioning, and certainly not in the detailed way in which I am discussing it here, if it did not conceal important matters. But simply as one example among many, it is sympto-matic of the way Karajan worked. This petty attitude reveals a trait of Karajan's that seems to be typical of the man. But more about that and other traits later on.

If one stood up to Karajan, insisting on one's own point of view, he turned away in indignation and set a mean-spirited series of manoeuvres in motion. It was a method based on conscious hurt, neglect, injury and even defamation, used in tandem with little comforts, just long enough for the victim to become com-pliant.

Wooing and flattery continued, and closeness and familiarity were granted and feigned just long enough for a goal to be reached. If Karajan encountered resistance in the process, he broke through it with the gentle power of sublime pressure, or with harsh repul-sion and rebuke. If this failed, he was insulted and wounded, without any understanding for the situation and arguments of the other party. The slightest insult was sensed immediately. That was what made dealings with Karajan so difficult, so wearing – unless one either joined in the tiring game, capitulated or gave up dealing with him at all. Often giving up was the only option left. For who, feeling constantly wounded, could avoid being unforgiving? Karajan stressed over and over again that he was not unforgiving in the slightest: all truly unforgiving people do that. It wouldn't occur to anyone else.

12

So my letter to Karajan, dated 20 December, read as follows:

Dear Herr von Karajan,

In view of the publication of my book in Berlin, it would seem to me to be sensible to give you my position on the Econ Verlag matter.

There are two main points on which we plainly disagree. One of these, concerning the simultaneous publication of books on the same subject by a single publishing house, will not be discussed here, since it has no relevance in this context. The other, namely that no changes should be made to the manuscript, seems, in contrast, to have become a cardinal point and requires clarification.

Let us remember quickly: you had asked me whether I was interested in writing a book about you. It was the fact that you had approached me with the proposal, not the other way round, that made the project interesting to me in the first place. I was thus able to assume, among other things, that you would use all your powers to help the project along – always according to the premise that my judgement about your work would be inviolable.

It was agreed from the very beginning that I would be given a free rein in the shaping and use of the material; indeed, you repeatedly stressed that you (as you rightly suppose) place a particular value on my critical and independent judgement. That naturally rules out your control over the manuscript's content.

Following my most recent conversations with yourself and Herr von Wehrenalp, however, I have been forced into the impression that you wish to avoid a possibly unfavourable evaluation by controlling what has been written (involving corrections, for which read censorship).

I had come to Berlin with the honest intention of bringing about a quick solution. Herr von Wehrenalp made me certain stipulations that have nothing to do with the agreement we made at the Frankfurt Book Fair. You, for your part, forbade me to be present at the gramophone recording of *Parsifal* (the reason for my journey from the USA). That strikes me as senseless. For as early as November we had agreed to give particular emphasis to your working style in the context of the *Parsifal* production.

If my working method can claim to be based on certain principles, then they are those of fairness and independence. I do not deviate from these principles. In this case they rule out

13

control over the manuscript. In my work in public relations I have made these principles my constant guideline. For I do not see life as a process of inner freedom in constant decline.

If I was mistaken in my assumption of mutual agreement with regard to control over the manuscript, then I am the wrong man for you. I need the book about you neither to satisfy my vanity nor for material reasons. If I write it, it is solely out of curiosity and the related fascination with finding out the motives behind your unparalleled career.

I am interested in the psychological background of your life's work. The biographical discussions, which we have been having for a long time now, are intended to provide the book with a framework for the psychogram of your career and hence of you yourself. A book constructed in this way would be meaningless if you or the publisher were to influence the result. The book stands or falls on our all being prepared to take the risk and allow ourselves to be surprised by the result.

I shall write the book. And I am keen to start on it. But only under conditions that make it possible for me to write it at all. If it should prove impossible to permit these conditions, other solutions would have to be sought in the interest of the project.

Dear Herr von Karajan, I do not wish to close this letter without telling you how hurt I am by the direction events seem to be taking. But I close with the certainty that you finally understand and acknowledge my point of view; and with the confidence that together we shall finally bring this book to its conclusion . . .

And what did Karajan answer to this letter, which, for all its long-windedness, is still clearly comprehensible? On 18 January 1980 Karajan replied from his winter residence in St Moritz:

Dear Herr Bachmann,

I do not understand your letter of 20 December 1979. Herr von Wehrenalp told me that, with regard to the simultaneous publication of books, your wish is being carried out, and a six-month delay has been granted. There is the possible publication of a book about my stage productions in words and pictures, but the latter book would never overlap with a work by yourself.

I do not think that your assessment of the problem of 'control' is correct. It is not a question of what you write, but of whether the information that you have received from me is valid.

Even if I should be pleased to grant you papal infallibility, I cannot claim the same for myself.

We have spent many hours together, and I have told you my opinions on many matters, and given you facts from my life. It is obviously possible that in many of my statements I might have said things which, upon closer reading, do not reflect my opinion.

This is the sole point on which we must ask for your understanding, as a book of this kind should be free of errors.

I think that once this matter has been cleared up it would be time for you to come to an actual agreement with the publishing company.

With best wishes
pp. L. Salzburger
(Herr von Karajan left after dictating)

An astonishing letter. Remarkable and revealing in many respects. It is not surprising that Karajan did not understand my letter: he had no wish to understand it. Because he would then have had to take a stand on it. But worse than this is his statement that he might have uttered things that he didn't mean. We do not intend to be mischievous and suggest that Karajan didn't know what he was saying. On the contrary: he knew it all too well. If it were otherwise, he could not be taken seriously, and all the conversations stored on well over a hundred tape cassettes would be worthless. For what is an author to do with material which he must assume corresponds to a state of *non compos mentis*?

No – what is expressed in the letter is plain fear, namely the fear of being tied down to one's statements. It is Karajan's characteristic fear of commitment, the terror and hesitation when faced with any finality in the personal sphere (less in the artistic one, where he is able to escape into vagueness). Karajan was always evasive. Here he was trying to do it by means of revocation. Where a manly act was required – 'a man is as good as his word' – Karajan became evasive. His problem here was that he could not stand by what he had said. What is revealed here is wavering, fussing and twisting rather than manly declaration. Austrian fussiness aside, in other spheres too what constantly comes to light was quite the opposite of manliness.

The degree of insecurity and lack of self-confidence expressed in his letter would tend to arouse one's suspicions. Characteristically, the letter was not signed in person (as if he himself did not want to stand by it). We could pass over that. But we can also ask what is hidden behind an apparent piece of trivia such as this. I believe it is a mixture of superciliousness and arrogance, suspicion and fear. Knowing as we do that Karajan liked to embellish even unimportant letters with a dramatic signature, its absence cannot be unimportant in a letter concerned with a project in which a great deal of time and interest had been invested on both sides. Once again, what appears, and what is supposed to strike the reader, is the aspect of pettiness, fuelled by arrogance, towards the recipient. Towards his secretary, on the other hand, he showed the suspicion that prevented him from entrusting her with blank signatures, as is customary at executive level for the smooth running of an organized correspondence.

Karajan was an incredibly cautious and fearful man as far as his private life was concerned (something, one is tempted to suppose, that was in any case non-existent). This general fear of intimacy determined his dealings even with people who were very close to him. So it is not surprising that he should not have wished to open his heart to such people as he involved in the writing of his life story. From the very start Karajan systematically resisted questions about his origins, the milieu in which he spent his youth, about anything that might have provided information about his inner life, as soon as his interrogator wanted to penetrate beneath the surface of the Karajan image.

But that is not all: when I wanted to bring private matters to light indirectly, via close acquaintances, Karajan attempted to put a stop to that too. For example with the singer Irmgard Seefried. They had known each other from their time in Aachen, when Seefried was starting out on her stage career and Karajan was making his career as Germany's youngest general musical director. Frau Seefried first of all made a conversation contingent on Karajan's agreement. When approached about the matter, Karajan immediately set his conditions: 'In that case I must, of course, see what is suitable in it and what is not, otherwise I can't do it . . . Then she suddenly says something, do you see what I mean? . . . If you ask her things that create a particular kind of atmosphere that I simply wouldn't like to have in a book, then it's pointless.'

I encountered similar reactions with regard to the master's court astrologer, Francesco Waldner, who similarly wanted to check with Karajan first. 'No, no, no, I wouldn't like that' – this was the original tone of the reply. Walter Legge, to whom Karajan was largely indebted for his post-war career, did himself out of the chance of giving me important material about this and about his relationship with Karajan straight from the horse's mouth. He refused a conversation for the reason that Karajan did not want this, and that in any case he himself was planning a book on the subject. Months later Legge was dead too. The plan remained unrealized.[5]

I have no wish to continue the list of similar cases. Those mentioned may suffice. Obfuscation, obstruction, concealment, creeping off instead of trustingly opening up, over and over again and all the way down the line: this was Karajan's attitude whenever he felt he was being placed under the microscope. Although he was willing, for example, to tell me all about his sailing ship *Helisara VI*, he never let me on to the ship, as if there was something to hide there. Although even the bedrooms and private studies of his St Moritz villa were readily displayed for the benefit of all the journalists from the glossy magazines, I was never given the opportunity of learning from Karajan the relationship between himself and the objects with which he decorated his most private surroundings, what they meant to him, what stories had grown up around them. It could have provided indications, pointers, to his inner world – and this was precisely what was to be avoided at all costs. Well, I nevertheless found access to the places where Karajan didn't want me to be. But that is another story, which does not belong in this book.

Karajan's answer was always a great silence – for all the talking that was done. Silence particularly where questions about his childhood, his feelings, his view of the world were concerned. What he tells us about his childhood is reproduced as a series of collective experiences, and in general expressions which convey nothing personal about him. He was able to say nothing about his own personality. This is starkly opposed to his request that we should work together on a book which would finally provide information about him, after all the superficial literature which, as he knew, had been distributed about him. But as his entire emotional life was concentrated in music, he had no other possible references. Defensiveness and insularity at every level. And that is how the inability to form relationships is expressed.

What kind of person asks one to write his biography and then maintains a consistent silence? Who repeatedly seeks and accepts contact with a view to a conversation, and then refuses to have one?

Was I too timorous perhaps, did I ask the wrong questions, was I over-cautious? Should I have been more ruthless? Would he then have spoken of his longing for love, of his undeveloped emotional world, of his inability to form relationships, his inhibitions where love was concerned? Would I have reached him then?

Or would I only have reached him if I had been a psychologist? In that case the first question would have been: is he unable to talk about himself in other circumstances? Is he capable of communicating anything only in the context of psychoanalysis, with the full certainty, the total guarantee that not a word of it would pass to the outside world?

We cannot suppose even this, unfortunately. To take analysis he would have had to be much more open, much less fearful. Even if he was only able and willing to reveal himself in analysis, then he would necessarily have dealt with his problems in some way, and would have been able to talk about them.

But Karajan refused, because he was unable to open up. And he would probably not have wished to do so even if he could. Characteristically, he was unable to speak about music either. 'I'm afraid of flogging things to death,' Karajan said in self-justification. For this reason we don't learn anything about his relationship with and his understanding of music, anything about his relationship with the works of the world's musical literature, which had constantly occupied his mind (and, we might hope, his heart) over half a century. He was afraid of committing himself with a statement, for 'it all comes to a standstill then, it becomes lasting, it is a statement that has been made. And it is then called "valid". And from that point on everybody is justified in turning your words around. For that reason: I don't like being watched when I'm cooking.'

Karajan, or the big silence: it is difficult to accept the limitations of a revered figure. It is doubly difficult in the face of his desire, both egocentric and reckless, to have the great biographer Richard Friedenthal as the author of his biography; at least that is what Karajan told me he wanted. (The Munich writer Friedenthal, the child of Protestant pastors and a Jewish family assimilated for many generations, was forced to leave Germany.) This very wish, which borders on the inappropriate, shows that Karajan understood nothing, or wished to understand nothing, of the demands that a biographer makes, and is permitted to make, on his material. Neither had he understood that a book can't simply be written in a minute, that it takes time, that it has to mature, that it cannot (as he once said, when he was pressing for the book and threatening to sever relations between us) be compared with the schedule of a theatrical production? Perhaps he meant the book simply to be a part of his self-dramatization. But he chose the wrong man for that.

He would have to do that work himself – and, as we know, he spent years working on his own book. If I understand him correctly, this book was supposed to deal with all the deepest secrets of Karajan's inner character that he withheld from his biographers. That could mean only that a responsible biographer would have had to wait for that book before he could write his own. But if Karajan, given that he was the way he was, wanted to write a book about his true self, then his plan was fairly ill-conceived, because he lacked the strength to be himself. But that strength would have been the book's initial premise. Karajan as the tragic man, who wished, without any prospect of success, to place his life in a more thorough context, who made human wholeness his life's goal without achieving it, although he imagined he had been working on it his whole life long, came no closer to fulfilling this precondition than did his demands upon his biographers. Karajan, for the most part letting himself off the hook with Salzburg *politesses* and incapable of a genuine exchange of opinions, was unable to fulfil these demands because he remained silent when everything depended on his speaking. He grew loquacious only when listening was unnecessary. That at least was my experience: in the course of the ten years, more or less, of our conversations, we barely touched on a single topic that did not crop up sooner or later, in similar or identical words, in an interview with a press, radio or television journalist. Occasionally I could not help having the impression that he was quoting from one of the books that he had supplied with his authentic and to some extent 'facticidal' statements. These striking repetitions of statements to a great number of people have the character of incantations and invocations, as if Karajan had been seeking, by perpetuating the message, to lend support to its truth content. This is just as striking as the Karajan phenomenon as a whole: there was, after all, nothing about him that was not striking, and he was, almost tragically, one thing above all: he was striking. I do not, of course, mean this in any diagnostic psychiatric sense.

There is no point in writing a book that would fall in with Karajan's ideas. But the book that would do justice to Karajan, to his work and his complex personality, could not be written during his lifetime. For such a conclusive account we lack the broad view that can be provided only by distance in time. We still lack other evidence, his letters, accounts by friends and by his family circle, which could supply further information. His own statements about his character and life history are vague enough, and overlaid with the tendency towards obfuscation rather than helpful clarification – whether consciously or unconsciously is an open question. It would take a psychologist to break through that. He would have to seek out the causes of Karajan's behaviour. The prototype of the artist in the age of threatened self-identity, Karajan represented the type of genius devoted exclusively to his own work, and also, perhaps, to those people whose function is something like that of satellites, whom he could experience as a part or an instrument of his work. But it is quite uncertain how much light psychology can throw on the complex and shadowy phenomenon of Karajan. While we still lack a unified theory of human behaviour, the field is left open for speculation. I shall refrain from roaming that deceptive terrain. It is enough to portray Karajan's behaviour. Because of Karajan's refusal to communicate, we are only inadequately informed about the central events of his life-story, influenced by complex peripheral conditions. Finally, in his case, we run into the phenomenon of incomprehensibility.

The motivating forces of human behaviour, particularly the behaviour of those who, like Karajan, represent power, lie to some extent in the unconscious, and can therefore be only fragmentarily understood. For there is little point in explaining Karajan's performing genius on the basis of the qualities of his character. But we can convey a picture of the great interpreter which, for all the annoyance it will obviously entail, still appears warmer in a human sense than the portraits painted with the usual tendentious biographic idealizations and glorifications.

More can be achieved, I believe, through due care and the wish to establish probability rather than claiming complete certainty, than for example by tracing all psychological problems back to the experiences of early childhood, as occurs in Freudian psychology and the theories that its various schools and adherents have derived from it.

In a letter of 6 November 1980 I did tell Karajan of the need to work out a biographical method appropriate to the material using psychological methods. However, I must confess that we should beware of this method for the reasons mentioned – reasons which admittedly make their restrictive appearance only later on

– and it is better avoided. Quite regardless of this, I would be incapable of work of this kind. In my letter, which, incidentally, remained unanswered, I proposed certain reflections on the book project, and it might be illuminating for me to reproduce an extract from it here:

Dear Herr von Karajan!

As our project is being considerably delayed, it will certainly not be inappropriate for me to jot down some ideas about the project in a kind of interim report.

Having seen the almost unmanageable amount of material that has already piled up, the question quickly arises of the biographical method appropriate to the material.

The method based exclusively on historico-critical consider-ations would certainly not do justice to the object of the research. All that would produce would be the record of a career. To do only historical work about you would mean delivering you up to the sterile meticulousness of the factual account, and would also mean depriving an extraordinary artist of the aura of extraordinariness. So that will not be the aim of my book; rather I shall seek to provide the presentation of a character, a glimpse into psychological structure, conditions and conditioning factors.

For a person is more easily distorted and condemned than understood. How easy it has been in the past for biographers to become hagiographers or (perhaps a lesser evil) pamphleteers. It is, without a doubt, a perilous ridge that we are walking here, from which we can plunge into the depths on either side. In order to maintain one's balance here it takes certainty and trust, but also the boldness of the experienced mountain-climber (which would connect with my less dangerous passion – less dangerous because in mountaineering tne dangers, subjective and objective, can be gauged more precisely than they can in writing, where the only certainty is uncertainty of resonance). So the historical and critical basis must be extended.

This can be brought about most meaningfully and purpose-fully by means of the – let us say it jokingly, even if it is not at all a laughing matter – 'psychological-apostolic' method. This deprives the historian of his hero, in the interests of psychologi-cal work. And that is something that must be done, because given the context of your achievement, your gift exceeds the measure of mere biography.

Of course, a part of my task will be to show the fact and

nature of your achievement. But that cannot suffice. It is not merely attractive, it is necessary to reveal how your nature, based on a particular 'gift', portrays itself, and, in portraying itself, becomes all the more certain of its own qualities and gifts. Then the biographer can, to quote J. G. Droysen, 'do nothing else but enter into the personality that he is portraying, so to speak, in order to reach that personality's horizon, preoccupations and range of sensibility'.

My way of treating a subject that interests me is to turn it over and over, to examine its effect on me and my effect on it, until I have grasped it in all its aspects, in the true sense of the word – precisely because it has assumed a graspable form in the process.

So nobody should be surprised if I approach the object of my research in the role of the conductor, enter into it from its most specific domain, the podium. This method contains no threats to the project itself. For should the attempt prove unsuccessful, even that is instructive as far as the project is concerned. There are experiences that cannot be described, that can only be experienced through one's own actions. Conducting is one of them. You know that much better than I do.

So when I was in London a few days ago I undertook just such a practical experiment – 'active research', to some extent, into the portrayal of the psychology of a phenomenon . . .

Admittedly, the method is very expensive. But it pays for itself far beyond its immediate purpose . . .

What the individual person really is, what he is and can be in all his historical singularity, in his quite personal freedom and bondage, for good and ill, is something that no scientific system has as yet been able to answer. The task of interpretation does not at all mean plunging into the often murky swamp of psychological speculation.

This is not – and this should not be misunderstood – a matter of dismantling Karajan. All that is being dismantled is his legend. He has been placed on the wrong pedestal. To take Karajan down from the pedestal is to fetch him back from the world of myth and place him where he belongs: on the pedestal of esteem and gratitude for that part of his work that is capable of pleasing us, and not on the altar of adoration.

However, this book seeks not only to increase our understanding of the difficult figure of Karajan, but also to provide pointers to two related questions: what are the particular historical circumstances which have favoured Karajan's career? And in what way does the characteristic personality of the charismatic leader, which Karajan so distinctively possesses, fit in with those particular historical data?

I have indicated the difficulties that such questions are likely to run into. It is punishing work to write the life-story of a man in flight. Karajan, always fleeing something, also fled from himself, into silence. Even when he did talk he was in flight, to escape the hand of the biographer. Was it the past that he feared, was it his almost compulsive striving after praise and recognition that led him to drape his illusory dream-world, his 'reality' over the facts of his life-story, protecting and concealing it? An examination of the taped accounts has, comparing the facts with Karajan's statements, brought so many contradictions and vaguenesses to light that not all statements made within this book can be verified. Factual considerations stand in the way of such an endeavour at the present time, when much about Karajan's biography still remains shrouded in darkness. This work will be reserved for a more extensive publication.

So this book must remain a fragment. It makes no claims to completeness or clinical objectivity, but rather risks subjective exaggeration, where this promises a greater chance of understanding Karajan the man. These observations on the career of an artist significant for our time can illuminate his life, his character and the age in which he worked and developed, what he is, only in a fragmentary fashion. If this is an attempt to track down the Karajan phenomenon from various different angles, it is done without feigned anxiety or obfuscatory caution. For it must be permissible to question the historical reliability of Karajan's memories. Even Karajan himself would have been keen to find information about the causes and forces that shaped and defined his actions. One thing continually emerges throughout this process: the figure of Karajan (and I too have no wish to deny him my admiration), its reality as well as its myth, remains the single most prominent phenomenon of the musical life of our time.

1

Beginnings

'Viva Toscanini', it rang from the stalls and the balcony. The audience was wild with enthusiasm. It was calling the maestro out before the curtain at La Scala, Milan. Thunderous clapping, storms of applause, ovations. They were all celebrating the successful first Italian staging, initially marred by loud protests, of Debussy's setting of Maurice Maeterlinck's drama *Pelléas et Mélisande*. The work was just six years old, the original performance of Debussy's only opera having taken place on 30 April 1902.

Since 1898 Toscanini had been musical director of the Teatro alla Scala in Milan. Later he would always describe this staging of *Pelléas et Mélisande* as one of the most significant that he produced during his time at the theatre. A week before the much-lauded première on 25 March, at which Debussy made a speech of thanks to the conductor, Arturo Toscanini had turned forty-one. The whole world knew the fiery little conductor. His name was on every tongue, and that same year he was preparing to go to the Metropolitan Opera in New York, where Gustav Mahler was already firmly engaged for the 1907–8 season. Many of the Met's stage stars were far from delighted by Toscanini's impending arrival: the inevitable arguments and strains that would be involved in working with the famous Italian fireball, relentless and rigorous as he was, were all too familiar. After hearing of Toscanini's appointment, Caruso, the New York audience's favourite, went to the Met with the intention of dissolving his contract with the most famous opera house in the New World. Happily it was not to come to that.

In that April of 1908, then, Toscanini was gradually taking his leave of La Scala with a much-fêted performance of Maeterlinck's drama, to further his fame at the Met, where he would shock the orchestra at their first meeting by rehearsing Richard Wagner's *Götterdämmerung* without a score, thus winning immediate respect and admiration from the American musicians.

On 4 April, two days after the celebrated Toscanini première in Milan, the weather in Salzburg was changing. It was Saturday. Moderate cloud-cover thickened towards evening into a solid bank of cloud. With slight winds, a grey bank of stratus clouds gathered over the city on the Salzach. In the night of 5 April the rain set in: Salzburg weather as it always has been. They quietly put up with it in the rather sleepy provincial city on the periphery of the Habsburg Empire. Vienna, the turbulent centre of the Danube monarchy, lay to the east, while progress lay to the west, and so the citizens of Salzburg quite liked to cast westward glances, as they always had done, across the border. From 1809 until 1816, after all, they had been a part of Bavaria. Later, after the collapse of the monarchy, the barriers between themselves and Bavaria were lifted in a spurt of initial enthusiasm, only to fall again just as quickly, and were finally swept away with the annexation of Austria by Germany, only to be reinstalled after the brief dream of the thousand-year Reich. The people of Salzburg are accustomed to change. They react to the political storms and changes of climate as calmly and as naturally as they react to the weather.

Each downfall of steamy rain is still followed by sunshine – festival weather, they would say these days. The people of Salzburg were thoroughly capable of adjusting to it, quickly, effortlessly, inconspicuously, as quickly as the weather changes, without any injury to themselves. They were adaptable to the point of self-disownment, they moved with the wind, not against it. The world was fine here (was it really?). They were Catholic. The Protestants had been purged under Archbishop Freiherr von Firmian in 1731 and 1732: some 20,000 Protestants had been forced to emigrate from the city and the countryside, most of them settling in far-off East Prussia. Although there was turmoil everywhere in the world, no revolution from Salzburg was to impinge upon world affairs. Salzburg was something of a byword for constant adaptability.

On the morning of 5 April, 4.1 mm of precipitation were recorded. A rainy, gloomy Sunday. The work-places were at rest, the only hives of activity were the churches, their bells stridently calling the faithful to prayer and to mass. It was still Lent. The weather outside was inclement, that cold, wet Easter in Salzburg. Drizzly weather, bringing colds and catarrh. People stayed indoors. The soothing monotony of the rain fell across the city and its princely residence as it went on with its rather rural life. The day ended in the comforting clatter of the steamy rain, whose myriad little drops fell whimpering to their deaths on the city's historic roofs and pavements.

The night that was falling was historic, too: it was to provide the city with its second great son – Herbert von Karajan.

Its first and greatest son, Mozart, left his city, which had treated him so shabbily, at night. They come and go in the dark, the great sons of this still often ungenerous city.

Herbert von Karajan was Sunday's child in the true sense of the word. Was he also blessed by fate, as the popular belief has it? The time of his birth is unclear. Was he born at 11 o'clock at night or shortly before midnight? Karajan himself didn't know. He mentions both, and when his mother later told him, 'You're my Sunday's child,' she meant more than the simple words revealed. She probably also wanted to indicate how much she loved him, and perhaps also that she loved him more intensely than her firstborn son, Wolfgang, one year and nine months his elder.

Whether it was 11 o'clock or midnight, the weather was unchanged. At that time it was overcast, the air temperature was around 4 degrees Celsius, and a light rain was falling.[1]

The Emperor had a new subject, at any rate. The nobility had not yet been abolished, the monarchy was still in existence, and so the entry was made in the register of births: Heribert Ritter von Karajan. Heribert – the name seems to have been chosen quite intentionally, seeming to anticipate the future. It's all in a name – *nomen est omen*: Heribert derives from the Old High German *heri* meaning army and *beraht* meaning glorious. The name brings with it an obligation, and the obligation was to be fulfilled: glorious in his fame, he was one day to lead the armies of his listeners and orchestras to the joys of Western music.

But not only the name; the life of the newborn infant seems, with the foresight of predestination, to be prefigured and determined in the family crest: in this crest, on a green hill under a red heart stands a simple crane. Two helmets are graced by this natural, watchful crane and a fallen, two-branched black anchor with a ring entwined three times by a green olive branch.[2] Crane and anchor: a symbol of the restlessness, the wandering flight of his life on the one hand and on the other the need for the security of custom, of an anchoring in tradition; but also of his readiness to seize the future, his mobile involvement with the achievements of the new century. Flying and sailing were later to become very real preoccupations for Karajan. And the red heart? What does it stand for? Let us be noble, and say: the glow of his inner flame.

Heribert's antecedents came from Greek Macedonia. The progenitor of the von Karajan line, Georg Johann von Karajan, the son of Joanes Karajoannes (year of birth unknown, died before 1764), came into the world in the Karstic Mountains of Macedonia, not far from Olympus, in Kosani (Kozané), in 1747. At the age of twenty-four, 'black Jan' (*kara* means black in Turkish), clearly equipped with an astonishing business sense, travelled to Vienna, soon moving on from there to Chemnitz in Saxony. There he founded cotton-weaving mills and factories for Turkish yarns. In so doing, he and his brother Theodor Johann had a hand in establishing Saxony's textile industry. For this pioneering work, for his services to the industry and trade of the Electorate of Saxony, he and his brother were raised to the nobility of the German Nation of the Holy Roman Empire by the Elector Friedrich August III of Saxony, during the imperial curacy of 1 June 1792. Until the end of the eighteenth century Georg Johann von Karajan stayed in Chemnitz as a businessman. He finally left the Chemnitz factories to his brother and returned to Vienna where he became a textile wholesaler. He died on 2 June 1813.

One of his sons, Theodor, struck out on an academic career. He led a scholarly life as Professor of Old German Philology and Historical Research at the University of Vienna. He was curator of the Imperial Court Library, held office at the Imperial Academy of Sciences in Vienna, was a member of the upper chamber in the *Reichsrat* and, in 1848–9, a member of the constituent assembly in Frankfurt am Main. Not much was lacking, and Theodor, Heribert's great-grandfather, would have relished the honour of being made Dean of Vienna University. The faculty had put him forward for this. But the Minister for Education, Graf Thun, stood in the way of the appointment because Theodor von Karajan was a member of the Greek Orthodox Church. Consequently, von Karajan relinquished his professorship and resigned his offices. The family von Karajan doubtless had a certain tradition of being snubbed by the authorities, and of reacting in just such a resolute and confident way. In recognition of his great services to science, in particular his work over eighteen years as Vice President of the Academy of Sciences, as well as 'his loyalty and devotion, revealed in his work at every opportunity, to the Austrian Imperial House',[3] Theodor von Karajan was awarded the Knight's Cross of the Austrian Order of Leopold on 11 July 1869, and was raised to the Austrian knighthood. Theodor had experienced satisfaction late in life. He died in 1873, and contemporaries said of him that he held the masters of music in the highest esteem. It was in him, then, that the musical inheritance dormant in the depth and breadth of the Karajan soul first came to light.

He had his sons Maximilian and Ludwig Maria, Heribert's grandfather (not Maximilian, as Löbl's and Haeusserman's biographies incorrectly have it), baptized into the Roman Catholic Church. Privy Councillor Ludwig Maria, born in 1835, married the Viennese Henriette von Raindl. He was a doctor of medicine, worked as government councillor and health adviser for Lower Austria, and died in 1906. So Heribert was never able to know his paternal grandfather.

They were stubborn climbers, the Karajans, and successful in their climbing. Having fled the Turkish yoke, they quickly made themselves useful to Franz Joseph's empire, winning honours, titles and respect. In the eighteenth century these immigrants became successful businessmen and traders within a short time. In the nineteenth century they shone as scholars, academics and jurists, and in the twentieth century they were to find fulfilment in music, medicine and technology. Their talents were many, and they knew how to develop their gifts and transform them into success. Their careers reveal stubbornness, persistence and the firm resolve to make something of themselves. They were competent, and they were rewarded for it.

Ernst, the oldest son of Privy Councillor Ludwig von Karajan, walked in his father's footsteps. He studied medicine and enjoyed a remarkable career in Salzburg, which made him, as senior registrar of the St Johann Hospital and later director of the State Health Authorities as well as State Health Consultant, a well-known and well-respected personality. Born in Vienna in 1868, in 1905 he married Martha Kosmać from Graz, thirteen years his junior. On 21 July 1906 she gave him the first of his two sons, Wolfgang. The firstborn was then followed by Heribert, on 5 April 1908. A good measure of paternal blood flowed in his veins. It was said to be Macedonian in origin. But it cannot be ruled out that it was, in part at least, Turkish. For from the end of the fifteenth century until the beginning of the nineteenth century Macedonia had been under the rule of the Turks, and was subjugated and ruthlessly exploited by them, with all the well-known consequences for the harassed population, who bore all with the endurance of centuries of slavery.

Heribert von Karajan was born into an era which bound him more strongly to tradition than the children of other eras. Heribert's father had still addressed his parents with the formal *Sie*. For Heribert he would always remain a patriarchal figure of respect. Authority and obedience were still given pride of place in 1908. But traditions were breaking down, and the new century was to bring with it Europe's retreat from world domination.

The twentieth century – 1900 – had begun with a 'supreme court banquet' in the Hofburg. With all the pomp and splendour of the Habsburgs' finest hour, intoxicated with the belief in progress and the pride of achievement, they crossed the century's threshold with confidence. The nineteenth century ended in a glorious twilight. But its by now unconcealable decadence was already leading, in places, to criticism of the ruling system. Its mainstays, the officer corps and the official sector recruited from the nobility, were rotten and unsteady. Increasingly the aristocracy, including the Karajans, was losing its position as the main source of support for the feudally structured monarchy.

There was creaking in the timbers of Austria-Hungary, of the whole of Europe, in fact, and Karl Kraus, who had been publishing *Die Fackel* since 1899, wrote: 'Nowhere in the world is the end being experienced as visibly as it is in Austria.'[4] In the soil of a rotting epoch, unshakeably exemplified by an almost mummified Emperor, fermentation was afoot. The nobility, born to uphold the throne, increasingly reneged on its duties. The instincts of the people were leading them towards a fatal nationalism, and in the Viennese literary café, the Central, Leon Trotsky was playing chess with Austrian Social Democrats. 'Vienna, the city held by so many to be the epitome of harmless jollity, the splendid room full of satisfied people, for me is sadly nothing but the vivid memory of the saddest time of my life,' Adolf Hitler was to write in *Mein Kampf*.[5] For: 'The miserable living conditions of the Vienna labourer are shocking. I still shudder today when I think of those miserable cave-dwellings, of hostel and mass-accommodation, of the gloomy images of refuse, repellent filth and worse.'[6] That is not the Vienna of the aristocracy, not the Vienna of the Karajans. It is remarkable enough that this Adolf, who failed as an artist in the Vienna of the imperial age, would later smooth the way for Herbert the aristocrat to rise to unimagined heights.

'Austria is in a state of latent revolution,'[7] lamented the ruler of Austria-Hungary, after Russia the second largest, and after Russia and Germany the most heavily populated country in Europe. The Habsburg Empire was about to lose its internal peace: the Hungarians were troubling the Emperor and the question of the Southern Slavs and the problem of Bosnia-Herzegovina were plaguing the old monarch. The Romanian author and politician Aurel Popovici from Siebenbürgen called for the division of Austria-Hungary into sixteen national member states in his book *Die Vereinigten Staaten von Großösterreich*, asking, 'Should the Empire of the Habsburgs exist or collapse?'[8] The battle was on, and Emperor Franz Joseph had to be reminded that conflicts of nationality had already, in the past, brought international complications in their wake and ended in wars which his empire, with all its many peoples, had lost: in Italy in 1859 and in Germany in 1866. With the annexation of the occupied territories of Bosnia and Herzegovina on 5 October 1908, which led to a difficult international crisis, Franz Joseph finally took that crucial step that was to lead the Habsburg Empire into the First World War and to the end of its existence.

So, born into the decline of the West foretold in Oswald Spengler's morphology of world history, *Untergang des Abendlandes*, between the years of 1908 and 1918, little Heribert grew up in the rather quiet and peaceful surroundings of Salzburg.

The century into which he was born was not only that of decline, of the great catastrophes, mass murders, holocausts and the most monstrous crimes against humanity, the century of barbarism, in fact – it was also the century of great freedom, of unrestricted mobility and communication. Gustav Weißkopf, alias Whitehead, carried out the first successful engine-powered flight in history on 14 August 1901 in Bridgeport, Connecticut. This was the first step in a development which few people dared predict and which has assumed dimensions far beyond the wildest imaginings. It has peaked in the supersonic planes and jumbo-jets of our own age, the first vehicles to make mass air travel a reality. Henry Ford contributed to the advance of the motor car by introducing conveyor-belt production; the first great heights were reached with the mass-manufacture, in its millions, of the Model T, affectionately dubbed the 'Tin Lizzie', produced in the year of Karajan's birth.

The development of electronic sound reproduction and radio

technology, the latter first successfully used by Marconi in 1897 in communicating messages, made swift progress, and the phonograph, developed in 1877 by the American inventor Thomas Alva Edison, thanks to the improvement of the system by the introduction of the gramophone, developed by Emil Berliner in 1887, ushered in the era of musical mass communication. Karajan was to seize this invention, still in the early stages of its development, and use it as no other artist has before or since.

The age now dawning was also that of the great simplifiers and revolutionaries, represented by names such as Einstein, Freud and Hitler. Albert Einstein, born in Ulm, where the young Karajan was to launch his career, forced our ideas of energy and the universe into the lapidary formula $E=mc^2$. With his 'Special Theory of Relativity', written for the *Annalen der Physik* in 1905, he completely overturned humanity's understanding of time and space and overturned the classical model of physics.

Psychology found its great apologist in Sigmund Freud, who set out to examine the unconscious with the theory of psychoanalysis which he had developed in 1900. Precisely two weeks after Karajan's birth Freud came to Salzburg, where he held the preliminary introductory meeting of the First Psychoanalytical Congress on 26 April 1908 and led the session the following day. There is a great temptation to make connections between the infant Heribert and the theory of Freud, the psychological investigator; it is tempting to inquire into the damage that he might have been suffering during this phase of early childhood by living in a house run along patriarchal lines, with an over-solicitous mother. We shall resist this temptation, and instead recall the definition with which the satirist Karl Kraus discredited Freud's already controversial teachings in the following year, 1909: 'Psychoanalysis is the very mental illness whose therapy it imagines itself to be.'[9]

Adolf Hitler, like Karajan a subject of Franz Joseph, as a twenty-year-old in Vienna around 1901 laid 'the granite foundation'[10] of those political views whose consequences would shake the entire world and the entire century. In *Mein Kampf* he writes about these years in Vienna, as portentous as they were unsuccessful, during which he sought in vain to enter the Kunstakademie:

Wherever I went all I saw was Jews, and the more I saw, the more sharply they distinguished themselves to the eye from other people . . . During that period my eyes were also opened

31

to two dangers that I had previously barely known by name, and whose terrible meaning for the existence of the German people I certainly failed to understand: Marxism and Jewry.[11]

Hitler already considered himself a German at this time, and in his mind's eye he saw himself as a citizen of a coming Greater German Reich, in which Austria would be subsumed. The consequences are well known.

Of course, in 1908, Heribert von Karajan knew nothing of all this. He grew up, well cared for by his affectionately solicitous mother, we suppose, at 1 Schwarzstrasse in Salzburg. The harmony of this family, four members in all, chimed with the last echoes of the aristocratic, late-bourgeois melodies of the fading imperial and royal monarchy. Harmony, if it did exist in the Karajan household, surely surrounded the child and shaped his nature.

Toscanini, Hitler and Franz Joseph, names from 1908, apparently unconnected. And yet they were to be crucial to Karajan's career. Might this be more than a random coincidence?

Toscanini was to be Karajan's model, his distant teacher. And in the imponderable, inconclusive and vague matters dealt with in Maeterlinck's drama *Pelléas et Mélisande* (performed by Toscanini in Milan), Karajan was to see a reflection of his own essence. Hitler was to smooth his path to world fame and shape his career. And as for Franz Joseph, impressed by the figure of the Emperor and the aura of unapproachability of 'His Apostolic Majesty', Karajan was to preserve in himself the courtly gesture of the imperial and royal monarchy for our own age.

Karajan recalls:

It was the Kaiser's birthday in Salzburg. The whole street was full of people. Then my uncle said, 'Here comes the Kaiser', and I was held up in the air a little, as I was tiny at that time, after all. I could just see the Kaiser from the chest up. His head floated away over the heads of the others. For me he was no longer a human being, and he probably considered himself to be somehow other than human.

This early encounter with 'His Apostolic Majesty' was to make a deep impression on the child. It is one of the few childhood memories that Karajan has revealed spontaneously and with an evident emotional involvement. It is unclear when this encounter occurred. Franz Joseph's last official visit to Salzburg took place in 1909. It is doubtful whether Karajan would be able to remember so far back. It is possible that the Emperor, while staying in Bad Ischl, where he used to spend the summer until a few years before his death in 1916, had come to Salzburg on a private visit.

The Karajans lived in the Schwarzstrasse. The house bore the number 1, but the entrance to the living-quarters was around the corner in Johann-Friedrich-Hummel-Strasse, named after a director of the Mozarteum, on the narrow side of the building. It is an impressive building, baroque in tone, reflecting the Belle Epoque. Confident architecture from the late phase of historical architectural styles ornamented the building with one main dome and, in harmony with its outline as it tapered towards the east, three smaller domes. The Karajans' palace in the city could not have been better situated. The south-facing front looked on to the Elisabeth-Kai, with the Salzach flowing past it towards the west. The east side of the building faced the Platzl, from where the Staatsbrücke led over the river straight into the heart of the old city. To the west the row of buildings that began with the Karajan house now continues with the Hotel Österreichischer Hof. The Karajans' domed building is an exception to the otherwise feudal rigour of the façades on the right-hand shore of the Salzach. With its domes and towers it has an independent and playful look. Not exactly out of place, but striking, like so many things about the Karajans.

They lived on the first floor. The generous building was divided between the Imperial Government Councillor, Privy Councillor and Senior Registrar, Dr Ernst Ritter von Karajan, and his wife, and his colleagues, Dr Max Strohschneider (ground floor), a doctor in the State Hospital, and a dentist, Dr August Schwabe-Schwabe, who lived and practised on the second floor. All three doctors had their private practices in the house. The stately building is now owned by the Raiffeisen Bank, Salzburg. It was sold in the seventies, after the brothers Karajan failed to agree about their other inheritances.

Heribert's father was well known and loved in the city and its surroundings. His work as Senior Registrar of the St-Johann-Spital and later as Director of the State Health Authorities brought him into contact with a wide range of people. He was, in the true sense of the word, a popular doctor, a doctor of the people. He operated on Salzburg's goitres, his speciality. Karajan tells us:

His most prominent feature was his humanity. There was not a single farmer on whom he had not operated, and they were

– I often experienced this myself – simply tremendously affected by his goodness. He was not one of those surgeons, so plentiful today, for whom operations are simply a balancing act. He cared for people both before and afterwards. He was simply one's idea of a true doctor. He may have suffered because he was not given a teaching post, something which, quite certainly, he fundamentally deserved.

Actually Heribert's father had wanted to become an actor, but had joined the medical profession at the wish of his parents. In Vienna, where he grew up, the family ran a cultured, musical house, quite in the style of the period. Music-making in the home, in its fine old sense, was held in great esteem, uniting the domestic, family aspects of life with its musical side. That was to remain the case in Salzburg. Ernst von Karajan was an enthusiastic player of domestic music, being considered very musical, and playing the clarinet reliably enough to be able to play, for sheer pleasure, in the orchestra.

My father himself played quite passable piano in middle age, and his great passion was the clarinet. And when he had the time he went to the Stadttheater, which at that time was more or less at the operetta level, and sent the clarinettist off – he was happy to have a free evening – and played there for his own relaxation.

Without any doubt, Heribert von Karajan's eminent musical talent is inherited from his father. He said of the musical inclinations of his mother:

My mother understood it intuitively. She didn't know very much about it, but she was an ardent admirer of Wagner, and probably had a very deep temperament. It seldom emerged, but when she was listening to music it was quite clear that she was truly enthralled by it.

Heribert's first musical impressions came from music played in the home. And the stimulus to play himself came from his rivalry with his elder brother Wolfgang. His brother, himself a highly talented musician, was given his first piano lesson at the age of five. That was enough to make little Heribert want to have the same. In retrospect Karajan did not see his brother as dominant,

34

as the big brother, in fact, that he certainly was. 'Absolutely not, not in the slightest.' But then he continued:

I was always too small to do anything, too weak and too inadequate or something of the kind. I was devoted to him and wanted to do everything that he had learned to do. Everything that he had had, I wanted to have too. When he was given piano lessons, I wanted piano lessons as well. And then they said, 'No, you're too young, you can't do that yet.' Then I hid myself and listened to what he was playing. I always hid behind the curtains. And then I tried to copy him. And of course once I actually did have piano lessons I caught up with him in five weeks. Then he stopped and took up the violin.

If we consider what Thomas Mann terms 'prenatal merits', for Heribert these include the ambition of his paternal forefathers, their iron will to create something and to do it better than anyone else, as well as an infallible sense of quality – the Karajans never left anything unfinished – and a happy mixture between a business sense and musical inclinations. It is only logical, if not self-evident, that the Karajans' musical gifts should have come to fruition in the sons of Ernst von Karajan. We may only speculate on the extent to which Salzburg, the city of Mozart, with the incomparable flair and the indescribable aura of artistic exhilaration generally attributed to it, stimulated a specifically musical aptitude already in existence. In any case it is certain that among the first sounds and noises that reached Heribert's ears from outside, the clatter of hooves from the *droschkes* must have been among them, moving down the Schwarzstrasse past the house, across the Platzl and the Staatsbrücke, or in the opposite direction. But not only that: the call of the 'Bull of Salzburg', the pipe organ in the castle of Hochsalzburg, also echoed through the open window into the nursery, so clearly and distinctly that Wolfgang, the older brother, could later learn every note and play it on the piano.[12]

Along with the Bull of Salzburg and the trotting of the horses, the ringing of the city's many bells was among Heribert's earliest musical impressions. The call of the Bull of Salzburg is traditionally preceded by the thirty-five-bell Antwerp glockenspiel, built in 1702, that rings from the tower of the royal residence. In Salzburg one is never far from a church, and if on Sundays and holidays the strident tones from the Catholic churches, which claim and enjoy special privileges here, rang out from the Cathedral, or from the nearby Dreifaltigkeitskirche, then no doubt the resonant harmony and richness of the sound of bells, with all their overtones, took root in one way or another in the mind of the sensitive boy.

Childhood memories: what does a child really understand about the era in which he grows up, how clearly does he comprehend the events of the day and their meaning? Ranking alongside the experience of seeing the Emperor Franz Joseph there was the memory of Halley's comet. Its arrival in 1910 was awaited with fear and trembling, and the end of the world was much spoken of. 'It made a terrible impression on me with its huge tail. It looked like a Christmas tree decoration. I hope I shall live long enough to see it again.' Since 239 BC the lonely wanderer of the heavens has been observed every seventy-six years. On 11 April 1986 it neared the earth for the second time this century, and spread its imposing tail against the firmament, in the constellation of the Wolf. Did two-year-old Heribert, at the sight of the comet, become conscious of man's connection with the cosmos? Probably not. Man's sensory connection with the universe as a whole would only occur to him later in life. These are dim presentiments, if that. Is it perverse to see, in the magical power of the appearance of the comet and the fascination of everything distant, unattainable, lonely and superterrestrial that emanates from it, those powers that would later awaken Karajan's desire, expressed in many and varied ways, for cosmic harmony, which he was then to seek in music and the religions of the Far East?

From the moment his parents realized that Heribert was musically talented, he too was given piano lessons. We cannot rule out the idea that there was a certain amount of defiance involved in this as well, along with an urge to match his brother. Heribert also had his first visit to the opera during this time. The Karajans lived quite close to the Stadttheater. It was only a short walk away, so the little boy, barely four years old, was taken along to a performance of *Die Meistersinger von Nürnberg*. He was allowed to experience the overture and a few minutes of the first act, and the proud knight and his lady stayed in his memory. At this time the boys were also playing with the picture-paper theatres that were popular at the time, cutting out the gloriously coloured pieces of paper, sticking the sets together and bringing the main actors – robbers, knights, rogues, noble ladies and the whole inventory of the classics – to life in their home-made paper theatre. Thus the childish imagination developed, and if in future the director Herbert von Karajan was to see himself as the best of his own dramatic works, this may have been the origin of the idea.

On 15 April 1912, ten days after Heribert's fourth birthday, the most dreadful traffic accident of all time occurred. Early on the crow-black night of that Sunday, at around twenty past two in the morning, the 46,329-ton luxury steamer *Titanic* sank. One thousand, five hundred and seventeen passengers, mostly second- and third-class travellers and not members of the money aristocracy and the nobility, drowned in the ice-cold water of the North Atlantic. The Titans' rebellion against the gods had ended in Orcus. The accident shook the world, and was taken as a symbol of the coming holocaust. Karajan vaguely remembered the mood that the news of the catastrophe spread throughout the house: 'There was something threatening about it.'

At the age of four and a half Heribert appeared in public for the first time. In a restaurant in Morzg, south of the city, he played a rondo by Mozart during a benefit event, in the presence of his parents. This was still a playful presentation of a child's enjoyment of music. When he played in public again the following year he was built up into a child prodigy. Parental pride and the spirit of the age may have had something to do with this: it was, after all, the age of prodigies. Claudio Arrau, born in Chile in 1903, came to Berlin at the age of seven. He had his début there in 1910, and, as a pupil of Martin Krause, caused an uproar. The Hungarian Ervin Nyiregyhazi, born the same year, played as an eight-year-old prodigy before Queen Mary in Buckingham Palace. Since Mozart, Salzburg had been without a prodigy and now clung to anything that seemed like one. But Heribert was not a child prodigy in the true sense. His performances, even later as a pupil at the Mozarteum, were quite unexceptional demonstrations of talent within the context of his training, finding proof in public performance. They were auditions, and not at all prodigious. And happily that is how they were received by the Karajan household.

Heribert was six years old when the shots rang out in Sarajevo. They led Emperor Franz Joseph to take swift action against Serbia, and were finally, on 28 July 1914, to lead to a declaration of war against Serbia, whereupon the disaster of the First World War, Europe's civil war, was unleashed. Heribert's mother spent the summer of 1914 with her sons on a little island in the Channel of Fasano opposite the island of Brioni. Here Heribert saw the sea for the first time, and was 'deeply impressed'. The island belonged to a Viennese named Kuppelwieser. He had bought it because the doctors had advised him to find a mild place by the sea. He had irrigated and planted the island himself, and turned it into a little paradise.

The boys were able to run wild here. They charged down the even gradient of the island's hill, over and over again.

They stayed in the only hotel on the island. They had barely arrived when Archduke Franz Ferdinand of Austria-Este, the heir to the throne, and his wife, Duchess Sophie von Hohenberg, were shot dead in the street by a Serbian from Bosnia, Gavrilo Princip. Heribert's worried father sent his brother-in-law Kiepach to bring the family home.

Before their return, the family watched the funeral convoy steaming through the channel towards Trieste bearing the mortal remains of the murdered Duke and Duchess.

There were four warships. They came up from below and passed through the channel, right in front of our hotel. When I saw the four ships one after the other, with black flags at half-mast, my uncle behind me said to my mother, so clearly that I heard every word: 'Mark my words, there'll be war now.' That left a deep mark on me. It struck me as really strange. I had no idea what the word meant. But it was spoken with such an emphasis that I had an idea of its meaning. For the same reason I believe in other languages too. As when a dog hears you talking: he knows what you mean. I thought of war as some terrible thing. That tore me out of my childhood for the first time. It was something unfathomable for me.

Then I went to my aunt's farm. My mother's sister had married a certain Baron Leutzendorff, who had a very fine property – Schloß Prankh near Knittelfeld in Styria. It was a joy for us to be able to go out to the farm. There we had this really unfettered life, horses, animals in general – that was actually what I had always wanted. I always liked being in natural surroundings. My father was exactly the same.

Thus Heribert and Wolfgang experienced the start of the war at the home of their aunt, where Heribert was happier than he had been in the city. For in the city both school and a home run on patriarchal lines demanded conformity, subordination and achievement. But even there they always found time and opportunity for boyish pranks and adventures. They joined forces with the Hueber boys and formed a quartet, being always seen together, engaged in all kinds of likely and unlikely projects. Igi and Edi Hueber were the sons of the prominent specialist Dr Hueber von der Mauer. Descendants of minor Tirolean nobility, they were the Karajan boys' true childhood companions. Eduard Hueber was Heribert's childhood friend. Later Professor Hueber, he died of cancer of the larynx in the seventies.[13]

The boys' aunt in Styria had a Hupfeld Phonola, a semi-automatic piano with a mechanism which turned rolls of paper. It was thus at his aunt's that Heribert first became acquainted with a medium for the technological reproduction of music. He listened to original recordings by Rachmaninov and other great and important composers. 'I naturally spent hours sitting in front of it.'

The first years of Karajan's life coincided with a period of change, an age that was also in search of new forms of artistic expression. Braque and Picasso had been tracing the world of objects back to stereometrical basic forms since 1908. They called the result Cubism. The artistic community 'Der Blaue Reiter' was striving for a renewal of art from its origins. The painter Kandinsky was one of the most prominent representatives of the Almanach founded in Munich in 1911, which combined all the arts, visual art as well as music and poetry. In 1914, with his book of short stories *Dubliners*, James Joyce covered new ground, enriched by his technique of interweaving the world of objects with various levels of consciousness. In 1916, in Zurich, Dadaism came into being, mocking the traditional bourgeois culture that had been thrown into question by world war. In 1919 Walter Gropius founded the Bauhaus, a school with workshops in architecture, handicrafts and the visual arts, the source of decisive impulses for new building and the design of utilities.

In music, Arnold Schoenberg was discovering new territory. His *Five Orchestral Pieces, opus 16*, 1909, caused a scandal at their première in 1912. 'Schoenberg is the cruellest of all composers, he must be tone deaf,' was one of the malicious critical commentaries at the time. Freudian psychoanalysis found expression in the musical monodrama *Erwartung* that Schoenberg wrote in three weeks in 1909. The libretto, by Freud's pupil Marie Pappenheim, reads like a text spoken on the psychoanalyst's couch, and the music sounds like a colossally extended enlargement of the closing moment of *Tristan*. On 31 March 1913, before a laughing and noisy audience, Schoenberg performed the *Six Pieces for Orchestra, opus 6*, by his pupil and friend Anton Webern.

Also in the spring of 1913, Igor Stravinsky, with his ballet *Le*

Sacré du printemps, which had its first performance at the Théâtre des Champs-Élysées, unleashed the musical scandal of the century. In 1905, with *Salome*, and finally in 1908 with *Elektra*, Richard Strauss opened the way to new areas of sound and expression, taking them to the furthest reaches of polytonality.

There was, in fact, a great deal happening during these years. There was an oscillation between tradition and progress, and occasional attempts to reconcile the two. This was also the case in the performing arts. In Bayreuth, in 1908, the year of Karajan's birth, Siegfried Wagner took up his inheritance. In the same year Gustav Mahler composed his major work, *Das Lied von der Erde*, and on New Year's Eve 1908, he began his career as a conductor at New York's Metropolitan Opera with *Tristan und Isolde*, after having been driven from Vienna, as the long-haired director of the Vienna Hofoper, in 1907. Also in New York, Toscanini was preparing himself for his conquest of the musical world. In Tsarist Russia, the composer Sergey Koussevitzky was fulfilling every conductor's dream. He founded his own orchestra and his own festivals. Long before Karajan, he realized the idea of the autonomous festival *en permanence*. And during the years before the outbreak of war, his wife's fortune gave him greater independence than any conductor before or since.

Until the first few years after the war, Salzburg was still a provincial backwater without any real cultural perspectives. The only important musical events were guest performances from outside the city. In the spring the Würzburg Stadttheater visited Salzburg as part of their tour. That gave the schoolboy Heribert the opportunity to become acquainted with the medium of the opera. The first opera he heard was *Walküre*, and it made such a profound impression on the growing boy that he was unable to tear himself from the work of Richard Wagner for the rest of his life.

A great deal of music was played in the Karajan household during those years of breakdown and the foundation of the republic, those years of change and transformation.

In my childhood there was barely a single Sunday when friends and relations didn't come after dinner. We then played symphonies eight-handed on two pianos. So, at the age of six or seven, I came into contact relatively early with a very extensive repertoire of symphonic music. Where was one to hear it otherwise? But because my old aunts could no longer master it with their arthritic fingers it was played slowly, and if it was heard

40

in the original tempo they would say, 'That was much too
agitated.'

Another of the guests was the music scholar Bernhard
Paumgartner. At these family musical events he played viola or
horn. The playing often continued late into the night. The boys
slept close to the the music room, and so they went to sleep
surrounded by the muses conjured up by the family music-making
– if they could get to sleep at all.

On 21 November 1916 Emperor Franz Joseph died after a sixty-
eight-year reign. The decline of the empire was edging closer.
Before it met its end, Heribert appeared in public as a pupil at the
conservatoire of the Salzburg Mozarteum. On 27 January 1917,
Mozart's 161st anniversary, Heribert von Karajan, not yet ten
years old, played Mozart's Rondo in D major K 485, on a Bösen-
dorfer grand piano in the great hall of the Mozarthaus. The programme gives an unambiguous instruction: 'one curtain call only'.
Heribert's teachers in the Mozarteum were Franz Ledwinka
(piano), Franz Sauer (harmony) and Bernhard Paumgartner (composition and chamber music).

The dissolution of the Habsburg monarchy after the military
defeat in October and November 1918 brought with it one crucial
event which had nothing to do with his musical career, but to
which Karajan would, particularly later, attach considerable
importance. This was the abolition of the nobility by the Constituent National Assembly in April 1919. Now, all of a sudden, he
had ceased to be Ritter von Karajan. If he later called himself
Herbert von Karajan, we need have no hesitation in referring to
this as his stage name. Anything that applies to an Austrian aristocrat loyal to the republic applies equally to him. His passport had
him simply as Herbert Karajan. In the years after the defeat, his
original distinguished Christian name, Heribert, was promptly
given a cosmetic correction, rendering it solidly middle-class and
republican. The i fell victim to conformity with the new age. From
now on he would modestly call himself Herbert.

The fourteen-year-old Herbert Karajan was sent to England for
his summer holidays in 1920. He learned the language so quickly
there that when he returned three months later he spoke almost
fluent English. He made steady progress at the gymnasium and
the conservatoire, always getting good marks for hard work. The

double burden of scholarly education and musical studies was an exhortation towards shining achievements.

Until their voices broke, the Karajan brothers sang in Paumgartner's choir. Herbert's voice was accurate, if not especially fine. Nevertheless Paumgartner encouraged him because he was reliable. They were friends and frequently played together, even later on, after Karajan's voice had broken.[14]

Bernhard Paumgartner was always a welcome guest in the Karajan home. During these years he became a paternal friend to the growing boy. Born on 14 November 1887 in Vienna, while he was still a child he met Johannes Brahms, Hugo Wolf and Anton Bruckner, who was a close friend of his father's. They were frequent visitors to the Paumgartners', just as Gustav Mahler was later to be a regular guest. Paumgartner's mother was the *Kammersängerin* of the Kaiserlich-Königliche Hofoper, Rosa Papier. His father, Dr Hans Paumgartner, worked as a writer on music, a critic and a composer. Bernhard Paumgartner saw Brahms weep over Bruckner's death. He enjoyed an excellent education in the spirit of the humanist tradition. During the First World War he researched and collected the soldier songs of the peoples of the Austrian monarchy. In the autumn of 1917 he was made director of the Salzburg Mozarteum, where Herbert and Wolfgang were trained. Herbert could really not have hoped for a better mentor. Paumgartner introduced Herbert and Wolfgang to the secrets of music, and opened up to them the treasures of the great musical literature of the eighteenth and nineteenth centuries. At the same time, and this was a fortuitous event in their education, he became their friend. He was a good twenty years older than they were, and thus occupied the role of a kind of mediator between their father, who was busy advancing his career, and the boys, who were in search of change and a father-substitute. Quite without a doubt, he was a figure of admiration and attraction, not least for the simple reason that he took the boys on his motorbike. Herbert had his first few rides on the motorbike under Paumgartner's instruction, and the interest in technology thus engendered was never to leave him as long as he lived. Paumgartner played sport with the sons of the Privy Councillor and Senior Registrar. He always found time for the alert and inquisitive boys. They played tennis and football. He went skiing with them on the nearby Gaisberg, and took them hiking in the mountains.

He took them to the south in his car, and, drawing on the reserves of his extensive education, told them about the artworks of Italy. And he took Herbert to orchestral rehearsals, to give him an impression of the meaning and nature of conducting. He let him sit beside him, and later supported him when he was mature enough to do it himself. During these important early years, Herbert witnessed the rise of the festival. He watched the rehearsals, and positively soaked in his impressions of theatrical, operatic and concert rehearsals.

The Greek educational ideal of the *gymnasion* and its Roman counterpart expressed in the phrase *mens sana in corpore sano* found happy fulfilment here, or so it seems in retrospect. It seems almost as though the polymath Paumgartner ideally filled the function of the ancient Greek sophist with his various kinds of educational care, a concept now fallen into disrepute. Bernhard Paumgartner: a happy presence for Herbert von Karajan, Sunday's child.

In 1920 Paumgartner had an important encounter with the director Max Reinhardt, and subsequently played an important part in the development and growth of the Salzburg Festival, a circumstance from which the budding student Herbert was to benefit, and which was to prove truly advantageous to the conductor Herbert von Karajan. Paumgartner, the Mozart scholar and Mozart expert, conducted and composed the incidental music at the first Salzburg performance of Hugo von Hofmannsthal's *Jedermann* on 22 August 1920, and over the next few years, until he reached a ripe old age, conducted the Mozarteum orchestra at the serenades and church concerts that featured in the festival, whose president he was until his death on 27 July 1971.

Attentively encouraged by his mentor and musical teacher, Herbert completed his training at the Mozarteum and won a distinction in his matriculation examination on 11 July 1927. The following credits were given for the individual subjects: piano – very good; theory of form – very good; instrumentation – very good; harmony – very good; music history – very good. Herbert, who attended the gymnasium with Wolfgang, matriculated and, with his certificate in his pocket, followed his brother to Vienna to pursue his studies at the Technische Hochschule.

Herbert's father had certain reservations about Herbert's plans to follow an artistic career. He himself had abandoned a career as an actor to become a doctor. He advised Herbert to learn a practical trade that would assure him economic stability, an all-too-understandable desire against the background of a worsening world economic situation. Herbert's father made a final attempt to direct his son's career. 'When it came to my becoming a student, my father said: "Shouldn't you find out about learning a practical job?" For at that time music was seen as impractical. So I promised him: "I will. At least I'll try," and studied technology for a term and a half.'

His mother was also concerned about his career plans. She asked uncomprehendingly, 'What will you do if you go deaf in your old age?'[15] His father tried to guide him, but without getting in his way, if we can believe what has been said. We know nothing about the conflicts that tend to arise in situations such as this, where the son wants to go a different way, one which his father sees as dangerous and insecure. That doesn't mean they haven't occurred. Karajan is so obviously silent about his youth that one is really tempted to find out more about it.[16]

What were his parents really like? What was their determining influence on the upbringing of the child until he was a young adult? How did their son see them? What was the atmosphere in which Herbert grew up? The answers that Herbert supplies are inadequate but psychologically transparent enough to provide certain pointers for the reader trained in such matters.

Which of his parents did he see as having had more influence on the shaping of his character?

> Which one? Well, you know Goethe's lines: *Vom Vater habe ich die Natur des Lebens ernstes Führen, von Mütterchen die Frohnatur, die Lust zum Fabulieren* [From my father I have my nature for the serious business of life, from my mother my cheerful nature, my pleasure in stories.] I think that my emotional depth, experiencing things deep within me, is something I certainly have from my mother.

Was he close to his mother?

> No – I must add, of course: she was a wonderful woman whose dearest wish would have been to look after the whole world. She was simply concerned with the welfare of all of us, my father included. That was her basic position. And I remember: once when I was brought home after breaking my ankle in a fall, she said, 'Thank the Lord!' I don't think it was 'Thank the Lord' because I'd come out of it alive, but because she had me back. So she was touching in that way.

Was he over-mothered?

No, I can't say that, it was kept within limits. It's just that –
obviously you can see in retrospect that it was done with infinite
love. And with my father as well, I think. His main concern,
again, was to educate us as well as possible. I started to learn
the piano at a very early age, and always practised the piano in
tandem with my gymnasium work until matriculation. So that
amounted to fourteen hours of work per day. If I hear people
these days saying they're overworked at school – well, perhaps
we were a little less overworked, but I played piano for between
four and six hours a day. And that left very little time for what
boys normally do at that age. And of course I craved all that,
but it couldn't be done.

With which of his parents did he get on better, to whom was
he able to express himself?

Our children nowadays can talk about anything – it wasn't like
that in those days. My father still addressed his father with the
formal '*Sie*'. And some of that lingered on. He was a patriarchal
figure.

Did he find his father dominating?

Never. At the age of five I had him in the palm of my hand.
No – he was very gentle by nature . . . He wasn't a bitter man
by any means. He was supported by the love of the people he
had helped. I only really understood the value of that later in
life. That's what I always think about when I think about him.
My father was someone who had a great deal to do and took
it terribly seriously. For each operation he took a twenty-
five-minute walk from our apartment along the Salzach to the
hospital. Even at three o'clock in the morning. Because he
said to himself: 'During that time I can prepare myself for all
eventualities. I recall all the possible operations that I have
carried out in the past – if something went wrong then, what
can I do to prevent it this time?' Then he would come back
and go to bed and sleep again at about half-past four. There
was that. And there was hardly a party that he wasn't dragged
off to. So we didn't get to see him very much. Of course, our
mother was there instead.

Did he miss his father as someone to talk to, to relate to?

Yes, yes – no, you couldn't say that either. As I've said: in those days, and I know this from many of my colleagues, it was impossible to have an exchange of feelings with your parents. You had to seek that elsewhere.

So who did he discuss his problems, his worries with?

Nobody, in fact. I stored them up in myself a lot. That happened much later on. But as for finding the right person to talk to . . .

Was that difficult for him?

Yes, it was. Very. I'm not a person who makes friends easily. Not at all. What you would describe as friendship between your colleagues at school is something quite different. I was naturally under a lot of stress from my piano studies alongside my school work. It wasn't just plonking away, I played in public every year. On the one hand it isolates you. And on the other, of course, it gives you a satisfaction that it would be very difficult to get from any other source. That much is clear.

Which parent made the decisions about his education?

Neither of them could make up their minds. If there was some-thing to be done, then it was, 'Ask your father!' And he would say, 'Ask your mother!' Then they would try to find a solution between them. In the end things stayed as they were, and I felt so hampered by this as a boy that I said I'd find the solution by myself. Those are things that you may not know at first. But you turn into the kind of person who says: I'd like things to be as decisive as possible. It was even like that at school. I wasn't born to be ordered around.

Astonishing statements. What do they reveal, and what do they hide? Do they tell us anything about what did or didn't happen in the Karajan household? Karajan's information conceals more than it explains. A great deal emerges spontaneously, but then, after it has been recognized as a revealing statement, it is retracted again. Much of it sounds as if it has been reproduced from the fantasy of a distorted adolescence. Most of it consists of sweeping generalizations, produced for the purposes of defence. In many cases Karajan is projecting backwards from the present on to the past. Karajan portrayed his past to his best advantage. Was he

46

really someone who had had his father, a considerable man, in the palm of his hand at the age of five? A father of whom it has been said that, filled with an aggressive brotherly love, he ruled like a despot both in the clinic and at home? And what is this hint about being ordered around? Who, if not someone who had been ordered around, would have cause to portray things differently, or even to mention it? Anyone who had been lovingly guided rather than ordered around would have no comments to make about this disagreeable experience.

Are these statements of Karajan's not rather wishes, belated invocations on the part of the younger child that Karajan was, and who, as he himself confesses, 'was always too small and too weak'? Might he not, in his often contradictory statements, be defending an image of his parents that he has laboriously constructed but which has little to do with the reality of his youth?

Did he share in the almost overflowing compassion and care that he ascribes, in memory, to his mother and father? Who was being taken under whose wing? And what characterized his relationship to his brother?[17] Herbert, the frail, almost delicate child, emulated Wolfgang, his big brother, in everything that he did. He played the piano because Wolfgang did so. He ate what Wolfgang ate. And in Vienna, already a young adult, he studied precisely what Wolfgang was studying: technical science. What was the source of this fixation, and what did it mean? Here the little, weak boy, and there the big brother. Wolfgang had always been physically superior to Herbert. As an adult, too, he was bigger and healthier. Throughout his youth he represented a constant challenge.

If a child is as small and weak as Herbert was, under reasonably normal conditions we might suppose that his mother cared for him to a greater or lesser degree. He describes her, after all, as a person who cared for others with an almost obsessive attentiveness. Was Herbert the younger, weaker boychild who often ends up homosexual in some way or other?

So what really happened in that household, Herbert's brother apart? What, aside from all his talent, led this self-confessed little weakling to distinguish himself in music at such an early age?

What is the cause of his striking tendency towards flight, which he proved unable to set aside throughout his life?

Why did he escape into music? Did he do this to live out his fantasies of greatness? In his own work, might he have been continually frustrated by the indifference of a musically un-educated mother? Is it here that we must look for his desire,

47

unsatisfied throughout his life, for attention and recognition? Is it here, too, that we will find the key to his insularity, and his inability to form relationships?

Did his mother perhaps live her own life in too strong an identification with her son, or was his need as a small child for tactile stimuli and loving care unsatisfied, consequently leading him to transpose this need into the realm of sound, which might explain his turning to music? And if this were so, would such acoustic stimulation actually be enough to compensate for the lack it was supposed to replace?

All of these questions, however interesting we may find them, are for the most part unanswerable. Karajan's statements are regrettably not the material to provide us with explanatory and conclusive answers. At best they supply fuel for conjecture and speculation. I shall avoid the latter, however, and shall not allow myself to be carried from feelings of plausibility to concrete hypotheses.

And as regards conjecture, I shall practise restraint to the best of my ability. We cannot know what psychological pressures and injuries affected Karajan's development. The totally formative effect of his childhood and adolescence cannot therefore be dissected. But it lies before us in the totality of his personality.

Psychoanalysis might be able to instruct us, in so far as we can expect anything from Freud's theory. And anyone who did so would still face the question of whether Karajan would be prepared to undergo such treatment, as he did not care for such things.

Karajan's statements shed no light on his background, but in many ways they provide confirmation of what he was: cold, anxious, incapable of ties and relationships. Always in search of praise, attention and approval. An artist who, chiefly because of his emotional coldness, was incapable of leading a real private life, and wanted to protect what little he had – actually non-existent – by defending it, always in terms of a career-mindedness that had its origins in sibling rivalry.

So Herbert went to Vienna, the city of symphonies, as the Viennese composer Ernst Krenek once put it: 'The short history of symphonic form is inextricably bound up with the Habsburg Empire and its centre, Vienna. In no other city have true symphonies been composed; the names of Haydn, Mozart, Beethoven, Schubert, Brahms, Bruckner and Mahler are proof of that.' But Herbert did not go to Vienna to become a composer. He studied technical science. At the same time he continued to study the

48

piano, with Professor Hofmann. At first he and his brother shared a room. Then, when the intensive practising disturbed his brother, they separated. Herbert arrived in Vienna with high ambitions. As his brother reports, he wanted to invent something progressive and sensational in the field of motor-car manufacturing: 'At that time Herbert wanted to replace all internal combustion engines with a new source of power.'[18]

He wanted a major success. The time was right. The way was open, for loners with brilliant ideas had right of way. New ground was being broken in the technical sciences. Charles Lindbergh crossed the Atlantic in an aeroplane. This gave air travel an additional boost. But the economic situation was unfavourable, leading as it was towards the great world economic crisis. But just as advantages gained from Herbert's father's position had helped the Karajans through the lean period of the last years of the war and the immediate post-war period, Herbert's time as a student was also financially assured. Also, relations of the family lived in the city.

Herbert soon gave up his studies at the Technische Hochschule. Information is contradictory about how long he was able to bear it there. At one point he mentions three terms, somewhere else two, and again elsewhere, one and a half.[19]

Methodical discipline such as that summoned up and employed by his brother was inimical to Herbert. Wolfgang, on the other hand, successfully completed his studies at the Technische Hochschule. Later, as a professor and certified engineer, he was to develop electro- and microcardiographs in his laboratory for electrotechnology in Leopoldskronstrasse, and make his name with this alongside his passion as an organist. As a cheeky youngster he had assembled one of the first portable long-distance radio sets outside the family apartment. 'Wolfgang set up the machine in the middle of the Staatsbrücke, and in the wink of an eye two or three hundred people were standing around us. It was indescribable, music coming out of a box like that. We couldn't imagine it. He was reported to the police and had up for disrupting the traffic.'

Perhaps it was not only Karajan's impatience and lack of self-discipline that made him incapable of going through the various stages required for dealing with dry pedagogical material. Perhaps the college must share the guilt for this to a large extent. For its students had to waste their efforts unnecessarily and engage in numerous digressions because nobody in the college taught even the simplest techniques of scientific learning and research. Left to his own devices, Herbert brought his phase of aimlessness and helplessness at the Technische Hochschule to an end and transferred to the less systematic science of musical interpretation. He attended lectures on music by Professor Dr Robert Lachs and joined the Academy of Music. Without doing him an injustice we may suppose that Karajan's dealings with academic musical study were not overly intense, but rather an interested if somewhat casual way of listening. Even later in life, Karajan barely attended to academic musical problems and questions of interpretation with any great seriousness. His reservations towards, indeed his dislike of the scientific treatment of music and of attempts to explain and interpret music using non-musical means such as language started early and stayed with him.

It is also striking that in all the stories, in all the commentaries, music is never discussed on its own account. He hardly ever mentions problems of interpretation or, for example, his attitude to the work of a particular composer and his estimation of him.

It's always been that way. In my view you should do it with the message of the music and keep quiet about it. I'm afraid of flogging things to death. In the book I'm about to write at the moment – I don't talk about it in there either. I talk about how you arrive at a particular interpretation, but not what I think about the individual composer. Words are too inadequate, and I think that is the power of music, that it starts at the very point where words stop.

So shall we not be able to expect any more penetrating analyses from him?

No, I work them out myself.

And does he not want to give them away?

No, I couldn't. The best part would probably get lost in the process. And one thing is most important: music is an art that speaks to many people, but speaks to them in various tongues. Many people could have very different opinions about a really important and valuable piece of music. Even if it is fundamentally the same one. Because in the end it all goes back to a single root of psychological drives and instincts that governs human life in general. But the way it emerges from the composer, the way in which it follows his particular laws, his formal rules, his harmony, the age in which he lived, quite simply – his view of all that then gives rise to various different interpretations.

Karajan now wanted to be a pianist. However, self-criticism soon told him that eight hours a day of working at the piano was not for him, and that he might not have the talent to build up the career of a great pianist.[20] So he finally turned to conducting. We might presume that in doing so he was taking the path of self-denial along the way of least resistance.

The tendency to avoid difficulties may have been a factor here. But it was certainly not the crucial one. The tendency to flight is fuelled, I believe, in other ways. It is the fear of failure, of tangible failure. A miscalculation is a miscalculation, whoever is responsible for it. In technical science this can have fatal and catastrophic consequences. A wrong note is a wrong note, whoever plays it. Inadequate piano technique and unreliable fingering are things that we often hear. A loss of memory during the performance ruins the interpretation at a stroke. For that reason the instrumental soloist is under constant pressure, the unremitting demand for dependability. If your hands fail you, you've had it.

But how does that compare with conducting? Here the occasional failure is easily concealed. The failure of the conductor is delegated to the orchestra. The danger of showing oneself up in front of the audience is slight. Even a temporary amnesia of a few bars can be covered up if the rhythm and dynamic of the music changes slightly or not at all. Often not even the orchestra will be aware of errors. In conducting, a mistake on the part of the conductor (as long as it does not involve the most elementary omissions and failings) is transferred to the orchestra. If the conductor makes a mistake the orchestra has to pay for it. The conductor salvages his image, and the halo of infallibility granted him by his audience remains intact.

Karajan need not necessarily have been aware of this. Those who are subject to the tendency to flight are not always conscious of it. But it governs their actions, and there is nothing to indicate that it did not govern Karajan's actions during his years as a student in Vienna, given that for the rest of his life one thing was true of him, and that beyond all bounds: he was in flight, a flight from himself into immortality. Was it not also the fear of failing as a pianist that led him to escape to the podium? For there we have him, small in stature though he is, a big man because he is

51

standing on the podium. While Herbert Karajan the music student might have been unable to see and acknowledge this (although I believe that he did see it), he quite realistically recognized the limitation of his undoubtedly extraordinary pianistic talent and adapted accordingly. He recognized it not least because he was afraid of showing himself up. The insecure man always devotes most of his efforts to avoiding exposure and disgrace. Paradoxically, in doing this, and in sniffing out the host of dangers that might menace him, he even develops an astonishing degree of security.

The great performers of the day gave guest performances in 1920s Vienna. The Russian Revolution drove a whole army of excellent artists westwards. Vladimir Horowitz was a legend even then. He played in Vienna with Milstein and Piatigorsky: they were the most famous trio of the time. Horowitz set new standards in piano-playing, against which Karajan had to measure his ambitions and possibilities. In Berlin, Claudio Arrau won himself world fame as an interpreter of Liszt and Beethoven. Herbert was self-critical enough to see that he could not compete. The actual importance of the constitutional weakness of his middle finger, which he claimed had ruled out a career as a pianist from the start, is irrelevant compared with the overwhelming competition he faced. Karajan quickly made the right decision: he did not risk the certain fall into abysmal failure and anonymity.

A major source of help at the crossroads between a career and a lost artistic calling was his mentor and friend Bernhard Paumgartner. He provided advice. When he became artistic director at the Staatsoper in Vienna, Herbert von Karajan was once more strongly indebted to his tutor Paumgartner for his advice, which pointed the way for him and decided the course of his life. He wrote to him on 20 September 1957:

My dear, esteemed friend!
If I have best wishes to deliver to you today, it should come in the form of a letter of thanks to you, to whom I owe a significant part of my career. You were, after all, a major influence on me, both musically and in other ways: your initiatives led me from my intended career as concert pianist to conducting. I still clearly remember the crucial conversation in which you explained to me that my particular way of listening to music is such that I could only find true satisfaction in conducting. So

52

it is you that I must thank for that crucial stimulus in my life, and my thanks go out to you together with the hope that your personality, which, as so rarely today, unites the whole intellectual historical flow of the past and the present, may give us all encouragement and help in our work in Salzburg.

In constant loyalty and affection,
Yours
Herbert von Karajan[21]

The conducting class at the Vienna Musikakademie was run by Professor Alexander Wunderer. After the departure of Clemens Krauss he was little more than a stopgap. Karajan made a virtue of this necessity: he learned by observation. Nowhere in Austria was better suited to this than Vienna. The Staatsoper was run by Franz Schalk. The building's administrator and house inspector was Emanuel Ritter von Karajan, later captain of the castle guard. The Privy Councillor and trained engineer was Herbert's uncle. This gave his nephew access to the performances and the rehearsals, often closed to the public, of famous conductors. He showed him the building and its technical apparatus, and familiarized him with the wonderland of grand opera. Here, too, we come across something astonishing that will recur with almost frightening regularity throughout Karajan's life-story. Call it luck, chance, fate or whatever you will. The fact is: whenever he needed them, the right people, the important people in Karajan's career, have been on the spot. Unasked. They are already there, they represent the 'relationships', the 'circumstances' that shape his life. In his youth it had been Bernhard Paumgartner, while now, in Vienna, it was his uncle who was in exactly the right place to give the up-and-coming conductor an exact picture of the possibilities of a leading opera house. Later on, other people fulfilled the same function.

Along with Franz Schalk, the most important conductors at the Opera were Richard Strauss, Felix Weingartner, Robert Heger, Wilhelm Furtwängler and Clemens Krauss. Karajan was deeply impressed by Strauss's interpretations of the works of Mozart. During this learning phase he was exposed to many different influences, many of them powerful. 'One was very easily influenced at the start, of course, quite clearly.' But he did not meet Strauss in person. 'I never tried to come into contact, because I always said to myself, What can I give them? I would only get in their way.'

53

Karajan met Richard Strauss only much later, when he was conducting a new production of *Elektra* in Berlin on Strauss's seventy-fifth birthday. By then he was in a position to give the composer something, and they had a conversation in which Strauss acknowledged Karajan. And that was the end of the conversation.

From Clemens Krauss Karajan first learned the older conductor's technique of achieving the maximum clarity and precision of ensemble playing and diction using the smallest and most economical gestures. This temporarily brought him the reputation of being Krauss's pupil, which was not actually the case. Karajan did not meet Krauss until later on.

In the absence of an orchestra, the circle of students prepared the works being performed at the Opera at the piano, conscientiously attending and analysing the works in the Staatsoper. The students would conduct in turn, while the others played the orchestral parts at the pianos with piano scores and joined in the singing, and still others sang the choral parts. In this way the works were picked up in a practical way. And it must be admitted: even today, despite the existence of gramophone records, this is still a good way for up-and-coming conductors to work through the opera repertoire. Because the conducting student has to enter into a rapport with the colleagues who are to play and sing according to his directions, it is a process which very quickly reveals who the master is, who is in control – or not, as the case may be. A training based on gramophone records lacks the advantages of this rather provisional and Spartan-sounding method, as the process is then one-sided, and goes in one direction only.

It was in this way that Herbert spent one and a half years of more or less intensive study in Vienna. He attended concerts and learned by observation. Conducting the Vienna Philharmonic, having succeeded Felix von Weingartner as their permanent director from 1927 until 1930, was the newly famous Wilhelm Furtwängler. The young Karajan went in and out of the Staatsoper, saw the great men of his time and quite certainly dreamed more than once of conducting there himself. On 17 December 1928, at a concert given by Professor Wunderer's conducting school, Herbert Karajan demonstrated what he had learned. He conducted the last item on the programme, Rossini's *Wilhelm Tell* Overture. It confirmed him in his belief that he had a feeling for the orchestra, that conducting was his vocation.

Two weeks before Karajan proved himself publicly as a conductor, Wilhelm Furtwängler conducted the première of Arnold Schoenberg's *Variationen, opus 31*. Almost half a century later, in

54

1974, Karajan would preserve these variations – these pieces which, with an extreme compositional rigour, display the entire tonal palette of the large orchestra – for posterity in a sympathetic recording – without ever having met the composer. During his time as a student in Vienna Karajan met Anton Webern and Alban Berg, of whose major works for orchestra he would give equally exemplary interpretations. 'I knew Webern when he was considered a complete fool. I knew Berg. In the early years. His widow always came to my concerts when I played works by him. She was a wonderful woman. Like a queen. Tall. He was a very beautiful man, too. They were a truly aesthetically beautiful, wonderful couple.'

It is striking that the rising conductor Karajan did not develop any ambitions to become creative on his own account. He abruptly abandoned his compositional experiments. Might fear of failure have played a part in this, fear of isolation as an outsider, of the risk of being exposed to general ridicule as an unrecognized genius, and of becoming the curiosity that so many people considered Alban Berg to be?

Or did he recognize that he was not a truly creative spirit? One thing alone is certain: when he opted for conducting, Karajan was choosing his career over the possibility of becoming a genius in his own right, as a composer. The basis for his decision was his own unerring sense of what was possible, his sense of success, rather than a feeling for life and an idea.

He concentrated with determination on this one thing. This aggressive concentration on a single goal, obliterating all others, would stay with him throughout his life. It would shield him from the admission of creative failure. Gustav Mahler and Richard Strauss were the greatest conductor-composers of their day. If Karajan admired Strauss during these years, it was not only the conductor but also the highly successful composer that he admired. It was Karajan's tragedy that in his chosen profession he was never to do anything truly creative. He remained the eternally striving, performing, interpretative artist, however great his application. The realization of this later on, before he had even reached old age, was the double tragedy of his career.

As far as we know, Karajan made no true friends during his time in Vienna. He did not keep up with any of his colleagues. Karajan went his own way, on his own. Throughout his life he was to make no friends in the generally accepted sense of the word, although he would always seek them. And if he did find people who might have been his friends, they were soon scared

55

off. But the essence and the meaning of friendship lie in the fact that it lasts, that it endures. Karajan said towards the end of his days:

I do feel friendship for a few people. But I can't show it as such. I'm very friendly with the pilots I've been flying with for twenty years, there's a lot of human closeness, a lot of intimacy. Then there's a certain closeness to the people I've climbed mountains with; you don't talk to each other a great deal, but you feel there is really somebody there for whom you exist. But I admit that this feeling has only arisen over the years. I used to be a cold and calculating person. But I have changed a lot.[22]

Having carried off the concert at the Akademie, Herbert Karajan now planned, in the glow of his first success, his début in his home town. All the wheels were set in motion by his father, his friend Paumgartner, friends, acquaintances. The concert was held on Tuesday, 22 January 1929, in the Great Hall at the Mozarteum. For the event announced as an 'extraordinary symphonic concert', Herbert's father and the family friend Paumgartner used all their contacts in true Austrian style. Paumgartner put 'his' Mozarteum orchestra at Karajan's disposal, his father made use of all his not inconsiderable social prestige in organizing the event. And in addition to the Salzburg theatre and concert agent, Walter Hofstötter, Herbert had his acquaintances sell tickets. In giving this concert he already knew what to do if success was one's goal. The highly esteemed state governor, Dr Franz Rehrl, was invited with the following letter:

Hochverehrter Herr Landeshauptmann!
Permit me respectfully to offer you tickets for the proscenium box for the symphonic concert by the orchestra of the Mozarteum to be conducted on 22 January in the Mozarteum by Herbert Karajan, the son of our Senior Consultant Physician, Dr Karajan.
It would be a source of quite particular pride to this talented and promising artist if you, hochverehrter Herr Landeshauptmann, would attend the concert.
I remain your trusting servant
Walter Hofstötter[23]

The programme included works that could hardly be more demanding for the début of someone barely twenty-one years old: Tchaikovsky's Symphony No. 5, Mozart's Piano Concerto in A major, KV 488 (soloist: Yella Pessl) and the tone poem *Don Juan* by Richard Strauss. (Wilhelm Furtwängler was even less modest: he reached for the stars immediately and chose Bruckner's Ninth.) This programme, aiming undisguisedly for effect, won him his expected success. The district governor, Dr Rehrl, sent Herbert Karajan, as his name still appeared on the programme, a laurel wreath as a gesture of his appreciation. But much more important than this gesture of friendship was the fact that Erwin Dietrich, the manager of the Stadttheater in Ulm, was sitting in the stalls. He immediately spotted the great talent of the gifted young man, and made him an offer, since the post of a second or even a first co-ordinated kapellmeister had fallen vacant. He invited Karajan to a rehearsal session. Karajan confessed that he had never conducted an opera, and suggested an entire production. Dietrich complied with his suggestion. Those who demand a great deal often receive it. Overjoyed, Karajan went to Ulm.

The review, in the *Salzburger Volksblatt* of 23 January 1929, of the concert that brought his fame to Ulm, lists the specific qualities that marked Karajan out from the start: suggestiveness, a finely tuned tonal sensitivity, a tectonic sense of form. Under the heading 'Extraordinary symphonic concert', the newspaper reported:

As a rising conductor, Herr Herbert Karajan is keeping the promises he made as a prodigy at the piano. The first public appearance at the conductor's stand, which the student from the Vienna Musikhochschule made at an extraordinary symphonic concert on Tuesday evening in the Great Hall of the Mozarteum, shows a strong and restrained conductor's will, capable of making itself felt. Music produced from instinct and intellectualism. This will is based on a tectonic sense of form, a sense, indeed, that governs all the intellectual trends of this age of engineers. Depth and refinement are achieved by intellectual means, while excessive outbreaks of emotion, a demagogic attitude and overdramatization are held at bay. The work's construction is openly presented to us.

The baton work and posture were restrained. Not a declamatory conductor, but a leader of suggestive power. Suggestion of a conviction that is not contrived but experienced. And above all, not a youthful runaway indulging in unnecessary extravagances or drowning in his own pathos. Examples of his

57

reflectiveness: the careful crescendi, the moderation of the middle passages, the fine sense of tone, the imperceptible changes in tempo, the caesurae in the phrasing, in short: the quiet determination in development, structure and performance. The vitalized musical formation is helped along by the intelligence of the Mozarteum orchestra, which over the last few years has made tremendous progress in its power and vigour, in the accentuation of its dynamics and in its ability to sense the conductor's intention. The effect of Tchaikovsky's Fifth Symphony and Strauss's *Don Juan* was inspiring.

The evening was, and this is said without local patriotism, a small and surprising sensation. Many aspects of the conductor's attitude may change as he develops, becoming clearer and more relaxed. Even the form in which ideas are conveyed may undergo changes. But what will remain important will be the primal power of Karajan's musicianship and the intuitiveness of his effect on the orchestra. These qualities make up the inner calling to the career of kapellmeister. Karajan has them, and exploits them with a healthy instinct, and this will probably enable him to win through. In what direction, it is difficult to say. In the openness and transparent clarity of his intense emotion he fleetingly recalled the young Clemens Krauss. But he will have nothing to do with imitation. He will probably go his own way, for the world belongs to the young, and the son now conducts his father. Particularly when the latter is cheerfully playing the clarinet in the orchestra.[24]

Thus praised and encouraged, the Austrian Karajan moved to Germany with the highest hopes. Germany, where another Austrian, Hitler, had already gone ahead of him, to rise to Führer of the German Reich. The quality generously ascribed to Karajan really applies to Hitler: a leader of suggestive power. Regardless of the diversity of the two men's aims, and the terrible consequences they were to have in one case, they were both careerists.

58

2

The Career

'I was always in charge.'[1]

Anyone who can say this at the end of his days, at the end of a long and great career, must be extraordinary. Extraordinary in his talents and gifts and extraordinary in the demands he makes upon himself and those around him. And there was never any doubt about Karajan's extraordinary talent. The only thing that was doubtful was whether and how it could be guided towards complete development.

A career often begins earlier than a superficial glance at the stages of a life might reveal. Karajan's career began in Ulm. It was here that he was given his first appointment, and here that he created all the preconditions for his later fairytale rise, both in an artistic and a robustly realistic sense. Ulm was the first stop on Karajan's rise to fame. If we are to believe his own account, he held the position of leading conductor from the start. He shared it with the conductor Otto Schulmann, a few years his senior. Even if this was not so, and Karajan was, *de facto*, the assistant conductor to start out with, it is unimportant. For from the very first Karajan saw himself as the decision-maker. He was not born to be ordered around, as he repeatedly bragged.

Karajan came to Ulm empty-handed. At just twenty-one years of age he had no practical operatic experience. From Vienna he brought memories of the powerful apparatus of the Staatsoper, equipped with all the facilities of the big stage. These memories were quickly replaced by disillusion. The musical life of Ulm, its artistic and practical facilities, were a very small-scale affair. Having moved from the Musikakademie in Vienna to Ulm, an

59

upstream journey in many ways, he fetched up in the depths of the provinces, in the upper reaches of the Danube. From the broad horizons of the Austrian metropolis, in the winter of 1929 the young aristocrat moved to the narrowness and limitations of petty-bourgeois Schwabian smugness. This was to be the year in which Karajan embarked on his long and successful career. It was the year in which the Graf Zeppelin flew around the world and Hugo von Hofmannsthal and Arno Holz departed it. And it was also the year in which Remarque's *All Quiet on the Western Front* became a bestseller and Thomas Mann won the Nobel Prize for literature. In Berlin the first experimental television broadcasts were being made, and Kodak brought colour film on to the market.

The Theater der Reichsfestung on the Danube had a choir of not three dozen singers and an orchestra more or less the same size, stocked up with a few extra when operas were on the programme. The piano replaced a large number of the instruments called for in the score. Improvisation was encouraged, and so was imagination. Playing was done with closed ears: one compensated in one's mind for the actual shortcomings. The stage was as wide as the average sitting room is long. The technical equipment, in so far as we might dignify it with the name, was inadequate and outmoded. The ensemble consisted for the most part of beginners or enfeebled, has-been singers, being looked after in their old age. We do not know what the young conductor thought when he became aware of the conditions under which he was to work. If he was shocked, we can only empathize. But if shock it was, he soon overcame it. A salutary shock.

Wagner had encountered similarly disillusioning conditions a good ninety years before, in Riga. The theatre there, tellingly called the 'barn', with its strongly raked stalls and deep orchestra pit, and the darkness of its auditorium, was a crucial stimulus behind the design of the Festspielhaus in Bayreuth.

After an intensive six-week rehearsal period, Karajan had his début on 2 March 1929 with Mozart's *Marriage of Figaro*. The result convinced the manager of the talent of the fresh-faced operatic conductor. Thus, the man who 'had proven, on the occasion of his guest performance, to audience and press alike, to be a spirited and sensitive conductor', as the *Ulmer Tagblatt* had it several days later, was appointed 'as the opera's kapellmeister for

60

the remainder of this year's season and for the Stadttheater's 1929–30 season'.

Karajan rose to the challenge of the unsatisfactory conditions at the Ulmer Stadttheater. He put up with life in the provinces, he gritted his teeth, and he did it so thoroughly that he lost for ever any appetite for anything half-cocked, dilettante, provisional or artistically provincial. In Ulm he conducted his way through the current repertoire. He grew familiar with the works using all those inadequate musical and technical resources that are nowhere more acutely and permanently affecting. He got to know the mistakes, the less accomplished passages in the works, in his daily analyses at the piano, where he rehearsed the parts with the singers, and in the evening performances, which constantly threatened to become over-enthusiastic. Anyone without the gift of adaptability must learn it very quickly, or else fail hopelessly as a conductor in a provincial theatre. For little attention is paid to the kapellmeister in such places; instead he has to adapt to the whims and fads of the people on the stage. Karajan brought this adaptability with him among his store of talents. In Ulm he was able to refine it to perfection.

The demands of the provincial theatre trained him in attentiveness. They made him sensitive to unpredictability, they taught him to recognize possible disasters in embryo, and to pounce upon them with lightning speed. He gained something without which his somnambulistic certainty, his absolute dependability in the orchestra pit would have been unthinkable: the trade, the craft of conducting.

Thus the years of apprenticeship in Ulm were the most important of his career, for it was here that he acquired the weaponry without which his later successes would have been inconceivable, without which a conductor who really wanted to master his trade would be absolutely unable to survive. He learned the current operatic repertoire and much else besides, inside out, because he had to approach it from every angle in an institution where the kapellmeister is repetiteur, singing teacher, arranger, gaffer, arbitrator and much more in one. In Ulm, he worked on the broadest repertoire, ranging from Handel to Richard Strauss. He conducted the *Meistersinger* – certainly with inadequate resources, but learning for his future life from his mistakes and shortcomings. He conducted, some of them for the first time in Ulm, *Rigoletto, Martha, Don Giovanni, Cavalleria Rusticana, The Barber of Seville, Carmen, La Bohème, Don Pasquale, Tiefland, Rosenkavalier, Undine, Tannhäuser, The Merry Wives of Windsor, La*

Traviata, Wildschütz, Julius Caesar, Lohengrin, Arabella and, in 1931, as part of the festival celebrating 150 years of the Ulm Stadttheater, *Trovatore* and *Madame Butterfly*.

When, more than a generation later, he conducted *La Bohème* at the Staatsoper in Vienna, in a full-scale and spectacular production with Franco Zeffirelli as director and stage-designer, the event took him back to a 'terrible evening in Ulm' where he had conducted his first *Bohème*.

> I suffered from it for years. It is that suffering in the depths of my soul that really brings the music alive in me. During certain performances I have often suffered physically because they were badly produced. Suddenly the music would seem too slow, dragging too much. No wonder I wanted to get it over with quickly. I simply couldn't watch what was going on up there any more.[2]

The fact that it was in Ulm that Karajan began his career, and not at a major theatre, almost in itself justifies the existence of the fast-disappearing, solid provincial theatre. If Karajan later worked with an adaptability verging on wizardry, and was apparently able without any lengthy preparation to bring works from different eras to the public ear at short intervals and in musically impeccable performances, this was directly due to his remorseless training in a deprived provincial setting. Karajan owed more than his mastery of the workmanlike aspects of the conductor's duties to his apprenticeship in Ulm. He was not dismayed by the inadequacy of the technical, organizational and artistic resources of a small theatre, or the shortcomings of an excessively small and feeble orchestra. Instead he took it as a challenge, to grasp the essence of a work in the space of a moment and, stubbornly and obsessively, to bring about the preconditions that he needed – in every area of his work – for the fulfilment of his artistic visions. His dissatisfaction with what was immediately available to him in Ulm distinguished Karajan, to his own profit and advantage, from those provincial kapellmeisters who so complacently come to terms with the given conditions, or simply become resigned. The young Karajan already held them in contempt. Improve things, adapt the given conditions to your own aims – such was Karajan's motto.

'The principle of circumventing a solution of problems by adapting to circumstances must not be allowed to obtain. Rather, what is necessary is to adjust circumstances to requirements.'[3] Those could have been Karajan's words. But these sentences were said some years later by someone who was soon to play a crucial part in the life of the young conductor. It was the motto of those who could only seek and produce perfection with external things, because they could not do it themselves. The statement comes from Hitler. It was spoken on 23 May 1939, addressing the heads of the Wehrmacht in the Reichskanzlei in Berlin. But as yet there was no recognizable connection between Karajan and the Third Reich.

If the stage in Ulm was too small for a Wagner opera, then it was only logical that Karajan, at the height of his powers, should get hold of the huge stage at the Großes Festspielhaus in Salzburg. If the orchestra turned out not to be adequate to the works to be performed, then it was only consistent to introduce what was, in the eyes of many people, and certainly in Karajan's view, the greatest, most musical and perfect concert orchestra to operatic playing. And if inadequate financial resources, philistine trade unions and unsympathetic authorities stood in the way of the deployment of first-class singers, choirs and employees, then the obvious next step was to use a media network, to exploit record and television companies to one's best advantage, to create the financial basis for the best possible artistic results. Ulm, the first stepping-stone of his career, was the beginning of a consistent career strategy leading to the utopia of the perfect illusionistic theatre. As an alternative to all the shortcomings of his work-places, whether they were Ulm, Aachen, Milan or Vienna, Karajan finally made this utopia a reality in his Salzburg Easter Festivals, the crown of his career.

But it was still a long way from Ulm to Salzburg. When Karajan asked his friends to support his festival idea and realized the project, which was becoming a real business concern, of consider-able economic importance for the city's tourist industry, he drew upon the indispensable and important experiences that he had already gathered in Ulm. Such experiences always leave their mark in some way or other.

To find subscribers for the concerts in Ulm, Karajan turned to the citizens of the city. He was confronted more than once by the Swabians' contempt for artists as a clan, and the response 'I'm not giving anything to a bunch of playactors', became a wound for which he was to seek revenge throughout his career. In Ulm in the 1930s it was not customary to associate with theatricals and strolling players; one went to the theatre, but apart from that one had nothing to do with theatrical people. So the young Karajan, already at a disadvantage because of his unsociable nature, grew

63

all the more isolated. This awareness of not being accepted injured his pride – after all he was the descendant of Austrian aristocrats. He was hurt by his experience of petty-bourgeois attitudes among the people of Ulm. But Karajan's wounds never healed quickly. 'I said to myself back then, if I continue to be treated as I predict I will be, I shall do everything I can to bring this profession the respect and dignity it deserves. The members of the theatre were outcasts . . . And back then I vowed: I'll get respect from the lot of you!'[4] Respect for him, his prowess, respect for music, for art in general, and for devoted, often selfless artistic work.

When Karajan, then more than seventy-four, attended a performance of Goethe's *Faust* in the Wasserkirche in Zurich, the insults, rejections and injuries of his years in Ulm must have risen up in his memory. For Gretchen was played by his daughter Isabel. It was her very first role. She began her career as an actress in a 'jubilee production for "Goethe year" ', which was very popular, but was still produced in a cruelly mutilated version and lacked everything that Karajan considered to be the ethos of his work: respect for the text.

The improvisations and shortcuts that typified this touring production, compromising both the work and the actors, must have reminded Karajan of his own beginnings in Ulm. There the increasingly experienced young conductor learned how to ignore the tone of the orchestra, its inadequacy and errors, the more intensely to listen to the imaginary orchestra of his inner ear. The production of *Faust* would have reminded him not least of the first time he worked at the Salzburg Festival, where, in August 1933, he conducted the music composed by his friend and mentor Bernhard Paumgartner for Max Reinhardt's production of *Faust*. And if the old Karajan in Zurich was able to cast his mind back, he must have thought of the great and moving Paula Wessely, and wondered whether his daughter would be capable of making that fraught and difficult journey from the troupe of strolling players to the all-encompassing world of the theatre, whether she would be able to make the transition from travelling player to great and sensitive actress.

Although he was rather isolated in Ulm, both privately and professionally, Karajan did not miss an opportunity to study the great men of his time. After being in his post for just three months, he travelled to Vienna in May 1929, where Toscanini was giving a guest performance with La Scala of Milan at the Staatsoper. Verdi's *Falstaff* and Donizetti's *Lucia di Lammermoor* were on the programme. These performances by Toscanini, then at the peak of his ability and his fame, were revelations to Karajan. He followed both productions from the fourth row, and gestured to the leader of the claque, who was unfamiliar with the works. When he was rehearsing *Falstaff* for his Easter Festivals, Karajan told me of the dismay with which he returned to Ulm from these performances, back to the podium of his inadequate theatre. He expressed himself in similar terms to his biographer Haeusserman. I shall therefore take the liberty of quoting Karajan in Haeusserman's version.

> From the first beat I was thunderstruck, I was completely astounded by the perfection that had been achieved here, especially in the *Falstaff*; we know that Toscanini had done a great deal of work on this *Falstaff*, polishing it up, rehearsing and rerehearsing it and constantly swapping the singers around. This production was already ten or twelve years old at the time [not even eight, in fact – R.B.], not 'old' in the true sense, but matured. For the first time I understood the meaning of the word 'direction'. Certainly, Toscanini had used a director, but basically the important ideas were his own. The congruence of the music and the stage production was something quite unimaginable for us; instead of people standing around pointlessly, everything had its place and its purpose. I don't even believe that the Viennese were fully aware, back then, of how great a contribution it was for La Scala to come to Vienna and demonstrate to us young people what can be done with an interpretation if everything is in its proper place.[5]

Rehearsing and re-rehearsing, polishing up the production, swapping the singers around until the best possible cast has been found, allowing a production to mature and bringing it into festival programmes over the years, constantly improving it – these were later to be characteristics typical of Karajan, taken directly from the model of Toscanini. 'I don't need to make a secret of it – for me it was the most fantastic impression of my life.'[6]

The up-and-coming kapellmeister used the annual summer breaks at the Stadttheater in Ulm to continue his training by attending rehearsals and performances at the Salzburg Festival. Bernhard Paumgartner, who played the Mozart Serenades with the Vienna Philharmonic, told him everything he needed to know about the festival. Knappertsbusch, Franz Schalk (one of Karajan's teachers, so they say), Bruno Walter, Clemens Krauss, Ernst von Dohnanyi, Robert Heger, Sir Thomas Beecham, Fritz Busch and

Richard Strauss were, along with Paumgartner, the prominent festival conductors during those years. The unchallenged and universally admired ruler of the theatre was Max Reinhardt who, between 1929 and 1932, directed Goldoni's *Servant of Two Masters*, Hofmannsthal's *Der Schwierige*, Goethe's *Stella*, and Schiller's *Kabale und Liebe*, as well as Somerset Maugham's *Victoria*. Karajan came under the spell of this theatrical director, unchallenged in his artistic authority. Later, when Karajan began to stage his operas himself, he would repeatedly mention the name of Reinhardt and his artistic legacy.

In Salzburg the young musical director was given his first assignments. He worked on the conducting course started in 1929, along with Lovro von Matacic and Lajos von Rajter, as an assistant and instructor. He soon had the opportunity of passing on the experience he had won in the provinces, learning new things at the same time. When Toscanini conducted *Tannhäuser* and *Tristan* in 1930, and *Tannhäuser* and *Parsifal* in 1931, Karajan spared himself no hardship in that economically insecure time: 'In order to hear him I cycled from Ulm to Bayreuth . . . Karl Muck had fortunately managed to get me a ticket.' It might have been Salzburg that he cycled from, Karajan could not remember exactly – he circulated both versions.

If we are to believe Karajan and his biographers Haeusserman, Löbl, Robinson and Lorcey, his career proceeded as follows, in a summarized version. Dietrich, the manager of the Stadttheater, refused to renew his contract for 1933, and Karajan was to leave Ulm. However, he managed to change the manager's mind and persuaded him to retract his dismissal. He kept his appointment for a further year. On 31 March 1934 his contract finally expired. Karajan wandered, desperately in search of a new post, through Germany, and danced attendance in Berlin's artistic agencies. It was there that he met the Aachen theatre manager Dr Groβ, who was looking for a conductor. Karajan managed to obtain a trial period. In September 1934 he introduced himself to the audience of Aachen with *Fidelio*. In 1935 he was made Generalmusikdirektor, succeeding Professor Peter Raabe, and thus became the youngest in Germany. Complying with a Third Reich formality, which required membership of the Party for the position of Generalmusikdirektor, Karajan was obliged to join the National Socialist Party; refusal would have meant the loss of his post. This, at least, is the official version put forward by Karajan's propaganda and publicity machine.

But as the facts tell us otherwise, we must have a look at the period coinciding with Karajan's first years as a musical director, and it is imperative that we should sketch out the political, intellectual and economic situation of the years leading up to 1933 in order to gain some understanding, from these events, of why Karajan's life actually took a different course from the one he and his trusty heralds would like us to believe.

The collapse of the Austro-Hungarian Empire led to political instability and economic misery. In an agony that lasted years, Germany's Weimar Republic was dying a slow death. Savings were being swallowed up by inflation. It shook the social and economic foundations of the middle class. With the start of the world economic crisis on 24 October 1929 (Karajan was already conducting in Ulm), the job-market situation became drastically intense. It was the age of public soup kitchens, of queues in front of grocers' shops and daily visits to the labour exchange. Even at the beginning of 1929 the number of unemployed in Germany had risen to just over three million for the first time. In September 1930 it reached the three-million mark again. In 1931 it had risen to almost four and a half, and at the beginning of the following year it already totalled more than six million. The social consequences of the world economic crisis contributed considerably to political radicalization in Austria and Germany. The mass misery of the armies of the unemployed spread like a consuming conflagration. It prepared the ground for National Socialism, which was chalking up increasing support among the millions-strong army of the socially and economically insecure.

In the wake of the world economic crisis many musicians were also left without an income. The job survey of 16 January 1933 revealed a figure of 28.9 per cent unemployment among manual and office workers. But in the group of musical directors, music teachers and independent musicians unemployment reached 46 per cent, and among singers and singing teachers, 43.5 per cent. There was a total of 23,889 unemployed musicians and 1,891 singers. In the face of these figures, which reflect the disastrous situation for practising artists if they cannot describe it, Karajan could consider himself lucky to be offered any post at a German theatre. When Karajan took up his position in Ulm, Hitler was forcing his way to power. In the masses of jobless and those on government support, poverty, hunger and despair had unleashed irrational longings and wildly burgeoning hopes of a radical change in their situation. For them, as they saw it, things could only get better. In his book on Hitler, Joachim C. Fest wrote:

> Charlatans, astrologers, clairvoyants, numerologists and mediums flourished. These times of distress taught men, if not to pray, pseudo-religious feelings, and turned their eyes willy-nilly to those seemingly elect personalities who saw beyond mere human tasks and promised more than normality, order and politics as usual – who offered, in fact, to restore to life its lost meaning. With remarkable instinct, Hitler grasped these cravings, and knew how to make himself the object of them. This was his hour in every sense.[7]

For a large proportion of the German electorate between 1929 and 1933, the promise of economically stable conditions and a fundamental renovation of society became an irresistible temptation, regardless of the fact that this promise was not fulfilled by the National Socialists. They proclaimed a classless society where life was largely to be led according to the tried and trusted maxim 'make way for the hard workers'. For those who were industrious and willing to conform, the Party promised all kinds of prestigious jobs and management posts: the Party would help anyone who wanted into the stirrups of a National Socialist career. During these crucial years the Party was attracting membership from all classes, musicians and intellectuals included.

Were they, the latter above all, victims of a complete misapprehension of the future policies of the National Socialist Party, were they misled by hollow promises of a 'rebirth' of Germany? Or was it indeed possible to be misled, did the National Socialists not make their intentions as clear as possible from the very start? Had Hitler not quite clearly revealed his 'programme' in *Mein Kampf*, long before it was carried out, had Goebbels not spoken clearly enough when he announced:

> We are entering the Reichstag in order that we may arm ourselves with the weapons of democracy from its own arsenal. We shall become Reichstag deputies in order that the Weimar ideology should itself help us to destroy it ... We come as enemies! Like the wolf falling on a herd of sheep, that is how we come.[8]

The Party's struggle for power did not take the form of a debate conducted in the airless arena of intellectual argument. On the contrary: from the first, agitation replaced factual, rational argumentation. Verbal agitation was followed by the physical variety. Gangs of thugs used the robust argument of crude force to convey the required emphasis. Street-fights and brawls between the gangs of the SA and the Roter Frontkämpferbund, the fighting organization of the Communists, were daily events. In March 1929, when Karajan had just had his début in Ulm, there was a confrontation in Dithmarschen, in the course of which two members of the SA were killed and thirty people injured. In August 1932 five members of the SA murdered a Communist. When they were condemned to death, Hitler sent a telegram publicly celebrating them as heroes.

State resistance to this covert civil war, 'which, until January 1933, left behind it a thin but steadily bleeding trail',[9] was a cowardly affair. In June 1930 a ban on the wearing of NS uniforms was passed in Bavaria and Prussia. A few days after the Reichstag elections in September 1930, in which the NS won 107 votes and thus became the second biggest party, a sensational case against three officers from the Ulm garrison was brought before the Federal Court in Leipzig. In contravention of an order of the National Defence Ministry, the officers had recruited for the National Socialists. Hitler, called as a witness, declared his support for complete legality in the political struggle in unsettlingly ambiguous terms. Asked about his countless threats against the 'traitors at home', Hitler replied, to applause from the gallery: 'I stand here under oath to God Almighty. I tell you that if I come to power legally, in my legal government I will set up state tribunals which will be empowered to pass sentences by law on those responsible for the misfortunes of our nation. Possibly, then, quite a few heads will roll legally.'[10] That is clear enough. What Hitler meant by legality he later exemplified by creating the People's Courts, controlled by Roland Freisler, among other ways. In 1930 it was not even necessary to know who it was that Hitler saw in *Mein Kampf* as the parties responsible for the misfortunes of the German people. In speeches, Party pamphlets and terroristic acts against undesirables it soon became clear what kind of future the Party was ushering in. Extensive coverage of the trial for high treason against the Reichswehr officers was also carried by the newspapers in Ulm, where the accused had been based and where Karajan was rehearsing the opening concert of the new season; on 1 October the coverage even coincided with a discussion of Karajan's new production of *The Barber of Seville*.

It was evident early on where the Party's cultural politics was headed. Thus, in April 1930, the first National Socialist minister of a German state, Wilhelm Frick (Minister of the Interior and Education for Thuringia) introduced a 'bill against Negro culture and for German folk culture', banning 'modernist' films, books and plays. In addition, he had all 'modernist' paintings removed from the Schloßmuseum in Weimar. Amid tumultuous scenes, the Reichstag was opened in Berlin on 13 October the same year. Howling and making gestures of protest, the NSDAP members entered the chamber, provocatively disregarding the current Prussian ban on uniforms. Brownshirts and Communists brawled outside the parliament building, and Goebbels staged the first organized riots against Jewish businessmen and passers-by. On 17 October, the famous lecture 'German Pronunciation – A Call to Reason', delivered by Thomas Mann in Berlin's Beethoven-Saal, was disrupted by SA members sent there by Goebbels.

In this climate of intolerance, intimidation and latent terror turning more and more into open threats, Karajan was working in Ulm and enjoying his first triumphs. He was learning to come to terms with the conditions dictated by poor financial funding. To be able to perform concerts at all, the orchestra had to be supplemented by military bands, by musicians from the Young Pioneers, from the infantry and the artillery. Karajan had the orchestra pit covered over by a concert podium, and worked hard in all his areas of responsibility, constantly making improvements.

To what extent National Socialist ideology affected Karajan during this tentative period, while he reaped his first harvest, is uncertain. Before the NSDAP became a mass party, its popularity among the younger generations gave it the appearance of a mass youth movement. In 1931, for example, some 70 per cent of Berlin SA members were under thirty, and in the other districts the proportion was similar. 'Hitler's enlistment of the young proved to be a canny policy. He also saw the wisdom of entrusting them with high positions. Goebbels became a gauleiter at twenty-eight, Karl Kaufmann at twenty-five. Baldur von Schirach was twenty-six when he was appointed Reich youth leader, and Himmler was only two years older when he was promoted to chief of the SS.'[11]

Although many people, while Hitler was seizing power, still clung to the hope that a government with strictly monarchist tendencies, such as that fought for by von Papen in 1932, would keep the National Socialists within bounds, the pointers for the future were clearly apparent to anyone with eyes, ears and a brain. On 2 June 1932, Wilhelm Kube, a member of parliament, said in the Reichstag: 'If we make a clean sweep it will make the exodus of the children of Israel look like child's play.' And, in case that was not clear enough, he added that 'A people that has a Kant cannot tolerate an Einstein in its midst.'[12]

In order to gain a better understanding of the cultural political situation in which the young Karajan found himself in the spring of 1933, the political influences to which he was exposed and the events that determined the state of Germany at that time, we should at this point give a brief account of the events of the previous few months.

On 30 January 1933 Hitler attained his provisional goal: he was made Chancellor by the aged President von Hindenburg. On 1 February Hindenburg dissolved the Reichstag elected in November 1932. New elections were set for March. On 4 February, Hindenburg passed the 'Emergency Act for the Protection of the German People', thus paving the way for the use of terror in the fascist election campaign. It gave the government the right to prohibit, on ill-defined grounds, events and press conferences organized by the competing parties. It immediately set about doing this with draconian rigour. On 17 February a horde of uniformed brownshirts invaded the State Art School in Berlin-Schöneberg, burst into an exam which was taking place at the time, threw out four Jewish and Marxist examining professors and set about the students who tried to protect their teachers. On 22 February the Prussian Minister of the Interior, Göring, set up a 50,000-man-strong auxiliary police force. Equipped with white armbands, pistols and truncheons, they were to spread terror and fear with a violent series of arrests. In a speech at a Party meeting on 3 March, Göring said: 'My measures will not be sicklied o'er by any bureaucracy. It's not my business to do justice; it's my business to annihilate and exterminate, that's all.'[13]

In the meantime the National Socialists staged the most expensive and reckless election campaign of the age. In order to suggest omnipresence, Hitler once more began to fly around Germany. In the election campaign waged with increasing intimidation by Göring's police apparatus, Goebbels' plan of action included the massive deployment of every technical means at his disposal. Alongside the extensive use of radio, the banner marches and parades organized across the country by the Nazi propaganda

71

machine tried to recruit the masses to the Party using highly theatrical devices. A considerable proportion of the expenses for the election campaign came from industrialists and bankers invited to the palace of the Reichstag President. The Adolf Hitler Foundation for German Business, organized by Gustav Krupp von Bohlen and Halbach, brought in at least three million Reichsmark.

On 27 February, coinciding nicely with the National Socialists' plans for dictatorship, came the fire at the Reichstag building in Berlin. The National Socialists immediately put the blame on the Communists and exploited it for propaganda purposes, launching a wave of arrests whose victims included undesirable writers such as Carl von Ossietzky and Egon Erwin Kisch. The next day, prompted by Hitler, Hindenburg issued the emergency decree for the 'Protection of the People and State'. As the decisive legal basis for National Socialist power, it gave Hitler the tool he required for his despotism and rule of terror. This emergency decree, complemented by a further law 'against treason to the German people and treasonous machinations', was to be the most important legislative act of the Third Reich. It formed the actual legal foundation of the regime, and replaced the constitutional state with martial law. It remained in effect, unchanged, until 1945. On the basis of this law, on the grounds of the Reichstag fire, by March more than 10,000 arrests were estimated to have been made in Prussia alone.

Although the election on 5 March did not bring the majority Hitler expected, the swastika was hoisted on public buildings. In a series of surprise actions Hitler won power in the states. In Württemberg, the state containing the city of Ulm, the government was forced to resign. Gauleiter Wilhelm Murr, made state president of Württemberg after a rigged election, frankly announced: 'The government will strike down with all brutality anyone who opposes it.'[14] On 9 March Wilhelm Frick announced the building of the concentration camps. Three days later, on 12 March, Hitler revealed in a Remembrance Day radio address that the colours of the Weimar Republic, black, red and gold, were to be abolished, and that in future the swastika and the black, white and red banner were to be the state flags. From now on the swastika fluttered over the Stadttheater in Ulm, in the mounting political storm. A few days before, on 8 March, with the support of the population of Ulm, troops of brownshirts hoisted the flag of the New Germany over the Rathaus, the Grenadiers' barracks, and other municipal and state buildings in Ulm. 'Indescribable jubilation surged through the crowd. National comrades, and not only women and mothers, were seen with tears in their eyes',[15] when the swastika flags bearing the symbol of the German liberation movement rose up the poles, as reported in the *Ulmer Sturm*. This organ of the Ulm NSDAP had ten days previously blessed Karajan with an excellent review of his second symphonic concert on 22 February, in which, for the first time in Ulm, he played Mozart's Piano Concerto in D Minor as conductor and pianist, with his own cadenzas, and won thunderous applause.

In Ulm, on the occasion of the opening of the German Reichstag on 21 March, 'to give visible expression to Germany's awakening and national rebirth for the present day and for times to come',[16] Einsteinstrasse, named after the city's great and now ostracized son Albert Einstein, was renamed Fichtestrasse: the 'German national' philosopher Johann Gottlieb Fichte was honoured anew. Was this event, publicized as it was in Ulm's daily newspapers, as well-hidden from Karajan as the hounding of other prominent representatives of German intellectual and cultural life, and their expulsion from Germany?

Despotism and lawless anarchy, which defined the political events of those March days, also spilled over into the supposedly unpolitical realms of music. On 7 March in Dresden, the SA forced Generalmusikdirektor Fritz Busch to call off a performance of *Rigoletto*, as reported in the *Schwäbischer Volksbote* which was available in Ulm. A concert with the Gewandhaus orchestra in Leipzig, scheduled for 16 March, to have been conducted by Bruno Walter, was prohibited by the government. Similar things were later to happen to the Jewish conductor in Berlin, where he was to have conducted a concert with the Berlin Philharmonic on 20 March. The state secretary in the Ministry of Propaganda, Walter Funk, decreed that the concert was to go ahead under a different conductor. At the wish of Bruno Walter, Richard Strauss, hesitant at first, had agreed to conduct it. He did this not so much 'for the slimy little scoundrel Bruno Walter',[17] as he wrote to Stefan Zweig in a letter intercepted by the Gestapo, as to rescue the concert for the financially hard-pressed orchestra. Bruno Walter, having had a salutary lesson about what was to come, abandoned any further work in the Third Reich, as did Fritz Busch. The Leipzig *Signalen für die musikalische Welt* of March 1933 contained the following succinct account of his expulsion by the anti-Semitic regime: 'As reported, Generalmusikdirektor Bruno Walter will return to New York at the end of September 1933, to conduct forty concerts as Toscanini's sole partner with the city's Philharmonic Orchestra. This spring Walter is to give guest performances in Vienna, Budapest, Amsterdam, Prague and London, and in August he is to conduct at the Salzburg Festival. Walter has fulfilled all his German obligations.'[18]

The Austrian Karl Böhm, conformist and sympathetic to the regime, gladly took over the position that had fallen vacant in Dresden.

The exodus of the great men of German culture had begun. The expulsion of Jewish musicians was received with worldwide dismay and rage. In order to carry out the process of *Gleichschaltung* (forcible co-ordination) of the people and the government, Hitler, by decree of the Reich President, set up the Reich Ministry for Popular Enlightenment and Propaganda. Under the leadership of Dr Joseph Goebbels it was to become one of the most important tools of the Third Reich, and was most effective at forcing through the absolute demands of the regime in intellectual and cultural life. At the beginning of the spring of 1933, on 21 March, the German people were granted the 'Day of the National Rising' when, at a solemn state ceremony at the Garrison Church in Potsdam, above the tomb of Frederick the Great, in which Goebbels used all the propaganda effects at his disposal, Hitler had himself styled the 'legal' heir to the Prussian crown. On the steps of the Garrison Church Hitler and Hindenburg exchanged that handshake which was 'reproduced a millionfold on postcards and posters. It symbolized the longing of the nation for reconciliation. Without "the old gentleman's blessing", Hitler had said, he would not have wanted to take power.'[19] The same day saw the founding of the 'Deutsche Bühne', the Nazi theatre organization. And in the evening the politically naïve Wilhelm Furtwängler gave a festival performance of the Führer's beloved *Meistersinger*. The birthday of the new German Reich was also duly celebrated in Ulm: in the square below the venerable monastery, a crowd of thousands of enthusiastic people turned out to watch the march past of the parade troops, and in the evening the 'torch procession of national Ulm' appeared once more in the Münsterplatz, despite the terrible weather. Beneath the blue and red glow of the torches, spurred by the tirades of hatred delivered by Standardbearer Schwäble and Kreisleiter Maier against the 'Jewish agitators', the 'Jewish gutter press' and the *Untermenschen*, to the sound of the 'Horst Wessel Song' and the thrice-repeated chant of 'Sieg Heil', it made for the 'most powerful demonstration that Ulm has ever experienced'.[20] In the meantime, in the Stadttheater, topped by swastika banners in accordance with municipal regulations, the still unknown young kapellmeister Karajan was conducting the penultimate presentation of the season in honour of the day, a performance of Verdi's *La Traviata*.

Two days later, on 23 March, Hitler (having tellingly exchanged civilian dress for the brown shirt) presented his 'Law for the Removal of the Distress of People and Reich', the so-called Enabling Act. Against the votes of the Social Democrats, the Act was passed with the consent of all bourgeois parties. It gave the Nazis free rein, and allowed the government unlimited freedom of action. From that moment onwards, Hitler was able to pass decrees without the agreement of the Reichstag, in violation of the state constitution. The Reichstag was eliminated. 'The task of art is now to be the expression of the determining spirit of the age, of rising heroism. Blood and race are now to the fore,' Hitler said, summing up the new tasks of culture in his Reichstag speech, which was also extensively reported in the Ulm newspapers.[21]

Hardly had Göring announced the results of the vote on the Enabling Act (441 votes to 94) than the National Socialists rushed to the government bench, where, their arms raised in the Hitler salute, they began to sing the 'Horst Wessel Song'. The nation's internal break with Weimar was complete. On 29 March 1933 a further law was passed, the so-called 'Lex van der Lubbe'. It brought forward the law of 28 February, and hence the 'legalized' sentencing and execution of the Dutch Communist Marinus van der Lubbe, whom the National Socialists blamed for the Reichstag fire. Now there arose the issue of 'legality' of which Hitler had spoken at the Federal Court in Leipzig in 1930. Now the first heads were to roll 'legally'. 'Off to the concentration camp!' was the headline in the *Ulmer Sturm*, announcing the arrest of forty-three Social Democrat officials in nearby Göppingen.[22]

On 1 April 1933 came the first of the long and terrible series of official anti-Jewish measures which was to reach its full intensity in the eradication of millions of European Jews.

The first organized boycott of Jewish shops that Saturday heralded pogroms and genocide previously unknown in human history. The windows of Jewish shops and offices bore posters with calls for boycotts or insults: 'Germans defend yourselves! Don't buy from Jews' or 'Jews out!' Armed SA gangs underlined the calls for a boycott, and kept customers from entering the shops.

The Party's call to anti-Semitism failed to achieve the desired effect, in so far as large sections of the population, after an action so riddled with mayhem and illegality, tended to sympathize with the Jews. In the face of threats, further boycotts were abandoned. In his radio address 'Against the abominable agitation of the Jews',

Goebbels nevertheless announced a renewed attack the very same day, to 'annihilate German Jewry . . . Let no one doubt our resolution.'[23] The people of Ulm remained particularly enthusiastic about the nationwide boycott. As early as 11 March the 'People's Fury against Judaism' had been set up in Ulm, and had succeeded in closing Jewish shops. 'Even in the early hours of the morning,' the *Ulmer Sturm* proudly reported, 'a large number of national comrades were demonstrating in front of the building of the department store Wohlwert and the other Oriental Jewish hagglers and junk dealers, demanding the closure of the premises . . . Wohlwert was the first that had to give in to the furious demands of the masses. Later several other Jewish junk shops followed suit.'[24]

Exactly a week after the first organized pogrom by the Nazis against the German Jews, Herbert von Karajan joined the National Socialist German Workers' Party (NSDAP), being given Party Number 1 607 525 with Ortsgruppe V 'Neustadt' in Salzburg. The date was Saturday, 8 April 1933. That weekend the front page of the pro-Nazi *Salzburger Volksblatt* carried a report on the Civil Service Act passed the previous day by the Reichstag in Berlin, which meant that Jewish employees would lose their posts, leaving attractive vacancies open, even for conductors.[25] The announcement of the new law was broadcast the very evening it was passed, and the next morning it was in all the German newspapers, which were also on sale in Salzburg. 'Of course, it cannot be proven' that Karajan, the second kapellmeister of the Opera House in Ulm, 'heard the radio news on the Friday evening, or did not skip the front page of the *Salzburger Volksblatt* the following morning. But he acted exactly as anyone in his position would have acted on the basis of such a piece of news: he joined the NSDAP . . .'[26]

Three days before he joined the Party Karajan turned twenty-five. He was recruited to the Party by Party Comrade Herbert Klein of Lasserstrasse in Salzburg, to whom Karajan gave the sum of five schillings 'as a recruitment fee, and who also sent him the certifying registration form. Party Comrade Klein later handed in the registration form at the recruitment office in Salzburg, Schwarzstrasse 1.'[27] If, as the leader of Ortsgruppe V 'Neustadt', Mösel, said in a letter to the District Treasurer of the NSDAP in Salzburg, the Party's recruitment office was actually at Schwarz-strasse 1, Karajan would probably have been able to take the registration document straight home with him: for Schwarzstrasse 1 was the house where the Karajans lived. 'There was also a kiosk there, which sold, among other things, Nazi propaganda material,

Party pamphlets, Hitler's programme, a convenient way of finding things out without crossing the street.'[28]

Herbert Klein's parents ran the specialist rubber shop 'Gummi-Klein' at Sigmund-Haffner-Gasse 16, which still exists today. Although the Klein and Karajan families knew one another, Party recruitment officer Herbert Klein is not described today as a close acquaintance of Karajan, understandably enough. Klein studied and graduated in history. As director of the Salzburg State Archive and president of the Salzburg Society for Regional Studies, the later Privy Councillor Dr Herbert Klein led a respected life in Salzburg and died in the early 1970s.

Let us picture Salzburg and Austria at that time, the better to understand the political situation there: as a result of the severe crisis of capitalism at the beginning of the thirties, which led to a profound longing for a more just society in Austria as it did elsewhere, the myth of salvation invaded the political arena of the First Republic. In May 1931 the Credit-Anstalt collapsed, bringing Austria's economic crisis to its peak. The country was in economic ruins. In this situation, President Miklas gave the politician Dr Engelbert Dollfuss the task of forming a government. Just over five feet tall, Dollfuss was practically a dwarf, but his political ambition was all the greater. After a series of tough negotiations the first Dollfuss cabinet was formed on 20 May 1932. It too was unable to prevent a high level of unemployment and a proliferation of strikes. By March 1933 the Dollfuss government was over. It began its rule with emergency measures on 7 March, illegally abolishing the National Council. The first emergency measure led to intense restrictions on the freedom of the press. The menace of violence hung like a fog over Austria. The threat of civil war had become acute. Dollfuss was not a man for half measures. He represented the very Austrian clerical fascism of those days, and saw politics as a means towards the realization of the absolute. With the goal of creating a broad-based popular movement, the Vaterländische Front was founded in the spring of 1933. The goal was not achieved, however, as popular enthusiasm failed to manifest itself. Left without the mass base that Hitler had in Germany, Dollfuss simply put himself at the head of a commonplace dictatorship supported by the federal army and the police, achieved by a *coup d'état*.

Disagreements with National Socialism, a growing force in Austria, led Dollfuss to seek dialogue with Hitler, a man for whom

77

Dollfuss had little time. But negotiations with Hitler's confidant Theo Habicht, State Inspector of the NSDAP in Austria, about the possibility of integrating the National Socialists into a front of farmers and the bourgeoisie, collapsed, and there soon followed a wave of National Socialist terror in Austria. Bombs and grenades exploded. There were fatalities. Hitler introduced a visa fee of 1,000 marks for journeys to Austria, to which Dollfuss responded with a five-schilling fee. In consequence of this 1,000-mark fee the number of German visitors to the Salzburg Festival dropped from 12,983 the previous year to 796 in the summer of 1933. After a renewal of National Socialist terror, the Dollfuss government placed a prohibition on NSDAP activity, the Communist Party having been banned in May. But the Party continued its activity illegally. So it was in this climate of condemnation, expectation, longing, despotism, intolerance and terror that Karajan joined the Party in Salzburg, in that city which, in Thomas Bernhard's words, had been 'coarsely abused for centuries by Catholicism, and for decades brutally raped by National Socialism'.[29] As a 'profoundly religious man',[30] Dollfuss enjoyed a close relationship with the Catholic Church. This also explains the reprisals carried out against non-religious teachers during this period, and the obligatory list of sins distributed among school pupils, and also the official medical examination of the mental condition of anyone who left the Church, by now ruinously amalgamated with politics and in league with the unChristian, despotic rule of the Dollfuss regime.

All of a sudden Karajan was both a Catholic and National Socialist. A mutually exclusive and impossible union, one might think, between brotherly love and the will to destruction. Was Karajan, then, a part of what Thomas Bernhard describes as 'that form of humanity as an attitude of mind, most ubiquitous in Salzburg, and which completely dominates the city to this very day'?[31] At any rate, certainly, he felt a conflict of loyalty between his sense of the Austrian state and German culture and nationhood, to which he had to sacrifice a romantic yearning for the old imperial age – if indeed he had such a yearning, as we may suppose he did. He also entered into a conflict between morality on the one hand and a pragmatic striving for success on the other. But was he at all aware of this in April 1933? Did he ever consider at that time what it meant to be prepared, as a National Socialist, to sacrifice inner freedom for external power and greatness? In the spring of

1933 Karajan was just twenty-five. Twenty-five is no great age. It is the age at which one is allowed to make mistakes. But that is not the issue. What is important was his attitude towards his actions during that period, which he consistently refused to admit, up until his death. His attitude was one of disavowal, as we shall see later on. Hence the thoroughness of our examination of his time in Ulm and his subsequent career. For it would be fatal to lose sight of the reality of those days – which was also reality for the young Karajan – precisely because in his old age Karajan's sole concern was the effective denial of anything to do with reality.

During those days, weeks and months of the National Socialist seizure of power, did Karajan unwittingly succumb to the apocalyptic, morbid charm of Fascism and its aesthetic fascination (we should not forget that by 1933 Mussolini had already been in power for eleven years)? Did he simply slip, almost blindly, into National Socialism, culpably underestimating its power? Did he allow himself to be seduced and blinded by the aesthetic dimension of the cult of Nazism? Should we then benevolently exculpate such a distinguished young man, even allowing for an as yet unformed critical ability, of having had the faintest notion of his spiritual identification with power and much else besides, or might we for a moment recall Gustav Gründgens in Klaus Mann's stylized portrait?[32]

'Karajan in the Third Reich, or: Why I Became a National Socialist'; this chapter of his biography, the most important of his career, has until the present day been carefully expurgated, and a taboo has been imposed upon it by Karajan and his well-meaning admirers. But history knows no taboos. Karajan's behaviour during this phase of his life demands historical precision. For the murder of millions of helpless victims of persecution was brought about by 'a very large number of culpable individual decisions and actions', and demonstrates 'that it can certainly not be blamed, with the naturalness to which we have grown accustomed, on superiors and finally on the Führer himself. That everything that happened was allowed to happen is the product not only of miraculous qualities of leadership, but also of an "incredible obedience".'[33] Or might we say that everyone was his own little Hitler? And quite legally, under the cloak of external allegiance?

The *Gleichschaltung* of the states supervised by the Reich Governors and brought into effect on 7 April was followed on 11 April, three days after Karajan became a Party member, by the exclusion of Jews from public employment. It took Hitler less than three months to block his opponents. During those same three months Karajan finally decided to join the Party.

Karajan was one of the so-called 'March fallen', the contemptuous slang term for those who deserted to the Party after the events of March. Karajan did not resist the lure of mass desertion, the need for a sense of belonging that was spreading like an addiction, the persuasive rhetoric of the time. For as it seemed, the future belonged to the regime. It may be that the general optimism of reconstruction and the beginnings of a political upturn, the distinct improvement in national prestige as far as other countries were concerned, perhaps also Hindenburg's readiness to lend the support of his moral authority to National Socialist plans for the seizure of power, and the general mood of reorientation, with its accompanying readiness to make sacrifices, moved Karajan to join the Party. Or was it simply what we might call a youthful indiscretion? Or was it, perhaps, his addiction to his own greatness, as promised by the National Socialist future?

Was his conversion somehow connected, then, with his highly desirable post as kapellmeister? Karajan was a foreigner; like Hitler he came from Austria. Unemployment among musicians had reached a peak. Dietrich, the theatre manager, refused to renew his contract for the 1933–4 season. Karajan later told Haeusserman:

> That naturally came as a great shock to me. But then, when we travelled to Vienna together to appoint singers, I managed to persuade him to retract the dismissal and keep me on for another year. Many years later he told me the reason for this dismissal: 'I was only afraid that you might get stuck here.'[34]

That sounds good, at least. But is it true? In Karajan's 'de-Nazification' files we come across the lapidary statement: 'He was unsuccessful there for reasons of character.'[35] Might this have been the reason for his being dismissed? Did Karajan, who was primarily interested in symphonic concerts, make himself unpopular in the theatre by being too ambitious? At any rate, at Christmas 1931, on the occasion of the première of the opera *Schwanda the Bagpiper* by Jaromir Weinberger, there was even an attempt on Karajan's life, which was foiled by the double-bass soloist Fritz Kaiser. In the manager's office the violinist Willi Döpke, a 'touchy' leader of the orchestra whom Karajan had replaced, so to speak, with another musician, had his Browning – loaded and with the safety catch off – taken from him. Karajan only went on conducting after an emergency interval of half an hour, during which the furious violinist was sacked on the spot.'[36] And what, in fact, was Karajan's relationship with his co-musical director Otto Schulmann, a Jew baptized a Catholic?

> He had to leave in '33. We were great friends from the start. He had grown up in Munich, I in Salzburg, and we listened to music in the same way, simply because we had both been properly educated in the musical life of the big city. We got on famously, and naturally exploited the fact when we were sharing out the repertory.[37]

It must, to put it mildly, have been a strange friendship that linked Karajan, the member of an openly anti-Semitic party, and Otto Schulmann, exiled by the very same party. Karajan's emphatic and generous declaration of friendship possibly tells us something, against the background of his Party membership, about what friendship meant to him, ill-equipped as he was for forming relationships. Was it naked fear of losing his position in Ulm that drove Karajan into the arms of the Party? Or was he being coldly calculating when he joined the Party on 8 April, in the hope that his Party membership card might bring him certain advantages? On 7 April the law was passed that was to free him from his rival, Schulmann. Did Karajan hope to become the sole kapellmeister in Ulm after Schulmann's departure, did he want to secure his position by joining the Party? If that was his plan it misfired badly. Karajan had to share his post for the 1933–4 season with Max Kojetinsky. Did this lead to new conflicts, with the result that Karajan's contract was not extended in the end, so that he was, so to speak, kicked upstairs? But could we accuse him of finding his own problems more important at that time than the life-or-death circumstances of his friend and rival, Schulmann? Karajan paints a highly illuminating picture of his departure from Ulm. But does it tell us the whole truth? Schulmann, whom I managed to track down in San Francisco, will give nothing away. He remains silent even on the subject of his emigration and its consequences: his exile from Germany must have meant the collapse of all his hopes. He answered my request for a contribution to the discovery of the truth with an abruptness that revealed nothing, and only threw up new questions – why was he so eager to cover up his own past?

> The statement that Karajan and I were friends is the only one that is entirely correct, just as the fantasies of later jealous

and self-important people about an important man merit no attention from me. All I might add is that we are fine, more than fine, and that we have always wished him similar success, which he seems to have achieved on a major scale.[38]

Schulmann's refusal, whatever his reasons, to help us clarify matters, might remind us that there is also a psychological phenomenon of solidarity between victims and criminals.

It might be helpful, if we wish to draw a picture of the state of things in those days, to remember that, as the result of legal measures, within a year of the spring of 1933 almost 2,000 Jewish musicians and theatrical workers, around 10,000 lawyers, doctors and civil servants, as well as several hundred college teachers, were forced to leave their posts. And that some 60,000 people sought refuge abroad after the first incitements to anti-Semitism. Among these was Richard Friedenthal, whom Karajan would have liked to have as biographer. In his novel, *Die Welt in der Nußschale*, Friedenthal provided a striking image of Jews holding on to their German cultural legacy: under the baton of a conductor, *émigré* musicians in an internment camp on the Isle of Man, miming the playing of their scores without their instruments, play Beethoven's Eighth Symphony. Could Karajan see the consequences of Germany's anti-Jewish laws in the spring of 1933, did he foresee the exodus of Jewish intellectuals and artists, and did he, perhaps, exploit it?

This much is clear: on 1 May 1933 Herbert von Karajan joined the Party once again, this time in Germany. As Party Member No. 340914 he was accepted into the Ulm District NSDAP, Gau Württemberg, on the very same 1 May that Hitler declared a national holiday, the 'Day of Victory', and following which he put a block on new membership, since within three months more than one and a half million new members had pushed the 850,000 original Party members into the minority.

What was it that led Karajan to join the Party for a second time, as a kind of act of confirmation? Was it the coming prohibition of the NSDAP in Austria, the result of the state of the Party, which had ceased to look promising as early as April? This would have been a good reason for declaring one's membership for a second time in Germany, since it was impossible to know what might become of the Salzburg files in the event of a prohibition. Or did Karajan think it more secure, because he had still not

82

received his provisional membership card by the end of April (it was not to be issued until 30 May),[39] to join in Ulm as well, particularly since the Party had announced a block on membership? The date 1 May was the last on which it was possible to become a Party member in Germany. The block lasted until 1 May 1937.

Might it have had something to do with the fact that Karajan, although the season had finished at the end of March, was recalled from Salzburg for 'national labour day', to take part in the biggest procession that the city had ever seen? Were all members of private, municipal and state institutions called upon to participate? Picture the scene: from all the gables and windows in the little alleyways wave the flags of the new Germany, whole streets are adorned with the most splendid Nazi banners, and, where there is room, there are garlanded pines and maypoles. The face of the city is disappearing behind the decorations celebrating the national revolution. And through this decorated city, accompanied by 500 flagbearers, in a four-mile procession, the 'national community of the fifteen thousand' comes out to the stadium to witness, in the presence of the army, the solemn ritual of the dedication of the colours. The procession included thirty-five floats, most of them taking a national character from the themes of the guilds. The gardeners' float, for example, displayed, resplendent 'in two big green areas made of lettuces, two swastikas of radishes'.[40] Was this march of the guilds, this diversity of social classes, not the embodiment of Richard Wagner's *Meistersinger*? Did the shoemakers not arrive with their very own Hans Sachs? Might Karajan simply have been carried away by the National Socialist pomp of propaganda marches, the procession and the banners? Did he merely succumb to the terrible kitsch of this mass event, or did he farsightedly exploit this moment, perhaps only as an onlooker, to confirm his allegiance to the Führer and the Reich? We don't know, because Karajan would say nothing on the matter. We know only that on this rainy first day of May, whatever the circumstances, he joined the Party for a second time.

It is not easy – in the face of this confirmed allegiance to the National Socialist regime – to believe that Karajan had fallen prey to a political seduction that had entirely paralysed his powers of decision-making. With the *élan* of youth he enthusiastically threw himself into the arms of the Party once again – whether because of a lack of political education, the career-oriented need to form a pragmatic bond with the Nazis, or the fact, intuitively understood, that a golden future lay with Hitler.

83

Karajan did not in any ascertainable way resist his emphatically confirmed partisanship for the Nazis. During the spring of the fateful year of 1933, and also throughout the later terrors of the Third Reich, Karajan clearly felt no irresistible distaste for the Nazis, their gangs of thugs, their openly homosexual associations or their repellently philistine ideology. He, the future missionary of beautiful sound, of the aesthetic of the harmony of beauty in music as in life, did not find them despicable enough, at any level of his existence, either consciously or unconsciously, to keep him from becoming and remaining a member of the Party.

The Nazis exerted their fascination on many people in many different ways. We still do not know what led Karajan to join the Party. But his character as a whole and his behaviour would tend to indicate that an affinity for particular aspects of Nazi ideology might have been important factors in his joining. If this were so, could we then call Karajan apolitical in so far as being a permanent adolescent, who already bore within himself the structures of Fascism, he could not be held fully responsible for his actions?

The Nazis understandably exerted a particularly strong attraction on the character type of the 'eternal adolescent', with his inner complexity woven of delicate, feminine sensibility on the one hand and heroism on the other, in constant pursuit of his own manliness. A manliness, indeed, that the Nazis represented and practised only in a quite negative way, in the thoroughly inhuman character of their brutality. It is possible that Karajan was just as attracted by it as he was by the demagogic aura that emanated from Hitler and his Party.

We are not 'rummaging around' in his past, as Karajan once tearfully grumbled, in seeking to bring to light the facts of a phase of his life that was crucial to his career – facts repeatedly denied with every available means of distortion and obfuscation. We are not fruitlessly digging and poking in his history if we take Karajan's place and do what he himself stubbornly refused until old age to do: to face up to the past. And neither are we disparaging or insulting him if we present one of the great men of our time with the facts and circumstances that he persistently refused to see, because confronting them might cause him shame. The 'word of advice' from the German Evangelical Church on the subject of the Nazi trials in 1963 applies here as well: 'Past injustices cannot be settled by keeping them silent, and only ignorance can speak of soiling one's own nest, where it is in fact a matter of cleaning a nest already badly soiled.'[41]

It would seem to indicate a considerably disturbed relationship with reality for Karajan to present his biographers and interviewers with untruths even where they can be revealed as such by an examination of the facts. During a conversation we had on 9 January 1981 in his house in St Moritz, we came, as we had done on other occasions, to discuss his role in the Third Reich.

Bachmann: Does it hurt you that your Party membership is still held against you?
Karajan: I'm quite indifferent to it. But so indifferent – I really can't tell you.
Bachmann: Do you think you did something wrong back then?
Karajan: No, quite certainly not. I would do exactly the same again. I was given a position as Generalmusikdirektor in Aachen, and after I'd held it for a long time my secretary came and said: 'Listen, the district commanders . . .' That's what you can't explain to anyone. Nobody can understand it. For me that was as if you said: 'We're going up the Eiger now, but listen, you have to be a member of the Swiss Mountaineering Club.' Then I would join. And that was then – then they used to say: 'That's simply impossible, you are there, and you have to do it.' And the important thing for me was that I could finally have – well, in Aachen there was a big orchestra and a wonderful choir, a medium-sized theatre. I was able to do whatever I liked. And after all that I'm supposed to be some kind of murderer!

Karajan's words have a very familiar ring. Was it not Hitler's master-builder and future armaments minister, Albert Speer, who excused his partisanship with the Third Reich in a similar fashion? As he himself confirmed: 'For a big building I would have sold my soul, like Faust.'[42]
Anyone who, as a former Party member actively involved in the cultural propaganda of Hitler's new Reich after the crimes of Auschwitz, that most terrible example of complete inhumanity, compares membership of the NSDAP with belonging to a mountaineering club, who, after the murder of millions of Jews, can say that he would do exactly the same again, has grasped nothing of what it means to be a human being. Probably quite unconsciously he is, in his boundless inability to connect with the people around him, making a mockery of the ideal of humanity, and the victims of a regime which he himself loyally served. Either he didn't know what he was saying and doing, and had known it at no point in

his life, or he has never understood the catastrophe that occurred during those years, either internally or externally.

Is it unfair of us if, with the moralistic rigour of later generations, we cannot think of any other answer? Of course: the genocidal consequences of National Socialism were not easily identifiable in the thirties, and the diabolical forces, the dislocations to which its underlings would be subjected, were hardly apparent to those who saw themselves as blessed 'by being born in an age in which life is easier, in which the conquest of power has been fully achieved and which does not demand guilt from the individual conscience, or sacrifices that man's very nature resists'. Not everyone is born to heroic deeds, certainly. But are errors such as those revealed to us by the history of the Third Reich not forgivable only 'if they lead to a modification of wrong beliefs, as well as to actions that this modification demands'?[43]

Karajan's portrayal of the circumstances of his joining the Party falls under the heading of clumsy deception, since it can to a certain extent be debunked with a little inquiry. It is enlightening to read the account that he gives of himself to his biographers, and how they record and pass on his attempts at vanquishing the past.

In his book *Das Wunder Karajan*, Karl Löbl reproduces the facts as follows:

> He had been accused of two things: membership of the NSDAP and political activity. What had really happened? In 1935 Karajan saw himself as being presented with a choice either of losing the post of general musical director in Aachen which he had just taken up, or of joining the Party. He joined. Without scruple. His professional career was more important to him than anything else. He did not identify with the regime. Like so many other artists he was politically entirely indifferent. And like so many other people at that time he could certainly not know what difficulties would be raised for him ten years later.[44]

As we know, this version is entirely false. Anyone who joins a party is not politically entirely indifferent, but is acting in a political way. It is the very act with which he declares his allegiance to a quite particular political view embodied in the party, and thus becomes one of those responsible for it. It is difficult to claim of anyone joining a party that supports and represents the regime that he does not identify with the regime. The one presupposes the other. Anyone who works in a politically dominated culture also has a political effect, even if he does not wish this to be so. And even if it were the case, this political ignorance (the idea that party membership excused one for ever of moral indifference) demands to be analysed once more.

We can only agree with Fred K. Prieberg when he comments in his groundbreaking book on *Musik im NS-Staat*: 'Anyone who joined the NSDAP "without scruple" and for the sake of his career was not required in addition to identify with the regime; even less can he boast of his political indifference. Careerism of his kind renders special allegiance to the Nazi state redundant.'[45]

Arts journalist Löbl is certainly not the man to suspect Karajan of having exploited the Nazi state or confront him with his own facts, let alone bother the younger generation, who can still learn from history, with embarrassing information. Rather his sympathetic exoneration leads him towards a situation whereby only refined distortion of the facts preserves the appearance of truth. In his book, in fact, he speaks at one point about the protests by the American Musicians' Trade Union on the occasion of Karajan's tour of America with the Berlin Philharmonic in 1955. The trade union was trying to prevent the guest performance because of Karajan's role in the Third Reich. Löbl writes:

> The grounds given were that 'there is documentary evidence that Karajan was one of the first helpers and propagandists of the Hitler regime'. The following individual facts were presented: Karajan joined the NSDAP in 1933. The Austrian Karajan also joined the Party in Austria. Later, when the Party was banned in Austria, he moved to Germany, where he rapidly became the musical protegé of Ministerial President Göring. This is a conscious or negligent falsification of the facts.[46]

Having reached the very summit of insolence, Löbl overreaches even Karajan's own efforts to vanquish the past. Where Karajan 'simply' hushes up or retouches the facts, here they are distorted into their very opposite, and with an alarming bravura the documentary evidence is declared, with disarming brazenness, to be a falsification.

Similarly, Jacques Lorcey, another biographer of Karajan,

elevates himself to the status of moral judge, dispensing absolution for all personal responsibility, when he writes:

> *Interrogé pendant des heures par des militaires plus ou moins hostiles, il explique qu'en 1934, trois jours avant de signer son engagement à Aix-la-Chapelle, les responsables du théâtre lui ont dit: 'D'après le règlement, vous ne pouvez exercer des fonctions aussi importantes si vous n'êtes pas membre du Parti. C'est une simple formalité. Voulez-vous remplir cette feuille?' Désireux par-dessus tout d'exercer son art dans de bonnes conditions, Karajan a donné son accord – mais il n'a jamais fait de politique: cela ne l'intéresse pas.*[47]

Another author, likewise unable to see beyond the shadow of his idol, was the music journalist and conductor Paul Robinson. In sentence after sentence he, too, manages to sidestep historical events, skilfully comingling facts and facticides, with the intention of giving Karajan the justification that should come from the man himself. He writes:

> As a musician it could not have escaped him that Germany had been taken over by a Fascist regime of the most repressive sort. Conductors were forbidden to play works by Jewish composers such as Mendelssohn, Mahler or Schoenberg. Orchestras were not allowed to retain their Jewish members. In addition, it became customary to play the 'Horst Wessel Song', the Nazi anthem, before concerts, and to give the Nazi salute if officials were in the audience . . .
>   Nevertheless, Karajan joined the NSDAP in 1935, in order to become Generalmusikdirektor in Aachen. His membership was represented to him as a mere 'formality', but he was also given to understand that he would not be able to hold such a post without being a Party member. It must have been a somewhat desperate move on Karajan's part, for refusal would not only have meant an end to his career as a conductor, but would also have practically destroyed all of his previous efforts, and his personality, entirely dedicated as it was to music. It seems typical that inner inhibitions later kept him almost entirely silent about the matter, and led him to present a purely external persona, masking his vulnerability with 'arrogance'.[48]

In its skilful combination of facts and a vague construct of unctuous exoneration, this is the unparalleled content of the German version of Robinson's treatise on Karajan. It provides the sad proof that not only the author, but also the translator, feels obliged to act as the conductor's conscience, making improving alterations, retouching the text and doing donkey work for Karajan's publicity department which does not quite tie in with the truth. We might refer to suppression of the facts. A comparison of the German translation with the original version might clarify this.

Original:

As Winthrop Sargeant revealed in an interview with Karajan in 1961 Karajan's decision was made entirely for opportunistic reasons, as Karajan himself admits: 'I would have committed any crime to get that post' (*New Yorker*, 2 December 1967).[49]

Translation:

Das geschah zum Beispiel im Jahre 1961, als er in einem Interview mit Winthrop Sargeant 'zugab', er habe seine Entscheidung, Parteimitglied zu werden, ausschließlich aus opportunistischen Gründen getroffen. [That happened, for example, in 1961, when, in an interview with Winthrop Sargeant, he 'confessed' that he had reached his decision solely for opportunistic reasons.][50]

'I would have committed any crime to get that post,' is the quotation suppressed in the German version. The fact that the source is also covered up is explained by the process itself. With these glosses, this concealment, the translator is, consciously or unconsciously, practising a sublime form of corruption in the service of a supposedly higher truth, and in his self-censorship making himself an accomplice in Karajan's cosmeticization of history.[51]

What happens when the biographer presents his subject in the context of an interview, suggesting, as such a presentation does, a fascinating authenticity (in the false hope that thus and only thus would the facts be documented) can be read in Ernst Haeusserman's book, which quotes Karajan's version word for word, without question:

It isn't a secret, I was a member of the Party, and I joined in 1935 in Aachen, when I was to become Generalmusikdirektor. Three days before my appointment, when the desired goal was just within reach, the town clerk came to me and said: 'Listen, there is' – and these were his words – 'there is one more formality to be carried out. You are not yet a Party member. According to the *Kreisleiter*, however, you cannot take up a post of this kind without being a Party member.' So I signed.[52]

Fred K. Prieberg acutely formulated what we are to make of such convincing confessional courage:

This touching story elegantly feeds on its appearance of credibility. Whoever thought it up knew that membership dates put a different colour on things: the earlier one became a Party member, the more enthusiastic an admirer of Hitler one was, and 1935 was, in the eyes of the Allies, rather less grave than 1933. But people nowadays say with great conviction: Yes that's how it was in those days. If things are not presented so simply, a less useful, less subjective truth comes to light . . . the truth with which the American Musicians' Trade Union tried to boycott Karajan's guest performances with the Berlin Philharmonic in 1955 . . . Other conductors were less eager – and suffered no setbacks; but of course they didn't have careers as comet-like and fabulous as that of Herr von Karajan. I gladly allow that it is of no importance to the musical historian whether someone was a Party member or not, unless their membership made musical history, and this is the only issue, not new 'denazification' trials. But anyone who can lay the subject on the table, with no difficulty, in all its details – like Karajan and his court reporters – must expect to be checked up on, and to be critically judged as well. Talk of 'pure art', which is supposed to have been everyone's sole consideration, cannot shake the certainty backed up by documentary evidence: anyone who acted opportunistically was killed opportunistically – in a moral sense, I mean. That too is a fact.[53]

Stars have a public and a private biography. One is conscientiously and industriously publicized, the other hushed up and hidden. But an artist, and particularly an artist who, like Karajan, has become a star, is a figure in the public eye. He creates an effect, a theatrical effect. He bears the responsibility for his effect just as he does for his actions and omissions in connection with it and with artistic activity. This responsibility should be free of weak spots. Lest there be any misunderstanding: it is not a question of forcing an aged, honoured, esteemed, gifted artist of great merit to fall to his knees in repentance. But covering things up is an uncertain way out, and by taking it Karajan runs the risk of being toppled from his plinth by historical truth. What once happened in his life cannot be erased.

Karajan had good reasons for fearing historians, in so far as he twisted history to his own ends out of an urge to become and to remain successful. For this urge for success required a spotless image bearing no relation to reality, an imaginary memorial, in a way, during one's own lifetime. When he joined the Party in April and May 1933, Karajan concluded his pact with the devil, so to speak, as Hitler's master builder Albert Speer was likewise prepared to do.

Success in exchange for conscience. The deal assumes a Faustian dimension: for the price of his soul he demands musical world domination. If Karajan was at the time unaware of the implications of his actions, it still hardly excuses him. He could at any point in his career in the Third Reich have formed a picture of the unjust nature of the regime, and acted accordingly. He could have deduced, from the historical facts presented here, the knowledge required to act according to moral principles. But is is doubtful whether he wanted to know anything in any case, for understandable reasons. Yet not wanting to know something always means knowing enough – enough to know that one would not like to know more.

The *Ulmer Sturm*, which Karajan presumably picked up if he wanted to read excellent reviews of his performances, would always have kept him very thoroughly informed about the aims of the Party and the regime, if he had so wished. On 27 April, four days before he joined the Party for the second time, above a review of the *Princess of Csardas* (conductor: Herr Kojetinsky), and beside the announcement of the immediate prohibition on jazz music (of which Karajan had been such a splendid master in those days), and beneath the headline 'Protectors of the Jews', the Party organ removed any remaining doubts in big fat letters.

There are still people who consider anti-Semitism to be a subsidiary and marginal part of the National Socialist movement, who think that anti-Semitism is more or less a question of taste. The Jews themselves know better, but it cannot be stressed deeply enough that the Führer has recognized the removal of the Jewish influence from the public life of the nation as an indispensable precondition for its new rise. Anyone who places himself between us and the Jews as we progress towards the solution of this question is therefore an obstacle to our rise. The results will come about of their own accord.[54]

Ten days after Karajan joined the Party for the second time, on the night of 10 May, there was, in the public squares of the capitals and university cities of the Reich, a demonstration of anti-intellectualism which made quite plain enough the direction in which things were moving. In Berlin, Reichsminister Goebbels was personally present at the barbaric and inquisitional conflagration. According to William Shirer, Berlin became 'the stage for a scene that the Western world had not seen since the end of the Middle Ages'.[55] To the tune of 'patriotic' melodies by the bands of the SA and the SS, some 20,000 'un-German books' were publicly burned up and down the country. Among the works thrown on the pyre were works by Einstein, Lion Feuchtwanger, Sigmund Freud, Erich Kästner, Alfred Kerr, Egon Erwin Kisch, Karl Marx, Heinrich and Thomas Mann, Carl von Ossietzky, Erich Maria Remarque, Kurt Tucholsky, Theodor Wolff and Arnold and Stefan Zweig. 'The age of oversophisticated Jewish intellectualism is now over . . .' Goebbels gloated during the burning, framed by torch processions and the so-called 'fire-speeches' of swastika-bearing youths.

So Karajan had managed to get a year's extension out of Dietrich, manager of the Stadttheater in Ulm. In August 1933, as part of the Salzburg Festival, he conducted the music of his friend and mentor Bernhard Paumgartner, for the Walpurgis Night scene in four performances of the new production of Goethe's Faust. Max Reinhardt was the director. The set was designed by Clemens Holzmeister, the same Holzmeister who would build the Großes Festspielhaus after the war, making Karajan's dream come true. Here, once again, we see that very characteristic phenomenon of Karajan's career – meeting people early on who were to be decisive in the development and realization of his plans. Holzmeister was to build him the largest operatic stage in the world. It was Karajan's first involvement with the Salzburg Festival. He keenly followed the work of the Jewish director, whom the Nazis exiled first to Austria and then to America. When Karajan later sought the actor in the singer, he was returning to the impressions and experiences that Reinhardt's rehearsals had given him that summer and in earlier and subsequent festivals.

In Reinhardt, Karajan found a magician, a craftsman and

technician and a great organizer, all in one. In Max Reinhardt's theatrical world he was given invaluable lessons in the high art of psychological management. He was watching a director at work who was just as keen on making himself understood as on understanding others, who did all this in an atmosphere of peace in which not a single hurtful, loud or impatient word was heard, and who knew how to watch and listen, and to free the actors from stage-fright on the opening night. Karajan took all this in, and much of it would later feed into his rehearsals and directing. It is not mere chance or luck that is involved in such encounters. The enviable fact that at crucial points in his career Karajan always managed to track down the right people to stimulate and encourage him, the right teachers and models as well as the right colleagues, is nothing less than a significant part of his talent.

In Ulm Karajan shared his musical work on the 1933–4 season with Max Kojetinsky. The establishment of the Reichskulturkammer in 1933 brought all artistic activities into line with the cultural political aims of the Party. This controlling instrument of the regime, divided into several different divisions and run by Goebbels, soon rigorously enforced the Nazis' absolute demands in the intellectual and cultural realm, encompassing everyone working in artistic and promotional fields. All musicians were brought together in the Reichsmusikkammer, whose first president was Richard Strauss. The task of the Reichsmusikkammer, along with the gagging and *Gleichschaltung* of German musical life, was the eradication of everything Jewish in music. Anyone with Jewish parents, or a non-Aryan father or mother, was *de facto* excluded from the Reichsmusikkammer. But membership was a precondition of professional activity. Refusal of an application for membership amounted to a total exclusion from public employment. The rejection and purging of anything Jewish on the one hand, and the establishment of National Socialist musical organizations on the other were the two definitive themes of the Third Reich's musical policy. Both were enforced with that bureaucratic perfection often described as a particularly German quality. Both were to Karajan's advantage.

The yardstick for Party reliability was membership of the NSDAP, and that was something that Karajan was able to demonstrate. During those weeks, word quickly got around that one could advance one's career as a Party member, and musicians flocked to the Party as if bewitched, since it promised success and security. The dismissal of Jews and undesirable artists from important positions in musical life was in full swing, and left gaps which had to be filled. It was simply a matter of time before Karajan was able to exploit this. Among those artists fired, put on permanent leave, excluded from public positions, simply expatriated or otherwise forced to bear the consequences of 1933 were such prominent men as Jascha Horenstein, Hans Wilhelm (later William) Steinberg, Franz Schreker, Arnold Schoenberg, Hermann Scherchen, Bruno Walter, Fritz Busch, Otto Klemperer and Fritz Stiedry. Arturo Toscanini stated, from abroad, what he thought of the Hitler regime. On 5 June 1933 he pulled out of the Bayreuth Festival because of discrimination against Jewish musicians, after telling the enthusiastic follower of Hitler, Winifred Wagner, that he could no longer be counted upon.

In the spring of 1934 Karajan's job in Ulm came to an end. Without any new posts on the horizon, he left Ulm and went off in search of employment. The *Ulmer Tagblatt* honoured his five and a half years of work at the Stadttheater:

> Herbert von Karajan, first kapellmeister at our Stadttheater, is saying goodbye to his friends in Ulm this evening with *The Marriage of Figaro*. With his departure a phase of Ulm's cultural life has come to an end . . . The contributions he has made in our city are many and varied. Once he brought young and talented musicians to our orchestra, and consciously carried out educational work, with the result that we soon built up an ensemble which could, in operatic and concert performances, easily stand comparison with the orchestras of much larger cities . . . One special event was the last big concert with an orchestra of ninety musicians. The Strauss evening featuring *Don Juan*, the Orchestral Songs and *Heldenleben* was unforgettable . . .[56]

These were the works that were to constitute the core of Karajan's later repertoire. Another striking thing was his educational work, which clearly exceeded all expectations and left behind something that had not been there when he arrived. Karajan's very first appointment had displayed all the talents that were to distinguish his career throughout his life. When Karajan moved on, the things he left behind had always been transformed into something better. This was the case in Ulm, and it was to recur in Aachen, and later with the Vienna Symphonic Orchestra, the

94

London Philharmonia and, towards the end of his life, with the Berlin Philharmonic.

Karajan went to Berlin for the first time in his life. When he left the birthplace of Albert Einstein – whom Goebbels had expatriated along with Thomas Mann, Bruno Walter, Max Reinhardt and many others – he was, in fact, being gently elbowed out. If Karajan's story is true, the manager dismissed him because he was afraid the young conductor would get stuck in Ulm. He did explain his departure to the director of the orchestra at the Ulm Stadttheater, Fritz Kaiser, by saying that he no longer found Ulm interesting enough, and that 'from that point on everything would have repeated itself'.[57]

Berlin was the centre of the Reich, both politically and culturally. Here the young, unemployed kapellmeister von Karajan did what jobless artists always do: he traipsed around the agencies. He got to know the undignified side of artistic life the painful way, from his own experience. Even during the last years in Ulm, he spent his free days travelling from city to city in search of his next appointment. Nothing came of it, apart from polite rejection letters. 'This feeling that nobody else wanted me lasted for quite a long time. I wasn't even allowed an audition,' he recalled at the peak of his fame.[58]

Karajan had hit the first trough of his conducting career. Some four million unemployed were still registered in the Reich, and Karajan was simply one case among many. Foodstuffs, textiles and other necessities were running out and prices were going up again. With the law on organization of national labour and the law on the regulation of the labour market, as well as a work-creation programme, the number of unemployed was brought below two million within a year. With hard physical graft, the workers, demoted to helot status, built roads using the most primitive techniques – spades, picks and shovels. Their reward consisted of a warm meal and a supplement to their unemployment benefit in the form of coupons to cover minimum requirements. Times were not good, and anyone who was not a Party member could expect little. Karajan soon found himself at a loss in Berlin.

Shyness drove him into isolation. 'I arrived there completely forlorn and abandoned, I knew nobody. I've always found it difficult to make contact with people,' he confessed decades later.[59] But it is also easy to admit something so clearly and undeniably apparent. Introversion is by no means an aid to advancement

95

during difficult times. If it cannot be compensated for by the help of third parties, a young artist will often find himself in trouble.

Whether Karajan really did spend three months 'under the harshest conditions', and whether overwork as a *répétiteur* did lead to 'serious nervous exhaustion',[60] as Haeusserman claims, we have no way of knowing. In retrospect such things are easy to idealize and dramatize.

It is, however, likely that Karajan, emboldened by desperation, finally seized his opportunity upon hearing that a first kapellmeister was needed in Aachen. At the beginning of May, Dr Edgar Groß, who had been made the new manager in Aachen, had come to Berlin to look around for a replacement. Karajan was introduced to him via an acquaintance. As he had done once before and was to do more often in the future, Karajan found another of the coincidences that so happily determined his career. With a hypnotic persuasiveness, as he put it, Karajan talked his way into an audition in Aachen.

This took place on 8 June 1934. 'He tried to conduct a very lively and vivacious version of Weber's *Oberon* Overture, then the first movement of Mozart's *Haffner* Symphony, and finally, "quite opulently", the overture to *Meistersinger*,' recalls Willy Wesemann, first violinist in the City of Aachen Orchestra. 'Some of the older musicians in the orchestra thought the conductor too young, and had hoped for a more settled and experienced character. But I was overwhelmingly inspired by his brilliance.'[61]

Here Karajan was treated like any gifted young conductor, far above the average and with an inevitable aura of eccentricity: he was spurned by the majority of the orchestra. And what might have happened to the extraordinarily talented conductor Karajan if the orchestra had enforced this opinion does not bear thinking about. The orchestra's rejection of Karajan provides proof once more (should such proof still be required) that an orchestra is quite emphatically not the best judge when it comes to recognizing a truly great talent. An orchestra that is not of the very best and has therefore not learned from its own experience what it means to work with the best will choose the more settled and conformist, the less demanding applicant. The training of orchestras, particularly by young conductors, is beyond the pale. An unknown who makes idealistic demands, as Karajan did in Aachen, is bound to make himself unpopular. But the orchestra had to adapt itself to the conductor's demands, rather than the other way around. Against the advice of the orchestral committee, and, with one exception, the invited representatives of the press, Karajan was appointed.

It is not clear who spoke up for Karajan. According to Karajan it was a former member of the Berlin Philharmonic who worked for the municipal authority. If we are to believe the violinist Wesemann, the then bass *buffo* at the Stadttheater, and the critic Dr Wilhelm Kemp, Party member Albert Hoff claimed to have brought Karajan to Aachen. Hoff, short and plump and sometimes familiarly known as 'fat Albert', as District Cultural Officer of the NSDAP played a not inconsiderable role in the cultural life of the city. When, in the spring of 1934, the mayor, Quirin Jansen, fired the manager, Francesco Sioli, who had been elected for a two-year period by the votes of the NS faction, Hoff was to have been made director of the city opera, to ensure that the programme would comply in all respects with the regulations of the Prussian Theatre Committee. Sioli was finally fired without notice at the end of March, despite approaches to Göring. This situation occurred not least through the efforts of the devious singer and director Anton Ludwig, who recommended that Hoff should fire Sioli. Sioli's dismissal left the way open for a Party-loyal artistic director in the Stadttheater. In February Sioli had engaged the conductor Hans Swarowsky, after two guest performances of *Carmen* and *The Flying Dutchman*, as Aachen's new kapell-meister, subject to authorization from the president. But Swarow-sky did not take up his post in Aachen. Mayor Jansen, who wanted to decide, and in fact decided, who was to be put in charge of the Stadttheater, found a dependable vassal in the new manager, Dr Groß. A holder of the NSDAP 'Gold Medal of Honour' bestowed by the Führer, Jansen, a Party member from the very first, was considered especially dependable by the Party. The new manager, who came from Lübeck, had already made his presence felt by giving special performances for the Party even under a Social Democrat mayor. As a Party member, a prominent member of the SS and member of the Nazi Air Corps, his arrival in the spring of 1934 could not have been better timed, particularly as his wife was also able to make herself useful as district cultural officer of the Nazi Women's League. Groß returned to Aachen from Berlin, where he had been in search of new staff for the ensemble, with the young Karajan in tow. It is quite obvious that in Aachen, where the city's cultural life was securely in the hands of the Party, a Party member was particularly welcome as conductor at the Stadttheater. Bearing this in mind, the orchestra's original rejection is more or less insignificant, as long as Karajan was able to portray himself to the relevant bodies as an indispensable mainstay of a co-ordinated musical life. Having achieved this, he was convincingly able to remove any last doubts about his dependability by his unusually high level of efficiency and the necessary proof of racial purity.

In one desperate effort, the young Karajan managed what many older and more experienced colleagues never succeeded in doing. He hauled himself out of the trough of unemployment and up to a highly enviable position. He made the leap from provincial anonymity to the metropolitan fame of a confident, culturally lively border city with a proven musical tradition, which also helped the young Leo Blech in the furtherance of his career. Aachen – for Karajan it meant a seventy-man orchestra increased to ninety-strong for concerts, a choir of 300 singers renowned for its quality, a well-equipped theatre, a presentable concert hall and an audience capable of honouring extravagant artistic demands.

Aachen was the springboard to the major success that Karajan dreamed of throughout his life. If the orchestra had had its way after his audition, who knows, perhaps Karajan would have ended up being the architect commissioned to make great things: 'Not building houses. But twenty turbines in the Straits of Gibraltar, to irrigate the Sahara – that would be a great success.'[62] With his appointment Karajan's striving after power won early satisfaction. He would have murdered for the Aachen job, he would have committed any crime, said Karajan, probably meaning that nothing was more important to him at the time than the post, which was appropriate to his capabilities and his plans. If anything good came out of the fact that he was without a mentor during his time in Ulm, it was that nobody had brought him down to earth from his high-flown plans. He compensated in his mind for the real limitations of his circumstances in Ulm. Having become arrogant in this way, he moved to Aachen. In choosing him, the city had drawn the short straw, as he was soon to find out.

With all these new vistas opening up before him, why should Karajan have been bothered about political events in the country? On 24 April, with the establishment of the 'People's Court', the regime created the instrument with which, under cover of apparent legality, injustice could be perpetrated in style. On 30 June, in an action prepared by Göring, Himmler and General von Blomberg,

Hitler brought about the massacre of the entire leadership of the SA, led by the homosexual Röhm and gathered in Bad Wiessee. Following the murder of Röhm and his SA leaders, the SS units who had carried out the liquidation set about eliminating the people named on a 'Reich list' of undesirables, including General Schleicher and his wife, Gustav von Kahr, Gregor Strasser and General von Bredow. A group of Silesian Jews was also shot down for the entertainment of the local Gauleiter. The massacre, in which several hundred people were killed, was justified, in a later retrospective law, as self-defence on the part of the state. In Austria, on 25 July, in a National Socialist *putsch* that cost over 250 lives, Chancellor Engelbert Dollfuss was shot. Hitler legally combined the office of chancellor with that of president and, as 'Führer and Reich Chancellor' became chief commander of the Wehrmacht; total power was now his. Could all this have escaped Karajan in his delight at being called to Aachen?

In late summer the rehearsals for the new season began. The new company included the dazzlingly beautiful operetta singer Elmy Holgerloef. Hanover-born Holgerloef's relationship with Karajan was soon to be a very close one, more off the stage than on. On 21 August he conducted the Vienna Philharmonic for the first time, thanks to Mrs Moulton, a rich and eccentric American widow, who had engaged him for a private concert at a large party. The first part took place in the Large Hall of the Mozarteum. The programme consisted of Debussy's *Fantaisie* for piano and orchestra (soloist Ralph Lawton) and *La Valse* by Ravel. For the second part they moved to the open-air theatre of the nearby Mirabellgarten where the students of the Vienna Staatsoper ballet school danced Debussy's *Prélude à l'après-midi d'un faune*, choreographed by Margarete Wallmann, with Willy Franzel as the faun.

The Reich Propaganda Ministry had 'no reservations' about the concert, for which Karajan, as newly appointed musical director, had to seek authorization from the President of the Reich Theatre Chamber.[63] This despite the fact that Goebbels had that May refused to allow Richard Strauss and Furtwängler to perform at the Salzburg Festival, because this 'was in contravention of the Führer's policy towards Austria'.[64] Karajan skilfully negotiated this obstacle, justifying his application by saying that the main object of the concert, which was entirely private and closed to the public 'was to establish the acoustic conditions of an open-air stage'.[65] Karajan was later to use what he had learned at this concert in the context of musical events such as those held as part of the NSDAP district assemblies. From this point of view, the journey to Salzburg had been worth all the expense.

Two days after this extravagant concert, Toscanini gave his first performances at the Salzburg Festival with a series of three concerts. In the last of these he conducted the very same work that Karajan had played at the end of his romantic dance soirée in the outdoor theatre of the Mirabellgarten. A coincidence, certainly, but also a symbol of his elective affinity with the Italian conducting genius. It is somewhat surprising that although Toscanini was Karajan's model in musical and artistic matters, this did not extend to the human sphere. After Hitler's seizure of power Toscanini refused to conduct in Bayreuth again, and after the Reich's annexation of Austria he ceased to perform at the Salzburg Festival, difficult as this was for him. Toscanini's resolute rejection of National Socialism and Fascism, and the consistency of his actions after this, could always have been a model for Karajan, showing him the only humanly possible course to take: to run out on the regime and go abroad. But for Party member Karajan it was probably already too late.

When I asked him about this, Karajan told me, on 17 June 1980:

> Do you think it would have made any difference if I had gone to America two years before Hitler turned up? Quite certainly not. The moment they realized there was any competition it was a fight to the death. [And on 9 January 1981, he added:] You see, if I had gone away then, I wouldn't have found a big orchestra in America before war broke out. They were a real mafia, they wouldn't have let anyone get near them. It would have been enough to have been born there. They had erected *such* a blockade. Just as they did after the war.

Someone who, at the end of his life, portrays the situation at that time in terms such as these, is blind to the fact that he himself had a hand in things being that way. Karajan always had to look for a mafia whenever he was unable, with the best will in the world, to justify himself.

Yet again, according to Karajan, he fell prey to evil forces. He tended to externalize the powers of destruction, looking for them outside himself. Karajan was incapable of recognizing this, because he had no functioning internalized conscience. Quite clearly, he never went through that developmental process.

The first shots in the battle were fired by the twenty-six-year-old Karajan in Aachen on 18 September 1934: he got off to a brilliant start with his first performance of a new production of *Fidelio* in the border city. A few days previously he had introduced himself to Aachen's music-lovers at a promotional evening for the Stadttheater, giving an 'impressive rendering' of the Overture to *Die Meistersinger*. On 23 October he conducted the *Walküre*, and on 8 December, the day of National Solidarity, he gave his first celebrated concert in Aachen. The *Westdeutscher Beobachter* reviewer could not resist opening his article with a fundamental observation on Karajan's concert: 'That a conductor in charge of the most wonderful and subtle instruments should prove artistic and national solidarity, that he should be thankful to those who gave him this instrument . . . strikes us as an equally essential precondition for true inner artistry.'[66] Showing national solidarity was never to prove a great difficulty for Karajan in Aachen or elsewhere, as we shall see. At Christmas he conducted a performance of *Rosenkavalier*, and in the new year he confirmed his talent with *Tannhäuser*.

Karajan was still not in charge at the theatre in Aachen. But he very quickly rose from the throng of favoured mediocrities who had of necessity gained ground in Germany since the exile of the Jewish musicians. The Generalmusikdirektor was Peter Raabe, a man loyal to the regime. Raabe had been working in Aachen since 1920 and soon saw a young rival in Karajan. He suddenly refused to make way for him. Karajan's handling of this first test of strength was characteristic of the tactics he employed in pursuit of his aims. Knowing that he had been well received in Aachen, and that the authorities had no wish to lose him, he toyed with an offer of a post in Karlsruhe. The hint was taken, and he was assured of conditions identical to those offered by Karlsruhe. On 12 April 1935 the city press office had this to say:

A young, extremely talented and highly distinctive personality will in future, while fully maintaining his previous sphere of activity, also run the city's concerts, two major duties that Professor Raabe temporarily assumed for a period of two years, and which have, until now, been shared between two men. Aachen can congratulate itself on finding this solution to the far from easy question of who could and should be Raabe's successor. Herr von Karajan, who was 'discovered' by theatre manager Dr Groß, and who is fully appreciated by Aachen's most important personalities, has secured himself responsibility for Aachen's musical life for three years – resisting some very strong currents that almost carried him away from us . . . In

101

December the Reichsoper in Charlottenburg tried to woo him away for their most important position, and after a number of guest concerts in Karlsruhe in March, Baden's Minister of Culture and Education was keen to see the guest conductor from Aachen working as Generalmusikdirektor in Karlsruhe ... Herr von Karajan, who has grown fond of Aachen as a place to work, was able to leave the decision in the hands of our mayor.'[67]

Professor Peter Raabe left the field open for Karajan and moved to Weimar on 1 July. At twenty-seven Karajan was made Generalmusikdirektor. Great hopes were placed on his shoulders, the hopes of both the musical world and the Party. For Mayor Jansen, who believed he had had some say in attracting Karajan to his post as Generalmusikdirektor, was convinced that in so doing he 'was acting according to the spirit of Germany's cultural duties'.[68] During the run-up to Karajan's first season he had succinctly outlined, in an announcement to the people, the cultural and political programme of the Aachen Stadttheater, which Karajan would now dutifully carry out:

The National Socialist movement and philosophy, whose growth is due not least to the strength of its cultural insights and demands, requires that we should be as attentive to these cultural needs as we are to political needs ... The theatre of our border town has a more elevated mission, over and above this: to be the bulwark for all the artistic forces of the Third Reich against foreign influences alien to our nature. In so doing it is completing the belligerent circle of German theatre on the western borders of the Reich.[69]

All obstacles to Karajan's fairytale rise from being Germany's youngest Generalmusikdirektor to being the immediate rival of the Reich's leading conducting personality, Wilhelm Furtwängler, had now been removed. Peter Raabe had been satisfied with the Presidency of the Reichsmusikkammer, after Richard Strauss had been obliged, obediently and against his will, to resign the post on 13 July following a battle of wills with Goebbels, who, as Reich Minister for Popular Enlightenment and Propaganda, was in charge of the Reichsmusikkammer. Raabe revealed the kind of man he was at the musicians' meeting of the General German Music Association on 7 June the same year, at which he said: 'If music in the Third Reich is gradually – for things such as this take time and peace – to reach the people and bring them the joy required to steel them for their work and the struggle for existence, we must first, with brooms of iron, sweep away everything un-artistic that has befogged these people's minds.'[70] The first thing to fall victim to these brooms of iron, the policy of creative liquidation, was everything Jewish in music. The catalogue of those condemned included the works of Mendelssohn as well as those of Gustav Mahler.

As early as February 1934, the conductor and composer Peter Raabe, a fervent supporter of Hitler and member of the adminis-trative committee of the Reichsmusikkammer, spoke at the first working session of the newly formed professional association of German composers, supervised by Goebbels, on the subject of the leadership principle in music – the *Führerprinzip*.

> I don't know whether it has every struck you that hardly any other associations of working people have consistently, in two senses, acted so much in the interest of the National Socialist community as have the orchestras. It is here that the leadership principle has been promulgated in the purest way, the conductor enjoys unconditional authority; not as a dictator, however, but rather as the man who has the trust of his followers, and who must constantly re-establish this trust not by means of force, but by means of persuasion. And secondly, in every orchestral musician the man who works with his hands is united with the man who works with his head.[71]

Orchestra and conductor as precursors of the people and the Führer. Confronted with such a striking equation, it must have been more than tempting to forge ahead as a conductor in the Third Reich. For when the motto was, as it were, 'Every conductor is his own little Führer', it was permissible to behave accordingly and, setting aside all scruples, to act as though the sacred art of music was the only thing at stake. There was nothing embarrassing about being equated with the Führer, since the conductor embodied his principle in the so-called 'apolitical' sphere of the arts.

But anyone who paid any attention in those days – and amid the bombardment of Goebbels' cultural propaganda it was impos-ible not to – would at some point have heard that this was not the case. Art and the practice of art were always political in the

103

Third Reich, and that is how they were seen and proclaimed – for example, in one of the 'fundamental speeches' with which Goebbels instructed the German people and its artists:

> The artist undeniably has the right to call himself non-political in a period when politics consists of nothing but shouting matches between parliamentary parties. But at this moment when politics is writing a national drama, when a world is being overthrown – in such a moment the artist cannot say: 'That doesn't concern me.' It concerns him a great deal.[72]

That is, we might think, understandable enough. Anyone who tried later on, once the terrible spectre had passed, to talk his way out of the matter by using the exculpating argument of political ignorance and fully apolitical work dedicated solely to art, must be reminded of it, posthumously, so to speak. Talking one's way out of things is not a punishable offence, but it does discredit the speaker where he is most concerned with maintaining a moral claim to integrity. Wilhelm Furtwängler, Karl Böhm, Richard Strauss, Carl Orff, to name only a few prominent figures of National Socialist musical life, should really have known this. Thoroughly compromised, they afterwards donned the mask of sanctimoniousness and continued their careers in post-war Germany wearing this borrowed face, as if nothing had happened. Here I must unfortunately cut short this fundamental observation on the behaviour of certain of the great men of the Third Reich, for we must devote our full attention to Herbert von Karajan.

Once he had become Generalmusikdirektor, he readily allowed the Nazis to use him for their own ends. A participant in the promotion of culture for Hitler's new Reich, he was soon able to prove himself. At the NSDAP District Party Day in Aachen, for example, at the end of June 1935, after he had already conducted a festival production of *Tannhäuser* for the birthday of the Führer and Reich Chancellor on Easter Saturday and, ten days later, in a private performance for the Nazi association 'Strength Through Joy', Beethoven's *Fidelio*. At the celebrations on Saturday, 29 June, in the Katschhof, Karajan spent four weeks rehearsing an impressive programme of works unambiguous in tone for an audience of thousands, the glitter of non-local Party prominence being provided by Gauleiter Josef Grohé and Reich Inspector Rudolf Schmeer, among others. Among the works included, along with the festival hymns 'Licht muß wieder werden' by Otto Siegl and 'Unsere Seele' by Bruno Stürmer, was Richard Trunk's cycle *Feier der neuen Front, opus 65*, dedicated to Adolf Hitler, to a text by Baldur von Schirach, the NSDAP Reich youth leader and later Gauleiter and governor of Vienna. The individual movements of this state-commissioned work bear the titles 'Hitler', 'The Führer's Guardians', 'O, My Country' and 'Horst Wessel'. It conveys a 'powerful vision' in music: 'The image of brown masses of people surging forward, surrounding the flag after the hero's death, planting it in the earth and saving the country.' The consecrating concert in which Karajan celebrated Führer, Party and Reich in the historic Katschhof between the cathedral and the swastika-beflagged Rathaus, a 'National Community Celebration', was the artistic highlight of Aachen's District Party Day. For the City Orchestra, swollen to more than 100 players, and the 750 soldier singers of the mass choir, symbolized, in the glare of the floodlights, 'the massive solidity of a mass of men dedicating themselves both to a political idea and a major artistic concept'. On that remarkable summer evening, on which 'Herbert von Karajan placed himself at the service of that idea', he proved, as the *Westdeutscher Beobachter* appreciatively stressed, 'that he is the man who can give a direction to the new organization of our artistic life in the direction that National Socialism demands'. With the 'Horst Wessel Song', performed by Karajan, orchestra and choir, and a torch procession by the Hitler Youth, the 'most important event in the Westmark' was ceremoniously brought to an end.[73]

The following year (the laws for the protection of German blood and German honour, the so-called Nuremberg laws, forbidding marriage with Jews and relegating Jews to a lower social class, had come into force in the interim), Karajan acquainted the people of Aachen with Heinrich Gemacher's *Kameradschaft* for choir and obbligato instruments. The employment of soloists who fervently supported the regime was only consistent with enthusiasm of this kind. The choice of soloists for Karajan's Aachen concerts was an added appeal. In 1935 he engaged the pianist Elly Ney, a loyal follower of Hitler, for one of the concerts which, under Karajan's baton, were increasingly being given in the surrounding towns and the Dutch–Belgian border area. At a Beethoven evening in Düren she played the E flat major Concerto under Karajan. The very same Elly Ney whose wont it was, at her performances for the Hitler Youth or at Reich Youth Command events, to precede her musical recital with a verbose declaration of loyalty to the

Hitler state. The same Elly Ney who, in the Berlin of the 1960s, revealed herself to me to be entirely unaware of historical events, when she actually spoke of the Jewish conspiracy which, she claimed, had destroyed her post-war career. To the end she provided a fine example of the continuing existence of delusory projection on to the Jews. She was unable – and this, too, was her tragedy – to stop giving concerts when it was time to do so, and went on giving recitals when her fingers and her memory had long since failed their art.

On 20 August 1936, Generalmusikdirektor von Karajan received his identity card and letter of confirmation as musical representative of the Reichmusikkammer, and consequently the authorization to control and co-ordinate the city's musical life beyond the confines of his immediate sphere of activity, the theatre. Karajan did quickly establish new standards in Aachen. He engaged the 'best and most impressive names that had ever been within Aachen's scope',[74] as the *Kölnische Zeitung* said in December 1935. His operatic performances also quickly won an extensive reputation for high quality. He first performed the *Ring des Nibelungen* in Aachen (21–8 November 1937) and was to return to it repeatedly later in his career. He won renown with the performances of Verdi's *Requiem* (first performance 20 November 1935) and Bach's *B Minor Mass* (first performance April 1936) with the city choir, conducted by Wilhelm Pitz, and with which Karajan performed in Vienna after the war. Pitz's career led him to hold the position of choirmaster at the Bayreuth Festival for many years. A friend of Karajan's, Pitz gave the conductor one of the chief bases for his success in Aachen in the form of an outstandingly well-trained choir. In Aachen Karajan was already fully aware of what a Generalmusikdirektor needed to do. He shrewdly chose the right colleagues to support him in his work. This was especially indispensable with a programme whose season included six to eight operatic premières, six double subscription concerts, eight Volkssinfonie concerts and one or two special concerts.

'Of course Karajan only came to the main rehearsal, other people did all the preparations,' recalls Kammersängerin Irmgaard Seefried, who started her career under Karajan in Aachen.[75] He was already more feared than loved. He surrounded himself with staff, and always promptly disposed of them when they had fulfilled their duty. In Aachen he was able for the first time to develop his organizational talent to the full, and he did so with relish. He planned far ahead. He worked through the entire repertory of major works with the excellent city choir. He planned for his later career by assimilating the representative standard programme with which he would tour the world after the war. In Aachen the later Karajan was already apparent in his unwavering sense of direction, his fanaticism, his recklessness and his human unapproachability. He monopolized everything, intervened in the productions of his directors, turned everything upside down at his rehearsals and soon realized that he himself was going to be his own best director. In Aachen he was carrying out his preliminary exercises. His time there amounted to a dress rehearsal for things to come.

The border city of Aachen has always exerted a particular appeal, thanks to its traditionally high level of cultural activity, extending to both the Rhine and the Ruhr and into neighbouring Belgium and Holland. A highly successful performance of Bach's *B Minor Mass* with an ensemble of 450 singers and instrumentalists in the Palais des Beaux-Arts in Brussels on 26 April 1936, shortly after the occupation of the demilitarized Rhineland, launched a series of guest concerts with the Brussels orchestra. Thus within a short space of time Karajan had made a name for himself outside Aachen and the borders of Germany. On 3 February 1936 he returned to Ulm to conduct a guest concert. Five weeks later, on 14 March, he did pioneering work for the official music of the New Germany at a volkssinfonie concert in Aachen, acquainting his music-lovers in Aachen with the *Concerto for Orchestra* by Party member Max Trapp. Karajan's last performance of 1936 was a production of *Fledermaus* with the beautiful operetta singer Elmy Holgerloef, whom he was to marry two years later.

In June 1937 he made his first guest appearance at the Vienna Staatsoper at the invitation of Dr Erwin Kerber. Karajan could scarcely have dreamed that less than ten years after his student days he would be conducting *Tristan* at Austria's most important opera house. The production went ahead under the worst conditions that a guest conductor can be offered: without serious rehearsals. Karajan would in future avoid experiments of that kind. Immediately after the performance Kerber, a senior civil servant, sought to engage Karajan at the Staatsoper under Bruno Walter. But Karajan refused, having gained the impression that he would be given only a second- or third-level post. Who knows what course his career would have taken had he agreed: less than a year later Austria was part of the German Reich, and the Jews who had fled to Austria were exiled yet again. Generalmusikdirektor Bruno Walter and his kapellmeisters Carl Alwin and Josef Krips were forced to resign their positions at the Staatsoper in 1938. Their loss might have been Karajan's gain.

Discussing Karajan's operatic début in conversation with Furt-wängler after the war, Bruno Walter said: 'I told him at the time: "You've mastered the score, but you must go into it much more deeply." '[76] Karajan must have taken that very much to heart, for when he conducted *Tristan und Isolde* at the Berlin Staatsoper on 21 October 1938, he did it with such insight and conviction that the Berlin critic Edwin van der Null, later to die in the war, was inspired to write an enthusiastic review in the *Berliner Zeitung am Mittag*, with the headline: 'In the Staatsoper: *das Wunder Karajan*'.

This brought Karajan the attention he needed. Many things combine to indicate that this practically ecstatic report was part of a stage-managed programme designed to build Karajan up into a rival of Furtwängler. Before this, on 30 September, Karajan had had his début at the Berlin Staatsoper with *Fidelio*. The house was half empty. But after van der Null's review that changed abruptly.[77] The fact that the thirty-year-old Karajan conducted without a score and revealed a supreme control that recalled Richard Strauss and other great figures of the age rightly stimulated the curiosity of the astonished musical world. Great things were unquestionably happening in the Staatsoper under Karajan's baton. And if the extravagant reports (Goebbels had forbidden criticism) might, in addition, have been dictated from above, their praise was by no means feigned.

In the summer of 1938, on 26 July, Karajan married the attractive singer Elmy Holgerloef, eleven years his senior. They lived in a house in the suburbs, on the Eupener Strasse in Aachen-Burtscheid. After their honeymoon, Karajan opened the new season with *Lohengrin* on 18 September. Before the wedding, on 6 July, he applied, via the Cologne-Aachen Gauleitung, to the Reich Command of the NSDAP for his membership card. Had Party membership now become so important for him that he needed to have it constantly reaffirmed in the form of the membership card? Or was the application related to his marriage? Either way: the application for the card triggered investigations into his membership by the Party heads, as the files of the district treasurer for Gau Salzburg revealed arrears in Karajan's contributions going back a long way. As Karajan had joined the Party in Salzburg and in Ulm, the Party had to establish which of these two occasions related to his membership card. They wanted to know above all 'whether the application with effect from 8 April 1933, with delivery of provisional membership card No. 1607525, had come into force, and also whether and, if applicable, for how long after this application membership contributions had been paid'.[78]

The investigations dragged on, and Party Member Herbert von Karajan's application for the card was 'postponed until his membership had been clarified'.[79] The probe passed through several different Party departments. In a letter of 7 July 1939, one year after the application, the Reich Command informed the treasurer of the NSDAP's Cologne-Aachen district of the result of their inquiry:

We have in the meantime established that the membership of the above-named with effect from 8.4.1933 did not come into force. In a letter of 2.6.1939 the Salzburg Gauleitung informed us of the result of the investigation, showing that Party Member Herbert von Karajan made only one contribution of 5 schillings in April 1933. The above-named left the same month leaving no forwarding address.

The application of 8.4.1933 is therefore declared invalid, and Membership Number 1697525 is deleted from the Reich Command basic membership book. The above-named, who joined with Membership Number 3430914 on 1.5.1933, in the District of Cologne-Aachen, with the address: Aachen-Burtscheid, Eupenerstrasse, continues as a Party Member in the Reich files.

After clarification of his membership, the card application made by the Cologne-Aachen Gauleitung is granted, and Membership Card No. 3430914 will be issued to the above-named.

I request that the Membership Card herewith enclosed should be sent to Party Member Herbert von Karajan with due reference to the existing rules of registration and the regulations concerning payment of contributions. Heil Hitler![80]

1938 was not only a particularly important year for the German Reich, it was also the year of Karajan's real breakthrough. On 12 March, with the entry into Austria of 200,000 German soldiers, supported by the SS and the Luftwaffe, Hitler brought Austria back to the German Reich. On 8 April, a few days after his thirtieth birthday, Karajan conducted the Berlin Philharmonic Orchestra for the first time in a special concert at the venerable old Philharmonie. Two days later the Reich's annexation of Austria, half enforced and half welcomed, was confirmed by a popular vote. From now on the country was referred to as Greater Germany. What the Salzburger Karajan had been doing in practice for years was now a reality for all the citizens of Salzburg. There had already been a trial annexation of Austria to the German motherland after the collapse of the Habsburg monarchy, before the borders, which came down immediately after the empire's defeat and the proclamation of the republic, were erected once more.

Aachen was the home of 'an alert and strong popular and national awareness', where more than elsewhere in the Reich there was a sense of 'everyone making a great effort to testify to Adolf Hitler, to whom this formerly threatened borderland owes especial gratitude', where it is clear 'that one is in a German outpost'.[81] It was here that Karajan, and with him the whole city, celebrated Austria's return to the Reich in a quite special way. 'Celebrating Adolf Hitler's great act of liberation and the reunification of Austria with the Reich', Karajan performed, as the theatre management proudly announced, a new production of Beethoven's drama of liberation, *Fidelio*, quickly rehearsed over four weeks to celebrate the integration of the two countries. As it had the only stage for far and wide, Aachen broke with tradition on Good Friday, 15 April 1938, to celebrate, with Beethoven's monumental work of liberation, 'a culturally world-renowned symbol of the Führer's act of liberation', and 'as an expression of the greatness of this historical event', the incorporation of Austria into what was now the body of the Greater German Reich.[82] Five days later Karajan was once more given the opportunity to prove his mettle as a loyal Party member. On the occasion of Adolf Hitler's birthday, he paid an act of reverence to his Führer with a celebratory repeat performance of *Fidelio*.

Karajan's début with the Berlin Philharmonic was immediately seen for what it was: a great event. In the *Berliner Tageblatt* Heinrich Strobel reported a 'great philharmonic evening', the high point of which was the performance of Ravel's *Daphnis and Chloë*, Suite No. 2. The concert opened with Mozart's Symphony KV 319, and finished with Brahms' Fourth Symphony. In the *Deutsche Allgemeine Zeitung* of 9 April Robert Oboussier declared the young guest performer to be a 'man with a calling'. In his opinion Karajan appeared to be 'a completely independent, starkly outlined personality; an elemental passion of musical experience. A will of masculine force and intellectual concentration. . . . The evening was conducted with the force of an explosion. The audience applauded the young conductor with an enthusiasm which, while acknowledging his importance, also established a now irresistible demand.'[83]

What is this 'now irresistible demand?' Is it the demand that the young Party member, unquestionably far more talented than all the other young German conductors of his day, should be favoured over Furtwängler, who had been declared unreliable by the regime? Be that as it may, at his first concert Karajan had the utopian notion of one day being in charge of this orchestra, as he later said in his address to the orchestra which, after Furtwängler's death, actually did make him its conductor for the rest of his life.

These convincing successes led the manager of the Staatsoper, Hans von Benda, to invite Karajan to perform two further concerts in the coming season. Before his celebrated operatic début, on 27 September, he conducted a master concert with the Philharmonic Orchestra for the Berlin concert patrons and the Nazi association 'Strength through Joy'. The programme consisted of Sibelius's Sixth Symphony, Haydn's Cello Concerto (soloist Arthur Troester) and Beethoven's Fifth Symphony. The phenomenal success of his Berlin débuts led on 4 November to his being engaged at the Staatsoper by the Prussian Minister President General Field Marshal Göring, who was directly responsible for the opera house. After his initial success with *Fidelio*, Heinz Tietjen, general manager of the Prussian State Theatre, had already offered Karajan a new production of *Zauberflöte* with Gustav Gründgens directing.[84] The première took place on 18 December and entered the annals of Berlin's musical history as the 'perfect *Zauberflöte*', and as 'one of the greatest artistic evenings that we have ever experienced in Berlin'. Interviewed late in life, Karajan said of Gründgens' *Zauberflöte*: 'For me his staging is still the most consummate production of this opera.'[85] The invitation to be musical director of this congenial staging, which made operatic history, represented a one-in-a-million chance to provide an artistic justification for the trust that the Party placed in him. In particular, the fact that he was allowed to work on a production using all the best and most outstanding artistic talents of the Third Reich amounted to an honour from the regime that placed him under a great obligation. This great success brought Karajan his first gramophone record. With the orchestra of the Berlin Staatsoper he recorded the Overture to *Zauberflöte* for Deutsche Grammophon. This saw

111

the beginning of Karajan's recording work, to which he owed not only the majority of his post-war fame but also his economic success.

Karajan's appointment to the Staatsoper and his rehearsals for the new production of *Zauberflöte* coincided with one of the most terrible events of pre-war Nazi Germany. This was the pogrom against the Jewish population, known as *Kristallnacht*, which took place on 9–10 November 1938. On those gloomy November days, in a concerted action which took the form of a revenge against the Jews, synagogues and Jewish schools, shops and houses were set on fire and destroyed in countless acts of violence. Thousands of Jews were abused, many murdered. Over 20,000 were arrested. On 12 November an 'expiatory payment' of a billion Reichsmark, later raised to one and a half billion, was demanded from the persecuted Jews for the damage done by the SA stormtroops in the course of the pogrom. For thousands of Jewish families this meant financial ruin and the loss of their livelihoods. The same day an order from the Reich Cultural Chamber was passed, forbidding participation of Jews in German cultural events. On 28 November, with the passing of the 'Reich police ordinance concerning the appearance of Jews in public' known as the *Judenbann*, came the exclusion of the Jewish population from public events and school attendance, and on 3 December the requisition of Jewish property was decreed. The obligatory adoption of the forenames 'Israel' or 'Sarah' had already been enforced on 17 August. Anyone unblinded by his own success, by indifference, intolerance, inhumanity or selfishness could, by November 1938, no longer ignore the abyss into which National Socialist disruption was to lead. On 1 October the Germans had entered the Sudetenland, preparations for the annexation of Czechoslovakia had been under way since April, and the arms industry's production was in full swing. Where was this all to lead, if not to war?

Unconcerned and unmoved by the internal and foreign political situation, Karajan continued to soar ever upwards. The will to power had seized him too. But whatever reasons we might use to explain the emergence of this fanatical will in Karajan as an individual, they cannot fully account for his astounding success in the musical life of the Third Reich. For this success is not simply a matter of his internal make-up. Karajan's histrionic ego was inseparably connected with his audience, which responded to his act of self-assertion by granting him success. He was overwhelmed by his belief in himself, and this compellingly and fascinatingly reflected back on those around him.

On 28 January 1939 Karajan conducted the première of *Die Bürger von Calais* by Rudolf Wagner-Régeny at the Staatsoper. Karajan met Tietjen's offer of the première with demands that were so confidently exacting that the baffled Tietjen could not resist his curiosity and, after an audition, conceded Karajan's wishes. *Die Bürger von Calais* is a work entirely in line with National Socialist ideology, dealing as it does with the Nazi idea of the sacrifice of individuals for the many, constantly drummed into the masses by the Propaganda Ministry, so that they would act correctly once war was started. 'A subject worthy to be the basis of an opera in line with the new Germany, with a superior ethos, a love of the homeland, patience and a willingness to make sacrifices',[86] as Fritz Brust observed in the *Dresdner Nachrichten* of 30 January 1939. Might this have escaped Karajan? The opera was given six performances in Berlin.

Two days after the première, Hitler delivered his celebrated or notorious two-and-a-half hour speech to the 885 National Socialist representatives at their first meeting since their election ten months previously. In this address at the Kroll Oper in Berlin, he bluntly prophesied the 'annihilation of the Jewish races in Europe'.[87] It was directed at an audience of millions, listening enthralled by their radios at home or in the pubs and meeting-places throughout the Reich, which 'knows that in all probability a war is coming; and it is delivered by one who knows that his listeners know it'.[88] On 30 January 1939, after which no one in the Reich who had either heard his speech or learned of its contents (and was there anyone at the time who could have been unaware of it?) could claim that he had known nothing of the planned extermination of the Jews by the Nazis, Hitler made the following prophecy:

> The war that I am about to unleash is one in which we ourselves and not the Jews our enemies shall be victorious. . . . This war, in which our victory is the same as the annihilation of the Jews, is an inseparable part of my programme, in which domestic 'tasks' are continuous with international 'tasks', and will receive a single continuous solution. . . . The annihilation of the Jew, our common enemy, is the reward and the deliverance I offer you for following me into this war.[89]

Might this have escaped the thirty-year-old Karajan? Against all probability? It is not my intention to imply that Party Member

113

von Karajan, waiting for his membership card, was informed of the content of Hitler's speech, which was the focus of everyone's attention at the time, but it is infinitely difficult to believe the contrary.

A few days after the holocaust had been announced throughout the Reich, Karajan travelled to Belgium, not to flee the regime that was openly declaring its murderous intentions towards European Jewry, but as a cultural emissary of the Nazi State, in order, quite in line with Goebbels' propaganda machine, to herald the superior cultural power of Nazi Germany; a message of cultural superiority which was to be followed in May 1940 by a military show of power with the occupation of Belgium. On 10 February 1939 Karajan gave a guest performance of *Walküre* in Liège with his Aachen ensemble, and two weeks later he conducted the Belgian National Orchestra in Brussels. Wilhelm Backhaus was the soloist in Brahms' Second Piano Concerto. On 23 February a new stage in Karajan's career began when he was commissioned to run the symphony concerts at the Berlin Staatsoper. In so doing he came into direct competition in Berlin's concert life with Furtwängler, who was to dominate the musical world of a war-torn Europe.

On 15 March Karajan gave a guest concert in Stockholm. On the same day German troops marched into the remainder of Czechoslovakia. These regions were turned into the protectorate of Bohemia and Moravia. On 20 March, the Wednesday before Easter, in the courtyard of the headquarters of Berlin's fire-brigade, the 'unusable remnants'[90] of confiscated, so-called 'degenerate' art were burned: 1,004 oil paintings and pictures, 3,825 sheets of graphics, water-colours and drawings, including works by Emil Nolde, Karl Schmidt-Rottluff and Erich Heckel. On 14 April Karajan gave his third concert with the Berlin Philharmonic in the Philharmonie. Alfred Birgfeld wrote about it in *Signale zur Musik*:

> The very first work, the Haydn Symphony (E flat major, with the drum roll), that ushered in the special concert by the Philharmonic under Herbert von Karajan, gave a hint, in its sharply outlined rendering, that Tchaikovsky's Sixth with its third movement, that fulminating 'Cossacks' Victory March', would form an unimaginable, rousing climax. And that is indeed how it was: the movement – as indeed the whole symphony – was characterized by a controlled development of tone. At the centre

of the programme, the interpreter of Tchaikovsky and Haydn devoted his efforts to a performance of Debussy's *La Mer* with just as much stirring power![91]

What was so obviously apparent in the thirty-one-year-old Karajan, the controlled unleashing of sound and his predilection for a repertoire aimed at creating effect, remained a constant determining factor throughout his life. He recorded the *Pathétique* for Deutsche Grammophon: it was the first recording of a ceaselessly growing series with the Berlin Philharmonic. In 1939 five records were produced in all; apart from the Tchaikovsky Symphony, they were all recordings of opera overtures and intermezzi with the orchestra of the Berlin Staatsoper. Without a doubt, Karajan's market value for the recording industry was recognized early and unerringly, and full use was made of it throughout the war years. By the end of the war he had produced twenty-three records with Deutsche Grammophon, a remarkable number considering the technically limited possibilities of the age of shellac discs and the general political situation. It tells us something about the important status bestowed on Karajan by the Third Reich.

A week after the concert, on 20 April, the Führer's fiftieth birthday, in accordance with a suggestion from the Reich Minister for Popular Enlightenment and Propaganda, Dr Goebbels, Hitler's signature officially promoted Karajan to State Kapellmeister. This brought Karajan to the highest rung of his career in the Third Reich. He shared his work at the Staatsoper with Victor de Sabata, Werner Egk and Robert Heger. He conducted the entire repertory, including *Meistersinger, Salome, Elektra* and *Carmina Burana*. Richard Strauss attended the new festival production of *Elektra*, in honour of the composer's seventy-fifth birthday.

Richard Strauss himself came to the première, arranged for his seventy-fifth birthday.[92] Afterwards I was invited up: he was standing there. And when he was on the point of saying, as he did so often, that today's was 'the finest performance of *Elektra* that I have ever heard', I said to him: 'Herr Doktor, please don't say that, I would rather you would tell me what was wrong with it.' He gave me a penetrating look and invited me to breakfast in the Hotel Adlon for the following morning. Then, the next day, he started talking about a few little technical details and then said: 'You are very precise, so that one can

115

hear the singers as well, but the final song, which is basically a dithyrambic hymn, the liberation that means we can become human again, well we know that already.... And,' he said then, 'don't bother with that, just give it a good stir,' by which he meant, just let the orchestra play. Then he grew serious again: 'You wanted me to tell you what's wrong. You have spent three months on the work now. But I went beyond it decades ago, I grew out of it, outlived it. So which of us is right? Simply do what you did yesterday, that's the right way.' And then a mischievous smile crossed his face: 'And by the way, in five years' time you'll see it differently.' And that was the profound wisdom of a man who knew of the constant change in things. And the day one ceases to feel that, it is better to cease to live!'[93]

Unmoved by the events of the war Karajan alternated between Aachen and Berlin, collecting triumphs in both cities. In May 1939 he travelled to Berlin with the Aachen City Choir for the Brahms Festival, enjoying a triumphant success with the *Requiem.*

In June he even managed to top this triumph. In honour of the state visit by the Prince Regent and Princess Paul of Yugoslavia, the Führer invited guests to a festival performance in the Staatsoper on 2 June 1939. In the presence of the most prominent Party members such as General Field Marshal Göring, who greeted the distinguished guests in the opera foyer, Dr Goebbels, Dr Frick, Dr Ley and Reichsführer SS Himmler, Karajan conducted Richard Wagner's nationalist opera *Die Meistersinger von Nürnberg* in Tietjen's staging, with the ensemble and equipment of the Bayreuth Stage Festival. The performance of Hitler's favourite opera as an official artistic symbol of Nazism became, as the front pages of newspapers throughout the Reich declared the following day, 'a unique manifestation of German art and a great homage to the Führer's guests'.[94] Hardly had he returned to Aachen than Karajan voluntarily allowed himself to be harnessed once more, five days later, on 7 July, for the cultural political propaganda battle being fought by the Reich and the Party on behalf of German art. As part of the Party Day in Katschhof, that Wednesday at 6.00 in the evening, he repeated his Berlin triumph with the closing scene (*Festwiese*) of *Meistersinger*, bringing the city and region of Aachen's NSDAP *Kreistag* to an unforgettable climax. Might it not have occurred to Karajan that 'here on German *glacis*, before the thousands of foreigners, for the brothers of Eupen and Malmedy', he was conducting as a representative of

116

the Third Reich, in a German outpost, where 'the eyes of the people sweep critically and searchingly across from the nearby borders' to the imperial city of Aachen, the 'Führer's city', as a 'standard for Germany', a status to which it had been elevated on the occasion of the District Party Day two years previously?[95]

He began the new season late that summer with a new production of the *Meistersinger von Nürnberg*. For the first time Karajan was responsible for the direction. During the course of twenty-five orchestral rehearsals he tried to convey his ideas of what the music should sound like.

In 1940, according to Karajan's testimony to the De-Nazification Commission and later interviews, during a performance of *Meistersinger* in the Berlin Staatsoper at which Hitler was present, an event occurred which was always cited in later days when Karajan sought to exonerate his work in the Third Reich. Rudolf Böckelmann, in the role of Hans Sachs, messed up the part, apparently, as later accounts had it, because he was drunk. Karajan was conducting without a score, but he still managed to rescue the faltering performance. Hitler watched the production with displeasure. He assumed that the confusion had come about because Karajan was conducting without a score. Hitler told Tietjen of his annoyance, and made it known that he would not attend the Opera again if Karajan was conducting. If this story is untrue it is a good invention, because it was to be used at the de-Nazification proceedings as an indication that Karajan had fallen out of favour with Hitler. A sign that Karajan was not held in particularly high regard by Hitler, however temporarily, is provided by an entry in Goebbels' diary on 2 November 1940, where he wrote: 'He has a very unfavourable judgement of Karajan and his work as a conductor.'[96]

The war was well under way in the spring of 1940. In April Denmark was occupied and Norway forced to capitulate. 'Adolf Hitler is leading us to victory!' said the newspapers in red letters, announcing Göring's prefatory address on the Führer's fifty-first birthday. On 27 April, Karajan conducted Hans Pfitzner's romantic cantata *Von deutscher Seele* in Aachen. Then, on 1 May, at around five o'clock in the evening, the first bombs fell on Aachen. It was a spring of great victories and capitulations, according to which side one supported. The Netherlands capitulated on 15 May, Belgium on 28 May. France followed in June: on 14 May Paris was occupied, and on 21 May Hitler went to Compiègne for the German-French ceasefire, by which the 'profoundest disgrace of all times' was removed.[97] The legendary Battle of Britain began in the summer and lasted until autumn without the Luftwaffe achieving any of its goals.

At the end of 1940 Karajan was sent to France, conquered in the June blitzkrieg, to win sympathy and represent the German nation and its cultural superiority. 'German cultural policy in occupied Paris, as carried out primarily by the German Embassy and its affiliated German Institute was', as Manfred Flügge points out in a book about the author Friedrich Sieburg, who was in Paris at the same time working towards the incorporation of France into Adolf Hitler's future Europe, 'practically the centre-piece of the strategic policy of moderation and distraction.'[98] In occupied Paris, Karajan, as an artist of Greater Germany, carried out propaganda work that was to have a lasting effect, using culture as a means of political publicity and promoting Germany as a musical nation. Around Christmas time, between 16 and 19 December, Karajan performed Bach's *B Minor Mass* in the Trocadéro and the Palais de Chaillot. The first time, a performance organized in collaboration between the Propaganda Ministry and the Nazi association 'Strength through Joy', in front of around 3,500 soldiers, and the second time for the French audience as well. Among those present was the alcoholic and more or less philistine Reich Leader of the German Workers' Front and Reich Organization Leader of the NSDAP, Dr Robert Ley.

In March Karajan guested with the Berlin Staatsoper in Rome. Jubilantly fêted by the audience, here too he won the respect of an enthusiastic public as a cultural emissary of the Nazi State. In May he went several times to Paris to demonstrate the victorious cultural power of the Hitler regime. In the Opéra he performed Wagner's *Walküre* with the Berlin Staatsoper. As an introduction he had the Berlin Staatskapelle play the 'Horst Wessel Song'. In June the orchestra of La Scala Milan undertook a tour of Germany, building 'bridges between the peoples' in line with Goebbels' cultural propaganda. But now, for the first time, it was conducted by a German: Herbert von Karajan. The concert tour also brought him to Aachen with the star Italian orchestra, where it was given an enthusiastic reception. Karajan's appointment as State Kapellmeister meant constant commuting between Aachen and Berlin. His frequent absences from Aachen led to a gradual estrangement from his wife Elmy. But the Aachen theatre was also worried about its future with Karajan. After he returned from his guest performances in Paris the theatre began to look for someone to succeed him. They held the first auditions. On

13 September, after seventeen orchestra rehearsals, Karajan opened his last season in Aachen with *Rosenkavalier*.

In the programme preview he attempted to win further loyal allegiance from his audience in Aachen: 'It depends on every individual if we are to prove that our German people wants to preserve and further to promote its most noble cultural possessions.'[99] Karajan did not break this promise for a moment, right through to the bitter end. On 18 and 19 January 1942, he performed Beethoven's *Missa Solemnis* with the City Choir in the Berlin Philharmonie. Then there followed the last concerts in Aachen, and on 21 and 22 April Generalmusikdirektor von Karajan made his farewells to Aachen with Bach's *Matthew Passion* after eight years of fruitful work. Karajan's last season ended on 15 July 1942. In Aachen he had shouldered a very heavy workload: the Generalmusikdirektor, driven by the euphoria of success, had made up to 150 appearances a year. On 28 August the new manager, Otto Kirchner, who had held office since 1939, announced that Paul van Kempen, the conductor of the Dresden Philharmonic, a 'personal friend' of Karajan's, was to be engaged for two years as Karajan's successor.[100]

Karajan had outgrown Aachen. With the dynamism that was his trademark he was aspiring to the highest. Of course the idea of being the conductor of the Berlin Philharmonic was still a utopia at this point. As yet that was well beyond his range. But Karajan worked towards it, unerringly. It is normal for the younger generation to wonder when they can 'take over'. At least that is how it is in areas where the object of the profession is power, which is justified in this case by a desire to shape and to mould one's material. Of his departure from Aachen Karajan later said: 'It is mere weakness not to be able to leave something to which one is still attached, but whose importance for one's own life has vanished.'[101]

That also applied to his wife. Elmy quickly lost any importance for him. His travels, and his intensified visits to Berlin brought him in contact with different people. It was here that he met his second wife, Anna Marie Gütermann, familiarly known as Anita. The impulsive blonde of a wealthy family – she belonged to the silk-thread dynasty of the same name – was nine years younger and came from Cologne, where she was born on 2 October 1917. She too had a failed marriage behind her.

Anita had a fault that was unforgivable in the eyes of the regime: Jewish blood flowed in her veins. Not a great deal, admittedly, not even enough for her to be affected by the Nuremberg race laws, but too much to be beneficial to Karajan's career. Did Karajan think he could win the regime over to her? Or might it even have been one of his many career-conscious actions with an eye on what was to come later? Had he correctly calculated the political developments of the years to come? It was still an age of expansion, despite the slowly changing fortunes of the war. Reports of successes from the front, announced by the victory fanfares from Liszt's *Les Préludes*, were still the order of the day.

Berlin's musical life during the first years of the war was thoroughly marked by the artistic rivalry between Furtwängler, whom the Party both mistrusted and wooed, and the challenging young genius Karajan, who was loyal to the Party. Furtwängler, who considered the Philharmonic his own domain (although on 4 December 1935 he had resigned all his official posts and after a discussion with Goebbels would only appear as a guest at the head of the orchestra and at the Opera) was from the first suspicious of his young competitor, who was held in such esteem by the press. During these years he certainly did nothing to help Karajan, whom he saw as a rival. Rather he always found an opportunity when talking to Goebbels (who was in a sort of competition with Göring in that Göring was responsible for the state theatres, and Goebbels for, among other things, the Philharmonic) to sneer at his younger colleague. 'Furtwängler has been complaining about Karajan, who is being fêted too extravagantly in the press. I'll put a stop to that. Otherwise Furtwängler is being very well-behaved. And he is, after all, our greatest conductor,' noted Goebbels in his diary on 14 December 1940. A few days later, on 22 December, he went on, with reference to Furtwängler's somewhat uncontrolled attitude: 'Furtwängler furious about Karajan. Karajan is being praised to the skies in the press. Furtwängler's right. After all he has world stature. I'll put a stop to it.'[102]

This does not rule out the assumption that Karajan was to be used by the regime to be set against the sometimes politically awkward Furtwängler, to 'eliminate or at least to neutralize him on a cultural level'.[103] It was immediately assumed that Karajan was to function as a counterweight to Furtwängler after the publication of van der Nüll's famous critical article. In his review of Karajan's Berlin début with *Tristan*, van der Nüll wrote that some older conductors could learn a few things from him, which Furtwängler considered a personal affront and which led him to make complaints in high places. The attack on the ageing star, if

120

that is what it was, was not without effect. 'After the "Hindemith crisis", Furtwängler had returned to the Philharmonie, but not to the Staatsoper, and Tietjen was frantically looking for a great conductor. Hence the effort, if not exactly the "directive" to build Karajan up and turn him into Furtwängler's rival. At the time everyone was talking about it.'[104] During Furtwängler's de-Nazification trial at the Schlüterstrasse in Berlin, in December 1946, circumstances were discussed which indicated that Furtwängler's opponents in the Party had encouraged the critic van de Nüll to write his provocatively exalted hymn to 'das Wunder Karajan'.[105]

In December 1977 Karajan himself discredited this review, which termed him a 'miracle' and which was devalued by the suspicion of deliberate agitation against Furtwängler. 'I wasn't a miracle at all. That review caused me terrible difficulties, and in fact it only held me up. For it takes time before you understand that something endless has been put in motion . . . Only if you manage not to grow bitter in spite of everything, and say, about everything you do, not "I must" but "I may" – that is a criterion, and maybe even a miracle.'[106]

Although Furtwängler was not happy to see Karajan conducting the Philharmonic, particularly in the prestigious series of 'Philharmonic Concerts', he did repeatedly conduct them between 1938 and 1942, either in concerts or for gramophone recordings. In 1940 he played Dvořák's New World Symphony and Smetana's Moldau with them. His concert agent Rudolf Vedder repeatedly found him rewarding engagements despite facilities being increasingly restricted by the progress of the war. As Untersturmführer of the SS, Vedder had excellent connections with the SS Reich Leader, later Minister of the Interior and 'schoolmaster of crime' Heinrich Himmler, and 'might consequently have influenced the events surrounding the rivalry between Furtwängler and Karajan in Berlin'.[107]

After the war this rivalry was also the subject of questions related to Karajan's de-Nazification trial in Austria. The result of this was assembled and presented at US Headquarters by the American cultural officer Otto de Pasetti, obviously biased towards Karajan and inadequately informed about the true facts of his Party membership. This file says:

Karajan had developed into an excellent conductor during his time in Aachen. When a personal difference had occurred between Tietjen, the general manager of the Berlin Staatsoper, and Furtwängler, Tietjen appointed Karajan to the Berlin institution as a counterweight to Furtwängler. According to all the witnesses heard, it seems that this appointment is to be ascribed to Karajan's hard work. His membership of the Party was only a secondary consideration. It might, however, have played a part, since it intensified Tietjen's position with regard to Furtwängler. But it was mostly due to Karajan's musical abilities. In Berlin there now began a struggle between Karajan and Furtwängler, which finally ended with the latter's victory. Furtwängler, who is a master of intrigue and could not stand having any other conductor of high standing near him, used every means within his power in his battle with Karajan (whereby it must, however, be said that he did not act unfairly towards K). For a while it seemed as though Karajan was going to get the upper hand over Furtwängler. His concerts were very successful. According to the accounts of Berlin artists he grew from concert to concert.[108]

On 10 April 1941 the Berlin Staatsoper burned down after a bombing raid. Although Furtwängler protested, the concerts that Karajan conducted with the Staatskapelle were temporarily transferred to the Philharmonie. Furtwängler felt challenged and rivalled at the very site of his triumphs. It did not suit him at all, and he tried unsuccessfully to counteract it. Within a short time the Staatsoper was rebuilt. But in Karajan's place Furtwängler returned to Unter den Linden. This book is not devoted to the role of Furtwängler in the Third Reich, and his probably unintentional corruption and complicity with barbarism. But we might allow ourselves one observation: Furtwängler's advantage, if we might call it that, probably lay in the fact that unlike Karajan he was not a Party member. Until the last, clearly recognized by Goebbels as a man of world stature, he allowed himself to be placed at the service of the regime without first being compromised by an early and possibly unconsidered membership of the NSDAP, without being bound to the regime. He helped many Jewish musicians and steered the orchestra through the war, that much is true. But he also finally abandoned it, when the compromise that he thought he could make seemed to develop to his personal disadvantage during the last months of the war.

Furtwängler, who believed he was working for a different Germany as some kind of resistance, believed, as an 'apolitical artist, above politics', that by staying and working in Hitler's Germany he would be able to carry out 'active political work against National Socialism': 'It is the political function of art, especially

122

in our time, to be above politics,' he said in his own justification to the Berlin De-Nazification Commission. Although by his own account he had intimate knowledge of the Nazis' attitude towards the Jews as early as June 1933, he allowed himself to be harnessed into the cultural political service of the Reich until the last year of the war, either ignoring or failing, through political naïvety, to acknowledge that he was being misused by the Nazis for their own ends and hence would necessarily appear at least inconsistent in his rejection of National Socialism.

In 1934, for example, he was received and decorated by Mussolini while on a tour of Italy with the Berlin Philharmonic. In 1935 he conducted a winter relief concert in Berlin, at which he was photographed shaking hands with Hitler. In the middle of the war, in 1940, he sent the Berlin Philharmonic Orchestra off on a concert tour of occupied Holland, Belgium and France with a speech that most emphatically underlined the artist's cultural political mission:

> The great German masters of music have expressed in their music what we are trying to realize in the visible world. Thus we might say that a common responsibility to the great masters connects us with those who have the most difficult task and the decisive role in the construction of the New Germany: the men of our incomparable Wehrmacht.[109]

In 1940, the very lives and existences of the German people had been placed at the service of conquest and destruction. Concerts at home and in occupied regions always had the supplementary function of reinforcing fighting morale and morally arming the Wehrmacht soldiers beleaguered by their heroic struggle. Thus Uwe Sass was able to say of the Lille guest concert under Eugen Jochum on the same tour, in the *Feldzeitung der Armee an Schelde, Somme und Seine*, September 1940: 'They are playing on enemy territory, and they know it. But last night we saw with our own eyes how little heed they pay to it for the sake of the cause they are serving: bringing German soldiers relaxation and new stimulations.'[110]

The Philharmonic tour, on which the conducting was shared by Robert Heger and Eugen Jochum, took the orchestra to Antwerp, Brussels, Paris, Versailles and Fontainebleau, amongst other cities, and included Nazi stalwart soloists such as Elly Ney. The orchestra even gave up its leave in September, to travel into the war zone to the fighters in that great struggle for the complete renewal of Europe. The stimulus to this concert tour, and this is the interesting thing, comes from the desks of the orchestra . . . They wanted in this way to deliver their thanks to the front . . . In Langemarck they laid a wreath on the graves of the young Flanders soldiers, in a brief and moving ceremony. But the greatest experience for them was the concerts they performed for the German soldiers on enemy territory . . .[111]

Between 5 and 12 February Furtwängler himself accompanied the orchestra on a concert tour to Stockholm, Uppsala, Malmö and occupied Denmark, and afterwards reported back to Goebbels from this promotional tour for the Third Reich. On 28 February Goebbels confided in his diary:

Furtwängler comes to see me. He has toured Sweden and Denmark and is simply bursting with nationalist enthusiasm. This man has undergone a transformation that makes me extremely happy. I have fought for him for years, and now see success result. He thoroughly endorses my policy on radio and film, and most readily puts himself at my disposal for all my work. His opinion of Karajan has become much more mature; he does not involve himself in public disputes, but regards all these publicistic quarrels with a sovereign, mature confidence. During this discussion he makes an extraordinarily likeable impression. I am pleased to be able to get to know this side of him. The Philharmonic Orchestra is at its brilliant best. All its members have been exempted from military service because it has important domestic tasks to carry out, and because its existence is so valuable that it must not be broken up.[112]

In 1942, at the NSDAP ceremony for Hitler's birthday on 19 April, Furtwängler conducted a performance of Beethoven's Ninth in the Philharmonie preceded by the Air from Bach's Orchestral Suite, for a gathering of prominent party members and the highest representatives of the regime. Thus Hitler was fêted and affirmed by Furtwängler, the outstanding representative and harbinger of great German musical culture, in a consecrating act of public homage. This supposedly unpolitical man was needed more urgently that ever.[113]

Karajan suddenly saw himself as finished. The enigmatic, power-obsessed and scheming general manager Tietjen, who was also in charge of the Bayreuth Festival, may well have had a hand in this. The reasons for Karajan's neglect are still hidden from us. In a letter of 25 December 1966 the eighty-five-year-old Tietjen indicated where they might be found:

I fetched Karajan from small-town Aachen to the big state opera house with the wonderful Staatskapelle in 1936. He stayed there until 1942 and showed little gratitude for my having treated him, the unbridled genius, like a son. Until now I have remained silent about 'other things', and shall continue to do so, particularly now, when Karajan is on the point of bringing Wagner back to Richard Wagner; that's more important than 'all-too human' matters.[114]

Is it really? We still have the prejudices that emerged from that abyss of an all-too human humanity to thank for a catastrophe of global dimensions. Collectively enforced prejudices, as the Third Reich showed, can lead to the most terrible horrors. It would have been useful to find out something from Tietjen. Possibly Karajan, trusting to his compelling charm and his undeniable powers of persuasion, overreached himself in his dealings with Tietjen. This is indicated by an entry in Goebbels' diary for 5 January 1942: 'I discuss the state of the Prussian State Theatre with general manager Tietjen. The conductor Karajan has made excessive demands on Tietjen. He wants to use these demands to force through his struggle with Furtwängler. Tietjen seeks protection from me, which is granted without reservations.'[115]

So Karajan was suffering the fate of so many who served the regime with both vigour and calculation. He became a victim of the very National Socialist system to which he owed his career. He was at the mercy of rival groups and institutions. He was caught up in the machinery of their mutual machinations, of overlapping and competing areas of authority, of the controlled chaos of an organizational structure based on vanity, a lust for fame and a desire for power. Karajan was to take a lesson from this. What he learned from it he was able to use in an appropriate fashion after the war, when he set about building his own empire.

Along with the Staatskapelle concerts, Karajan was given other rewarding tasks outside of his public duties. In 1941 he recorded Johann Strauss's *Emperor Waltz* with the Philharmonic, and with the Staatsoper orchestra he played Beethoven's Seventh for the first time. Karajan now had to devote more of his work to concerts and recordings. It did not happen as Haeusserman describes it: 'Karajan could not think of concerts with the Berlin Philharmonic, because Wilhelm Furtwängler was the orchestra's head conductor.'[116] Well, no, we must say to that. In 1942 Karajan played Strauss's Overtures to the *Gipsy Baron* and *Die Fledermaus*, and at the end of the year he conducted Berlin's leading orchestra three times in a row: on 27 December in a benefit concert, on the 28th in a 'work concert' in Borsigwalde (Berlin) and finally on the 29th in a concert in the Philharmonie dedicated to Johann Strauss under the motto 'Winged Music'. These were by no means second-rate events because the respected Hans Knappertsbusch also conducted several such concerts between 1941 and 1943. In 1942 Karajan also found himself some work in Turin. With the EIAR orchestra he recorded three Mozart Symphonies (Nos. 35, 40 and 41), as well as overtures by Verdi and Rossini for Deutsche Grammophon.

For the Jewish population, the gypsies, Jehovah's Witnesses and other groups of people styled as 'vermin' in the German Reich and its occupied territories, the most terrible period of suffering in their history began in 1941 and 1942. On 1 September 1941 the police ruling on the labelling of Jews came into force. It obliged the Jews to wear the Jewish star in public. The stigma consisted of 'a saucer-sized six-pointed star outlined in black, made of yellow material with the black inscription "Jude". It is to be worn visibly sewn on to the left-hand chest of the item of clothing.'[117] On 4 November the Reich Minister of Finance ordered that Jews 'not engaged in economically important businesses'[118] be deported to the ghettos and concentration camps in the East, and that their property be seized by the Gestapo. The first gassing experiments were carried out in Auschwitz, and at the end of the year a permanent gas chamber was set up in Chelmo near Posnan. 'To the gas chamber', the turn of phrase that had come into thoughtless slang use, would later cross even Karajan's lips. On 20 January 1942 the head of the Security Police, SS Obergruppenführer Heydrich, revealed to Ministry officials, SS members and the police at the Wannsee Conference the guidelines for the 'Final Solution', in which the conditions for the 'practical implementation' of the eradication of the Jews were laid out. The draft 'concerning the organizational, factual and material requirements for the final solution of the European Jewish question'[119] was produced at the demand of the Reich Marshal, Hermann Göring, who, as Karajan's protector at the Staatsoper – his plaything, completely under his control – regularly and with all due pomp found relaxation there from his diabolical official duties.

In August 1942 the state secretary of the Reich Ministry of Justice and later president of the People's Court, Dr Roland Freisler, explained his proposal for further depriving the Jews of their rights in the following words: 'The ill-feeling, widespread throughout the Reich, about the fact that Jews living in Germany are still granted legal redress in criminal matters, and can still appeal to the decision of the courts against police rulings, is likely to weaken the German people's will to defence in the fight imposed upon them.'[120]

In Germany at that time, nothing was more conducive to a correct understanding of National Socialism than the fact of being one of those affected by its racial laws. Anyone brought into contact with those laws because of their Jewish origin or kinship would, at that point if not before, have had their eyes opened to the monstrosity and inhumanity of the regime, regardless of whether they fell within the definition of the law. This certainly applies to Karajan and his new bride Anita Gütermann, 'incriminated' as she was by her Jewish blood. It is difficult to imagine that neither of them – confronted with this shaming law in so far as they had to determine that they were not directly affected by it – gave a thought to its possible consequences.

On 22 October 1942 Karajan married for the second time. As a good Party member he settled for the civil ceremony, as he had done in 1938. This gave him the opportunity in 1964 to exploit the right to a church wedding, when he married his wife Eliette – whom he had married in a civil ceremony on 6 October 1958 – for a second time, this time in church.[121]

After the war Karajan told the de-Nazification commissions in Austria that he had been brought before a Party court in 1942 because of his marriage to quarter-Jewish Anita Gütermann, and that he had there declared that he was leaving the Party. This statement was to lead quite decisively to the lifting of his conducting ban in the post-war years. Because it was clearly impossible, in 1945 and 1946, to check Karajan's apparently plausible statements, the commission on the political investigation of Salzburg artists could not 'rule out the idea that in leaving the Party Karajan was trying to make up for having joined it'.[122] On the basis of these statements the commission reached the conclusion that Karajan 'had left the party in 1942 regardless of possible detrimental consequences'.[123] It also believed Karajan's story that he had joined the Party in Aachen in 1935 purely as a formality, clearly unaware that Karajan could not have done this because in 1933 the ban on Party membership had come into effect, as it remained until 1937, unless Karajan had already been a member of a Nazi association such as the SA or the SS . . .

So what should we make of Karajan's version? Is it true, or simply a defence strategy in the context of 'de-Nazification'? We still have no proof for Karajan's statements.

But perhaps this proof will turn up one day, and we will be presented with a truth quite different from Karajan's account of his resignation from the Party. It is not unthinkable, for example, that there might have been a Party trial in connection with his having married Gütermann, who was one-quarter Jewish.

What is certain is that marriage to a woman one-quarter Jewish brought with it certain problems. The Party's definition of what constituted an Aryan was restrictive; on the other hand the decree of the Reich Minister of the Interior to the Reich Governors, 28/VII/37, shows that Hitler did allow exceptions in certain cases. Karajan, as a protégé of Göring and Goebbels (Karajan had his conscription revoked as the result of a conversation with Goebbels, which tells us something about his privileged status)[124] might quite easily have been one of these exceptions. In that case the Party trial (for which no proof has emerged to this very day), if it ever took place, simply bore out the fact of this exception.[125]

One hint that a Party trial such as this – pardoning a National Socialist-Jewish misalliance – actually took place, might be seen in the fact that the Chancellery of the Führer of the NSDAP (Head Office for Petitions of Mercy) collected information on Karajan's Party membership from the NSDAP's Reich Treasurer on 19 November 1942.[126] It must have had good reason to do so. Might it be the case that Karajan, contrary to his claim that he had declared his resignation from the Party at the Party trial, had his marriage to the quarter-Jewish Gütermann sanctioned on an exceptional basis, as a loyal Party member, on the instructions of the Führer? And is it not rather likely that the career-conscious State Kapellmeister von Karajan avoided risking exclusion from the Party, which would have been damaging to his career – contrary to his statement to the de-Nazification commissions?

Would a politically dubious kapellmeister have been sent abroad as a propagandist of National Socialist cultural politics?

Another link in the chain of evidence might be a petition from Karajan to the Propaganda Ministry on 14 August 1944. We can barely suppose that an expelled member of the Party would declare his support for the Third Reich exactly three weeks after the attempt on Hitler's life, as Karajan did with his 'loyal regards to the Reich Minister' (Goebbels) and his 'Heil Hitler', quite uncontestably written down on paper.[127] Or did Karajan manage to swallow his pride, despite his relegation, and ingratiate himself with the Party leadership, following nothing but his own selfish instincts, in order to exhaust every single possibility of continuing his work as a conductor to the bitter end?

To complete the chain of evidence, and to lend support to our supposition that Karajan did not resign from the Party, we have Karajan's best-kept secret: the card from the NSDAP central records. This shows no indication that he resigned at any point, although every alteration in his membership status is precisely entered – the line set aside and marked for that purpose is empty. This much-vaunted resignation from the Party would be entered here if it had ever occurred, and under whatever circumstances. Thus a suspicion turns into a probability, backed up by documentary evidence, that Karajan's later statements about his membership and resignation were merely a devout wish, casting a veil over an embarrassing past.

No documents have so far emerged about the Party trial and Karajan's supposed resignation from the Party. The resignation of such a prominent Party member as Karajan would have been a fairly spectacular event, however, which would not only have appeared in the Reich records of the NSDAP, but would also, for example, have been communicated to the Reich Cultural Chamber. One thing is certain: no proof has as yet emerged to back up Karajan's statements. Indeed, despite all the obstacles it is comparatively easy to supply evidence to the contrary. Can it therefore come as any surprise that Karajan – despite his assurance that he resigned from the Party in 1942 – was still registered as a member with the NSDAP leadership in 1944? When Dr Goebbels' Reich Cultural Chamber learned that Frau von Karajan was 'one-quarter Jewish' under Nazi law they wrote to the Reich leadership of the NSDAP on 4 April and 12 May 1944 for information as to whether Karajan was a Party member.[128] On 25 May 1944 Oberbereichsleiter Schneider provided the Reich Cultural Chamber with detailed information and confirmed Karajan's membership:

'At present Party member Herbert von Karajan is registered in the Reich records as a member of local branch Aachen/Gau Cologne/Aachen, with the address: Eupenerstrasse.'[129]

Further evidence, which supports the earlier indications, that the marriage was tolerated by the highest authorities, is provided by the musicologist Paul Moor in his essay on the history of Karajan's career, in which both instances of Karajan's joining the Party are mentioned:

> His career's martyrdom to the Nuremberg Racial Laws, however, did not tax him for long: records at the Berlin Document Center show that the following summer – June 23, 1943, to be precise – none other than Propaganda Minister Joseph Goebbels himself sent out a personal order for Party zealots to lay off Frau von Karajan's family tree. From then on, Karajan had no more trouble.[130]

According to Moor's research, Goebbels clearly concealed the Karajan misalliance, and brusquely called off the Party comrades who were, with unusual eagerness, sniffing at Anita Gütermann's family tree for alien, non-Aryan origins. He, Karajan, was still more important to Goebbels than his proscription for a marriage that was less than pure in National Socialist terms.

Anyone who failed to toe the line in the Reich was abruptly called to order during the war by being conscripted. The same happened to Karajan, if we are to believe him, after his wedding to Anita. The call-up was issued by the Prussian State Ministry. What happened next is too fine a story to be withheld here, even if it appears in Haeusserman's book and Karajan himself has told me divergent and imprecise versions of it:

> I immediately spoke to a famous general in the Luftwaffe; I had a burning desire to fly. He told me: 'I can't train you to be a fighter pilot because you're too old. But you could be a courier pilot. Once you've made your decision, I'll try and get you for myself.' After things turned out so badly, I sent a telegram to the general in the Luftwaffe. The next day I went to Tietjen. I had his secretary tell him: 'I'm resigning and joining the army . . .' And I was out. Then I went to my dentist and asked him to check my teeth because I was going away in two days. The dentist told his daughter, who was Goebbels' personal secretary, she told her boss and he immediately put a stop to the whole thing . . . So I was free once more, but I didn't

conduct at the Opera again. After 1942 I only had six concerts a year with the Staatskapelle.[131]

According to the former manager of the Berlin Philharmonic, Wolfgang Stresemann, Karajan often spoke with bitterness of the enforced interruption of his career.[132] He used the time to study new works. With his scores in the big pocket of his jacket he went on lonely walks in the Grunewald, through wind and rain. Until the serious air attacks of 1944, which destroyed the Philharmonie and other buildings, Karajan lived with Anita in the bachelor flat in the home of the parents of their Dutch acquaintance Carl Gustav Rommenhöller, later a businessman. When the house was bombed they moved to the Hotel Esplanade. Soon even the least percipient grew aware that the war was lost. But some of them made particularly heavy weather of things during the last few months before the terrible end; Furtwängler, for example, as Reich Minister Albert Speer remarks in his *Memoirs*: 'Following the last philharmonic concert that Wilhelm Furtwängler gave in the middle of December 1944 in Berlin, he invited me into the conductor's room. With disarming unworldliness he asked me straight out whether we had any chance of winning the war.'[133]

For a long time Karajan too, it would seem, expected a reversal of his country's fate, and military victory for the Germans. In 1943, at least, he 'warmly applauded' a performance of Bruckner's Fifth Symphony in the Philharmonie.[134] The Staff Music Corps of the Waffen-SS was playing, conducted by SS-Hauptsturmführer Franz Schmidt. All reports agreed about his success, and the special compliment paid by Staatskapellmeister Karajan was certainly more than mere politeness. During the war Karajan was, of course, more than an attentive listener at events unambiguously devoted to the glorification of the regime. Carl Gustav Rommerhöller, who spent a great deal of time with Karajan during those years in Berlin, and who had known Anita as Fräulein Gütermann, recalls:

He was very keen – although he never made himself conspicuous – on going to other people's concerts. At every Furtwängler concert I went to, Karajan was somewhere about. But he was always careful not to be seen, if possible. He wanted to know what the others were doing. And you had the feeling that he was very intensely preoccupied by what the others were up to.[135]

131

Although in Berlin's musical life he was restricted to the concerts with the Staatskapelle, Karajan remained a bone of contention for Furtwängler. Furtwängler could not leave the younger, ambitious antagonist in peace. This led Goebbels to step in as an intermediary. On 29 May 1943 he noted in his diary:

I had a detailed discussion with Furtwängler. He has been ill, and still looks rather unwell. Nevertheless, he can't stop sniping away at the young conductor Karajan. I shall try to effect some reconciliation between the two. I should like at all costs to keep Karajan alongside Furtwängler or just behind Furtwängler in Berlin. In any case Karajan can certainly not be compared with Furtwängler as a personality. Furtwängler told me he wants to remarry. He has a lot of family worries. I shall help him to overcome them.[136]

As well as his Berlin concerts with the Staatskapelle, Karajan was busy in Amsterdam and elsewhere abroad. In Amsterdam, with the Concertgebouw Orchestra, he recorded *Don Juan* and *Salome's Dance* by Richard Strauss, Brahms' First Symphony, Beethoven's Third *Leonore* Overture and the Overture to *Freischütz* by Weber. With these five works Karajan concluded an impressive series of musical documents, which laid the foundations, in the experience thus gained, for his unique postwar productivity in the field of gramophone recording.

In 1944 his engagements grew rarer. In Paris in the spring he was given two more guest performances alongside the concerts he was presenting with the Staatskapelle. On 19 April, in the Théâtre des Champs-Élysées, he conducted the Orchestre de Radio-Paris. The programme consisted of Handel's Concerto Grosso No. 12, *La Mer* by Debussy and Beethoven's Fifth. Fate was knocking on Germany's door. Karajan once more delivered his impressive message of the German cultural will in the midst of the war on 4 May, with a programme of Ravel's *Bolero*, Schumann's Fourth Symphony, Bach's Second Brandenburg Concerto and *Don Juan* by Richard Strauss. Meanwhile the defeat of Germany was looming on all fronts.

In 1944, held up and interrupted by air-raid warnings, and 'with the then unique extravagance of thirty-two recording hours for orchestra and technicians', Karajan recorded Bruckner's Eighth Symphony in the Großer Sendesaal in Berlin. The broadcast was intended to go out on 19 November, in the series 'Immortal Music by German Masters'. Months before Germany's defeat Karajan intended to make use of this popular series, which reached a wide audience, to build up a kind of rivalry with Furtwängler. To this end he wanted to use the Reichs-Brucknerorchester, founded in 1943 and under the command of the Reichsrundfunk, both organizationally and financially. For this reason, on 14 August 1944, he sent a handwritten petition from Bad Kissingen, where he was recovering in the sanitorium of Dr von Dapper, to Goebbels' Reich Ministry for Popular Enlightenment and Propaganda. This is what he wrote:

Dear Herr Staatssekretär! Further to my suggestion with regard to Feldpost number 00080: I should like to request that the Reichsminister authorize the Reichs-Brucknerorchester to make recordings with me for the 'Immortal Music' series. I have conducted the orchestra recently and can absolutely vouch for its quality. My reasons: the increased possibility of the use of the orchestra and the lessening likelihood of recordings being threatened or jeopardized by air raids. I also believe it is in your interest to allow me to be involved in the recordings more than once during the run of the broadcast, which will soon have completed a year's run. The orchestra still has dates free. If your decision is positive I shall get in touch immediately. With my very best regards to the Reichsminister and best wishes to yourself – Heil Hitler – Herbert von Karajan.[137]

But Karajan's hopes were not to come to fruition, although in a memo to the head of radio, Hans Fritzsche, the Staatssekretär wrote: 'Karajan should conduct the Bruckner-Orchester as often as possible and make a number of recordings for radio!' In the event, the relentlessly changing fortunes of war finally shattered his high-flown plans.

On 8 November 1943 Hitler made his last public appearance, and proceeded, in his bunker, to prepare for the destruction of the country and the collapse of the Reich. With the declaration of war on America in December 1941 the politician had stepped down to make way for the mass murderer. The end was now merely a matter of time. Karajan, who had never at any point in his life seen military service, had instead made his most original contribution to the moral rearmament of the people and the army by readily taking over guest performances and events that unmistakeably served the regime. In this he held his own. In January 1944 he

133

travelled to Romania, where on Sunday, 23 January, he conducted a symphony concert by the Bucharest Philharmonic in the Athenaeum in Bucharest, which was broadcast by Radio Romania. The programme consisted of a Concerto Gross by Locatelli, Robert Schumann's Fourth Symphony and Respighi's *Pines of Rome*.

On 30 January 1944 the Philharmonie was burned to the ground, having already been severely damaged on 23 November 1943. The very highest authorities desired that the 'Philharmonic Concerts' would from now on be held in the Staatsoper. Consequently Furtwängler, whose 'German' style of playing predestined the Philharmonic, along with himself, to become the showpiece of Nazi cultural thought, got in Karajan's way. In a letter of 29 June 1944 to manager Gerhard von Westermann, Furtwängler took a stand on the Reich leadership's wish for ten philharmonic concerts in the Staatsoper that wartime winter:

> I believe that if we reduce them to eight, the minister will declare his agreement, particularly if Tietjen causes difficulties ... I really don't know what criteria should be used in the choice of further guest conductors. I am currently considering – to complete my own work – giving only one concert in the autumn, the opening concert, and the others only after Christmas. The guests could then come in between.[138]

The obvious idea of engaging the rather under-employed Karajan in a generous gesture did not occur to Furtwängler, jealously concerned as he was with preserving his halo. Because he could not find, or did not want to find, any conductors, he reduced the series from the originally intended ten concerts to half that number, and of the remaining philharmonic concerts he left only two to the guest conductors Clemens Krauss and Karl Elmendorff.

Furtwängler's health was already poor at this time, and nothing would have been more obvious than to set up a 'worthy' successor to him. He openly admitted to the theatre manager: 'I don't like talking about it, and would like to use all the means at my disposal to avoid being considered ill. But between ourselves I cannot hide the fact that I am very worried.'[139]

Furtwängler made things difficult for Karajan at every level, and did not balk at pointedly petty actions.

Karajan himself said on the matter:

> I am a very tolerant person. I should say that it's one of my chief rules in life: the tolerance, the intellectual freedom to do

134

what I like. And I don't see why I should criticize anyone. He does it that way, I do it this way. There is room for both. But persecuting someone because he does things differently? Let us remember what Furtwängler did: When I performed a piece he would come along two weeks later as if he wanted to say: let's establish how it's really done. Just as Goethe persecuted Newton with his theory of colour. I never understood that. That kind of jealousy of other people.

During that last wartime winter season Furtwängler was, contrary to his intentions, very active, as if he was concerned with using every last opportunity to conduct. He significantly began his farewell season to the Third Reich on the afternoon of 22 October in the Staatsoper, with a concert for the armaments industry, which was grateful for every kind of stimulation and moral support designed to bring the fully operative production of armaments (which, along with war costs, was swallowing up sixty-eight per cent of the national income) to its highest point. In January 1945 Furtwängler, warned of persecution and following a piece of advice from Albert Speer, leaving his orchestra alone in the miserable time of defeat, fled via Austria to the security of Switzerland.[140] On 31 January he sent a telegram from Vienna: 'Fractured skull from fall on back on head. Doctor orders several days' rest. Berlin concerts unfortunately impossible. Suggest instead postpone concert beginning April. Furtwängler.'[141] To the bitter end, then, the industrious and reliable Robert Heger held the position. On 16 April he conducted the last concert by the Berlin Philharmonic, abandoned by their great master, during the Third Reich. The programme appropriately concluded with Richard Strauss's tone poem *Death and Transfiguration*. Karajan likewise held out, if not quite to the end, at least until shortly before the general defeat of the German fighting forces. On 18 February he gave another concert with the Berlin Staatskapelle. As the Staatsoper had burned down for a second time on 3 February, the concert was held in the Beethoven-Saal.[142]

We do not know if Karajan gave this concert as a memorial to the thousands who had died in the inferno produced a few days before by the senseless destruction of Dresden by British and American bomber units. Neither do we know anything about whether and how he reacted to the misery and general state of urgency of those days of uninterrupted bombing and air attacks, whether he lent a helping hand, whether he helped put out fires in the neighbourhood when the allies were dropping their

phosphorous canisters and his co-inhabitants were falling, scream-
ing and wounded, their every possession destroyed, their bare lives
all they could salvage. We know absolutely nothing of whether and
how the horror of war affected and moved him emotionally.

Six weeks before the end of the war he managed to trick his
way into leaving Berlin for Milan, in the company of his wife. He
had persuaded the authorities to grant him a life-saving visa for
recordings at the German-controlled radio in Milan. It was not
to happen. At the home of the Milan architect Aldo Pozzi, an
enthusiastic music-lover who was often to be seen in the box of
the Milan Gentlemen's Club at La Scala, Party Member Herbert
von Karajan learned of the collapse of the thousand-year Reich.

It is an undeniable historical fact that Karajan was among those
artists who found success in the Nazi State, and whose development was unavoidably shaped by the political circumstances of
the time. It is not easy to overestimate the meaning of National
Socialism for his life. Inexplicable, but just as indisputable, is the
fact that as a member of the National Socialist Party he placed his
talents at their service. He was a member of the NSDAP for many
years, and not merely a pressed fellow-traveller. By joining the
Party twice in April and May 1933 he began the lie of a career
which, as far as the period of the Third Reich is concerned, lacked
a human goal and hence a meaning. As a supporter of Hitler he
was prepared, by ignoring it, to tolerate Hitler's inhumanity for
the price of his career. With his declaration of loyalty to National
Socialism he began his metamorphosis into a 'rhinoceros', as portrayed in Ionesco's play. That applies to him personally just as it
does to the majority of the German people. In the process he lost
the goal – if indeed it had ever been his goal – that must have lain
in a strengthening of his ego against the violence and the corruption of conscience that emanated from the Party collective. His
membership and his decision to stay in the Party were the
decisions of a free man, in favour of ideology, injustice and intolerance. Karajan was the object and the vehicle of a musical politics
that needed victims just as much as perpetrators.

As an obedient servant he played his part in the implementation
of that politics, whether because he believed he would win an
advantage from it, in the form of a position and prestige, or
because he endorsed it. By his actions, he provided the proof that
he was not opposed to it. 'Reality,' wrote Fred K. Prieberg, 'is
unsparing, and anyone who regrets this should bear in mind that
personalities now wishing to be spared, who have had themselves
spared or are spared out of sympathy, had already, on the basis

of their own resolve, having made their own decisions, however subjectively, played a part in that reality and exploited it for their own ends.'[143]

The conditions that made Karajan's rise possible have a very particular background. This cannot be grasped from his biographical details alone. Possibly his relationship with National Socialism lay beyond the level of superficial affinities and inclinations, or of political opportunism, in a meeting of true minds. It is possible that he was attracted by the subliminally feminine trait that appurtained to the representatives of the Party leadership and gave the entire movement a curiously obscene character, and also possible that the promise of economic stability and the total reorganization, the rebirth of German society to a certain extent, were attractive enough. Perhaps it was also Hitler's concept of world domination that impressed the young Karajan. Another possibility is that he, the Salzburg Catholic, had been sufficiently imbued with the anti-Semitic element in Austria and Bavarian Catholicism to find an identification in National Socialism. Perhaps, too, it was the particular stamp of the party, its historicity, its hardness, in fact, that fascinated him. For at the root of his being Karajan was effeminate – which, however, tells us nothing about the 'true' Karajan.

We do not know what moved him, perhaps even Karajan himself didn't know. We do know that he assumed a partisan stand, in the true sense of the word. But anyone who assumes such a one-sidedly partisan stand, who becomes a partisan for inhumanity, has some questions to answer.

Why did Karajan take such a prominent position in a regime that announced, as part of its very programme, suffering that can only be grasped in the abstract? Why did he join forces, of his own free will, with a regime that most emphatically violated every idea of freedom in every sense from its very beginning? Why did he become the fellow-traveller of a regime based on organized contempt for humanity? Why were the terror, the manifestation of oppression, the thuggery, the brutality, the inhumanity, not sufficient evidence for him? Why did he repress the time and its terrors, why did he allow himself to be harnessed as he did by a regime that expatriated and exiled Thomas Mann, Einstein, Bruno Walter, Max Reinhardt and with them the intellectual and cultural élite of Germany? Why did Karajan fail to realize the possibility of an individual personal opposition to a dictatorship that was finally preparing a fate for the Jews and the ostracized people of

137

the Reich which can, horrifically enough, be reduced to the short-hand of 'Jewish Star-Train-Gas'?

Why, for example, did he not employ cunning to withdraw from compromising appearances? Others managed it, and nothing happened to them. Anyone who wanted to could do this – admittedly at the price of losing the protection of the state. However, spinelessness was particularly widespread in the musical life of the Third Reich. Summing up the issue, Fred K. Prieberg says:

> Among the music-makers there were some particularly happy dispositions who allowed themselves to be troubled by the regime as little as possible, and tried to get from it the best they could so as to come safely through, even if that safety had economic and existential rather than moral value, which would in any case have been annulled by the compulsion or inclination to wave the baton. In the end, morality could be fatal.[144]

This was revealed in the case of pianist Karlrobert Kreiten, executed on 7 September 1943 because he had predicted to a denunciatory acquaintance of his mother's 'that the war was already practically lost and would lead to the complete collapse of Germany and its culture'.[145] But Karajan did not have to distance himself from the regime with such deadly prognoses. As well as the much-cited internal emigration there was also an emigration abroad, and there were enough models available to give Karajan some idea of what the correct course would have been from a human point of view. But that would have been too much to ask.

But the problems of his age, the unjust nature of the National Socialist dictatorship, were easy to dismiss or fend off if Karajan imagined he was concerned with higher things. By persuading himself that he was strictly apolitical, he became an agent of politics. He certainly never understood that. Escaping to the island – non-existent in the Third Reich, but still notional – of apolitical music, he imagined himself safe there. But the amalgamation of music and politics in the Third Reich was a part of the very system. Its musical policy was nothing less than human barbarism, implemented according to the criteria of the National Socialist aesthetic. The expulsion of the Jewish musicians from the German musical industry, the policy of creative elimination, was, fundamentally and in its very monstrosity, the unique and characteristic aspect of National Socialism.

The fact that the leaders of the Nazi state always saw even the most innocuous music as political action, and abused 'correct' music as a promotional medium, was confirmed by the establishment of the Reichmusikkammer within the Reich Cultural Chamber. As it grew stronger and brought the Reich's music industry almost completely under its control, music was given the role, beyond its artistic character, of expressing and promoting an ethos.[146]

Seeking his fortune in a Germany that was stultifying itself into the monotony of an enforced culture, Karajan too became a victim of the system. 'For the musical policy created numerous states of emergency by annulling lifelong experience, moral and intellectual standards, and awakening instincts of fear and flight, impulses to power and persecution.'[147]

However much Karajan, and not only Karajan, saw himself as an 'apolitical' artist, it remains a mere excuse in the context of the historical reality of the Third Reich, its artistic policy and the unforced labour of the artists who lived in it. He made himself work towards the most outstanding achievements, distinguished himself and seized every opportunity to reinforce his reputation. When he was almost seventy years old he admitted: 'I made a career for myself much too quickly, and suffered for years from being set up as a sensation.'[148] Well, he put up with it at the time. There is actually little point in plangently continuing the deception later on. No, Karajan's work made him a cultural political factor and, as such, responsible, when, for example, he performed works in conformity with the regime at Party events or, as he did at one of his guest concerts in occupied Paris, when he conducted the 'Horst Wessel Song'. Whatever and wherever he conducted in the Third Reich, it was inseparable from the task bestowed on him according to the terms of National Socialist cultural propaganda. 'World status – demanded by all dictators when state criminality calls for an artistic figleaf – was easily had, for foreign countries thought it certain that the Nazi state would preserve and extend the tradition of musical classics.' The practice of music 'was to allow that "human engineering" indispensable for the transformation and adaptation of society, particularly the conditioning of the feelings of millions of individuals into a unity of feeling, thinking, experiencing.'[149]

The musical policy of the Nazis, with its incredible deployment of people and material, used all the means at its disposal to consecrate its goal. The fact that the enormous investments in creative energy and money finally proved senseless is the consequence of the abuse of using music as simply a means to the end of deceiving the people and the world. One of these means was the young Karajan, striving ever upwards, marked by genius. Anyone who allowed himself to be harnessed may be called 'politically naïve' or even 'entirely apolitical', to use the formulae of exoneration, current at the time, from the responsibility incurred in the process. But his work and his actions were wrapped up in the ideology of the Third Reich and its cultural policy, and were consequently eminently political. Unpalatable though it may be, what Prieberg wrote in his book on music in the Nazi state – which should be read by as many people as possible – remains a fact: 'Furtwängler and the Berlin Philharmonic Orchestra in Copenhagen had a greater effect than all the open-air concerts put on by the military; Karajan and the Berlin Staatsorchester in Paris almost offset the humiliating "Great Last Post" of the *boches* in Versailles.'[150]

Without the co-operation, the indifference and the cynicism of broad sections of the population, who remained at best insensitive to the crying injustice around them, things could not have come so far. This is now one of the notorious facts of history. But Germany's postulated collective guilt for the Third Reich is not the issue here. Neither is the issue the apportioning of individual guilt. I cannot and will not cast that stone. This was the age when men such as Karajan were able to push their way to the top, when people with a certain desire for power were able to get it. Given the spirit of the age, Karajan made it, much as Hitler made it.

From a human point of view we can reproach Karajan, or his ego, with the fact that he threw himself into National Socialist ideology. There would even be some justification for his being fascinated by it if he had absorbed and packaged it to turn it into something truly significant. For in this sense the person has nothing to do with the work. Karajan was the man who was able to take this fascination and transform it into his music and his stagings, which in his case amounted to the same thing, becoming the mouthpiece of the age in the process. He was by no means alone in this. For example, Martin Heidegger, apostrophized by many as the greatest of German philosophers, made his career breakthrough in this regime in a very disappointing way from a human point of view, to the cost of his teacher Edmund Husserl who had, as a Jew, to leave the regime. Heidegger too is only one prominent case among many.[151] The time was ripe for people of that particular psychological constitution. They were able to assert themselves in that context, and find their feet. It was a time for geniuses.

The problem here is one of integrity. The question arises: how far can one go without betraying what one sought to do and to achieve? Or more precisely: How far could Karajan go under Hitler without being corrupted in his claim for *humanitas*, which he wanted to realize in his artistic work (let us grant him that)? The truly shocking aspect of his biography is not that he did it and that he allowed himself to be abused – namely in joining the NSDAP and being useful to the regime. But that he refused to face up to it. And that he learned nothing from history. That is the horrific tragedy which doubtless affected the rest of his life. C.G. Jung was great enough to admit 'afterwards' that he had slipped, a statement which shows that he had at least learned from history – and Karajan did not.

Whenever the conversation turned to his role in the Third Reich Karajan did not take the opportunity to clarify the matter and confess, but rather to indulge in some manipulative historical cosmetics. But what is this behaviour if not the admission of moral failure? Shame and the fear of being unmasked led him even in old age to take refuge in a tactic whereby he tried to dupe the historians by means of calculated silence, studious reinterpretation and false information. He consistently and completely overcame the past by means of denials and excuses, and held at arm's length the issue of his inner exoneration from possible responsibility and guilt. The chance of becoming himself in the process of maturity fell victim to the permanent censorship of his consciousness. For Karajan was alone in seeking to claim that he was everything he might have been. Karajan's disastrous urge to repress matters certainly also grew out of the fear of someone who had been there, who had made his career in the Third Reich, who had allowed himself to be promoted as a Party member and who had entered into compromises, and who, with his eminent talent and his fanatical hard work, held out his hand to the regime and was finally almost betrayed by it. Behind all this there lies a twofold shame: the fear of being unmasked both as a comrade-in-arms and as an outcast. 'No, I really don't feel guilty about that', and, 'It really advanced my career', were Karajan's answers to my questions about his role and responsibility in the Third Reich. And: 'I'd do it exactly the same way again.'

Once when we were discussing these matters and I happened to mention some emphatic statements by the pianist Arthur Rubinstein, the following dialogue ensued:

'But there is one person who still bears a grudge.'

'I don't know.'

'Rubinstein.'

'How can that bother me?'

'Well, Rubinstein said in an interview in August 1979, when you were both staying at the Palace Hotel in Lucerne: "It's true that I would never play with Karajan, would never shake his hand. He was a partisan under the Nazis." '

'Terrible! And I expect I'm supposed to jump off the top of Mont Blanc from despair. I can't tell you how little that affects me.'

This complete lack of emotion, this unbounded lack of understanding of the effect of his action on someone like Rubinstein who lost members of his family – his sisters, his aunts – in the Third Reich, is what makes it so terribly difficult to find access to Karajan the man.

The question of what led Karajan to take the path of concealment and dishonesty when he had so little need to do so is an unfathomable one. Why he made no effort to put his actions in the Third Reich into the context of the information available to him in his old age, in order finally to make peace with reality, why he made no effort to understand his past, that 'unconquered' past – we are still in the dark about these matters. Only one thing is clear: he refused to face up to them. Not facing up to reality as it is, even to one's own reality, indicates quite considerable personality disorders. Karajan had no need to say: I was more or less forced into joining the NSDAP. He would have had absolutely no need to play this undignified game of hide-and-seek, this concealment and twisting of his past, this botching and retouching of his history.

Karajan could simply say: Yes, all right, I slipped in those days. Hitler was the idol, and he became the idol of my formative years as a young adult. The apotheosis of solidity, of power, of strength, that fascinated me at the time. The choreography of the Party Days with their magnificent theatrical effects got under my skin. I succumbed to the suggestive effect of the marching processions, the hugely heightened parades, the fantastic effects of the domes of light, the monumental solemnity of the torchlight processions and funeral marches, the rustling of the forests of flags, the richly symbolic consecration of the flags. My immature, unstable and sentimental temperament at the time was receptive to it, like millions of others in those days.

He could have said: Yes, Hitler's hypocritical depictions of himself were inexplicable points of identification for me. In his profane liturgies I found what seemed to me to be a valid and credible substitute for the rite of the Catholic Church, which had become nothing but an empty formula to me. I was drunk on this beauty that seemed to emerge from power and strength, drunk on its brilliance and undeniable monumentality. I quite simply succumbed to the irresistible seductiveness of the National Socialists. With Hitler I saw myself surrendering to the mystery of power. His rapid journeys from one end of Germany to the other in high-powered Mercedes impressed me, I saw his overland flights from one Party gathering to the next as the epitome of omnipresence. I simply couldn't tear myself away. It was an ecstatic experience for me, a frenzy of escape from the self, from which I was simply unable to find my way back into human reality. I was the victim of abnormal experiences, I surrendered to them helplessly, was beside myself, out of control. I simply didn't have the capacity of thought that would have opened my eyes to the inhumanity of the regime. I fell victim to the weaknesses that afflicted me then.

Karajan could have answered: The early Karajan between the ages of twenty-three and thirty-seven is alien to me now. He was an incomplete person, in search of identity. He was misled by propaganda. He was politically inept and robbed of his moral standards by his unparalleled success. I have nothing in common with him, and will therefore not cover for him with false alibis. But I accept responsibility for the Karajan that I have lost. I shall stand in for him. I now thoroughly regret the things that happened in those days. I am profoundly sorry.

But that was not Karajan's answer. He refused the manly act of taking responsibility for himself. He continued to live under the illusion that an artist does not need to ask about the circumstances, to ask 'what' and 'how' and 'for whom'. He believed he was being a complete artist by pursuing his talent with a natural instinct. This illusion has long been asserted with particular stubbornness in the field of art. And wide circles of people still believe that all that counts is ability, not 'awareness'. With pitiable vehemence Karajan refused us the necessary and the required inner sympathy for his own behaviour in the Third Reich. He was not up to the tasks of understanding and integrating, the tasks of maturity. He refused them just as he refused to come to terms

143

with the denied contents of his past. He renounced the possibility of forming a mature relationship with himself.

But for me the profound human disappointment lies in the fact that Karajan was unable to muster the strength required to face up to his biography. His basic lack of inner greatness prevented it. Where he should have mourned, he practised deception. This has nothing to do with wisdom, goodness and maturity. In this incapacity, this inability to mourn, his true greatness was lost. He confronted history with fixed views, obtuse and curiously unbending. He was unmoved by the struggle in which he urgently needed to become involved – the struggle with his own conscience.

Hitler thought that conscience was a Jewish invention. Through unimaginably terrible actions he brought unspeakable suffering and left behind him a world destroyed. What he had destroyed was people, and with them the substance of a world.

On 17 June 1980, the Day of German Unity – which would not exist if the National Socialists had not come to power – after a concert in the Stadthalle, Hanover, in the course of a late dinner in his hotel suite at which he was attired in the virgin white of a housecoat, Karajan summed up his work in the Third Reich as follows: 'It did me no harm.' This cannot be called appropriate. It reveals an abysmal insularity and a frightening lack of understanding of events that did not personally touch him. How might such action and thinking be described? Amoral?

Did Karajan live by the maxim: *Nihil verum – omnia licent*, Nothing is true – everything is allowed?

3

The Empire

May 1945: Hitler is dead. The Third Reich is in ruins. Europe's age of glory is past. The German dream of world domination is over. The heady days spent as the chosen race are at an end. Germany has lost its status as a civilized nation. Unconditional capitulation has thoroughly overturned the self-image of a nation guilty of following the Führer, with unbounded arrogance, into the most terrible crimes against humanity. The Führer's failure means the failure of all his followers. They are guilty of crimes both of commission and omission. A rude awakening has followed the dream 'of belonging to a master race unfettered by the restrictions of conscience if conscience stood in the way of its "ideals" '.[1]

The fall from the heights of the delusory National Socialist world to the hard ground of post-war reality affected Herbert von Karajan as well. At the age of thirty-seven he faced the void. He quickly resisted his shame at having become – as a Party member – a disciple and servant of National Socialist megalomania by rigorously leaving his own past behind. With a seeming lack of effort, Karajan discarded the twelve years of National Socialist ideology as if they were a dirty and no longer fashionable shirt. Mourning, understanding, heartfelt and inner regret for everything that had happened during the Third Reich – there is no sign of any of this. He still saw no reason for it even thirty-five years later, so how could it have been expected of him just after the war? What he did presumably regret was the loss of his workplace, his position, his brilliant career prospects. 'Feelings only suffice to cover one's own person, and barely extend to any kind of sympathy. If an object of pity does arise, it is generally none other than oneself,'[2] wrote A. and M. Mitscherlich in their book on the incapacity to mourn and the German way of loving, a book which we might most sincerely wish Karajan to have read, because in his old age it might probably have been of some use to him, since 'without any overcoming of guilt, however long delayed,' the work of mourning could not take place.[3] But his subsequent statements lead us to conclude that Karajan failed to come to terms with the events of the past in order to continue his life as a human being and not as one of Ionesco's rhinoceroses. The past was not dealt with, but instead resisted. That is understandable from his point of view. It is based in the desire to continue a promising career uninterrupted. But without the process of denial this would be impossible, at a time when de-Nazification tribunals were putting obstacles in his path. Given this fact, insight and understanding would seem to be a better solution in the longer term. 'The confrontation with the insight that the violent efforts of the war and the monstrous crimes generated by an insanely inflated self-image had served a grotesquely exaggerated narcissim, would necessarily have led to a complete deflation of self-esteem and an outburst of melancholy if this threat had not been nipped in the bud by the process of denial.'[4]

Karajan immediately hurled himself into inner distractions so as to avoid allowing feelings of any kind of guilt or responsibility to rise to the surface. He forced his life into a rigid timetable of study and work. He read whatever came to hand, including a book about oriental mysticism, in which he was always to lose himself in later life whenever he wished to avoid facing up to things. He seriously and systematically set about learning Italian. As a conductor and director of operas in Italian it would later be inestimably useful to him.

> I was afraid that in a state such as that, if you have nothing to do, you can quickly become demoralized. So I drew up a timetable for myself as if I was at school, and kept to it rigorously until ten o'clock in the evening. If I deviated from my schedule at all I forbade myself even our meagre rations and didn't give myself anything to eat.[5]

If this is not to be taken literally and things are being glorified in retrospect, it still gives us an idea of how Karajan, through tough and stubborn hard work, progressed from an attitude of grudging defiance to the repossession of his career, once it could no longer be withheld from him. He concentrated entirely on the future,

146

which would help him to forget the terrors of the past and the discomforts of the present, which, like demons, harried his sense of self-esteem. 'This concentration also gave me the strength to emerge almost unscathed from all that business.'[6]

So Karajan did not see the past as a part of his own history, and therefore felt no need to face up to it. He turned to face nothing but the future. With impetuous brilliance and an almost manic determination he set about rebuilding everything that had been destroyed on its old foundations. In this he was no different from the army of those betrayed and abandoned by the Führer, who, after the material and moral catastrophe of German history, avoided recognizing the consequences of events in the Third Reich, escaping into the obsessive effort of reconstruction and the affluence of the 'economic miracle', created and increased so quickly after the war.

Karajan left behind the Reich of the great failed theatre-directors, Hitler, Goebbels and Speer, to reconquer it later on as a director in his own right. Driven by a strength of will that enabled him to realize all his ideas of imperial musical influence in the face of all difficulties and obstacles and against all resistance and disapproval, he set about regaining his musical power.

It was the second and the most important nadir of his career, and from it he was to rise to new success and fame. While the fall from the dizzy heights of National Socialism into the abyss of an existence mutilated both spiritually and materially brought the shameful downfall of many of the regime's accomplices and fellow-travellers, Karajan emerged from it apparently unscathed. Like a cat that always lands on its feet, he landed on the hard ground of facts, which he immediately appropriated. Is there an essential similarity between man and beast? Of all animals, 'what interests me about cats is when they want to jump up somewhere, they have a look, and when they jump they can get there. There's no doubt, or else they wouldn't do it.'[7] Neither is there any doubt that Karajan used precisely the same tactic. He never undertook anything that contained the risk of uncertainty. He made his calculations and used them as a source of support. He was not an adventurer, for an adventurer acts in the opposite way. He breaks free and goes his own way. Karajan's affinity with cats touches on another point – behind it there lies a fascination with the attraction of self-sufficiency, unapproachability, a fascination to which people with Karajan's psychological structure are particularly susceptible. For the same reason he later sought and found this attraction in his third wife, Eliette. The true motivation is not the need to love, but to be loved and to tolerate the people who fulfil that condition.[8]

Anita and Herbert von Karajan spent the summer after the war in sun-soaked Northern Italy. From being refugees they became internees. 'I was captured in Milan. We were interned in a hotel after the war. It wasn't a hotel, but rather a terrible, fifth-class boarding house. And we were given other people's leftovers to eat.' A table with two chairs, a cupboard and two beds, a mirror on the wall and something like a stove in one corner: that wasn't the grand and enchanting luxurious world with which Karajan had allowed himself to be spoiled months before in the high-class Milan hotel Principe e Savoia on the Piazza della Republicana. Soon he lacked even the most basic means of sustenance. Anita's knowledge of languages won her a job as an interpreter with the victorious Americans. Through them she had access to food otherwise available only on the black market. The pianist Edwin Fischer, of whom Karajan 'was very fond on a human level', anonymously sent aid when he heard of Karajan's desperate situation. That was an additional source of help to them. 'At the time I gave a lot of thought to the idea of playing in a dance-band or something of the kind.'[9] But he sent the multilingual Anita out to work. While she was interpreting and earning their livelihood, he studied scores. The months immediately after the war in Milan were thus a time during which Karajan was obliged to hold his breath. It was one of the very few periods of his life when he had to do so, and the most important one. He was fuelling up during this period, soaking up the scores of the works with which he was most intensely concerned. He was thinking while planning for the future. He disguised himself in order to enter a new life as the same man in a different form, that of the conqueror. 'During that interval I did a lot of thinking. And when I returned to music I was a changed man.'[10]

The brooding heat of the summer of 1946, which melted the glaciers to a lower level than ever before, turned Milan into an inferno. Karajan was then filled with longing for the coolness, freshness and clarity of the mountains. In the Swiss travel office there was a poster of the Matterhorn. Karajan passed it almost every day. He often stopped and stared at it, magically entranced. It was not only a longing for the solitude of the mountain summits that held his attention. What was behind it was a longing to climb, a longing for success, for peaks as yet unattained. His painful,

148

heartfelt wish was to be on top again. In the late years of the war he once attempted to climb the Matterhorn. In 1942 or 1943, he couldn't quite remember, and from Breuil, where he quite often stayed at that time. He only reached the shoulder of the mountain, before being forced to turn back. He never stood on the peak of the Matterhorn; it remained a dream. This is symptomatic of the entire course of Karajan's life. The concrete effort involved in a task such as climbing the Matterhorn is something that he never successfully achieved. He never attained the concrete goal of his effort. Just as he had failed to achieve the self-discipline required for the scientific and technical work he had undertaken as a student in Vienna, so he also failed to muster the effort needed to climb the mountain. The climbing of the Matterhorn is a concrete goal, and it requires concrete effort. But that involves the very concrete possibility of failure. Might this explain why Karajan never composed, in contrast to his opposite pole, Leonard Bernstein? Because then he could have been pinned down to his unsuccessful work. As an interpreter, however, he could always safely blame the composer for any failures bound up with the work.

One effort that Karajan actually did make was that of creating an illusion, of turning himself into an illusion. He managed this in the Third Reich and then maintained it for the rest of his life: he won fame, power and influence. He made this falsifying effort unstintingly and without any loss of intensity. But he was neither capable nor desirous of a real effort, such as the effort involved in becoming himself. For this was the content of the whole illusion: Karajan believed he could, by making the massive effort that should have been applied to himself and directing it outwards into a career that won him fame and success, somehow find his undeveloped ego. He 'achieved' an enormous amount on behalf of this illusion. But it was a deceptive achievement, because the goal was a false one.

Via Trieste, where he first conducted after the war, 'with that hunger that comes from not having conducted for six months, along with hunger from not having anything to eat', Karajan reached Austria in a transport of refugees at the end of September. He was travelling in open goods vans and thus had an idea of how the Jews and gypsies must have felt as they travelled to their deaths. The railway journey lasted twenty-six hours. The first snow already lay along the border in the mountains.

Back at home in Salzburg with his parents he found that the

investigations and hearings of the Allied Commission for the Rehabilitation of Austrian Cultural Producers were awaiting him.

Things did not look good for the rest of Karajan's future. As a Party member and a protégé of the regime he had to expect drastic sanctions, a prohibition on employment. His career had been suddenly interrupted: his aim was to continue it as quickly as possible. He was prepared to use any course of action to achieve this, following the motto that the end justifies the means. Karajan had not changed, and had remained true to himself in the sense that he had failed to develop in any way. Just as he had allowed himself to be corrupted in the Third Reich, just as he had been prepared to 'commit murder' for the post in Aachen, in the first months after the war he was prepared to base his future on the uncertain foundation of false statements.[11] Karajan told the Theatre and Music Section in Salzburg, set up for the political classification of artists, that he had joined the NSDAP in 1935 in connection with his appointment as Generalmusikdirektor, and that he had resigned again in 1942 after marrying the quarter-Jewish Güter-mann. This put him in a favourable position, providing his story was believed and nothing could be proven to the contrary. This was clearly the case: possibly the relevant files were inaccessible in the post-war confusion, or perhaps no one made the effort to test the truth of Karajan's statements. In any case the authorities concerned with classification and de-Nazification were uninformed about important points in Karajan's past. Thus it happened, for example, that the First US Cultural Officer, Otto de Pasetti (an Austrian emigrant), 'after initial research in mid-November [authorized] Karajan's exoneration',[12] in order to solve the problem of conductors in Vienna. In the justification for authorizing him to perform in Austria, as effective from 15 December 1945, it therefore states: 'The theatre and music division of the American news monitoring service takes the view that von Karajan, by taking responsibility for his racially persecuted wife and shouldering the related consequences, compensated for his membership of the NSDAP.'[13] On 21 December 1945 Pasetti published an announcement to the same effect in the *Wiener Kurier*, which brought him a warning from General McChrystal at US Headquarters, who was later to live in Salzburg and Vienna. In Pasetti Karajan found a kind of apologist, although Pasetti's judgement of him was less than favourable: 'Discussions with Karajan have given me the impression of an arrogant man who has set himself goals which he pursues with the most stubborn energy. In his dealing with people he is difficult. He is not conciliatory. He has consequently made himself a large number of enemies. This last circumstance is important when it comes to the question of his performing.'[14]

A few days after the announcement of his authorization to perform, three concerts with Karajan and the Vienna Philharmonic were announced for 12, 13 and 19 January. The announcement was made at the suggestion of the head of the Philharmonic, Professor Sedlak. But the Russians raised objections to Karajan. In the Vienna municipal authorities' notification of their having examined the programme, it states curtly: 'Concert authorized. Conductor Herbert von Karajan refused.'[15] In a conversation a few hours before the concert, in the Hotel Imperial, Vienna, Pasetti and Sedlak were able to change the mind of the Soviet censoring officer Epstein, who had at first justified his decision in rejecting Karajan by saying: 'Karajan is known as a strong Nazi.'[16] Thus on 12 January, at three o'clock, Karajan launched his post-war career in Austria with Haydn's London Symphony, Richard Strauss's tone poem *Don Juan* and Brahms' First Symphony. Although demonstrations against Karajan were announced, things were quiet at the beginning of the concert. Fewer than one hundred people applauded Karajan as he walked to the front of the orchestra. But after the closing piece, the Brahms symphony, there was wild applause. The enthusiastic audience included a certain Dr Egon Hilbert, who was to speak up for Karajan during the coming months. For Karajan's next concerts with the Vienna Philharmonic, scheduled for 2 and 3 March 1946, were not to happen.

> This time the American authorities put the entire blame for his performing ban on the Austrian commission. According to Hendrik J. Burns of the *Wiener Kurier* the Austrian government had decided to prohibit Karajan's concert. The American Deputy High Commissioner, Brigadier General Ralph H. Tate, also withdrew Karajan's Information Services Branch performing permit for the US zone, and the official Austrian investigating commission at the Federal Ministry of Education made the same ruling.[17]

What had started so promisingly for Karajan came to an unexpectedly quick end. He was condemned to inaction once again, and this time for longer than before. He even had to defend himself, before the allied de-Nazification bureau, against the accusation of having been a member of the Nazi German security service. The British representative had surprised the commission with the news

151

that in a requisitioned index Karajan had been entered as a security agent in Aachen, with the date given as 1943. 'Although Karajan rejected this accusation when asked, further investigations were launched, and at the end of January the American representative, Herbert Allen, declared that no connection existed between Karajan and the security service.'[18] In Salzburg Karajan spoke once again about his work in the Third Reich. He told the American officer Henry Alter his version of the performance of *Meistersinger* in Berlin, which was thrown into general confusion in the presence of the Führer because of the drunken singer Böckelmann, and about how he had fallen out of grace with Hitler. To the US officer Ernst Lothar, commissioned to carry out further questioning, Karajan repeated the circumstances of his membership of the NSDAP. In a memorandum Lothar summed up the decision and his impressions of the two and a half hours of questioning. 'This is a fanatical man whose fanaticism applies to the music that means his existence.'[19] What had Adolf Hitler said in his cultural oration at the Reich Party Day in Nuremburg in 1933, the Party Day of Victory? 'Art is a sublime mission which commits us to fanaticism.'[20] And what did Friedrich Nietzsche – to whom Hitler liked so much to refer – have to say on the matter? 'Fanaticism is in fact the only "strength of will" to which even the weak and insecure can be brought'.[21] Precisely.

Karajan considered his trial interrogation to be 'meaningless discussions' and 'cross-examinations'.[22] He told the investigating officer that he would wait until the matter had ceased to be under the control of the military government and was legally regulated.

I said I would conduct when I was invited to do so and when it was my right to do so, and not as a special dispensation. That's exactly what I said to the American officer. After seven officers had discussed the matter, I said, 'Right, I've had enough. I'm going to the mountains. And if there's a law I'll come back.' Then, all of a sudden, everyone wanted me to come back. And then I said, 'No, thanks a lot. I've had enough.'

Karajan moved back to St Anton. He made use of this fallow period in dedicating himself to the study of scores again. He thoroughly revised his interpretative ideas, so as to be armed for the time after this enforced break from professional contemplation and reflection. 'I prepared myself for the moment when I would be able to pick up a baton again. My career had happened far too quickly. It was like a balcony without any support. In Aachen and Berlin I had simply taken on too much.'[23]

Karajan must have felt very sure of his ground. In fact, if the whole truth had come to light at that time, it could have had incalculable consequences for him. For when the Russian officer Epstein gave his permission for Karajan to make public appearances, which had initially been refused, it was agreed in the report to US Headquarters about the discussions that if new incriminating information about Karajan should come to light, Karajan would face severe punishment: 'If some new evidence should be brought up against Karajan during the next week, the case will be reopened and Karajan will be liable to get severe punishment.'[24] The organization of Karajan's second career, his post-war career, depended quite significantly on his version being accepted. For it is questionable whether a Party member, who had joined twice on a voluntary basis, and who sought to use false information to achieve quick de-Nazification, could ever have been considered as head conductor of the Berlin Philharmonic Orchestra or artistic director of the Vienna Staatsoper. To a certain extent, Karajan staked everything on the card of plausibility, and he had invested an extraordinary amount in the de-Nazification commissions. As we know, the bluff paid off.

Why none of the authorities concerned with the verification of his statements examined the truth in them remains a matter for speculation. Did they want to make life easy for Karajan? Bearing in mind the generally known fact that between 1 May 1933 and 1937 there was a strict prohibition on new membership of the NSDAP, it must be said that they were astonishingly ill-informed if they believed Karajan's story of his Aachen membership. Did someone perhaps obligingly conceal incriminating material? Was it for this reason that Karajan could be so sure his version would be accepted as the true one? Might this answer the question of why Karajan, even as an old man, portrayed the historical facts as mere 'claims'? Did he live for decades in the false belief that all the incriminating documents from his past had been destroyed? Whether he did or not, through his lawyers he informed the author of the book *Musik im NS-Staat*, on 11 May 1982:

This book contains some false claims about Herr von Karajan. On page 19 you write with reference to Herr von Karajan: 'But the official did not need to do this, since in his files the artist was already listed as Party Member 3430914, joined 1.5.1933, NSDAP Ortgruppe Ulm/Gau Württemberg . . .' You will certainly be aware that you must provide proof for the truth of these claims against Herr von Karajan. We request that you tell us the sources on which you base your claim, and send us photocopies of the documents. We must be given the opportunity to find out how your claim was arrived at.

The historian and legal academic Oliver Rathkolb has carried out intensive research into the processes connected with Karajan's de-Nazification procedure. His investigations tell us that after January 1946 the Theatre and Music section led by Otto de Pasetti was increasingly pushed into the background. 'Obviously the prominent de-Nazification cases of a Wilhelm Furtwängler or a Herbert von Karajan had already assumed international dimensions.'[25] A central Austrian investigative commission at the Federal Ministry for Education dealt with these cases. This commission was appointed as an 'expert evaluative commission into the political attitude of artists, singers, musicians, composers and directors (soloists), either independent or employed by the national theatre, at the Federal Ministry for Education'. One of its members was Karajan's later co-director at the Vienna Staatsoper, Ministerialrat Dr Egon Hilbert.[26] The commission concluded, on 25 March 1946, that Karajan should be allowed 'to perform as a conductor, but not in a leading capacity', 'as he is important for the reconstruction of Austrian musical life'. Stating its reasons, it gave him political and moral absolution on the basis of his claim – since revealed to be false – about his Party membership and ended up by stating: 'The established lack of conducting personalities makes Karajan's work in Austrian musical life, particularly at the 1946 Salzburg Festival, all the more necessary since the invitations sent to four of the world's foremost conductors (Toscanini, Bruno Walter, Sir Thomas Beecham, Erich Kleiber) have been turned down. It is also beyond a doubt that Karajan is to be seen as a first-rate conductor of European stature.'[27]

The cryptic, typically Austrian decision of the commission, Rathkolb says,

brought the Allies into an embarrassing situation once again as they had expected unambiguous Austrian decisions. The starting-point for the expert evaluative commission's report was the Prohibitory Law, para. 17ff, according to which an 'illegal

154

person' cannot occupy a leading position . . . The first lawyer, Pastrovich, had stated that 'an Austrian citizen who, during the membership ban (1 July 1933 until 13 March 1938), was a member of the NSDAP or one of its branches, is to be considered illegal regardless of his place of residence'. The legal consequences were admittedly made more lenient with reference to the Prohibitive Law, para. 27, but the idea of employing the famous conductor Karajan in a non-prominent capacity ran counter to the very idea of the orchestral conductor. But from the very first Karajan had wanted to avoid precisely that classification as an 'illegal Austrian NSDAP member', and the working ban that would necessarily be legally imposed as a result, and had consequently remained intentionally silent about his membership of Ortsgruppe V 'Neustadt'. The Americans too, because of their 'efforts towards de-Germanization', tended to pardon an Austrian who had joined the NSDAP in Germany (solely for career reasons) more easily than they forgave an illegal Austrian National Socialist.[28]

Although the Karajan lobby spoke up for the conductor, who they claimed was urgently needed – or perhaps because they did so – on 21 June 1946 General Tate told the Austrian Chancellor Figl, via the head of the 'Directorate for Internal Affairs of the Allied Commission on Austria', P. Nott Bower, that Karajan 'was to be excluded from all official appearances in Austria because of his National Socialist connections'.[29] The Chancellor then requested a reappraisal of the stage ban by the commission of experts. The commission's main argument – still unproven – for its positive verdict was 'that Karajan resigned from the Party in 1942 following his marriage to a woman not purely Aryan, thus proving his anti-National Socialist stance'.[30] It was hoped that Karajan would be free to work in the Salzburg Festival, but despite all the efforts of the commission of experts, biased in his favour, this was not to be. However, with Salzburg deviousness and cunning they arrived at an 'Austrian solution' whereby the stage ban, designed as a ban on public appearances, was interpreted very loosely, a fact immediately exploited by the festival's director. Thus Karajan was able to work at the rehearsals 'actively as a director, visible to all those present'.[31] He took part in the rehearsals and performances of *Rosenkavalier* and *The Marriage of Figaro*, which he had been helping to prepare for weeks. He conducted the performances from the prompter's box, while in the orchestra pit the substitute conductors Hans Swarowsky and

155

Felix Prohaska worked according to his instructions. The situation was like a gift from the heavens: 'I did everything, musically and to some extent theatrically, together with Oscar Fritz Schuh and Caspar Neher. We reached a very satisfactory agreement. Most of the women singers were young and beautiful.'[32] Did this compliment extend to Irmgard Seefried, who sang the part of Susanna and who, in Aachen, had refused to follow Karajan to Berlin?

Clearly Karajan took too much of the limelight at the Salzburg Festival. On 6 August the US Headquarters issued an unambiguous order preventing Karajan's public work as a director and musical adviser. The American theatre and music officer, Ernst Lothar, wrote to Baron Puthon:

> Mr von Karajan was present not just as a spectator, but as a stage director, whose remarks were put down in writing, by assistants. This is contrary to the understanding reached between you, Mr Hilbert and myself. I then pointed out that Mr von Karajan should not show up in any capacity at the Festival, in which he was banned to take part. I have orders to ask you to put an immediate end to these very unfortunate activities.[33]

On the same day the baron, a clever tactician, justified himself in the following terms:

> The instructions that you gave myself and Herr Ministerialrat Dr Hilbert at the time regarding General Musical Director v. Karajan contained the prohibition both on conducting and on leading and directing rehearsals; but they do not extend to his activity as an artistic adviser to the directors of the Salzburg Festival. The directing and running of rehearsals is carried out at all operas by our own conductor and director, but we could not manage without the valuable advice of Herr v. Karajan, who had already led the rehearsals for all three operas in Vienna before the ban. In accordance with your wishes, however, I shall request that Herr v. Karajan arrange his artistic advice in future in such a way that he does not appear before the public. I have informed the district commissioner of this incident, and he is taking further steps on his own account.[34]

From now on Karajan delivered his instructions, considered

indispensable, from the wings and the prompter's box. District Commissioner Hochleitner believed that he could circumvent the stage ban by giving a private concert with Karajan for invited festival guests. But the head of the propaganda department of the US occupying forces, Ladue, stood in the way of this too. Although the Austrians, along with Ernst Lothar, called for a retrial and the authorization of Karajan's performances, the Allied Commission's Directorate for Internal Affairs held to the stage ban and told Chancellor Figl on 17 September: 'The Directorate therefore requests that you take the necessary steps to ensure that Herbert v. Karajan be debarred forthwith from all public appearances in Austria.'[35] This decision was accepted and enforced by the commission of experts, with the result that on 4 November the Chancellor was able to tell the Allied Commission that the 'stated decision according to which the conductor Herbert Karajan is to be excluded from all public appearances in Austria has been carried out. Karajan has been required to abandon a public appearance. The Federal Theatre authorities, the presidium of the Salzburg Festival and the most important musical societies have been informed of this decision.'[36] But Egon Hilbert, clearly biased towards Karajan, would not let things go as easily as that. In January 1947 he began a renewed attempt to win an authorization from the Americans for Karajan to perform and in March the US officer Ernst Lothar granted permission on the grounds that Karajan was absolutely required to relieve the conductor Josef Krips at the coming Salzburg Festival. But this time, all of a sudden, it was the French who raised objections against Karajan's performing in Salzburg. 'Apparently they could not forgive him the fact that he had conducted at the Paris Opera in 1941, and played the 'Horst Wessel Song' as an introduction.'[37] Thus no further interventions were made on Karajan's behalf during the 1947 festival, as adequately renowned conductors were available.

Condemned to be a passive observer, Karajan had to watch his former rival, Wilhelm Furtwängler, throwing his weight around in Salzburg during the summer of 1947 and joining forces with the Vienna Philharmonic. Even Karl Böhm was forbidden to conduct in Austria again that summer, because during the Third Reich he had 'made at least two glowing declarations of devotion to Hitler, which were not private, shamefaced, qualified or preformulated by NS officials, but exhortations aimed at the German and Greater German public, once on the occasion of the "election" on 29 March 1936, and then again on the occasion of the "plebiscite" on "Austria's homecoming" on 10 April 1938, this time

157

delivered directly for the Gau Propaganda Office of the Vienna NSDAP', and because in March, on the occasion of a guest concert in Vienna, he had mounted the podium and of his own accord given a Hitler salute.[38] Karajan felt cheated and hard done by.

During Karajan's conducting ban he met Walter Legge, the artistic director of Columbia Records, later EMI-Electrola, who was in search of a conductor for the London Philharmonia Orchestra which he had just set up. He was a godsend. As he had already done in the past, Karajan now hit upon just the right partner once again. With Legge he quickly found his way out of the post-war trough of inaction and banishment from the conductor's podium. Via the detour of gramophone records, the two set about building up a new career. The old references from Aachen and Berlin had become worthless. They remained shrewdly unmentioned. New ones had to be found. With gramophone records, Karajan would make a name for himself once again, and be presented to an international audience as the phoenix emerging rejuvenated from the cleansing ashes. He began a spate of intense work in the recording studio. In the autumn of 1947 he played a series of various works with the Vienna Philharmonic, including Brahms' *German Requiem*. This brought Karajan together with the famous choir of the Gesellschaft der Musikfreunde in Vienna.

From the very first it was truly 'love at first sight' . . . ; in the wake of this whole enterprise the Gesellschaft der Musikfreunde, supported by the personal courage, incredible by the standards of the day, of President Hryntschak and General Secretary Gamsjäger, declared that they were making me their lifelong concert director. That was during the time when I was not allowed to make public appearances.[39]

Now everything came together, one thing following on from the last. It was as if the floodgates were being opened, the great masses of water suddenly being liberated. Karajan's musical energy, held in check for two years, was worked off during the months and years that followed in a frenzy of production which was to be unique in the history of performing artists. The conducting ban was lifted in October 1947.

At the end of that month he appeared before the public in a concert with the Vienna Philharmonic which included Bruckner's Eighth Symphony. In the score which he gave to Walter Legge as a memento of the event, which was so important to him, he inscribed the following dedication: 'To my second musical self and dear friend in memory of a long-awaited day. Herbert von Karajan, 26.x.47.'

On 20 December, in a concert with the Philharmonic, Karajan conducted Beethoven's Ninth Symphony. In the *Österreichische Zeitung* of 24 December, Dr Hajas took an emphatic stand on this. His review is notable for the ambivalence of the feelings unleashed by the demonstrative appearance of Karajan before the Vienna Philharmonic during the Christmas period two and a half years after the end of the thousand-year Reich.

To a sell-out house last weekend Beethoven's Ninth Symphony was given the frenetic applause due to a première. It was not, indeed, the first time since the end of the war that it had been played in a Viennese concert hall, and this year too it might have been an opportunity to declare one's enthusiasm for it. But until now it had been performed only in the 'unofficial' part of Vienna's concert scene, so to speak, which is not powerful enough, politically or otherwise, to raise the temperature convincingly. 'Fortunately' it has now, at last, finally found Herbert von Karajan for the Philharmonic Concerts too, and through his 'version' ensured a sensational success brought not so much by Beethoven's as by Karajan's 'Ninth'.

The demonstrative applause at the end of the concert proved that we should remember the importance of this date: Karajan's 'Ninth' is the victory of interpretation over the work and brilliant proof of the possibility of a new and 'timely' sense being provided by the conductor. For only through Karajan has this musical drama of humanity turned into a military parade, the revolutionary declaration of freedom become a call to arms (as one delighted voice in the press has already mentioned), the titanic inspiration of an enthusiastic love of mankind been transformed into cold 'demonism' . . . The result of this was certainly rich enough in tone and noisy enough – but it had little in common with Beethoven because almost all of these new, sensational effects were purely external in nature. Nowhere did this appear more brutally than in the adagio, whose warm and soulful singing was lost in an unemotional frivolity, and in the finale, where the conductor put the choir and orchestra through their paces, so to speak, to show that they had learned their lesson well. Or was this what met with such triumphant acclaim in the fully attended auditorium, the fact that the peace that will unite mankind, which Beethoven joyfully proclaims with shawms and cymbals, is now being performed in military march time?

There is no doubt that in the interpretation of a conductor whose career began in the Third Reich, the spirit and taste of the Reich are involuntarily finding new expression: in the musical sphere, star-oriented individualism and superficial aesthetics become too integrated within the polish of cultural propaganda, in the service of a political ideology which has never been afraid of distorting even the most sacred cultural products for its own ends. In the face of this, it is important to bring Beethoven's monument to joy and humanity back to an audience that has grown estranged from his legacy, and to challenge an interpretation which, through simple arrogance, has turned the will of its creator into its very opposite.[40]

The year 1948 brought the long-awaited breakthrough into intense activity. In Salzburg Karajan gave the summer festival new artistic impulses with grand performances of Mozart's *Figaro* and Gluck's *Orpheus and Euridice* in the Felsenreitschule. In unstinting and obsessive rehearsals, which were nothing but hard-nosed pedagogical work driven by ambition for success, he welded the London Philharmonia into a body of sound which could master the future tasks of Legge's ambitious recording projects with a seeming lack of effort. The same is true of his work with the Vienna Symphony Orchestra, who chose him as their conductor and travelled with him in the winter of 1950 (1948, according to Karajan) into a Germany laid waste by war. But everything was still organized in a very makeshift way. True reconstruction was only to occur very gradually. The clearing-up was still being done. 'In Essen – it was wintertime – we played in an unheated circus. And nearby there were the lions who grew terribly fascinated when I was changing.' There they were together, in a chance and unexpected way, in real life for once and not merely in the metaphorical sense: the animal tamer and the beasts. In a very real sense Karajan was entering the world of travelling entertainers, artists and actors of whom he – the great magician, virtuoso and stage manager – was certainly the most elegant. For the world of the circus, sensation based on effect and craft, was always a part of Karajan's being, and would never be entirely eradicated. The tour brought him back to Aachen where, after eight years and the collapse of a whole world, he performed again for the first time on

160

25 January 1950: in the 'Eden-Palast' cinema the former General Musical Director of the old imperial city gave a much-fêted guest concert.

At the end of 1948 Karajan conducted the Salzburg Festival production of Mozart's *Figaro* at La Scala Milan, and subsequently took charge of the city's annual 'German season'. Until he took over the artistic direction of the Vienna Staatsoper in 1957 he retained intensive professional connections with La Scala, and this work was also continued later on, although in a different form. At La Scala he came together with the prima donna of the century, Maria Callas. Her performance in Donizetti's *Lucia di Lammermoor* established a fruitful if all too short collaboration that led to recordings of Verdi's *Trovatore* and Puccini's *Madame Butterfly*, the interpretation of which set new standards and testified to an artistic partnership whose heights would never be reached again.

In 1949 Karajan received his first invitation to the International Festival in Lucerne. There he conducted the Swiss Festival Orchestra, a disparate ensemble combining elements from all parts of the country, which never attained a satisfactory homogeneity. He would always remain loyally and affectionately grateful to the people of Lucerne, because 'they were the first people after the war to say: "What they said about you and did to you after the war doesn't concern us at all. You are welcome with us and can come whenever you like." I'll always remember that.' In 1969 the city thanked him for his loyalty by awarding him the art prize of the city of Lucerne. Inviting Karajan to Lucerne had been a fortuitous idea, as he was to give the festival there his own definite stamp for decades to come.

In Salzburg Karajan gave another two concerts in the summer of 1949, but the opera houses suddenly spurned him. What had happened? Furtwängler, quite the old and jealous adversary, far from generous where such tangible interests as festival engagements and benefits were concerned, informed the directorship of the festival that he would not tolerate the preferential or equal treatment of Karajan. As conductor of the Vienna Philharmonic, which was working as an operatic and concert orchestra in Salzburg, Furtwängler found a soft option in the Austrians: they played along with his mean trick so as not to annoy the master. Karajan was pushed into the background. He would not play in the Salzburg Festival again until 1957, and he broke with the Vienna Philharmonic in 1950. On the other hand the world was opening up to him. He was soon given a tour of South America, the Festivals of Lucerne and Bayreuth were to invite him, he celebrated triumphs at La Scala which made his name known throughout the world. And there were also the London Philharmonia and the Vienna Symphony Orchestra.

In Vienna Karajan concentrated entirely on his collaboration with the city's second orchestra. Within a short time he had made it one of the most famous orchestras in Europe and a serious competitor for the Philharmonic, which often seemed overly absorbed in its main function as the orchestra of the Staatsoper.

Performances of Bach's *B Minor Mass* and *Matthew Passion* during the 1950 Bach Festival in Vienna, on which Karajan had worked in countless rehearsals, were major and unforgettable musical events of the day. Months of detailed work preceded the impressive performances. They were also connected with a filming of the *Matthew Passion*, which Karajan had made the previous year with André Mattoni. As Karajan's private secretary, Mattoni became his right-hand man. He relieved him of the administrative tasks and duties that were piling up. Mattoni became his intermediary and mediator, his protector, the master's assistant, acting with either diplomatic skill or frigid directness, whichever seemed the more opportune. Karajan tended to hide behind Mattoni, using him as a front man whenever he considered it appropriate, in the struggle for the extension or preservation of power, to stay in the background and if necessary to involve himself in intrigues from that position of security.

Having seen himself ejected from Salzburg's operatic scene, Karajan switched to Bayreuth. In the summer of 1950 he gave a concert in the Festspielhaus for the general meeting of the Society of the Friends of Bayreuth. For the coming year he was invited to perform *Meistersinger* and the entire *Ring* cycle. The production of *Meistersinger* was recorded and remains one of the most impressive musical documents of its time. The critic Karl Heinz Ruppel sums up the essence of the musical impressions as follows:

The actual event of the production, however, was Karajan's conducting début in Bayreuth. From the first note of the overture an enchantment emanated from the conductor's stand, something that occurs none too often even in this lofty hideout for great and very great conductors. There was a brightness and clarity of tone, a filigree finesse of orchestral polyphony that had never been heard even in the wonderful acoustics of the Festspielhaus. How constant was the flow, how convincing the tempi both in themselves and in their proportions, how unpathetic it all was, and how 'meaningful' in Goethe's sense of the word![41]

In 1952 Karajan, now forty-four, conducted the new production of *Tristan und Isolde* directed and designed by Wieland Wagner. It was to lead to an early departure from Bayreuth.

Bayreuth: the idea of an authentic reproduction of works, unhindered by the restrictions and contingencies of traditional operatic concerns. This idea must have been extraordinarily attractive to Karajan. In Bayreuth he saw realized what he would later optimize in his Easter Festivals in terms of his own requirements. In Bayreuth Karajan finally made his name as the most important post-war Wagner conductor – and it was thoroughly logical that so promising a collaboration should be granted continuity and cultivated in the long term. But it was not to be.

Karajan, obsessed by ambition and the conviction that he would become as outstanding a director as he was a conductor, was not satisfied, after his own first directing experiences, with working only from the covered orchestra pit. He wanted everything. But Wieland and Wolfgang Wagner, into whose hands the running of the festival had fallen after the war, wanted Karajan the conductor, not Karajan the director. Direction was Wieland's domain. He was clearing Bayreuth of dead wood, and would brook no interference. He did it so radically, right to the very roots, that Karajan did not wish to follow him. His ideas about the unity of music and representation on the stage were geared in quite a different direction. The incompatibility of their artistic conceptions clearly surfaced during the new production of *Tristan und Isolde*. Karajan argued with Wieland Wagner. 'I said: "Herr Wagner, you will have to write some new music, because this music doesn't fit what you are doing on the stage. People can't see it any more."'[42]

Wieland Wagner's conception of *Tristan* shocked Karajan to the point of rejecting it. Karajan could do nothing with the raked disc of the stage, the monochrome stretched backdrops, the completely empty, bare stage. In his head he had a quite opposite vision of the opera, enlivened by people and objects. He saw himself confronted by a contradiction from which he could only retreat. In the discussion of the possibilities and limitations of a timely production of Wagner, Karajan took the stance of the custodian. Karajan was as far as possible from the position of negation from which Wieland Wagner approached his grandfather's work. In the obvious discrepancy between the on-stage action and the music, in the contrast between musical ecstasy and theatrical asceticism that appears in Wieland Wagner's productions, Karajan could see no meaningful way of mastering and appropriating Wagner's work. Wieland Wagner's suffocating attempts to de-romanticize the works, his wilful stagings against the spirit of the score went against the grain as far as Karajan was concerned. Karajan could not agree with the elimination of romanticism from Wagner's work. So they went their separate ways.

Karajan could not complain of being under-occupied elsewhere. He was busy recording the entire popular repertoire with 'his' London orchestra for the British company, Columbia. The production of gramophone records, impressive not only in numerical terms, spread and established his reputation. Many recordings from this time, and indeed from the whole period of their collaboration which lasted until 1960, are exemplary in their artistic quality and importance. They reveal Karajan's genius as a conductor in combining his two musical yardsticks, Toscanini and Furtwängler, into a synthesis of precision and imagination. The fifties were Karajan's great, his golden years. Everything he did later is simply an improvement of details, an increasingly sophisticated refinement, in which he ran the risk of losing sight of his goal while searching for the ideal to which he came so close in the fifties, and losing himself in details through his obsession with sound.

All his interpretative ideas were already unshakeably formed in the late forties and the fifties, and so were his dramaturgical conceptions. Until his old age, which would not produce a new 'style', there were only slight deviations in his work. Once he had recognized something as being correct he would keep it as it was. There were no experiments. In his best recordings from this time, particularly those of Beethoven's and Brahms's symphonies, he attained a conclusiveness and a compelling persuasiveness in his renderings which he was unable to surpass in later versions of these works. Although they were to become richer and more mature in certain of their details, they did not grow any more logically consistent. In addition, they lost the freshness and flexible verve and brilliance of the first efforts.

In the spring of 1952 Karajan led his first tour with the London Philharmonia, which took him via cities such as Turin, Geneva, Bern, Zurich and Basle to the musical centres of Europe: Paris,

Milan, Vienna, Munich and Berlin. He showed the continent that as the violinist Joseph Szigeti summed it up, 'even a big orchestra can play with the perfect precision of a good quartet'. His concerts with the London orchestra were already something extraordinary. They were infused with the exciting atmosphere of a true sensation. They also took the form of a search for a new partner. For Karajan set his goals high: he wanted to go beyond his previous achievements and attain the very best. That was to be found in Vienna and Berlin. He went to those cities, announced his presence, introduced himself, got himself known again. There the 'wonder' of the thirties showed that he had not taken the path of child prodigies, which so often dwindles to nothing. There he demonstrated his supreme ease with the trade of which he was legitimately a master.

But in Vienna and Berlin Furtwängler exercised his control over the Philharmonic. He did so in a strange way, exploiting the fact that Berlin felt it could not do without him. Soon, however, questions were flying around about who Furtwängler's successor was to be. For Furtwängler was ill, had been away from Berlin for far too long and wanted to spend more time on his composing projects. He no longer reluctantly emerged to conduct a large number of concerts in Berlin. Until his death the orchestra courted the conductor, who kindly welcomed their requests, and practically pleaded with him to appear more often at the head of the orchestra. It was almost a form of undignified begging. An open letter in 1950 voiced criticism about Furtwängler's rare appearances in Berlin. It said:

Not only do you have rights, you also have duties! . . . Unfortunately, however, we are forced to realize, again and again, that you hold this position only nominally and do very little to demonstrate it to the outside world. You do set a high value on being involved in the selection of conductors . . . This would, as such, be your inalienable right if you would move the centre of your activity to Berlin.[43]

Once again, Karajan was affected by the right that Furtwängler claimed for himself in Berlin. He had been approached as early as the beginning of 1950. The correspondence between the committee member delegated to represent the artistic interests of the Berlin Philharmonic Orchestra, Ernst Fischer, and Furtwängler on the subject of Karajan gives us an informative picture of the conflict between rejection and recognition laboriously achieved, in which

165

the unforgiving Furtwängler saw himself threatened by his younger rival. On 28 February he wrote:

> The only colleague about whom I have any complaints is Karajan. No objections can be raised, of course, about his conducting with you in Berlin. But I would not recommend him for touring. Tours with a conductor are always a sign of close collaboration and this matter should not only be decided according to the conductor's market value, but according to the relationships between the conductor and the orchestra . . . As far as Karajan is concerned, there is, of course, as before, and contrary to what the press reported, no kind of rivalry towards him on my part. Why should there be? Unfortunately it is a different matter on his part. In Vienna he prevented the choir of the Gesellschaft der Musikfreunde being put at my disposal for the *Matthew Passion* in the planned Bach concert by the Vienna Philharmonic, and the society yielded to him, as it was depending on him for its major Bach Festival . . . [44]

It was probably right to give in: Karajan had, in fact, prepared the *Matthew Passion* in countless rehearsals, and naturally he did not want the conception on which he had spent so much time working with the choir to be ruined by a performance that Furtwängler was organizing outside the framework of the Bach Festival, as a Philharmonic subscription concert. Furtwängler would also have refused such a request. During the war he had already proved uncooperative where far less important matters were concerned, for example when Karajan wanted to transfer his concerts from the temporarily destroyed Staatsoper to the Philharmonie, and took a negative, even intransigent stance when Karajan later requested a repeat of this transfer for acoustic reasons. The letter makes plain what Furtwängler's real concerns were during those years: he wanted the world to see him appearing as the head of the orchestra, and to accompany it on the tours he desired so much, but to leave the important work in Berlin to other people. Karajan was good enough for that – but he had to be kept away from the tours. Furtwängler was playing a disagreeable game both with Karajan and with the orchestra. A year later, on 10 March 1951, Furtwängler returned once more to the event in Vienna:

> Although I had a very bad experience with Herr von Karajan last year from a 'cooperative' point of view, this does not mean that you should not involve this talented conductor; on the

contrary, in your position I should recommend that you try everything to have the priority on this appointment [...] The only thing I have to say about Karajan is that he should not be given special treatment over the other outstanding conductors . . .[45]

Without a doubt, the orchestra was seeking contact with Karajan, while Furtwängler, on the other hand, was resisting the plans to entrust Karajan with more important tasks. Furtwängler was told on 1 March 1950: 'We have not yet heard anything from Karajan. We might consider one or two concerts in Berlin, but otherwise we do not have any extensive plans with him . . .'[46] But a year later, on 14 March 1951, Furtwängler received the following information from Ernst Fischer:

We ascertained from your letter that you have no objections to Herr von Karajan conducting. But your view that Herr von Karajan should be treated no differently from other famous conductors can probably not be carried through . . . The whole world knows that the Berlin Philharmonic is seen as your orchestra. We have patiently waited for you for five years in the hope that you would one day return entirely to us. But if a development should occur with the aim of having Karajan in Berlin more often, we will be unable to resist it, as we have nothing to show but our empty hands . . .[47]

That was said tactfully and in a roundabout fashion, and it enabled the orchestra to achieve what it was aiming for, even if it was a drawn-out process. Furtwängler declared himself ready to take on four subscription concerts as well as two special concerts during the 1951–2 season. But the situation was still unsatisfactory. The orchestra was in search of a conductor who would not only take on a handful of concerts, but would form and shape it by working with it on a regular basis. Furtwängler had not yet been reinstated as the official conductor of the Berlin Philharmonic Orchestra. That was not to happen until 1952, although nothing changed as a result. But the orchestra had to think about its future. Sergiu Celibidache, whom Furtwängler favoured, and who had led the orchestra after the war, since Leo Borchard's death in an accident, was increasingly less of an option for the orchestra. On the one hand his salary demands were too high, and on the other there were repeatedly disagreeable scenes during rehearsals. He later even accused the orchestra of non-cooperation, a lack of discipline and provinciality.

Karajan waited quietly, apparently relaxed. But his silence was deceptive. For Karajan was waiting for the right moment. In the meantime he was winning influential friends who made things easy for him, and on whom he would call when the time was right. He was still hesitating. There were certainly a number of reasons for this. In 1950–1 Berlin was no longer the musical metropolis of Europe, and was yet to be so again. The city was in ruins. The orchestra had no home there. In the politically altered landscape it was suddenly no longer the centre, but was isolated, far from events to the extent that Karajan's current work was able to develop much more strongly and emphatically in the cosmopolitan triangle between London, Vienna and Milan. Celibidache saw things much the same way. For him too Berlin was now only one among several possibilities. Karajan kept his eye on the Berlin Philharmonic, but he did not impose himself. In the meantime he increased his fame by means of a great deal of touring work, winning greater respect for himself and bolstering his already excellent reputation as a trainer of orchestras and a profound musician. This was a clever career strategy. Karajan was able to wait. He waited, we might say, as a big cat waits, often for days, for its victim, studying its every movement, ready to strike at the crucial moment of weakness.

In the spring of 1952 he finally talked to the representative of the Berlin Philharmonic on the occasion of his Berlin guest concerts with the London Philharmonia. On 3 June Ernst Fischer told Furtwängler, who was ill again:

> Following the concerts I have now spoken with Herr von Karajan about our plans with him. The result was, like our previous correspondence, quite inconclusive . . . This was the crux of his explanation, just as it was in the case of Herr Celibidache. Both gentlemen seem to find the tours more important than the Berlin concerts . . . He hinted that he might withdraw from the Vienna Symphony because he has no exclusive contract with them, in order to do the tour with us, which I found 'touching' of him! We have informed the Senate of these inconclusive discussions, so that no misinterpretations or distortions may be circulated suggesting that you or the orchestra did not wish Karajan to come to Berlin . . . [48]

Shortly after this Gerhard von Westermann took over the post of manager, which he had already held from 1939 until 1945. Dr Joachim Tiburtius was on the Senate. Both meant Karajan well, and so it could only be a matter of time before he had his chance.

On 8 September 1953 he conducted the Berlin Philharmonic Orchestra again for the first time since the war. In the first festival concert he conducted Bartok's Concerto for Orchestra and Beethoven's *Eroica* before a full house in the Titania-Palast. Eleven years had passed since their last encounter. In the meantime he had fallen, and risen again just as rapidly.

That summer Karajan had learned to fly in Swiss Ascona. This event demands to be given the same importance as his conducting activities. For Karajan, flying was more than simply a means of moving around using a different means of transport – that is only the superficial aspect of it. It was a way of rationalizing his tendency towards escape. Karajan saw the aeroplane, the symbol of our century's unlimited mobility, as the vehicle of the age. It was twenty years since Hitler had created a sense of omnipresence with his flights around Germany. From now on it was Karajan, his own best promoter, who sought constant presence through his flights across Europe.

The following year Karajan conducted the Berlin Philharmonic once more. On 23 September, back in the Titania-Palast, he conducted a special concert as part of the Berlin Festival. The programme consisted of Bartok's Third Piano Concerto with Géza Anda as soloist, Mozart's Symphony No. 35 and Brahms' First Symphony. Friedrich Herzfeld wrote about it in the *Berliner Morgenpost*:

Karajan has basically changed not at all. He still prays like a saint while conducting, and smiles like a *conférencier* when taking his bow. The virtuosity of his orchestral palette is almost without compare . . . In the past he has been played off against Furtwängler. And that has remained the case, even in musical terms . . . A triumph for virtuosity! Thus we are constantly interested but not actually gripped, since he lacks the true tragic sense necessary for Brahms' First Symphony, as indeed for all classical music. He is not a priest but rather a magician, although one who is privy to a wonderful kind of magic.[49]

What Herzfeld is addressing here is something that Karajan was to hear throughout his life, and he would chafe against it in a tragic way. A few days previously, on 19–20 September, Furtwängler opened the 1954 Berlin Festival in the Titania-Palast. Apart from Beethoven's First Symphony he brought his own Second Symphony into the public eye six and a half years after its original performance. It was to be Furtwängler's farewell concert to Berlin and the world.

Karajan never spoke in any detail about Furtwängler's attitude towards him. He went no further than hints, brief comments and the observation that he never understood jealousy in matters artistic. But the depth of the injuries, and their failure to heal, are revealed in the fact that Karajan never conducted any of the memorial concerts dedicated to his predecessor. Furtwängler's newly appointed successor passed the memorial concert on 26 January 1956 to the ever-helpful Joseph Keilberth, who assumed responsibility for the première of Furtwängler's unfinished Third Symphony. Karajan delegated the conducting of the memorial concert on 30 November 1979, the twenty-fifth anniversary of Furtwängler's death, to Lorin Maazel, who also performed the Third Symphony. Karajan's intentional absence was greeted with incomprehension in some quarters, and the press was not sparing in its accusations. In 1957, shortly after Toscanini's death, on the other hand, he conducted Mozart's *Masonic Funeral Music* to the memory of Toscanini before the production of *Salome* at the Vienna Staatsoper. And when, on 16 January 1967 in Milan, the tenth anniversary of the day of Arturo Toscanini's death was commemorated, Karajan found himself wholeheartedly prepared to extend posthumous gratitude to his distant teacher and admired model with a gripping performance of Verdi's *Requiem*. There is no clearer way of expressing one's esteem or its opposite without wasting any words.

In the late autumn of 1954, on 21 and 22 November, Karajan once more conducted the Berlin Philharmonic. The programme included Ralph Vaughan Williams' *Tallis Fantasia* and Anton Bruckner's Ninth Symphony. H. H. Stuckenschmidt confirmed the forty-six-year-old's ability: 'Today Karajan has a capacity for taking very deep breaths. He is able to arrange tensions and relaxations in such a way that the inevitability of the massive form shines through, and the jutting massifs of the adagio can be seen in their entirety.'[50] We might jokingly say that it was his pilot's vision that allowed him to survey the broad symphonic form. The deep breaths that Karajan had taken during the weeks and months after the defeat of Germany were to help him negotiate the hazards of haste and impetuosity and reach the concentrated gaze of maturity.

Karajan, the first true embodiment of the concept of the 'touring conductor', went to Rome after the concerts in Berlin. In Berlin, in the meantime, Celibidache and the orchestra finally separated. On 29 November he told the manager that ' "if he was called" he would first throw out all the superannuated and completely incompetent musicians and would then demand absolute power to take musicians who behaved badly during rehearsals and quite simply show them to the door . . . that, if he was called, "heads would have to roll!" '[51] Following the rehearsal on 30 November, at an orchestral meeting, it was only by an effort of will that von Westermann, the manager, could prevent 'a decision rejecting Celibidache as conductor being made at that very meeting'.[52]

That Tuesday, when the orchestra had taken its stand against Celibidache and absolutely rejected him, Wilhelm Furtwängler died near Baden-Baden at the age of sixty-eight. '*Le roi est mort, vive le roi!*' said an anonymous telegram that Karajan received in Rome. He sent his secretary Mattoni out for a newspaper. It contained the news that Furtwängler was dead. Karajan's model, teacher, adversary, rival and competitor was no more. Suddenly perspectives had changed. At the vanishing point of Karajan's new central perspective, there gleamed all of a sudden the shining possibility of the Berlin Orchestra, deprived of its master. The previous year, von Westermann had already sounded out Karajan to discover whether he was ready to undertake the long-planned American tour of the Berlin Philharmonic should Furtwängler be prevented from doing so. 'I said that I would rather work with his orchestra than anything else.'[53] Now, after Furtwängler's death, he was telephoned from Berlin. Quite unambiguously, Karajan answered, 'With the greatest of pleasure – but only as a designated successor, as the artistic director and successor of Dr Wilhelm Furtwängler!'[54]

Chancellor Konrad Adenauer stressed the importance of the American tour in a letter dated 13 July 1953, urging Furtwängler to conduct on it:

I am especially pleased that Berlin, whose fight for freedom is followed and admired particularly in the United States, is to appear in America as an ambassador of German culture. Considering the great importance that this first guest performance by a leading German orchestra holds for German-American relations, I and the German public would be delighted if you

171

could finally also decide to conduct the American concerts of this orchestra whose name, connected with your own, remains a reliable and beautiful concept throughout the whole world.[55]

Ambassador of German culture – that was not a problem for Karajan. What Furtwängler could no longer achieve was now to become Karajan's work and triumph. He had clearly formulated the demand he would make on the orchestra. He wanted the succession to last throughout his whole life. 'I will only discuss a lifelong contract.' It was most fortuitous that the tour's American organizer, Columbia Artists Management, sent Karajan a telegram immediately after Furtwängler's death to the effect that the tour would only go ahead if he agreed to conduct. Unseen hands had manoeuvred the orchestra into a tight spot. Karajan had a bargaining counter with which he could push through any demand he wished to make in Berlin, for in that city they knew enough about Columbia to know that the guest tour would go ahead with a German conductor, and that this conductor would have to be 'accepted and confirmed' by Columbia.[56]

Thus Karajan had the whip hand. No one wanted to jeopardize the American tour under any circumstances. Too much prestige stood to be lost. On 13 December the Berlin Philharmonic Orchestra passed a unanimous resolution in favour of Karajan. It read as follows:

All full members of the Berlin Philharmonic Orchestra believe they see in Herbert von Karajan the artistic personality capable of continuing the tradition of the Berlin Philharmonic Orchestra. They therefore request that their manager, Dr von Westermann, begin negotiations with the aim of transferring the conducting of the major philharmonic concerts and tours to Herbert von Karajan for a period still to be decided.[57]

The period on which Karajan was insisting had already been formulated, and thus Karajan was able to accept this serious offer 'with the greatest of pleasure'.

With the orchestra's decision Karajan had everything he needed. His preparations in reaching for the stars had been brilliant, everything had been set up with the greatest of care, and if managed correctly it could still last for a whole lifetime. But one obstacle remained. Karajan had accepted obligations at La Scala Milan, which clashed with the period of the American tour. Mattoni was given the difficult and delicate task of persuading La Scala's

172

manager, Ghiringhelli, that he would be doing a good thing if he freed Karajan from his obligations. 'That was my first really delicate mission' – Mattoni carried it off with diplomatic aplomb.[58] It comes as no surprise to learn that he had earlier considered a diplomatic career. The agreement of La Scala and its general manager released Karajan from the rehearsals for *Walküre*. ' "I understand," he said, "that this is a chance that you will never have again; you can go!" I shall always be grateful to him.'[59] Of course, he insisted on taking on the highly important tour as Furtwängler's official successor. The tour was to be a gesture of thanks from Berlin for the help they had been given during the blockade. In the winter of 1955 Karajan prepared for the tour with intensive rehearsals. The closer the departure date approached, the more worried he became: he had still not been officially engaged. Karajan, cautious and wary as the result of certain surprises early in his career, suspected intrigues. Wolfgang Stresemann, who spent many years as von Westermann's successor, managing the orchestra, noted in his fine reminiscences of great conductors:

> Karajan, highly suspicious by nature, believed that the Senate was hesitating intentionally to see whether the American tour was a success or a failure, a suspicion that he voiced to me on many occasions, but also once to the very well-meaning senator Tiburtius in my presence. Things reached crisis-point. Karajan went to Ernst Reuter [the ruling mayor at the time] and threatened to pull out of the tour. Finally they agreed on a solution that satisfied Karajan. The contract was to be signed after the American tour, but a press conference was held before it, at which Tibertius publicly asked Karajan if he would like to be Furtwängler's successor. Karajan accepted 'with the greatest of pleasure' and went to America with the Philharmonic.[60]

The American tour, patronized by Chancellor Adenauer, was a total artistic success, which led to another and even more extensive tour being organized for the following year. The tour was to cross the USA from Washington to Santa Barbara on the Pacific (from 7 October until 19 November 1956). The fact that Karajan and the orchestra's manager von Westermann were, on the first tour (27 February to 1 April 1955), exposed to violent protests did not stand in the way of a second tour. In New York the musicians' union demonstrated against the first guest tour. Members of Jewish organizations demonstrated against Karajan in front of Carnegie Hall, and tried to disrupt the concert. 'No harmony with Nazis',

'More good music without good Nazis' and 'They helped Hitler murder millions', read the demonstrators' banners.[61] They distributed leaflets to the people attending the concert, who were given heavy police protection. The leaflets conjured up Karajan's and Westermann's pasts, for example: 'Dr Gerhart von Westermann, manager, joined the Nazi party in 1933, serving in the key propaganda post of Deputy Director of the Munich Radio', or 'H. von Karajan "was an Austrian who went to Germany in 1932 . . . joined the Nazi party when he was under no compulsion . . . at a time when it was proscribed in his own country . . . an illegal Nazi . . ." As between the two musicians (Furtwängler and Karajan) on the record, Karajan is the more notorious Nazi . . . (Wm. E. Ringel, Chief of Security Section of Counter Intelligence in Austria).'[62]

With headlines and demands such as, 'The musical directors of the Hitler regime', or 'Music lovers, do not attend tonight's bloody concert', attempts were made to intimidate the audience and keep it away from the concerts.[63] Understandable as these protests may have been, it is difficult to endorse them. They were aiming at the wrong goal. Music is an apolitical art. The fact that it was interpreted by a former Party member did not change its nature. On a human level, Karajan's past could be held against him. But it could not be held against Karajan the artist. Anyone who believed that they could not or should not take on board music interpreted by Karajan was faced with only one alternative: to do without it, by refusing to attend concerts or listen to records. But they had no right to prevent others from doing so because of their own unforgiving attitude. That would mean summoning up the very same demon against which the actions were directed. Wolfgang Stresemann was right when he said:

> The deep wounds inflicted by Nazi Germany have still not healed completely – how could it be otherwise? – and to this very day a furious minority will not hear of the moving human examples set by such as Yehudi Menuhin and Bruno Walter. Anyone who spent the war years in New York will understand the attitude of this minority without endorsing it, in the hope that harmony and reconciliation, so appropriate to music and musicians, might still affect those people who are so justly embittered.[64]

It was no less a figure than Bruno Walter who extended the hand of reconciliation to Karajan in Vienna after the war.

When he came to conduct I told the president of the Gesellschaft der Musikfreunde, whose lifelong concert director I already was: 'You have a word with him. If it's unpleasant for me to be there I won't come to the reception.' And Bruno Walter said: 'Yes, but why? I will extend the hand of friendship to anyone who shares my opinion that people should get on rather than tearing each other to pieces.' And a very nice relationship came out of it in many ways. I had terrific admiration for him as a person . . . I also went to his rehearsals, watching how it was done. And what he had was this truly human warmth and goodness. He asked the orchestra to do things, the way you ask children; or with the pleading gesture of Mary – an invitation. That was something very strong with him. Very strong.

The close contact between orchestra and conductor throughout the American tour, and the success that resulted from it, swept all doubts aside: the orchestra recognized Karajan as their future conductor. As the bureaucratic wheels of the Berlin Senate turned slowly, the Berlin Senate's contract appointing Karajan as 'permanent conductor' of the Berlin Philharmonic Orchestra was not signed until April 1956. It was the most important contract of Karajan's artistic life. It made his career-utopia a reality. This contract made possible the realization of an artistic idea which was still vague at this point, and which was later to take shape in his Easter Festival. Karajan's contract was signed by cultural senator Tiburtius on the 24th, by Karajan on the 25th and by financial senator Haas on the 26th. The contract retrospectively established Karajan's post with the orchestra as of 1 September 1955, and obliged him to do nothing more than an annual schedule of six concerts with up to two repeats of each, as well as a tour of Germany and abroad involving some twenty concerts. This is almost incredible when we consider what Karajan managed to achieve on the basis of this contract, which placed him under the minimum obligations. Although Karajan was later successfully brought closer to his orchestra, the contract was not as yet formally modified. It still committed him to only half a dozen concerts a year. Karajan was later happy to exploit this state of affairs whenever he wanted to do anything that might be of use to him. Stresemann, who worked with Karajan as the Philharmonic's manager for nineteen years, notes:

Karajan was by no means disinclined to employ threats whenever he encountered resistance or when things did not go as he had planned, a sure sign of insecurity . . . The number of threats I heard Karajan make during the course of my work is considerable. Even his speech of thanks for the freedom of the city of Berlin concealed a threat, if a veiled one. It consisted in a comment – which, fortunately, no one noticed – to the effect that he could fulfil his contract (six double concerts) in a single short period, a possibility which he frequently used as a threat on other occasions.[65]

But now, when the contract was being signed, Karajan was not concerned with threats. Happy to have achieved his life's wish, he declared to the assembled press, 'I have the honest intention of continuing this work until I can do it no more, or until I die.'[66]

This declaration of loyalty to the orchestra and to Berlin was put to the test a few weeks later. Following the first major European tour with the Berlin Philharmonic and two concerts at the Mozart Festival in Vienna, as well as a celebrated guest concert by La Scala Milan with Maria Callas as Lucia at the Vienna Staatsoper, it became known that a contract had been signed between Karajan and the Austrian Federal Theatre authorities, making him artistic director of the Vienna Staatsoper with effect from 1 January 1957. Rumours immediately started circulating that Karajan had only used his Berlin post as head conductor in order to gain a foothold in Vienna, and that he would sooner or later abandon Berlin. The denials followed immediately. Karajan sent a telegram from Vienna: 'There is no question of any reservation with regard to this connection, which is dear to my heart. As I have proved my complete loyalty I should now request that the authorities involved finally leave us in peace to work and finally abandon the pointless intrigue of causing ructions between the orchestra and myself.'[67] And the management was quick to respond, 'without reference to all previous communications', that 'our conductor Herbert von Karajan' would conduct sixty-nine concerts during the 1956–7 season, and that he would conduct the Berlin Philharmonic for the first time at the Salzburg Festival in the summer of 1957. 'The close connection that he feels with Berlin is borne out by the fact that apart from his concerts in Berlin and our representative annual foreign tours, conducted by him, he will direct the conducting courses at the Berlin School of Music.'[68]

Everything was temporarily in order again, and the incensed and concerned Berlin public was put at its ease. Karajan would actually preserve his connection with the orchestra with exemplary loyalty. During the years to come he would put it at the head of the world's best orchestras, turning it into a high-powered machine made up of around a hundred instrumental soloists, with which he would achieve the luxury of perfect sound. He also had the luxury of doing whatever he wanted, whatever entered his head, as well as the luxury enshrined in his contract: 'The true luxury is that I need never be afraid of not being appointed again.'[69] Such awareness often leads to self-satisfied complacency – with Karajan, however, it became a stimulus to give his best and find existential meaning in the perfection of artistic work. He was primarily interested in artistic quality, even where others suspected the motivation of commercial interests.

He now had years of rapidly won fame behind him, while before him lay a musical paradise. With the signing of the Vienna contract Karajan had made a temporary peace in his unparalleled campaign, battling through every musical sphere of interest to win the most important positions in Europe's musical institutions. From 1957 until 1960 Karajan was at the zenith of his power. He was artistic director of the Vienna Staatsoper, lifelong concert director of Vienna's Gesellschaft der Musikfreunde working alongside the Vienna Symphony Orchestra, as well as lifelong chief conductor of the Berlin Philharmonic. He directed the London Philharmonia and was closely connected to the Vienna Philharmonic; he worked as director of the Staatsoper with La Scala Milan, and for this period he was appointed artistic director of the Salzburg Festival. A plethora of official positions and power such as Karajan now held single-handed was something entirely unique in the history of practising musicians. Nothing like it had ever existed before him, and it will probably not happen again for a long time as things stand at present. 'A single person should do the lot,' he told an acquaintance while he was still a young 'prodigy'.[70] Now he was that single person. 'So what does Herbert want this time?' his mother had asked, unable to hit upon an answer.[71] She never really understood her child. But it was so simple: Karajan wanted everything, for Karajan was synonymous with absolute demands. If we compare the course of Karajan's life with that of Hitler, we will make the astonishing discovery that both of them had attained dominance from absolute zero within around two decades. Hitler was forty-five years old when he was named 'Der Führer' in 1934 after the death of President von Hindenburg. Karajan was forty-six when he reached for the stars, his appointment as lifelong chief conductor of the Berlin Philharmonic Orchestra. Both careerists,

Hitler and Karajan, achieved their rise to power in Germany: and for both men, born under the sign of Aries, Berlin became the centre of their power. It took Karajan only ten years and no more to rise from the pit of post-war helplessness and despair, from the hunger and unemployment of the years of ruin, to reach the top. To win for himself the most important and influential institutions and to create the biggest musical empire ever to come under the sway of a single interpreter.

There is a basically frightening will to power behind all this, a striving for the greatness of a Caesar, and for imperial power. Karajan had achieved everything imaginable. But had he reached his goal? He was only starting. He was now standing at the bottom of his career, not the peak. Only now could be begin to build, artistically. Would he now be able to tackle the ideas in his head – the synthesis of perfection with a spiritually imbued rendering, the unification in a single person of interpreter and director, the 'democratization' of music, the global presence of his musical ideal of harmonic beauty in the service of the masses? Now, after he had won everything he thought he deserved, only now did the true work begin. Only now was life really beginning for the fifty-year-old Karajan. Everything that had gone before was merely a sloughing of skins, from which he always emerged strengthened and better armed for the fight. He assimilated everything that had been valuable to him at each phase of his development. He retained the good in everything. Even the Third Reich had brought him some 'good'. It was there that he learned, through daily observation, the techniques of propaganda and self-stylization. Now he had the opportunity to apply what he had learned in a grand manner. Karajan, who had never seen military service, set out on his campaigns armed with achievement on a solid foundation of quality.

But at what price did Karajan achieve his rise to power? The sloughing of his skins, which left behind a stronger armour every time, also extended to the private, interpersonal sphere. Soon after the stormy relaunch of his career, Karajan and Anita grew estranged and finally separated. Just like Elmy, Anita was unable to follow Karajan into success. They both lost him because they wanted him too much for themselves. That was an understandable but ill-considered attitude. Anita soon switched to other interests, and even other men. Karajan, for his part, gave as good as he got, particularly during their time in Milan. Around 1951–2 the crisis surfaced. Anita was impulsive, a woman who was very sure of herself, and also very dominant. When she entered a room she filled it. She turned the people present into supernumeraries to her entrance, pushing them into the corners, rendering them insignificant. This often removed the sympathetic aura that seemed to emanate from her at first glance. It was plain that this marriage would not go well in the long run.

Carl Gustav Rommenhöller, who knew both of them from their first years in Berlin, described the relationship between Herbert and Anita as follows:

> Actually Anita was the real Frau von Karajan. She was basically the right wife for him. However – and she told me this herself just before the wedding, she said: 'You know, you can work it out, of one hundred per cent of Herbert's life ninety per cent is made up of music. And women, sport, speed and other interests are divided up in the remaining ten per cent.' She really understood that, but at a particular time in her life it wasn't enough for her. She is a very strong personality, open-minded, not easy either, she was always difficult. I met her when she was eighteen. Perhaps she didn't recognize clearly enough that one part of Karajan's ten per cent is more than a hundred per cent for many other men. She probably understood that too late.[72]

Faced with the intensity with which Karajan pursued his career, which he saw almost as a mission, Anita felt, at the peak of her physical maturity, that Karajan did not need her enough. A vacuum inevitably formed, which Karajan was neither willing nor able to fill. Like her predecessor Elmy, however, she did not marry again. She would otherwise have lost the resonant name of Karajan, and perhaps everything that made up her life and her personality.

> She was Karajan's only wife. The first one certainly wasn't, and the third one isn't either, according to Anita. She doesn't say she is still in touch with him, but she occasionally talks about things that have happened with Herbert: 'Herbert phoned me and said this and that,' so as to give the clear impression that she is still in touch with him. There is such a thing as wishful thinking.[73]

From 1958 Eliette Mouret would have her own experience of

179

the difficulties involved just as much in being Karajan's wife as in being Frau von Karajan. On 6 October 1958, in Mégève, Karajan married his third wife, the attractive blonde Frenchwoman. With this former fashion and photographic model he succeeded where he had failed with his first two wives: he fathered two daughters, Isabel and Arabel. But did he find happiness in this marriage?

The years of his rise were also the years of painful loss. At the age of eighty-two, Privy Councillor Dr Ernst Ritter von Karajan died unexpectedly of an inflammation of the lung. He was not to experience his son's great successes. In 1954 his mother died of a carcinoma. Karajan had to be fetched from Milan, where he was rehearsing *Figaro*. He stayed away from his sick mother's deathbed.[74] In so doing, was Karajan perhaps emulating another Olympian, Goethe, from whose biography we know that he avoided touching sick people and attending funerals? We shall not delve further into Karajan's dislike for imperfection at this point, but rather take a look at the further progress of his career.

Karajan set about organizing his empire. Now that he had everything he was able, from his position of strength, to abandon certain things. He rearranged his possessions. Anything superfluous was cut back. His collaboration with the Vienna Symphony was curtailed and finally cut off entirely, with the result that the orchestra, deprived of Karajan's discipline, returned to the ranks of solid mediocrity. The Philharmonia also fell victim to new, better and more dependable possibilities. The last concert with the orchestra to whom Karajan to a very large extent owed his rise took place on 2 April 1960. It had now served its purpose. Otto Klemperer took it over. Both orchestras were basically mere substitutes for things still to come.

On 26 July of the same year Karajan opened the Großes Festspielhaus in Salzburg with an opulent production of *Rosenkavalier*. The set was designed by Clemens Holzmeister, to whom Salzburg owed the world's largest operatic stage. The width of the main stage portal was increased from fourteen to thirty metres. There were 2,371 seats in the auditorium. What Karajan was opening was his own opera house. A few years later, once he had full control of the stage, he would realize the dream of his youth, the dream of his own festival. Paul Czinner captured the opening performance on celluloid, and less than two years later it was released in the cinema, the recording of an unforgettable staging.

180

For Karajan it was the stimulus to do things differently, and, as he saw it, better.

With the Staatsoper, Karajan took over a somewhat dilapidated institution which still remembered former glories. Routine and slovenliness were coupled with ill-will and intrigues into a conglomeration of incompetence and indiscipline that took a heavy toll on artistic work. Karajan came along to clear away the shambles and quarrelling that had taken root there. He was eventually to fail in this. Only in the sphere of his own activity did he succeed in putting across his ideas. What were his goals when he came to Vienna? Paul Robinson sums them up as follows:

> In response to his suggestion, leading opera houses like La Scala and the Vienna Staatsoper were to exchange their best productions. The Scala could thus be assured of idiomatic German productions, while Vienna would be able to enjoy idiomatic Italian performances. On top of this, the Salzburg Festival and the Vienna Staatsoper would reach an agreement by which the productions of the Festival, which took place in the summer, would be brought to Vienna in the autumn of the same year. The result would be an equal reduction of expenses for both, since they would share the costs of the investments; Vienna would thus be able to show festival-standard productions. Karajan also promised to engage leading conductors for a few months and thus get rid of second-rate kapellmeisters.[75]

His exchange programme with La Scala and his own productions in Vienna were personal triumphs. Many of them entered the annals as peaks of the age. Karajan, the egomaniac, took over the opera house so as to find artistic fulfilment there. What he failed or refused to see was the fact that during his absence the house needed somebody to take charge of it. He overlooked the fact that the time he claimed for his own projects was time lost to the necessary repertory work. He ignored the fact that an opera season cannot consist of a series of new productions and premières. And he failed to notice that the standard, the quality of an opera house is measured much more accurately by the level of its repertory performances than by outstanding luxury productions. He mistook the everyday work of the opera house, which relies to a great extent on its being responsibly run, for the passing fancies of a festival, which are almost entirely free of social concerns. Quarrels arose with the trade unions. Karajan's adversaries and those who envied him found him easy game. Vienna, the city where the conspiracy was invented, made life difficult for Karajan. Nowhere else in the world are people praised and reviled with such intensity and in such quick alternation. Karajan was not up to dealing with these conspiracies. His power slipped from him. In autumn 1961 the unions of his technical staff prevented the orderly running of the schedule with a series of strikes. Chaos had returned after a few years' absence. Karajan resigned, and was tempted back to his conductor's stand after a whole catalogue of new conditions had been fulfilled. The opera was to be autonomous, as he demanded, the areas of competence of the state authorities were cut back, and Karajan finally had the power to dispose of a proportion of the opera's budget. So that the administrative business might proceed as it should, a co-director was appointed, in the person of Walter Erich Schäfer. After one season Schäfer realized that he was unable to help. Egon Hilbert replaced him. That was the final straw. Hilbert quickly assumed responsibility in artistic matters, it was said. He thwarted Karajan's intentions.

Why? Was it a matter of revenge, its causes known only to Hilbert and Karajan? Or had the differences arisen solely out of different artistic visions? Let us remember: Hilbert was a member of that commission of experts that had stood up for the lifting of the stage ban on Karajan after the war.

Karajan was unable, while at the Vienna Staatsoper, to realize his plan for an international operatic association, a working community of leading opera houses which would exchange their best stagings on a rotating basis. Later too he was also unable to manage this because it was simply impossible to co-ordinate dates between singers, orchestras, conductors and the other artistic staff within a reasonable space of time.

After various internal disagreements, in June 1964 a difficult conflict arose between Karajan and the Austrian Minister of Education, Theodor Piffl-Percevic: after eight years of controlling the Vienna Staatsoper Karajan irritably picked up his hat and coat and left Vienna in a sulk.

When I saw that everything I had laboriously built up over eight years was not to be continued according to my wishes, when I was not to be granted the working conditions I demanded, I came to the obvious conclusion . . . I was probably the last individualistic operatic director with full responsibility . . . I shall not be swayed by anyone where artistic matters are concerned . . . Of course it helped me a great deal. For the first time in my life I didn't have to think about myself, but about 600 people: choir, orchestra, ballet, the entire staff; when you really have to deal with their problems it's wonderful. I told Lorin Maazel, my successor: 'It doesn't matter whether or not you like it, whether it's good, whether you have the feeling that it's wrong – you have to stick it out for as long as possible, for you'll see that things pick up incredibly for you afterwards.' But my time was over. And things happened to the whole structure after which it just wouldn't have been possible any more. Something like that, done in that way, wouldn't be possible today. I started in Vienna, and thought I might be able to do a festival there as something like my daily bread. It took me maybe four or five years before I saw it didn't work. Because they can't keep the best people there tied to the opera house for ten months. And it took me the last two years to see that if it's possible then it isn't desirable. Because a normal person can't bear every day being a holiday . . .

I will certainly never take over the running of an opera house again, because the existing system of the so-called repertory opera is growing increasingly dubious from the quality point of view. The years in Vienna finally demonstrated to me the impossibility of the opera business. I also doubt whether it will go on for much longer. And I see no reason why something should be kept alive when you've been convinced for ages that it can't survive for much longer, for the simple reason that the relationship between costs and the quality on offer is no longer correct. If a state is ready to supply the extra money needed for true quality, then the only possibility lies in finally spending that money on a truly perfect, wonderful production on television. Then everyone gets something out of it. I'm not arguing for the closure of the opera houses, far from it. They will always be there. But the opera with its repertories strikes me as terrible, which is why I finally said: there's no longer any point to it.

While Karajan may not have seen things that way during those years, in retrospect at least his Vienna regency appears simply as a further step on the path towards perfection. In Vienna he dealt as a director with Richard Wagner's musical dramatic works, using the possibilities provided by the best-equipped operatic stage in existence. What was for others the goal, the end of their careers, was for Karajan merely a stopping-point. Vienna became his rehearsal stage, on which, in the lap of luxury, he once more put himself to the test, at the highest level, before he finally reached perfection in Salzburg with his own festival. Or that, at least, was what he claimed.

In retrospect things looked a little less heated. In Vienna in 1964, however, heated they were. Karajan was deeply hurt that his demands were not met at the Staatsoper, and that they created such difficulties for him that he thought he had to draw his own conclusions. He saw it as nothing other than a personal affront. He did not see the actual forces behind it. And in all probability he did not want to see that the Staatsoper was not simply a luxury toy which you can pick up and throw down as the mood takes you, or some mediocre private institution at which you can play around according to the motto *Après moi le déluge*, but rather an enterprise every area of which demands careful administration and organization. It is impossible to avoid having the impression that Karajan misused the Staatsoper to some extent by subjecting it to his highly personal artistic demands. In any case he did not succeed in employing the most outstanding colleagues, either conductors or directors, although this would have been a minimum precondition for the continuous improvement and care of the business. Nothing outside his own activity as a director and conductor interested him particularly. Conflict and finally separation were inevitable consequences of his appointment. For the age of absolutism is past, even in a state opera house, in a society based on democratic principles and in which the unions increasingly call the tunes.

In a last attempt at communication after his resignation Karajan wrote to the Austrian Chancellor, Dr Josef Klaus:

> ... I feel obliged, especially since I was the first to tell you of the untenable situation in the Staatsoper, to inform you of a letter that I sent to the Minister of Education, in which I present new and important reasons why collaboration with my co-director finally became impossible. During the last few weeks I have put off negotiations proposed to me for as long as possible, and believe that in doing so I proved my interest in the matter and my deep loyalty to the opera house. If no satisfactory solution is found I will have to accept, to my regret, that the preconditions necessary for my artistic work will not be granted me in Austria, and that I shall be forced by this to draw the necessary conclusions.[76]

The satisfactory solution of appointing Oscar Fritz Schuh as

Herbert von Karajan with Germaine Lubin, Paris, 1941

On becoming head of the Vienna Opera House, 1956

With Eliette, 1963

Flying his private aeroplane, Salzburg, 1964

1958

Arriving at Orly with Eliette, April 1966

the new operatic director was not to be. On 23 June 1964 Karajan published the following explanation of the matter:

> ... After the collapse of all previous negotiations I was asked on 16 June 1964, on behalf of the Ministry of Education, to suggest figures whom I trusted. I nominated Professor O. F. Schuh – a suggestion that met with the most positive response throughout the whole world of music and gave me the guarantee that the artistic standards of the Vienna Staatsoper reached over eight years of work would be maintained and continued. I agree with Professor Schuh that the negotiations with him collapsed. Under these circumstances I see no assurance that the agreed preconditions for my artistic activity have been met. Out of loyalty and a desire to stand by my contract I shall fulfil the obligations I have already entered into. After eighteen years of work in the concert hall, after sixteen years in Salzburg, eight years as artistic director of the Vienna Staatsoper, on 31 August my work in Austria will come to an end.[77]

Imperially vexed, Karajan threw in the towel with a dramatic and theatrical gesture of unbridled fury. Insulted, he turned his back on home, fatherland and people. He punished the entire Republic for refusing him what he demanded. How is such behaviour any different from that of the child who turns away defiantly because its mother doesn't give it what it wants? On an earlier occasion in Vienna another Karajan had resigned all his offices when he didn't get what he saw as his natural right. It was Karajan's great-grandfather Theodor. Because the Minister of Education, Graf Thun, withheld from him the honour of making him a dean of the university in 1851 he resigned his professorship and offices. There was a tradition for this: the Karajans had had a tough time with the Ministry of Education. What the great-grandfather was unable to do his great-grandson finally succeeded in doing via a circuitous route. He finally went over the head of the Ministry of Education, if only to win justice for himself and his ancestor.

A great era was coming to an end. And also a time of misunderstandings and intrigues, as well as highly emotional public appearances. As artistic director of the Vienna Staatsoper Karajan conducted a total of 234 performances in the most important music theatre of the time, an annual average of 29. The naked figures cannot convey the musical glories, high points, failures and triumphs hidden behind them. And now they seemed to be of no

185

importance. There was sulking on both sides. Even the Vienna Philharmonic, with which Karajan went on a world tour in 1959, felt cheated when it came to their attention that Karajan had signed an exclusive contract with Deutsche Grammophon which would bind him for several years to the Berlin Philharmonic. The Viennese, on the other hand, were exclusively committed to Decca, so that the successful collaboration was temporarily interrupted. In the press Karajan was accused of a lack of love for his homeland and of 'Balkan morals', since he recommended that the Vienna Philharmonic break their exclusive commitment if they placed any value on future collaborations. Insulted yet again, the conductor followed his absolutist, inviolable sense of himself and produced the heaviest artillery in his own defence, finally firing his cannons on the noisy and ill-disciplined sparrows that tormented him:

> Because of the 'Balkan morals' which refer to Karajan's ancestors and the unscrupulous trading habits of Greek merchants, Karajan took the case to court. He denounced the journalists who had coined the phrase with regard to him. At the first hearing Karajan's case was dismissed. 'Balkan morals,' according to the court's definition, 'can be taken to mean rather crude morals, something like coercion, which may be feasible in a legal sense but are morally untenable and impossible amongst cultivated people.' Karajan brought the case again. This time the newspaper which had put forward the claim of 'Balkan morals' was found guilty.[78]

In Salzburg they immediately recognized the opportunity presented by Karajan's furious departure from Vienna: 'The people of Salzburg would rather not be considered Austrian than do without Karajan, the city's greatest son, "the greatest since Mozart",' was how the Graz newspaper *Neue Zeit* glossed Salzburg's loyal welcome.[79] The president of the Salzburg Festival's board of trustees, Landeshauptmann Dr Hans Lechner, sent a telegram to Karajan on 24 July:

> At once, with deep regret over your decision with regard to your work as director of the Vienna Staatsoper, I should like, in the name of the Salzburg Festival, to thank you for your loyalty to the festival! Salzburg will give you every assurance that in future you will find all the preconditions here that you require for your work, and which will perhaps enable you to consider your decision about Salzburg as other than final.[80]

Karajan was only waiting for this invitation, this excuse, so to speak. He did not need to be asked twice. It had actually been worth playing Austria off against his work in Berlin, and Vienna against Salzburg, which now became the beneficiary of the troubles in Vienna. In a letter of 5 August Bernhard Paumgartner, president of the festival and an old friend of Karajan's, suggested to the president of the board of trustees, the same Landeshauptmann Lechner, that Karajan be made one of the festival directors. 'I hope that from now on, in connection with the other directors, a team of like-minded artistic men will apply its forces fully and entirely to the achievement of the very best from the Salzburg Festival.'[81] Paumgartner closed his letter with a request that the necessary steps be taken by the board of trustees.

All of Karajan's operatic powers were now directed solely at Salzburg. With his departure from Vienna the collaboration between La Scala Milan and the Vienna Staatsoper also came to an end, and Karajan soon severed his ties with Milan as well. From now on he concentrated entirely on the project of his own festival. Here in Salzburg all his requirements were catered for. Only here could he realize his idea. He had three years to do so. In Salzburg he was also able to reap what he had sown. For here his imagination was not hindered by the narrow-minded matter-of-factness of a state theatre administration. Here his primacy was acknowledged. He was assured of the conditions necessary for the fulfilment of his demands for the highest quality. There was no room for mediocrity in Karajan's Salzburg.

A few things had changed in Berlin in the meantime. The Philharmonic had moved into a new building in October 1963, the new Philharmonie on the Kemperplatz. Hans Scharoun's boldly designed, ingenious architecture had become the model of a new form of encounter between audience and orchestra. Surrounded by spectators on all sides, the conductor stood right at the centre of events. It was a conception that met with Karajan's total agreement, regardless of the fact that the architectural division of the space, which took little account of acoustic concerns, impaired the hearing of the music from the very beginning. Might the opportunity for self-portrayal in a space conceived on the model of the circus have been more important to Karajan than an equally satisfactory acoustic experience for his audience wherever they happened to be sitting? Karajan used his full authority to back up Scharoun's design from the very start, and pushed it through, with vehement partisanship, against a hesitant majority in the session when the decision was made.

Was he perhaps exercising pressure, referring to his minimum contract and the disastrous possibilities that this could have had for Berlin's musical life? Over the coming years Karajan would reply to Mies van der Rohe's aphorism 'less is more' with an aggressive musical 'more is more'.

From 1959 Karajan resumed the collaboration with Deutsche Grammophon that he had started in 1938. From December 1961 until November of the following year, after a first mono version, he recorded Beethoven's nine symphonies once again, this time using stereo processes. It was one of his greatest financial successes. By 1977 1.2 million LPs of the Fifth Symphony alone had been sold, bringing Karajan and the orchestra a gold disc, a rare honour in the field of classical music. Karajan saw it as proof that his idea of the 'democratization' of music had fallen on fruitful and no less profitable ground.

Karajan's production of records with the Berlin Philharmonic Orchestra grew beyond all bounds over the following years. On his seventieth birthday he was able to show a catalogue of his recordings with Deutsche Grammophon that included the whole popular repertory, with repetitions in some cases, covering everything from light classical music to the showpieces of the great classics, and including more than 330 works on more than 200 different records. This is, of course, only Deutsche Grammophon's share of a production that had assumed colossal proportions. His recordings for Columbia, Decca and EMI-Electrola are legion. Until 1973 the recordings were made in the Jesus-Christus-Kirche in Berlin-Dahlem. Then they finally transferred to the Philharmonie, once all the requirements for the very highest level of excellence had been satisfied. Karajan's recording work with the Berlin Philharmonic was not connected to his contractual commitments as its head conductor. It was, all artistic considerations aside, a financial enterprise between conductor, recording company and the orchestral musicians, who participated on a private basis as the 'Berliner Philharmoniker', outside of their working duties as the 'Berliner Philharmonisches Orchester'.

This prolific recording work repeatedly led to accusations directed at Karajan and the orchestra that they were abusing their position supported by the state of Berlin in order to increase their private wealth. Along with this accusation went the demand that they should use part of their income from recording to offset their state support. It was said to be intolerable for taxes to be squandered on an institution which was clearly something of a goldmine in its own right, and which was actually self-supporting. Be that as it may: we still have Karajan and the 'Berliner Philharmoniker' to thank for a series of impressive interpretations, exemplary in their conception and artistic bravura.

In the mid-1960s Karajan began to approach the media of film and television in a practical sense. It was the next logical step towards his expansion into a global musical presence. Karajan was quick to recognize the importance of the medium of television for the communication of his musical message of the beauty of perfection. Leonard Bernstein's television concerts in the USA, often preceded by loosely written introductions, and in which he also sometimes performed as a piano soloist, had become something of an institution. His popularity, particularly among the young, was overwhelming. But he wanted to make more out of the possibilities offered by the new medium. Colour television had not yet been introduced to Europe. They made do with the aesthetic means provided by black and white contrasts. The series began with a timid experiment in the studios of the Freies Berlin channel, using Richard Strauss's *Till Eulenspiegels lustige Streiche*. Karajan was sounding out the televisual medium. Then he collaborated with the French film director Henri Clouzot. Among the films they made were Beethoven's Fifth Symphony and Schumann's Fourth. Now the Vienna Symphony Orchestra, which he had neglected over the past few years in favour of the Vienna Philharmonic, did pioneering and pacemaking work for him once again. It was a period marked by the yellow powder that was rubbed over Karajan's face and hands to prevent him casting a false glow on the screen.

In the studios of Vienna's Rosenhügel a period of ambitious filmic transpositions of symphonies and concerti was beginning; Yehudi Menuhin was another of those taking part. Clouzot and Karajan were concerned with portraying the compositional idea using the medium of film. They were studio films using the playback process, not television productions using the electromagnetic medium for recording images and a technology designed to create a completely new screen aesthetic. Karajan later abandoned the playback process when the technical facilities made live productions with no reduction in quality a possibility. These films were intended as a visual interpretation of what was heard, and it was hoped that the viewer would participate in the 'burning glow with which a score was translated into sound'. Karajan wanted to abandon the unconceptual filming of reality, the aimless tracking shots around the orchestra and the close-ups which he saw as arbitrary, the traditional visual communication of concert music. I remember many hours of testing, of lighting experiments, trying to find the right angles, at Karajan's first experiment in Berlin and during his filming with Clouzot[82] or his recordings in the Philharmonie, the endless patient waiting until Karajan seemed satisfied with the shot, only to see that it was unsatisfactory during the next attempt. No sooner had a shot been captured than it was rejected again. No sooner had Karajan found the right clip than he found one that was even more convincing. They were wearying hours of waiting for those unable to gaze fascinatedly, from behind the camera, into the wonderland of the very contemporary medium. In their best films the Karajan-Clouzot team succeeded in what they were trying to do: capturing the musical idea on a visual plane.

Karajan became the pioneer of the concert music film. When he thought he had learned enough from Clouzot he set up on his own. For Karajan was incapable of sharing. He had to do everything himself. Total artistic control was his motto. Karajan put all his ambition into the production of music and opera films which was to bring him unheard-of resonance and publicity. His concert tours in Japan with the Berlin Philharmonic in 1957 and 1966 opened his eyes to the opportunities presented by the televisual representation of music, barely exploited in any meaningful way in Europe.

In Japan, thanks to television, he built up what was perhaps his most loyal and largest congregation. The concert tours in the seventies were entirely in thrall to the medium, now in colour. In film and television productions Karajan completed what he had begun in the field of gramophone records: Karajan's empire increasingly extended beyond the confines of his local and institution-bound work. He first achieved a far greater effect through the medium of records. They had given him an unparalleled reputation in Europe early on, and finally won him an audience worldwide. To win an audience: this may be one of the main stimuli behind a production unlike that of any other conductor in the history of the performing artist. In the seventies Karajan set about recording live concerts by the Berlin Philharmonic.

'Out of the studio and into the concert hall' became his new motto. He sought to capture the directness of musical performance, of a conductor and an orchestra playing in a rapport with the audience. He wanted authenticity. And in the field of the operatic film, too, Karajan struck out in new directions. This process started with the filming of the première of *Rosenkavalier* for the opening of the Großes Festspielhaus in Salzburg in 1960. That was not how it was to be done. But neither was it to be done the way Joseph Losey did it with his filming of Mozart's *Don Giovanni*. 'I told Losey: "Some of the images were done wonderfully from a filmic point of view. But – it has nothing to do with the opera." ' For Karajan, the way to achieve an appropriate translation of opera into film lay somewhere in between these two poles. Opera films or filmic operas? The question is an empty one when applied to Karajan's idea of the right way to capture operas for the cinema and television screens. He attempted to display what he meant by this in his film versions of *Otello*, *La Bohème* and *Rheingold*.

> The visual representation of symphonic music is one of my main concerns. I am not after reportage, but rather the translation of music into images using aesthetic means, a visual interpretation of music with its moments of tension, its lyrical and dramatic values – allowing it to have a more intense effect on the listener. In the field of cable television and the video cassette we are facing tremendous developments. The new processes arising at present, some of them even extending to the field of holograms, mark an enormous step forward. It is quite clear that the development can no longer be stopped, and it is simply curious when people still behave so critically and want to return to a time long past. That is the future, it is going to come, and there is no longer any chance of stopping this development.
>
> The involvement of all the technical means we have at our disposal is justified by the very fact that only thus can our enormous demand for music be sated. I would need to live several times over if I wanted to reach as many people in the concert hall as I address in a single television broadcast. Music is a language that the whole world understands today, and which goes to the heart. I do not agree that it should be the preserve of a few connoisseurs – I find it unjust if only a little circle of people are able to go to operas and concerts. In this area we should think socially, in the good sense of the word, and give those who are less privileged, who don't have the opportunity of going to a concert, a chance to which they have a right. The musical experience should not be withheld from them. That's why I am so keen on these things. For the message

conveyed by music has an uplifting effect. It uplifts everything that is touched by it – it has the power to raise us from the lowest depths to the purest beauty.

On a walk on the outskirts of Salzburg I once fell into conversation with an old farmer who had recognized me and couldn't believe that he had met me there in the forest. 'I watch all your concerts, all of us always stay in,' he explained to me. The degree of openness and the education of people who haven't read anything before, apart from the Bible, perhaps (if they've read it at all), for me – and this encounter made that very clear to me – that is one of the finest achievements of our time – and the fact that anyone who feels like it basically has the opportunity not only to find out about everything, but also to experience it. The letters I get from viewers also indicate that we are going in the right direction with music films. For almost all of them say: 'The fact that we are able to watch has given us a far better listening impression.' If it's conveyed in the right way, anybody can understand music. That's why I'm very optimistic about this direction.

The 'democratization of music' and 'media connections' were the main concepts behind Karajan's striving for worldwide omnipresence in sound and images. Like no one else, before or since, he knew how to organize and technologize the making of music. He was constantly in search of new techniques of musical massproduction. He was fascinated by the idea of total musical information.

His departure from Vienna left him free to devote himself entirely to this idea. The first step in this direction was his tireless work at the microphones in the recording studios. He was to take the second, much more difficult step in the mid–1960s. The energies which had been misplaced in the quarrels at the Vienna Staatsoper were freed for the endeavour that was to crown his career as a conductor: the Easter Festival in Salzburg. Using all available media and means, Karajan set about realizing the festival. The obstacles were many and varied – there were people who envied him in Salzburg, too – and his influence was no less significant for that. Karajan finally won through. His idea was the organization, every Easter and on his own account, of annual operatic productions and concerts at the very highest artistic level in the Großes Festspielhaus, using the Berlin Philharmonic as his opera and concert orchestra. The endeavour was to be financed by the advance production of records of the operas to be performed. This was designed to bring the rehearsal schedule down to a reasonable level. The musical aspect would already have been prepared by the time the stage work was being done, which is where the already available recording was used, replacing the barbaric piano on the stage, with the *répétiteur* thumping out a parody of the score with the tempos all wrong. Karajan saw the production of the record prior to the performances as the ideal starting point for everyone who worked on the project, particularly the singers, who were able to concentrate entirely on the events on the stage. An association of sponsors, whose members each received a signed record, were able to attend a rehearsal held especially for them and enjoyed preferential rights to buy tickets, was to give Karajan further means towards ensuring the completion of his ambitious plan.

> I imagine the future of big musical productions for the theatre as follows: first a gramophone record, so that the music is already there down to the smallest detail when we are doing the subsequent staging. After that comes the film and television recording . . . Everything I have in my head will be made possible in Salzburg in an ideal way. I feel committed to the house as to no other: here I was born, and here I should like to work.[83]

That is how things stood on 19 March 1967. That Palm Sunday, at five o'clock in the evening, Karajan picked up his baton, to make musical history with the production of *Die Walküre*. Hitler's disciple from the Bayreuth Festival, Winifred Wagner, gave the master her devoted blessing after the general rehearsals: '. . . I must request your permission to tell you how happy so inspired a rendering made me from the first note to the last. You conducted the work with the anguish of your soul . . . For me the climaxes were 'Winterstürme', the scene with Fricka, Wotan's Narration and his Farewell! – For this rendering my most enthusiastic thanks.'[84] A lifelong dream of artistic independence was being fulfilled. It was the moment of great and intense satisfaction. The performance was a single powerful exhalation after a life of stubborn effort. The city's great son, who had travelled the world as a young and unknown conductor in order to make his fortune, had found his way home to conclude his career as the world's most celebrated and famous conductor. Karajan *père* had had the teaching post he had deserved withheld from him. The insult to the father was an insult to the son. Karajan wrought his revenge. He had won the world's attention. Now he stood right at the top, there was nowhere higher to go. He was answerable to no one, because he was standing up there at the summit, with his own blessing. It was his festival and his responsibility. It was the result of decades of work on the music and the best possible rendering of the music. In Salzburg he reached perfection in terms of his internal and external possibilities, and in this perfection he found fulfilment.

At the age of fifty-nine Karajan returned to the city of his birth in order to experience his monomaniac dream of the Festival of Festivals. In the years that followed he produced his interpretations, matured over decades, of Richard Wagner's music dramas under his total artistic control as conductor and director. Along with his set-designer Günther Schneider-Siemssen and a little team of very close collaborators, Karajan created an artistic triumph with the staging of Wagner's *Ring des Nibelungen*, which made up for all the setbacks that had afflicted him throughout his life. It was the truly great success for which he had always striven, for which he had lived.

Now, as he himself never tired of saying, he was

entirely happy and content. Because in Salzburg we are working in an atmosphere that could not be created in a normal opera house. There you are in the midst of chaos. In Salzburg we practically get a year's work done in nine days. There is a true team-spirit atmosphere. And that is ensemble theatre as I see it: people melting together because they are working together on a single task.

The inner harmony with which one does one's work, for example, at the Easter Festivals – which is basically a pure pleasure, and in which the month of rehearsals passes as if it were two days – couldn't come about anywhere else. After eleven months of preparation and excitement you are truly brimming over with it – and I live on it again the next year. I can't imagine, now I'm on the point of working through all of Wagner with my orchestra, that I could ever have been happy with anything else. For in Salzburg I am working under conditions which allow me to say: that expresses my idea, that's how it must be. If it doesn't work after that then it's all my

194

fault, because I wasn't forced into any compromises. But the fact that I can realize something the way I imagine it is something that makes me happy.

Karajan's unconditional belief in progress went hand in hand with an infallible gift for identifying the most feasible way of going about things. In the Easter Festival he created a working space that allowed him to flourish to the full. Only having to answer to himself, and freed from the handicaps of conspiring bureaucracy, the conductor and director of this big idea annually invited the friends and patrons of his festival to the most exclusive music festival in the second half of the twentieth century.

The idea of a festival of one's own, and if possible the most extraordinary one in existence, is not a new one. It is the interpreter's dream *par excellence*. On one earlier occasion this century a great man of music made this idea his own: Sergey Koussevitzky. What Karajan had fought and worked for for over thirty troublesome years came to the Russian conductor in a more pleasant way: through his wife's fortune. In Berlin in 1906 Koussevitzky first conducted his own orchestra. There, too, he founded the Russian Music Publishing Company, publishing new composers of the day such as Igor Stravinsky, Serge Prokofiev and Alexander Scriabin. Koussevitzky's musical empire expanded quickly. In Russia he founded his own eighty-five-strong symphony orchestra as well as a large choir. With these the eccentric conductor, far ahead of his time, oscillated between the cultural metropolises of St Petersburg and Moscow, where he organized his own series of concerts. He was the first musical organizer to put together music festivals dedicated to the work of individual composers, such as Bach, Beethoven, Tchaikovsky and Scriabin. He introduced series of chamber music and popular Sunday concerts, as well as the reductions for schoolchildren and students that we now take for granted. More than any other conductor in his country he worked for the communication of Russian contemporary music. His interest in new and very new music centred particularly on the work of Scriabin. In 1910 he overcame the initial resistance of the orchestra in London to give an enthusiastically received performance of the *Poème de l'ecstase*, and in 1911 he conducted the première of the *Poème du feu*, Scriabin's last orchestral work.

Koussevitzky's cultural missionary zeal reached a peak in his

195

musical tours down the Volga. They lasted five or six weeks, and led, in a steamer chartered for the purpose, from Yaroslavl or Tver to Astrakhan on the Caspian Sea. In this way Koussevitzky and his orchestra covered more than 2,000 miles. In all the larger cities such as Simbirsk, Tsaristsin (now Volgograd) and Kazan they stopped and usually gave two concerts: one of western European, the other of Russian music. The first Volga trip in the spring of 1910 was lent particular weight by the collaboration of the composer Alexander Scriabin. A second trip into regions otherwise cut off from high-art music was carried out in 1912. The third trip in 1914 was also the last: the war got in the way of Koussevitzky's plans for missionary work and colonization. In the end the revolution shattered all hopes of continuing the musical tours organized so magnificently and certainly to satisfy the most selfish pleasures. Koussevitzky then went to America, where he became a leading personality in the musical life of the New World until the end of his life and also devoted himself to future generations: his most prominent pupil was no less a figure than Leonard Bernstein.

At the beginning of the century Koussevitzky had made his vision of cultural missionary work a reality unparalleled in its eccentric originality. In this he was superior to Karajan. Koussevitzky recalls the failed rubber producer Fitzcarraldo who steamed upstream into the South American tropical forest in a lunatic endeavour to live out his ideal of grand opera. Koussevitsky went to the people as an ambassador of both new and old music. Karajan took some asking, before agreeing to a luxury offering of things tried and tested. His experiment did not lie in the communication of the new and the unknown, but in an attempt to obtain the best possible rendering. Where the former had been concerned to unite the pleasant with the useful, the latter sought a mixture of the culinary with the perfect. They matched one another in their efforts to bring music among the people. In his day, Koussevitzky had to travel to the people if he wanted to do something for the dissemination of music. In our own time, Karajan had records and television and other media of visual and acoustic dissemination at his disposal. Like Karajan, Koussevitzky was also a master in the use of publicistic media, but in his day only limited paths were open to him. He invited journalists, music writers and painters on his Volga trips so that they would promote his musical tours in western Europe and America. What Karajan achieved with his Easter Festival Koussevitzky had already, and with great originality, anticipated with his exquisite steamer trips through the

196

endless expanses of the Russian landscape. The thought of having his own festival had been an *idée fixe* for Karajan since his days in Ulm and Aachen. Where Richard Wagner had had the Festspiel-haus built in Bayreuth for the appropriate reproduction of his *Ring*, Karajan now matched him. The Großes Festspielhaus was 'his' opera house. Its stage was 'his' stage. The Berlin Philharmonic was 'his' orchestra. Even the works were 'his' compositions because, as he and many others believed, it was only through him that they attained true and valid reproduction. And as far as direction was concerned, all the demands he had made on himself found fulfilment: he was the director of his festival.

This is only logical: for anyone who, like Karajan, comes after decades of operatic practice to see that there is nothing more senseless than putting theatrical realization and musical interpret-ation into different, often conflicting hands, will be forced to conclude that the two areas should be united in his own person. Anyone who, like Karajan, sees himself primarily as a theatrical impresario will find nothing more natural than being director and conductor in one. This made things easy for Karajan's enemies, and often difficult for his friends. As his status as a conductor rose, his reputation as a director fell. Karajan the director was not, unlike Karajan the conductor, held to be the greatest.

It was not at first certain where Karajan was going to be able to organize his festival; Geneva was considered first, but this was quickly recognized as a compromise solution, abandoned in favour of Salzburg as the ideal situation, once certain obstacles had been removed. Karajan's decision to produce operas in Salzburg (some-thing that the Vienna Philharmonic saw as their privilege) with the Berlin Philharmonic, known to be a concert orchestra without previous operatic experience, first met with incomprehension and rejection. To a certain extent he brought the largest stage in the world to the city of his birth. It was thus his stage, and because this was the case, he was actually the only person who could place the opera house conclusively at the service of art. In a letter of 26 November 1965 to the opera house's architect, Clemens Holzmeis-ter, Karajan discussed the matter: 'Permit me in any case to tell you once again – as I have told the whole world – that your brilliant design and the equally brilliant realization have made possible the only building in which I can express myself. This is also the source of the idea of a new festival in which I shall find artistic fulfilment, both in preparing and in running it.'[85]

Karajan had every reason to show his gratitude to Holzmeister. During the building stage, in fact, he showed Holzmeister, who

197

had gladly taken up Karajan's suggestion of a projecting room, his less friendly side. Swearing by the acoustician Keilholz, Karajan thought little of Holzmeister's acoustic concept. There were tensions and quarrels. 'Karajan was suspicious of me; he was influenced by Keilholz,' remembered ninety-two-year-old Professor Holzmeister. 'He received me very frostily, very reticently. And Herr Keilholz was there as well.' Only after the final acoustic inspection of the Festspielhaus did Karajan agree to Holzmeister's work. ' "The rehearsal is over," Karajan cried into the auditorium, and turned towards me, where I was watching the tests from the stalls. "Herr Professor, I'm fascinated!" that was it. Not another word . . . The work was not easy – with the people of Salzburg and these small minds.'[86]

Vienna taught Karajan that meaningful artistic work as he understood it is not possible in an opera house in the longer term. The fights and quarrels with unions, staff councils and salary scales were unacceptable demands as far as his ambitions were concerned. Karajan set his model of the Easter Festivals against the increasingly ponderous and inefficient apparatus of subsidized theatre strangled by salary scales. The two things are incompatible, but success confirmed Karajan in his view that it was the right concept, at least for him.

What the actor Will Quadflieg said in his memoirs also applies to Karajan's understanding of theatrical work:

The extreme nature of theatrical work does not stop, for anyone involved in it – whether they be stage hands, hairdressers or lighting men – at being a simple employee. A theatre is not a factory . . . In the theatre it is not enough for everyone to deliver his piece of work in a clean and orderly state, keep to his working hours and receive his wages to the last penny. Anyone working in the theatre – not only the actors, directors and stage designers, but also the technicians, cloakroom attendants, craftsmen and administrators – needs enthusiasm. They have to stand by the matter at hand, the common effort. If, instead of this, they think only of their wage packet and their forty hours a week, something will quite certainly be lacking. Seen from this point of view, interests are too clearly contradictory. For what connects an unskilled worker, a hairdresser and an actor if not the common conviction that art and the theatre are extraordinary things which merit extraordinary personal commitment.[87]

For all his good intentions of complete financial independence, Karajan too was soon obliged to go in search of subsidies for his theatre.

I see nothing disgraceful in being subsidized. The grants for the Easter Festival have become necessary for the quite simple reason that the expenses – and this is something that many people will not understand – have risen continuously while ticket prices have remained more or less the same. I would have to raise prices, but I cannot do so out of loyalty to the festival in August. This would not be able to match the expenses. We started out with two hundred sponsors – and now I have more than two thousand. I could still get up to three thousand; but to do so I would have to throw out my loyal subscribers and tell them: I can't take you any more . . . I would rather chop off my own hand. I am now in a tight spot, whereby I could actually have a lot more money and have to throw it out the window because I can't use it because it would mean generally overhauling the structure. That's where the others have to come in. And also we're bringing in millions of schillings for Salzburg's tourist industry.

In Salzburg the catchphrase 'indirect viability' went into circulation. Karajan, the only interpreter capable in recent times of organizing a festival solely around his own person, fell back, after a short period of absolute autonomy, into the state of dependence from which he had attempted to free himself using every available means.

After intense attacks, chiefly from the Austrian public, which became increasingly frequent after the artistic débâcle over the performances of *Trovatore* at the 1978 Easter Festival, Karajan decided to make his escape in the spring of 1982 and after the end of the festival he gave the following explanation:

On 10 April 1982 members of Salzburg's provincial government and municipality held a conference with me in which we discussed the 'so-called' future of the Easter Festival. Contrary to a promise that I had been given, the result of the conference was leaked to the press, without my being previously informed. The result of this: factually incorrect, consequently misleading and entirely in line with the trend of the age, according to which, in the field of culture and particularly in the musical sector, people talk about things they don't understand. I alone had the idea of the Easter Festival, and over sixteen years I carried it out both artistically and from an organizational point of view. I see it as my duty to continue going down the same straight path. Nothing and nobody will change anything about that, and consequently as of today I assume full authority and responsibility for the financing of this institution as well.[88]

After the completion of the *Ring des Nibelungen*, his lifelong aim, Karajan scoured the operatic repertory for other suitable works; the Easter Festival, having been called into existence, had to go on, and the continuity of the work had to be maintained at the highest possible level. It was plain that Karajan would return, with his Salzburg productions, to something that he had been unable to continue in Vienna: the attempt to set up a pool of operas. He managed to win over Rudolf Bing of the Metropolitan Opera in New York for his plan. Their intention was to perform the individual works of the *Ring* for the New York audience in the autumn, after their première in Salzburg, in a gala week of opera. In November 1967 *Die Walküre* was performed thanks to the support of Eastern Airlines who contributed half a million dollars, and met with a rather reserved critical reception. The following autumn, on the other hand, Karajan had a genuine triumph with *Rheingold. Siegfried* was planned for 1969. But the collaboration which had just come into being was shattered by the strikes which paralysed work at the Met in the autumn of 1969.

Karajan did not manage to bring the impossible under his control. The idea of a working community of leading opera houses, circulating Karajan's staging, was primarily impracticable because both the various local conditions and his intended system of rotation encountered insuperable organizational problems.

Everyone wanted to do his own thing. At one point I had offers from six opera houses: La Scala Milan, Paris, Berlin, Vienna, Salzburg and the Metropolitan. But it was basically impossible because it looked as if each opera house was going to do a staging which would then simply do the rounds ... I only wanted to know how the others would react. Basically they were all insulted. And then each of them said: 'I can do it much better.' It happens every time: if one starts, then the others all

200

start copying him. That's what happened with the *Ring*: everyone wanted to do a new *Ring*, stagings no longer had anything to do with the *Ring*.

In 1970 Karajan included Beethoven's *Fidelio* in the Easter Festival programme. In the years that followed Wagner was honoured once more with *Tristan und Isolde, Die Meistersinger* and *Lohengrin*. While in *Tristan* he summed up the experiences gained during a lifetime's interpretation, his overwhelming theatrical success came with *Die Meistersinger*. In the closing *Festwiese* scene he managed to bring stage, orchestra and audience together in a single, like-minded festival community. He sympathetically exploited the massive dimensions of the stage, which extended into the auditorium on either side, and successfully gave visible and stirring expression to the idea of the music and the action. With *Die Meistersinger* Karajan achieved (at least in the closing scene) perfect harmony, both theatrically and musically, between idea and reality. The audience became a part of the staging, and was integrated within it as an element of the community experience that the production sought to convey. And at the centre of events, as paterfamilias, stood Karajan, guiding the whole production. Here he was the happiest man alive. You should give up while you're ahead, they say, when the climax has been reached. In 1974 and 1975 had Karajan not reached the stage of *non plus ultra*?

In 1976, at the ten-year jubilee of the Salzburg Easter Festival, discordant noises disrupted the harmony of Karajan's collaborative partnership with the singers and musicians of his grand festival, and for the first time they reached the outside world. The first commotion was caused by René Kollo's resignation from the title role of *Lohengrin*. He had difficulties with Karajan's directing, and perhaps also with the work itself. In the 1980s Kollo caused similar problems in the same role at La Scala Milan.

Kollo said in self-justification,

If partners work together, it must be possible to talk about different interpretations. I wanted to discuss things with Karajan; maybe I would have accepted his interpretation, after all, everything can be done in different ways. But he simply ordered me around. But I can't work without contact, for singing is something spiritual. Karajan is certainly one of the greatest conductors – no, he's the greatest. So I would have needed his recognition all the more.[89]

201

In Salzburg Kollo's departure was followed by the announcement by the bass singer, Karl Ridderbusch, who was singing the part of King Henry, that he intended to fulfil his contractual commitments in Salzburg but then resign from the Easter Festival, on which he had worked from the start. The tensions between Karajan and the two singers were made public with a certain degree of hypersensitivity after a serious illness which had left Karajan bedridden and unable to work for three months. Karajan had had a disc operation in the Kantonsspital in Zurich, had been treated there for arthritis and kidney stones and therefore had to call off all concerts between 7 December 1975 and 7 March 1976. At the end of the first concert after his recovery, in which Karajan performed Tchaikovsky's Fifth Symphony with 'his' Philharmonic in the Philharmonie, the long-missed head conductor was enthusiastically acclaimed by the cultural and political dignitaries in the audience (from the mayor downwards), and given standing ovations.

It may be that the severe illness and the risky operation on his lumbar vertebrae made Karajan even more sensitive. His delicate sensitivity extended beyond the sphere of music. There were entirely material reasons for his now public disagreements with certain singers. These concerned artistically divergent interpretations of the roles. As the conflict could not be overcome in the material way, however, because in artistic matters Karajan neither tolerated nor accepted either criticism or protest, it carried over into his private life. But this did no one any good. Democracy and participation cannot be implemented in art, at least not under the artistic primacy of someone such as Karajan. One person has to make the decisions: Karajan was right in this. But whether he always reacted in a humanly appropriate way when he encountered criticism, reservations or rejection is quite another matter.

In 1977 and 1978 Karajan was in addition forced for the first time to make artistic compromises. The desolate state of the market for singers obliged him to do so. For quite a long time he had been planning his new production of *Parsifal* – but the singers weren't there. Karajan tried to fill the gap with earlier Salzburg Festival productions. The alternative would have been to abandon the festival until the best possible conditions had been restored. Karajan decided in favour of compromise, and the critics, for factual or personal reasons which could hardly have been well-meaning, could not forgive him. In taking on the 'ancient production' of *Trovatore* from 1962, with which Karajan had toured Europe in the 1960s after resigning in Vienna, the 'paradox of the festival repertoire' came into evidence, wrote the music critic Reinhard Beuth with some vexation, reasoning:

> The important thing is not the Salzburg Festival rip-off. Worse things are at stake: namely the bankruptcy of an idea. The idea, namely, of allowing a man who is perhaps the greatest conductor of our time to work under the best possible conditions in order to achieve the best possible artistic results. Art cannot be calculated. Not even for Karajan. Art is something human. Karajan, who moved to Salzburg at Easter to teach the opera world the meaning of astonishment, has failed: the private concern has to be subsidized, the Wagner Festival has turned into an Italian *stagione*, the level of the festival has sunk to repertory standard. With the transfer of Verdi's *Don Carlos* from the summer repertory to next year's Easter Festival, the last trace of independence and importance will also be lost.[90]

The Viennese critic Franz Endler, too, who, as he himself said, never passed up an opportunity to 'point out the absurdity and illogicality of the Easter Festival as an institution', presented Karajan with his assessment of his festival on his seventieth birthday:

> Read Karajan's declaration of intent and the first eulogies of important critics who once brazenly compared the conductor with Georg Friedrich Händel . . . In these they spoke of financial balance, of the very best artistic conditions, of the most intensive rehearsal time. In 1978 the Easter Festival used up as much subsidy as any other spectacle in Austria . . . Here we must, I believe, establish once and for all that in the long run it is detrimental to the reputation of Austria, the land of music, if music lovers speak either angrily, or with boredom or pity, about the offerings of a man who is everywhere described as the incarnation of Austrian music. Herbert von Karajan is the only interpreter of recent times who was capable of conjuring up a festival from nothing entirely around his own person. He has the duty towards his audience to make this festival disappear again if his confidants can say that he himself is also no longer happy with the productions. He alone can do what no one before him could do. He can make sure that there are no more Easter Festivals. Might this possibility, which is also something new for him, not perhaps have a certain allure?[91]

In the *Salzburger Tagblatt* the critic Horst Reischenböck wrote about the Easter Festival as the 'Left-over Utilization Co.', which kept the entire production of *Trovatore* at a mediocre Staatsoper level, and considered this 'gastronomy-friendly, flogged-out production in its current version as an absolute low point in the history of the Easter Festival.'[92]

Joachim Kaiser, too, otherwise above suspicion as a critical admirer and eulogizer of the master, found praise difficult when he collected and formulated his thoughts about the return of Karajan's production of *Fidelio* to the Easter Festival programme. His article on 27 March 1978 in the *Süddeutsche Zeitung* was not much of a birthday present:

> We have experienced a catastrophe in sonic dimensions – comparable to the disproportion which, on a large and overly open stage, has already dominated Karajan's *Trovatore* and *Die Meistersinger*. And no production which showed personal relationships with the insistence of a Götz Friedrich could compensate . . . Thus things went no further than a mammoth, *Walküre*-like stage-set (Schneider-Siemssen), a sparse Karajan theatrical arrangement, with singers whose reward will be in heaven and with an orchestral brilliance that was sometimes forced, sometimes magnificent. It was almost tragic: the more violently and bitterly the maestro, no longer as silky smooth as he was, hurled himself into the matter, the worse was the failure of a *Fidelio* which, with reasonable sonic relations, could have been an event . . . [93]

What Kaiser is indicating here is Karajan's problem *par excellence*: that of correct proportion. Anyone who derives his sense of proportion from excess, as Karajan does, naturally runs the risk of never finding the right scale. At the beginning of the Easter Festival Karajan wrote the following message to his audience in the programme:

> If we consider what is constant in the sphere of interpretation, in the city where Hofmannsthal, asked in 1923 about the Festival which was still a novelty at the time, considered it possible 'at Easter or Whit or whenever', and wanted to include in it everything 'that is great drama: Shakespeare, Schiller or Richard Wagner', if one has the most beautiful and functional opera house imaginable at one's disposal for the purpose, and a team

of artists and colleagues all filled with a striving for the very best realization of an artistic aim, and constantly bring about that phenomenon that barely exists any more – the ensemble; if all of these forces, all this readiness and effort meet with the unique understanding of an audience that does not only receive, that does not only 'consume', but also inspires, if one can realize all of this in that city that gave one life and music, then one will feel the truth in the inscription on that Roman mosaic that was once found during the digging of the foundations for our Mozart monument: HIC HABITAT FELICITAS.[94]

Had Karajan been deserted by the happiness that lives in Salzburg just as much as anywhere else in the world? Were success and his life's work – one and the same thing in the case of the seventy-year-old Karajan – running through his fingers like water, through those hands that once had controlled his world? Was he now being forced to pay the price for the disappointment of his demands, for betraying his idea of a festival *en permanent*? Was he being reproached for letting his festival, designed to be the best, the most exclusive, the grandest in the world, sink to the level of a common-or-garden event, and slip into the ordinariness of the highly refined international music and festival industry? Would what Thomas Bernhard once wrote about the Salzburg Festival now, all of a sudden, also apply to the Easter Festival? A graduate of the Musikakademie and bound to Salzburg in a love-hate relationship brought about by early injuries, Bernhard warned in the mid-1970s that

> we should let nothing deceive us, for the art of mystifying the world, in whatever field, has been mastered here more than anywhere else, and thousands and tens of thousands, if not hundreds of thousands of people annually fall into the trap . . . In the summer, under the name of the Salzburg Festival, universality is feigned in this city, and the medium of the so-called 'art of the world' is nothing but a medium for deceiving away, just as everything in the summers here is nothing but deceiving away and dissembling away and playing away and so-called high art is abused during these summers by this city and its inhabitants for no other purpose than their common business interests, the festivals are set up to cover over the morass of this city for months at a time.[95]

Karajan's anti-Bayreuth had, beyond a doubt, got into a crisis in the second half of the 1970s. It brought 'a whole chain of disappointments',[96] as Hans Heinz Stuckenschmidt noted. The Nestor of German-language music criticism had extremely sceptical things to say about Karajan's idea of a luxury and élite aesthetic, which Karajan was at that time developing in a 'wonderful dialogue' with Joachim Kaiser:

> If what he is striving to do is realized, it will mean the collapse of the great culture of our ensemble and repertory theatre, which has lasted for almost two hundred years. Karajan cheerfully wants to sacrifice it to the festival and the idea of the star. I find this 'manager' concept extremely dubious. An aesthetic and a musical practice in which talk of mass media such as gramophone records and television is treated with the same seriousness as money, boxing and Karajan's insurance contracts with Lloyds (which forbid him to go lion-hunting or parachute-jumping), necessarily leads to the victory of civilization over culture.[97]

With the much-awaited production of *Parsifal* in 1980 Karajan set new standards once again, continuing the artistic success of the *Ring* cycle. He managed, at least musically, to penetrate the work, to bring out the score with a chamber-music precision that can only blossom from a musical intelligence honed and matured by experience. With *Parsifal* Karajan provided the interpretative summation of his work with Wagner. It was the balance of half a century of engagement with Richard Wagner's complete work, in the hypertrophy of which Karajan's addiction to grandeur and striving after power found a musical and theatrical equivalent.

Along with his Easter Festival, Karajan, who had very close connections with the Salzburg Festival as a member of its board of directors, also placed himself at the festival's disposal as a conductor and director. It is impossible to note all the numerous performances that Karajan presented before the Summer Festival audience. We might mention as the most outstanding events, milestones in his career as an opera conductor, Mozart's *Figaro* with Jean-Pierre Ponnelle directing, Verdi's *Don Carlos*, once with Gustav Gründgens in the Felsenreitschule (1958) and in 1975 in Karajan's arrangement, then *Boris Godunov*, magnificent in the fullest sense of the word, with the wonderful bass Nicolai Ghiaurov in the title role, and finally *Otello* and *Carmen* and, a thoroughly successful production, *Salome* by Richard Strauss with Hildegard Behrens, her strongest achievement under Karajan.

In the summer of 1981 Karajan brought out a new production of Verdi's farewell opera, the work of his old age, *Falstaff*. It was the opposite pole in Karajan's musical universe: in Verdi's most mature stage work Karajan the actor now came into consideration, the director who laughed along from his conductor's podium as the events on the stage went their twinkling way. *Falstaff* was the work in which Karajan was able to develop and display all the facets of his artistry. It was the work in which he found himself again, more than in other masterpieces of the operatic literature. If there was a cheerful Karajan, it was the one who conducted *Figaro* or *Falstaff*. It was here that he managed to get beyond himself and enter into the work, here that he effected the inter-relation between subtle cheerfulness and the intelligent indulgence that turned the rigid, inhibited star of the podium into Karajan the human being. But these were fleeting moments, and they were dissolved in the music and the irrevocable here and now of a successful performance. On the celluloid of his music and opera films, in the grooves of his records and the binary codes of his digital recordings he could not keep alive these moments of immediate presence, the unfathomable flair, the aura of his playing and the inexplicably brilliant charisma of his conducting and his formal organization, or the characteristically oscillating radiance and fascination of his personality as it blossomed through the transient development of his interpretation.

His work on *Falstaff* dated back to his years in Ulm. At that time the twenty-year-old Kapellmeister Karajan had first seen Toscanini on the occasion of his guest performance in Vienna with La Scala Milan, with *Falstaff* and *Lucia di Lammermoor*. It was a crucial musical experience for him. The degree of perfection and the harmony of the music and the theatrical presentation, in which Karajan found the true concept of direction, affected the young conductor, after the initial shock, like a drug which he craved from then on. When, a few years later, Toscanini performed *Falstaff* in Salzburg with Mariano Stabile in the title role, Karajan went to all the rehearsals and performances and fully absorbed the work in Toscanini's interpretation.

He continually changed the cast and actually went on working on them. I heard him do the work some forty times in bits. And that lingered with me and went on working, that is quite clear. Then I staged it myself at La Scala and at the Salzburg

Festival, and finally at the Easter Festival. If you keep working on these pieces for such a long time, you're so familiar with the problem that it actually resolves itself of its own accord. That was simply my luxury: I wanted to have an ensemble that really only consisted of actors, and I managed it. I am unshakeably convinced that Taddei, as he is now, is much better than Stabile was at the time, because he does not play the role: he *is* the role. Tying on a false belly won't work, you have to have a real one. And he has such a succulent way about him . . .

In the lifelong process of digestion and transformation he internalized the work so that in his old age he was able to bring it forth as something that had become a part of him. 'It's simply under your skin, I can't even think and there it is.' Having become one with the work like this, it was an artistic legacy that Karajan left behind, when, at the age of seventy-two, he captured *Falstaff* on record and then staged it again at the age of seventy-three, making it the most solid and mature musical and theatrical rendering of his career: the concentration of his lifelong work in the service of opera, and a résumé of his career as the most important operatic conductor of our time.

In 1964 Karajan had angrily turned his back on Vienna. He had 'finished with Austria'. But the people wanted its emperor back. He was wooed with promises that were worth nothing because they came from Vienna. He was courted. Karajan played hard to get. Chancellor Bruno Kreisky himself joined in the general efforts to win back the raging demigod. But first some old accounts had to be settled: outstanding compensation. The sum of three million schillings was mentioned. But there was also the matter of inner satisfaction. The return of the renegade was growing difficult. Karajan was playing for high stakes. If they wanted him, he thought, then they should be prepared to offer him something reasonable. He had long been prepared to conduct in Vienna again if they guaranteed him the artistic and technical conditions he demanded. At the beginning of the 1970s serious discussions were held. The idea of his return was soon generally flogged into the ground. The negotiations petered out. Karajan had clear demands and intentions: new productions in Vienna were out of the question. Instead, because of 'economic considerations', he wanted to transfer his Salzburg productions to Vienna, where they would be 'exploited to the full'. The productions were also to be made 'accessible to the broadest sections of the population using the most modern mass-media techniques', as the agreement finally worked out between Karajan, the Staatsoper and the relevant Ministry has it.[98] In addition, he only wanted to spend a few days every year in the site of his former triumphs.

Karajan was primarily concerned with television recording and the worldwide transmission of his Staatsoper performances. His return to Vienna was designed to strengthen the position of multimedia power that he had built up in the meantime. After a long period of discord and bargaining over new areas of power and money, by 8 May 1977 Karajan was fêted with ovations by an enthusiastic, hysterical audience as he returned to the podium of the Vienna Staatsoper after thirteen years of scornful self-exile. Before he raised his baton for the celebrated production of *Trovatore* with Leontyne Price, Christa Ludwig, Luciano Pavarotti and Piero Cappuccilli, he assuaged the keen desire of his thirsting soul with the thunderous waves of frenetic applause with which they greeted him. The picture of Karajan turning to look at the audience across the balustrade of the orchestra pit, his mouth half open and his eyes gleaming, travelled the world as an icon of return, the drunken joy of the moment. The return of the city's lost son – lost because he had been driven away – lasted nine days. Karajan put Vienna in a whirl with the model staging of *La Bohème* with Mirella Freni and José Carreras and Ponnelle's Salzburg staging of *Figaro*. After thirteen years of cosmopolitan ordinariness the opera house saw, for an extended week, the Karajan paradox of extraordinariness that was now the rule. It conjured up a transfigured and irrevocable era in whose reflected glory Vienna would bathe for longer than its envious pride was willing to allow.

Karajan had not come home, as Vienna imagined, he was only visiting, to avenge the wrongs he had suffered there. His return came too late to be a true return. A pall quickly fell on the musical joy that Karajan brought to Vienna. In 1978 a scandal occurred, when the planned Eurovision broadcast of his production of *Trovatore* was called off because the tenor Franco Bonisolli threw in the towel at the general rehearsal. In the spring of 1980 there was great trouble. 'The classic TV experience', as the advance publicity for the Eurovision broadcast of Verdi's *Don Carlos*, scheduled for 9 May 1980, grandly announced to the world, was called off. Broadcasters in fourteen countries who wanted to take the operatic spectacle either directly or in relay, had at short notice to dig around in their archives for replacement programmes.

What was going on? According to Karajan's version there were no legally valid contracts for television transmission with the singers taking part. Describing the embarrassing incident, he said:

I should first like to know why people sell products that they don't have. In the jargon that's called piracy. The Vienna Opera was not in a position to employ the singers, and in consequence they put a stop to it. There's no point in beating about the bush. For I myself have five unsigned contracts. Only so as to be entirely secure, I said, three days before the end of the Easter Festival: Please, I'd like to see a photocopy of the contracts and confirmation for the singers' rehearsal time. Then five void contracts turned up. No! For a moment I thought I was mad. Whereas in Salzburg we had arranged everything three years before the start of the rehearsal period, six days before the start of the rehearsal period they didn't even have contracts and dared to present me with that. Of course they all immediately wrote that I'd cried off. There was talk of contracts having been broken, and one wondered whether collaboration would ever be a possibility. And Herr Bacher from the radio station said: 'Let him have it, and perhaps we'll still get him.' Herr Bacher attacked me. At the same point I must be able to say how it really was. We wrote a communiqué but they didn't publish it. When we asked for an explanation they told us: 'Look, if you want to know exactly: we decided not to publish it, because Herr Jungbusch has to be right every time and you can forget what Karajan's been saying. Also we want all that to be dead and buried . . .' In Austria it really is just the way it is in Albania. There somebody can say anything they like with impunity, and the victim can't defend himself at all because nobody listens to his version. That was the first time in my life that that had happened to me.

That is Karajan's account of the Eurovision broadcast that never happened. Whatever inscrutable intentions might have been concealed by these equally obscure manoeuvres, the losers were the people they always are, and who they were once again – the world's opera-lovers. Once before, in 1977, Karajan blocked a Mondovision broadcast of *Don Carlos* from La Scala Milan, referring to exclusive rights over the singers, whom the television film and production company, closely connected to Karajan, would not release in this instance. The music-lover does not inquire into the background behind cases such as this. All he sees is that he is the loser, the one at whose expense the big deal is done – if necessary, even if it involves sacrificing what was originally intended. In furious articles in the press Karajan was accused of 'colonialist conduct'.[99] And the *Frankfurter Allgemeine Zeitung* commented on the non-event, under the headline 'Monopoly Culture', as follows:

> ... But in the most recent conflict about the direct Eurovision broadcast of Verdi's *Don Carlos* from the Vienna Staatsoper to fourteen countries, scuppered by Karajan, the crux of the matter is not the great Verdi conductor Karajan, but the apparently limitless high-handedness of the impresario, dictating to tax-subsidized culture what is to take place and what is not ... Whatever the individual personal situations and legal and financial structures may be, the annoying thing is that the very same musician who has in many ways stressed the importance of the communication of music through the media, via television opera broadcasts, for example, has been crucial in blocking these activities on the part of La Scala Milan and the Vienna Staatsoper, RAI and ORD. The private economic interests and the exaggerated monopolistic ideas of an artist, however important he may be, are coming into increasing conflict with the mission of publicly subsidized culture, and thus leave Karajan's idealistic and humanist messages looking threadbare.[100]

Karajan and Vienna: these were two things that would not go together, however much they tried. Something in the very depths of Karajan's soul and the soul of the Viennese ensured that there would always be trouble. There emerged feelings and actions which might be generalized into the abstract concepts of 'resentment' and 'conspiracy'. Playing people off against one another, secret deals, plot-hatching and backstabbing, envy and denigration; they cannot be imagined away because they are a part of the climate of Vienna, a city that has sickened and contaminated anyone falling for the ludicrous notion that it is possible to live in Vienna and remain a human being. The illness of that city which, in its effeminate fussiness, is constantly sinking into quarrelling, rows, envy and troublemaking, and which has engulfed in this morass everyone who has not grown up on it.

Once in Vienna, the same thing happened to Karajan, the most Habsburgian of all Austrians, having kept alive the *éclat* of the dynasty throughout our conformist century, having set up his own highly personal and absolutist, Habsburgian, Tsarist, Napoleonic, Caesarean regime, and taken the liberty of making excess the

211

measure of all things; he too landed in the Vienna morass, where, in a cut-throat, love-hate relationship, they heap all available filth or praise on one another, leaving each other either besmirched or anointed. Gustav Mahler and Karl Böhm had to suffer it, and much the same happened to Lorin Maazel. Karajan learned to live with it because, quick-witted as he was, he learned quickly. He lived well on it, because he was always able to turn a bad compromise to his own ends. But throughout his life he was pursued by the agitators of this swamp terrain on the banks of the brown Danube, people who call themselves cultural administrators and critics and, with pathological persistence, hurl themselves headlong into their great and unrequited love, unaware that if placed alongside the good, even the tawdry loses nothing by being denigrated.

If Vienna had ever realized that it is this characteristic and deep-seated complex that has always allowed the city and consequently the whole country to drive out everything great and outstanding, it would have recognized the case of Karajan for what it always was as far as Vienna and Austria were concerned: a stroke of luck. However, trapped in its morass, the city was too narrow-minded ever to resolve the Karajan misunderstanding. It failed to recognize that everyday and commonplace categories were now inadequate, and it would have had to make a massive effort of memory, thinking back to its great and long-gone past, in order to find the preconditions for unlimited suzerainty; it should have allowed itself the luxury of a generous soul and given Karajan what he desired. But a city, a people, a nation, which allows itself the luxury of a State Opera and at the same time drives out someone like Karajan has not deserved him. For Karajan Vienna was the murky pool from which he returned cleansed into the world, his world, the megalomaniac, melomaniac world of his Salzburg Festival, the philharmonic world of *Schönklang* and the synthetic world of the levelling, palliative and stultifying mass media.

A year after the Easter Festival was set up, Karajan founded the Herbert von Karajan Foundation in Berlin. His early media crossover work, in which no one else even approached him, was completed and continued in terms of scientific research in the service of music, and the encouragement of young people in the broadest sense. At the Research Institute of the Karajan Foundation for Experimental Musical Psychology at the Psychological Institute of Salzburg University, scientists examined the principles for a heightened understanding and experience of music both in the present and the future. This research investigated new directions in music therapy, as well as establishing and examining the principles of the preconscious perception of form. In annual symposia the foundation's scientific employees met for working discussions with invited representatives from various scientific areas, and answered questions about their current research.

The encouragement of the young was given new stimuli by the Berlin conducting competition, and by youth orchestras which met in rotation. The foundation of the Berlin Philharmonic Orchestra's Orchestral Academy as well as a singing college in Salzburg were designed to encourage and train talented instrumental soloists and singers. Karajan was quick to recognize that the training of qualified young people for orchestras and the operatic stage, particularly in Germany and Austria, his spheres of influence, was an urgent matter because it had for so long been neglected and inadequate, and in a far-sighted decision he therefore concentrated this distinguished pedagogical task, for the benefit of his orchestra, in his foundation – established with similar far-sightedness to nurture and transmit his posthumous fame.

Alongside the Easter Festival, from 1973 Karajan regularly sent out invitations to the second Salzburg festival that he alone controlled – the Whitsun Concerts. This three-day series of concerts quickly became an indispensable part of the Salzburg Festival. Every year Karajan performed a programme with the Berlin Philharmonic Orchestra, either thematically coordinated or concentrating on the work of a particular composer.

The loss of his position of power in Vienna in 1964 forced Karajan to consolidate his musical empire. He had used his position cautiously and to his advantage: less became more. As he grew older and developed a greater understanding of how to concentrate on important matters, he rid himself of unnecessary ballast. His former wild and hectic switching between foreign orchestras, his rushed concert work with the various orchestras under his control was from now on increasingly restricted to his work with the Berlin Philharmonic. With them he entered the world as the ambassador of great music and a noble craft. In the 1970s alone he made four extended trips to Japan, his largest market outside Europe. In 1979 he accepted an invitation from China, and at the end of October and the beginning of November gave three concerts in Peking to an enthusiastic Chinese audience. This successful cultural exchange found its finest expression in a concert in which the Berlin Philharmonic joined forces with their colleagues in the Philharmonic Orchestra of China to enjoy the

213

experience of making music together: this attempted *rapproche-ment*, this striving for a new understanding between mutually alien cultures, became the demonstration of the idea of international understanding through the conciliatory medium of music.

Karajan increasingly slowed down his collaboration with other orchestras from the sixth decade of his life. At the end of the 1960s he indulged in a two-year flirtation with the Orchestre de Paris. After a few records and concerts the love-affair was over. They parted as friends, and avoided each other from then on. Sporadic periods conducting foreign orchestras only underscored the tendency to fall back entirely on his Philharmonic. In 1967 he conducted a few concerts with the Cleveland Orchestra, drilled into world fame by George Szell, a man he admired. In 1971 he conducted the Czech Philharmonic in Salzburg. He played *Die Meistersinger* with the Dresden Staatskapelle and presented the East German orchestra to the Salzburg Festival audience in 1972 and 1976. This was enough for Karajan. These were nothing but episodes.

From now on he contented himself with the Berlin Philhar-monic as the concert and operatic orchestra for his Easter Festival and Whitsun Concerts, and the Vienna Philharmonic as the orches-tra for the opera productions he put on as part of the Salzburg Festival. The fact that he restricted himself to the nucleus of his collaborations doubtless has something to do with the difficult operation on his spinal column in the mid-seventies. If the concept is at all appropriate where Karajan is concerned, during the several months of his convalescence he passed through a kind of contem-plation of what he was doing, where he stood, what remained to be done.

> The operation was not only important as such, but really marked a clear break in my life. It wasn't so certain whether I would come out of it alive or as a cripple. Of course, that tore down a lot of barriers. At the same time there was also the simple matter that the practice of my profession has changed from the sometimes hectic effort it was to the pure joy it is today. I always have the feeling of sitting down to a prepared meal. Well, for many years I prepared the meal myself. But today I enjoy carrying out my work as I never enjoyed it before, and never could have enjoyed it, because one was simply confronted with too many details, which doesn't happen any more. If my hands work when I'm playing the piano, I don't give a thought to what my hands are going to play now. I have

214

a feeling, and it just happens automatically. Then it's basically easy to perform in a more relaxed and simple way . . .

A further painful event a few years after the operation on his spinal column may also have contributed to the process of contemplation and self-discovery that had slowly begun. In September 1978 Karajan fell off his conductor's chair during a rehearsal. 'I can't do anything about the fact that I've fallen down,' Karajan apologized. But it was an accident that could have been foreseen. Karajan liked to rest his feet against the side of his desk in a relaxed and easy posture. The inevitable happened, through a momentary lapse of attention, a clumsy shift of weight or a slipping of the desk or the chair: just having recovered from an operation on his vertebrae, as he grabbed at his baton, which had slipped out of his hand while he had been playing with it absent-mindedly during a short pause, Karajan fell heavily on to his bottom between his desk and his chair. It was pure chance that he did not shatter his pelvis and sprain his spine. Two nerves were injured, trapped. After that Karajan had problems walking and climbing stairs, and no longer felt safe on polished floors. He appeared at the desk of the Philharmonie at the Berlin Festival in 1982 wearing comfortable shoes specially made by a sports-shoe manufacturer. Even before he had properly mounted the podium, he stumbled, righting himself just in time. Karajan had grown truly frail. But the performance of Gustav Mahler's Ninth Symphony that 30 September 1982 was a memorable and great moment in the philharmonic musical spirit. In the closing adagio he created the impression that in the execution and sympathetic understanding of this work, perhaps Gustav Mahler's most profound music, he was achieving a renovation of the past, 'the gradual relinquishment of what has been, his acceptance of the irrevocable, his willingness to leave the past as something that cannot be brought back – in order, precisely in this way, to make it a part of his self-development'.[101] It would appear that Karajan, approaching his seventy-sixth year, was starting to mourn as well as to hope, something that had to occur if such performances, apparently filled with burning pain and heart-rending passion, were to be credible and meaningful.

On the occasion of his twenty-five-year jubilee with the Berlin Philharmonic Orchestra on 7 December 1980, Karajan addressed the following words of thanks, of which we reproduce an excerpt here, to 'his' orchestra in a ceremonial act during his concert in the Philharmonie:

215

Twenty-five years is a long time. In my imagination those years are suddenly condensing into a single second. In my life I have never been granted the opportunity to look backwards, I have actually always stood at the bows of the ship, and now that all of that is behind us, the countless efforts, the work, the joy in my work, joy in my contact with the orchestra, with which I have gone all the way around the world, everything has now combined into a single second, and is nothing but the awareness that the future lies before us. If you climb a mountain, the higher it gets the thinner the air becomes, and every step is more of an effort, sometimes ten times more. That is how things are for us now: the slightest improvement is a terrible hardship, because quite naturally there is that quality that can only be achieved over long, long, long years. But for us today, I may say, it has become our possession, and for that reason it is easy to look into the future and see how we could make it even better . . .[102]

Karajan's career is the story of an attempt to find truth and beauty in music by coming as close as possible to the ideal of perfection. Karajan believed the equation that beauty is perfection. With every available means, and in the face of all resistance, he devoted himself to this ideal with an obsessive courage and fanaticism. He prepared his own meal, so to speak, with infinite hard work and tireless effort. In his old age it was his constant source of nourishment, to the benefit of music. 'I have had a wonderful life. I have been through everything. And I am tremendously happy now, simply making music.' Is a man who can say such things about himself at the end of such a long and successful artistic life really what we might call happy?

'Yes, certainly. I wouldn't change places with anybody. Quite certainly not!'

4

On Staging

In the foregoing chapters I have tried to give a rough outline, with no claims to thoroughness, of Karajan's development and the most important stages in his career. Here and there I have indicated connections between the external and internal characters of this career. In what follows I should like to attempt to cast a little more light on these connections and reveal the close interrelations between Karajan's external and internal biography, since his professional career was inseparable from his private life. The two were densely interwoven, and their mutual influence was great. However considerable the risk of failure, I should now like to set about digging away, one by one, the many and various layers piled up on Karajan's personality, so as to penetrate to the core of his being.

Let us sum up: in the first chapter we learned something about the sibling rivalry between Wolfgang and Herbert von Karajan, which was subliminally present throughout his whole life and which stabilized into a fraternal relationship whose superficial character, geared towards mutual avoidance, was quite apparent. Wolfgang was always 'the big brother', and also saw himself in this role. Herbert vied with him throughout his youth. His musical ambition, awoken early in his life, at first appeared secondhand, and even the decision to study technical science in Vienna as his brother did leaves the impression of a kind of emulation. Beyond a doubt, Karajan was something of an outsider in his youth. He never found it easy to make friends or confide in other people. This fear of human contact intensified his feelings of loneliness, which drove him into the arms of music for consolation. He found refuge there. His tendency towards flight also appeared during his days as a student, at a time when it was very unusual to change one's course of study. After his failure in the field of technology he first of all wanted to launch out on a career as a pianist. Then, once he seemed unlikely to attain any degree of success in this field, he fled to conducting. Here discipline and dependability, which seemed to be absent from his technological studies, could comfortably be demanded from the orchestra. Thus the demand for perfection which he had originally made on himself found external expression.

The opportunities that a totalitarian state presented to an artist if his career was more important than anything else are revealed in the second chapter, dealing with Karajan's breakthrough and rise during the Third Reich. The way in which Karajan, once defeat had occurred, dealt with the conflict with his conscience that must have arisen from consequences of the Third Reich reveal a deep-rooted and highly stunted insularity and lack of insight. His inability to mourn was apparent in the way he replaced the past with fiction, denying it rather than dealing with it.

The third chapter, devoted to the construction of his musical empire, describes Karajan's rise, marked by power-seeking and unscrupulous ambition, to the top positions of European musical life. In his noisy departure from Vienna, intensified, by way of punishment, by the announcement of his withdrawal from Austria's musical life, Karajan's touchiness became apparent. The Easter Festival was revealed as a work of grandiose self-dramatization, realized with the unparalleled demands that he made in his monomaniacal efforts. This brings us to the true theme of this chapter.

What distinguished Karajan from all other conductors was the degree of self-dramatization which deflects the listener's attention from the music to the man, and turns him from an artist into a trademarked commodity. No conductor has outdone Karajan in self-stylization and self-dramatization. Herein lies his genius. But to separate Karajan the artist from his self-dramatizations, from his mystical fussing, his ritual incantations and dramaturgies, seems just as illegitimate and impossible as it is to separate flame from fire.

The discrepancy, so often apparent in artists, between inner ability, talent and the surface scenario presented to the outside world, was absent in Karajan. His talent was his outward persona, his outward persona his talent – because everything was dictated by self-dramatization. Karajan's primary talent was that of staging, of dramatization. His life was its own dramatization, and his person was turned by dramatization into a virtual personality, whereby Karajan seemed to be his presentation of himself. It was only through an act of dramatization, of staging, that Karajan became what he was. The Karajan phenomenon was less musical than it was dramatic. It was identical with the phenomenon of self-dramatization. Dramatization, of course, in the broadest and most complete sense. That was what he achieved in his life. Karajan's true 'achievement' was that of self-dramatization. It was there that he was great. But did he ever get beyond it?

It can come as no surprise that Karajan considered himself just as capable, gifted and outstanding a director as he was a conductor. Karajan never left any doubt that he saw himself as being more than merely a conductor. He was always concerned with the realization of an artistic presentation that went far beyond pure music. The idea of the *Gesamtkunstwerk* preoccupied him throughout his career. He saw it as being realized in the unification of the conducting, staging, sponsoring, entrepreneurial, researching and standard-setting artist in a single person. Part of his extraordinariness lay in the fact that he only ever followed his own lead, unerringly, in the long forward planning of a final goal, which he achieved in his Easter Festival and his worldwide omnipresence through the media of the electronic age.

No interpreter ever strained and organized his talent, his power and opportunities to such an extreme point in order to translate them into effects. No one else has ever made himself as ubiquitous as Karajan did, and no one else has ever won so much power and influence. Certainly no one else has summoned up such a continuous effort of will and such an extreme application of forces in order to become the person he wanted to seem. His desire was to play a leading role in the world theatre of the twentieth century, and his goal was to live that role. But the energy that emanated from him was not so much based in the essence of a powerful character as the show of strength of an insecure character, always in search of confirmation and recognition, oscillating curiously between suspicion and the need for communication.

On closer inspection the Karajan phenomenon, that of self-dramatization, leads straight to the problem of greatness. We might wonder wherein his greatness lay. For it is not easy to be great in every field. Doubtless the concept of greatness is related to a measure of consistency, the purposeful intensification of one's

219

work and one's character. Barely any other conductors have been the subject of such countless legends, misunderstandings and misinterpretations. His work was to a large extent intended as a supreme exertion and effort, taking everything to its extreme. The absolute and clear recognition of unimagined possibilities, with which he pursued and to some extent realized projects almost megalomaniac in scope, such as his festivals or the unparalleled large-scale deployment of electronic media for an all-encompassing worldwide concert of 'music for the millions', reveals the multi-faceted nature of his greatness. However extraordinary his achievements and successes may have been, the problem of his greatness in terms of his powers of understanding and substance was determined in a different way: his motive for action was entirely personal. It was the obsessiveness of personal power.

The passion for power and command, including the sense of having art at one's command, was more apparent in Karajan than in almost any other interpreter, and was revealed early in his career. He had a lifelong romance with power. His great love was power, rather than music. He loved music too, but it did not come first. He loved music through the power that it brought him. Karajan's will to power, his will to totality, expressed, for example, in his demand for total artistic control, was an urge to power that overrode all morality: it was the will to totality at any price – even the price of integrity, as borne out by his behaviour in the Third Reich and its influence on his biography. His lifelong courting of power, however, was such a strenuous, absorbing passion that it left neither time nor energy for intimate dealings with human beings. Thus his relationships with other people always failed, were never anything but phantom relationships. He sought to balance the deficit left by this failure by achieving power. Other people were only ever objects whom he could organize in formulaic situations or roles.

He was just as incapable of true and lasting relationships in the private sphere as he was at making interpersonal relationships credible on stage in his work as a director. This is also the core of all criticism of Karajan the director. If singers such as René Kollo, Christa Ludwig and Karl Ridderbusch rebelled against Karajan, their rebellion was not directed against Karajan the conductor, but at Karajan the director. His 'inability to see beyond opulent surface effects in order to place the characters in appropriate relationships to one another', which had grown over the years, slowly became the downfall of the Easter Festival productions after the completion of Karajan's *Ring*. '*Lohengrin* and *Die*

Meistersinger suffered from blatantly faulty dramaturgical connections, and almost worse than this, mistakes' occurred in *Parsifal* where Karajan's direction was seen 'once more as the camouflage of the undistanced reproduction of disorganized core ideas'. 'Karajan's work suppresses the reactions between one person and another, and fails to deal with the breakdown of groups into individuals', and the 'aestheticizing, ritualizing vision' of his direction was sealed in *Parsifal* and the 'descent of the work to a panorama free of conflict, a consecrating drama with a dance interlude'. With the example of a late work Karajan demonstrated his own late theatrical style. 'Salzburg,' as Peter Cossé summed up his analysis of Karajan's art of directing, 'is also the place where the emaciation of the "opera" genre through to this *Parsifal* was subjected to a drastically falling curve. If displeasure was appropriate before, now all that remains is the stale after-taste of boredom.'[1] Where it was a question of passionate feelings and tenderness, Karajan's presentation was often curiously rigid and inhibited, frequently almost ridiculous. His arrangement of the scene gave the impression that there was someone at work here who was either afraid to unleash feelings (and what else is at issue in grand opera?) in the process of staging, or who could communicate absolutely nothing about them, because he perhaps lacked the necessary personal experience.

'Many years ago I became aware that I can only make music for a staging that I see as the visual expression of the music I am conducting. I need complete harmony. Today the stage is often merely an end in itself,' Karajan said. For that reason he located the work 'in the music, that is where it came from and that is where it should stay'. Karajan invoked the perfect harmony of musical expression and theatrical form and action without getting beyond the level of invocation. Kundry's kiss in the magic garden in *Parsifal* is one example among many. In Karajan's arrangement of the scene it did not appear at all, as if he was keen to resist everything that might, through its very passion, give some clues as to his own psychological make-up. The critic Karlheinz Roschitz summed up Karajan's style of direction in the production of *Trovatore* as 'puppet theatre', and thus characterized the problems and weaknesses of Karajan's stage arrangement.[2]

The striking lack of connection between the plot and the events on the stage, the lack of any psychological penetration of characters also makes its appearance in another sphere of his direction: in his music film productions. They strike us as so unrealistic and artificial because the images often bear no relation to the musical

221

events. They have a will of their own. 'In Herbert von Karajan's own television films the music is predominantly accompanied by Karajan's hands, Karajan's curls, Karajan's neck, Karajan's silhouette or Karajan's closed eyes.'[3] Karajan in close up: the imploring gestures of beautiful hands, a temple ostentatiously entering the picture, the skilfully styled, silver finery sitting atop it like a crown, and a transfigured or grimly resolved expression, assuming the attitude of a high priest's authority. But the inner glow of music-making cannot be captured in this way. The images turn into set-pieces, they are interchangeable and could be used equally well for any recording. For long stretches the images in Karajan's music films run parallel to the music, without any congruence ever occurring between the musical events and the action on screen. What we see is an almost motionless face, engrossed in itself, closed eyes indicating inner processes never transformed into images.

Karajan's dramaturgy in his music films is borrowed from the ritualized dramaturgy of self-dramatization, here placed at the service of a cult of visualized meditation and mystical experience. This is why his films finally leave us unmoved. The aura of extraordinariness that made Karajan's concerts such incomparable and unforgettable events is absent from his films. In the films, in their place, we are presented with the dramatization of the sensation of what it means to give a concert. For Karajan, television and film were just as much the playthings of his power as the opera and the orchestra and – in his private life – his aeroplanes and his ships, all of them subjected to his great will.

Karajan's appointment to the Vienna Staatsoper and his first concert tours with the Berlin Philharmonic in North America coincided with the last great flowering of Hollywood. It was during the years of the unfettered cult of the stars that Karajan managed to rise to the most powerful positions of European musical life. It can hardly come as a surprise that the over-sensitive Karajan picked up the currents of the time with his unique receptivity, and adapted them to his own uses: nothing worldly, glittering, sensational or poster-like was alien to him during those years, and so it was to continue. The construction of his career went together with the construction of a stylized world. In this Karajan was helped by his talent to use institutions and powerful groups of people for his own ends.

In Vienna he was able for the first time to use the psychology of the grand entrance, which he had already witnessed and had the opportunity to study in the Third Reich, to its full extent. He

222

ruled there like a self-confident prince imperial. The eight years of his regency were the restoration of the empire in the private sphere, its courtly veneer and gesture kept alive by Karajan, the emperor's former subject, into the second republic. From Vienna onwards, Karajan never kept this gesture out of his lifestyle. He integrated the formative experience of his early childhood, his encounter with 'His Apostolic Majesty' Emperor Franz Joseph, into his personal reality. He surrounded himself with an imperial household, a completely devoted staff, which confirmed his greatness. One does not become an emperor by means of imperial gestures, but by means of the fact that one's servants, household and people bow before one. The imperial household gave Karajan the support that he, insecure as he was, could not find in himself. It was also a means of escape, of withdrawing, of screening himself off behind the protecting wall of his very close colleagues.

Karajan's cachet as a ruler was not entirely of his own making – it was a product of the interdependence he shared with a submissive environment. Fame and success exert a magical attraction on grovelling people. They were attracted by Karajan's super-gravity, and hurled themselves at the master as stars hurl themselves into a Black Hole, from which there is no escape. The constellations closest to him were a collection of devoted people who were constantly around him and constantly at his service. They were the attendants at his Salzburg court, the Großes Festspielhaus, where Karajan occupied the first floor of the management section, whence he ran his empire. If one deals for a lifetime with devoted people, one becomes a mock emperor. For that reason Karajan could only employ colleagues who did nothing but what he wanted them to do. If this proved not to be the case, trouble quickly ensued.

Karajan was fundamentally a theatrical being. His life was largely determined by dramatic intentions. The older he grew the more intense it became, turning into a monologue about the relationship between the person and the mask, the individual and the role. It had, we might say, a fictional character, rounded out with borrowed ideas. These he found in the figures from the world's great operatic literature. When Karajan conducted the *Ring*, for example, or *Tristan und Isolde, Boris Godunov, Don Carlos, Falstaff, Otello* or *Don Giovanni*, it seemed as if he found himself in their characters. Then Karajan was Wotan, Siegfried, Loge, Tristan, Falstaff, Othello, the King of Spain, Tsar Boris or

223

Don Giovanni. It looked as though a vacuum was being filled with borrowed characters, stories, music and self-dramatizations: Karajan or the mastery of illusion over being.

Without a doubt: the opera, as the world of illusion, was the world in which Karajan lived. In opera, even more than in the concert-hall, he fulfilled his dream of the heroic life, of omnipotence over things and the mastery of the world, albeit the illusory world, of the theatre. In the opera his visions of omnipotence and greatness found total fulfilment. Not for a single hour of his life did Karajan abandon the primal mechanism of satisfaction that came from the pleasure of living out fantasies of omnipotence and greatness. In this world of illusions Karajan was released from the responsibility placed on his shoulders of entering into real relationships. In this fictional world of passion, tragedy, evil, beauty and greatness he was able to construct and live out his illusory relationships, without fear of the consequences. The entire illusory construction of his fantasy world fell with the curtain.

The world of opera became the stronghold of concealed identifications. The opera was Karajan's medium because it is the medium of the mock emperor, 'for the reproduction of everything visual. He was very strongly visual. And opera is, after all, the medium for putting the visual on display. That cannot be done with the orchestra alone. Opera is perfect for that,' said Andreas von Bennigsen, himself a minor master in the guild of existential illusionists. 'He would never hide in the orchestra pit. No. His hair at least had to be visible . . .'[4]

It was only logical that Karajan should have brought his Easter Festival on to the largest stage in the world. In the Großes Festspielhaus he could spread himself out in the true sense of the word, more than on any other operatic stage in this world. Mastery of the apparatus, the machinery, the co-ordination of the most diverse simultaneous sequences of events, the combination of all the individual actions and events into a solid, perfect whole – that was what fascinated Karajan about the theatre. He wanted the perfect, magnificent staging. And this was something that he had been able to experience in the Third Reich, where a 'New Germany', not without effect, was staged using every conceivable means. In Vienna and Salzburg what Karajan staged was personal omnipotence and indispensability. His artistic life followed the dictum 'all or nothing', in which excess became the measure of all things. He saw the world in which he lived only as the extension of his private universe, like a potentate, free from compromise –

224

and he was even right to do so. For once one starts to make compromises, one's artistic endeavours come to nothing. The consequences would be nothing but a string of problems from first till last, the search for solutions encroaching on the time due to one's own work. Rather than treading water, Karajan opted for an absolutist lack of compromise.

For Karajan, who was not good at making friends, the opera became the instrument through which he sought contact with people, an alternative to his reality – the incapacity to form relationships. Podium, stage and screen were the places where he felt safe. It was here that he acted out his parts. He played the director as well as the conductor or festival entrepreneur. As a theatrical being, Karajan was necessarily completely dependent on his audience. This forced him to make the effort to appear worthy of them, not to disappoint them, to satisfy their expectations. In order to achieve this he established his own standards, against which he measured himself and others. The demands he made on himself and others were never small – always absolute. His standard was the aristocratic ideal of achievement for the community. Accordingly, this led him to demand recognition, honour, dignity, the right of disposal and influence. Conflict ensued if these demands were not fulfilled. When the Viennese refused him his demand for greater influence and authority he first of all resorted to the threat of resignation as a means of exerting pressure. Deeply hurt when this too failed to work, he decided to punish the entire republic. The people were to pay for the fact that he was not to be granted what he demanded, led by his rigid ethos of achievement, in order to carry out his plans. Karajan never forgave this insult. When, on his return to the Vienna Staatsoper in 1977, some verses about Karajan appeared in the magazine *Neues Forum* 37, *Schnadahüpfl*, he reacted as insecure and humourless characters do: he was insulted beyond measure. Karajan demanded satisfaction. He made his reappearance on the opera podium contingent on a public apology from the then Minister of Education, later Chancellor Sinowatz, who had no option but to broadcast a nationwide apology for the literary attack of his cultural political adviser Fritz Herrmann on his Mock Imperial Highness. What blasphemies had been uttered by the author of these satirical lines? One of Herrmann's verses reads as follows:

Es scheißt der Herr von Karajan
bei jedem falschen Ton sich an

und wascht sein Arsch im Goldlawur,
anal sein g'hört zur Hochkultur.

[At every bum note Herr von Karajan craps himself, and washes his arse from a golden jug – you have to be anal for high culture.][5]

To insult Karajan is to insult the throne. And that called for the harshest punishment. Regardless of the fact that finding satire and satirical verses at all worthy of note is actually the sincerest way of thanking their author. Other of Karajan's contemptible attempts to preserve his cult of untainted dignity and greatness, whatever the cost – even the good impression that he was trying to sustain – are also on record. Thus Sir Rudolf Bing, the former director of the Metropolitan Opera, New York, reports an incident which brought Karajan's collaboration with the outstanding soprano Birgit Nilsson to an undignified end.

After the *Walküre* in the 1968–9 season she made a few pointed comments about how difficult it is to work with a humourless man like Karajan, and it got into the papers. Karajan wrote to me and complained because I had neglected to admonish Frau Nilsson; he demanded that she should publicly declare that she was entirely in agreement with his musical and artistic achievements. In my attempt to extricate myself from this dilemma I committed the big mistake of mentioning in a letter to him that her disagreement dated from the time before her work at the Metropolitan. Then [Ron] Wilford [Karajan's agent] wrote to me: 'The maestro says this claim is simply not true – during the fifteen years of his collaboration with Frau Nilsson he never had a single difference of opinion with her.' But if the lady in question 'would not express her regret about the comments attributed to her by the press, this would mean that she considered herself outside the group of artists that is a part of Maestro von Karajan's artistic world'.[6]

In his memoirs Bing also describes his personal experiences with Karajan, in which no human *rapprochement* was possible because of Karajan's incapacity to make personal friends.

I was never able to have a personal relationship with him . . . When . . . the first act of *Walküre* did not match his expectations at rehearsal, he did not, for example, come to me to discuss this problem, but telephoned his agent. I then received the following letter from Ron Wilford: 'Maestro von Karajan has just called me about the main rehearsal for the first act of *Walküre* which took place in the Metropolitan today. He asked me to write on his behalf and tell you that he found the standard of today's rehearsal unacceptable to him.' It is difficult to develop warmer personal feelings when collaborative work occurs on a basis such as this.[7]

Oversensitivity and humourlessness on the one hand and the inability to make friends and the fear of relationships on the other point to profound insecurity. 'I hate being surprised by things for which I am unprepared or which I do not understand,' was the admission of a suspicious and entirely insecure man – insecure because profoundly thrown – whose lack of self-confidence never let him risk entering situations outside his control. The desire for total control is all too understandable given such an excessive level of insecurity. Things unforeseen, surprises, had no place in Karajan's life. In order to have his world under control at all times he consciously arranged everything so as to render himself irreplaceable. In his Easter Festivals he achieved and consolidated this condition of irreplaceability in all important matters.

Karajan subordinated his work and life to a dramaturgy that peaked in an uncompromising self-fulfilment. Self-fulfilment exaggerated, in the visionary calculation of his own career, into an ego-trip, in constant search of nothing but his own ego. Karajan showed barely any understanding of the desires or needs of other people if they happened to stand in the way of his intentions. In contrast, his sense of the legitimacy of his own desires was all the more intense. The festival, the peak of this self-fulfilment, became the high mass of self-invocation and self-worship. The man in his life was Karajan himself. In the lonely fanaticism of his self-love everything that was not Karajan went towards nourishing an insatiable subjectivity. In the individualism of his unlimited self-fulfilment, apparently free of any human bounds, he strove to become divine.

The picture that Karajan painted of himself for decades, an image circulated by the million, was a self-stylization into which he had put a great deal of effort. It was the mask behind which he hid his own defencelessness. But the concealment and trans-formation of his own character was one of the fundamental efforts in his life. There can have been few people who have stylized themselves so stubbornly and ruthlessly, making themselves impossible to find in the process. Always concerned with erasing his traces, he lived in the constant fear of being unmasked. If this occurred, as, for example, when it was proven that he had twice joined the Party, both times early in the day and both times voluntarily, rather than being content to show his reverence for historical truth and factual proof, he made his escape into the realm of fiction.

Another fundamental effort in his life was his desperate search for recognition, praise and admiration. Constantly on the lookout for approval and acclamation, driven by an unassuageable urge and thirst for publicity, he did not manage to engage in any personal contact with his environment. Between himself and those around him he installed a dramatic staging through which all contact was first filtered and drained of its spontaneity. The following extract from a conversation is on the one hand characteristic of the difficulty that Karajan had in engaging in a relationship along any route other than that of his artistic work, and on the other hand it gives an idea of his fear of laying himself bare, a fear to which everything in his life was subjected. For self-expression and self-revelation would have been, for Karajan, a quite straightforward profanation of his personal dignity. We might also recall here, and not coincidentally, that Karajan was not a dancer. The conversation concerns the mountaineer Reinhold Messner.

Karajan: I don't know him. I would very much like to meet him. What he writes in the book about K2 has actually never been written before. A man laying himself so bare and writing with such openness: I'm really carried away by this.
RCB: So how would he get in touch with you?
Karajan: Well, we might hope that things would work out better. But he's probably setting off again – I heard that he rests for three months and sets off again.
RCB: He found his goal in mountains.
Karajan: Otherwise he would be brought down by his complexes. Goethe once wrote that he would have been capable of anything if he hadn't written. And conducting *Tosca* three or four times a year, or *Sacre*, completely takes these aggressions away from you.

When psychologists speak of rationalization they mean a process like the one expressed in these statements. It was not because

228

adverse circumstances made contact impossible and because Messner was setting off on another expedition that this meeting failed to take place. But rather because Karajan was incapable of making contact. He wanted to, but was unable to. He transferred the initiative to Messner, who knew nothing of Karajan's intention. As a meeting was completely impossible, it was necessary to wait for things to 'work out better'. And when Karajan mentioned Messner's complexes, might he not also have been referring to his own, which would have destroyed him had he not always had the refuge of music to escape to?

Did Karajan recognize in Messner – who said of himself: 'I'm an anarchist: I define my own boundaries and rules as far as possible' – his alter ego? Messner's confessions such as: 'I'm a Sisyphus' and 'I always have to start again from the beginning' could just as well have come verbatim from Karajan.[8] He recognized himself in Messner, who managed to accomplish the concrete efforts for which Karajan strove throughout his life. To be up where the summit kisses the sky, where nothing lies beyond: at the highest height, exposed to the final solitude, in order to find oneself.

Karajan masked his inability to engage in relationships by withdrawing, by turning away. He learned evasiveness and distance as a means of avoiding the dangers that insults represented to him. If Messner had proved uninterested by his invitation to talk: would this not have come as a terrible insult? Or was he perhaps afraid of a conversation with the 'emperor' of another sphere, who would have had no reason to bow before the maestro? Would he have been able to hold a 'human' conversation – for this is what it would actually have been? So the avoidance of human closeness was also a protective device. Keeping his distance, cutting himself off, staying in his shell; this was all the product of a correct estimation of his vulnerability and his incapacity to deal with reality. A refusal, the absence of expected approval or a lack of interest in his work and his character would have shaken his equilibrium, laboriously accomplished and preserved and constantly jeopardized. All his efforts went into averting this existential threat: 'The fear of rejection is very strong in me.'[9]

So Karajan was always in search of praise, and praised himself as the greatest. He constitutionally required this praise, the mass applause of the festival audience, the promotion campaigns of the record companies, the publicity in the glossy magazines as well as the approval of the critics. They kept him in a state of high tension, driving him ever onwards. Certainly his heightened self-esteem

229

was only confirmed by approval from other people. His dealings with the powerful men of his time, whether they were in the world of finance, politics or culture, bear witness to that. When he invited the former German Chancellor Helmut Schmidt to stay with him in Salzburg or St Tropez, or spent time with the former British Prime Minister Edward Heath, when he showed his reverence to crowned heads of the world, when he went for an audience with the Pope and exchanged a twinkling smile with Khrushchev, and when the international money aristocracy entertained him in their houses, the reason, beyond all possible affinities and interests, was that it was thus that he could stay closest to the formula of the highest prestige.

Always keen on international superstar glamour, Karajan used the self-same standards when choosing the sites for his houses. His summer house was in a sheltered bay on the Mediterranean beach of St Tropez. It was here that the world of beautiful illusion and idleness had its home, and where for years its most conspicious representatives, Brigitte Bardot and Gunter Sachs, had provided hot copy for a press in search of gossip. It was here that Karajan, with his yacht *Helisara* (which he exchanged for ever-larger models, ending up with *Helisara VI*, which brought him up to the supreme maxi-sloop size) was able to impress a sensation-loving and publicity-seeking audience and win attention for himself. It was here that he was able to dramatize his masculinity at the tiller and wheel of ships that grew in size as his success increased, sailing into the little harbour of the former fishing-village and berthing by the bobbing yachts of the *crème de la crème*, the top ten thousand. It was in this milieu of effect, of exhibitionism, superficial chatter and hedonism, in this world of elegant illusion that Karajan – and it should come as no surprise – first met Eliette Mouret, later the third Frau von Karajan.

Often unprompted, Karajan hardly ever failed to stress in his interviews that he was not a member of the jetset. It was an accusation that preoccupied him, and an accusation entirely without foundation. Nothing could have been more unjust than to call him a member of the jetset. Karajan was too refined for that, for he belonged to the super-élite. The jetset was important to him only in that he himself had become its supreme goal. Thus the jetset met, for example, at the Karajan festivals in Salzburg, where Eliette, the Maestro's delegate, assumed the social responsibilities and, as an intermediary, privately established the necessary, compensatory balance between art and commerce.

Karajan's winter residence was in St Moritz. Furtwängler had a house there as well. He loved the quiet of the landscape, the peace of nature. Far from the bustle of a busy world he drew on the experience of nature. Otherwise there could have been no reason for his house to be sited in the unspoilt, gentle wooded area between the Lake of St Moritz and the Stazer See. Karajan, on the other hand, resided at the other end of the fashionable wintersports metropolis: on the slope of Suvretta, lined with luxury villas. It was here that all the people who perpetuated the myth of St Moritz lived and mingled. The rich and powerful people of the time – Niarchos, Onassis, Agnelli, Conte Rossi, Heineken and whoever. On the Stazer See the unsettled and restless Karajan would have been engulfed in silence and terrified. In the social network of the illustrious society of the Suvretta community, however, he felt secure and concealed. Here, where hardly anybody knew the first thing about music, it was all the easier to talk about the important thing that moved his world: himself. Here he was also able to exchange information about the luxury private jets and helicopters with which these people flew into the frozen, white paradise of the lakeside landscape of the Upper Engadine. When is the Upper Engadine at its most beautiful? When, beneath a deep blue sky, in gentle sunlight, the larches give a golden glow and the air grows thick with the rich scent of resin. In autumn. But in the autumn Karajan's house was always empty. And in the autumn most of the houses on the slope of Suvretta are empty.

Friedrich Nietzsche, the lonely walker of Sils Maria, discovered the Upper Engadine as a refuge from the world's incomprehension. Karajan, at least in his own stylized version, followed him on his walks through the clear mountain air. But the staging of Karajan's solitude sinks into farce, because it corresponds not to the profound feeling of solitude born of the experience of contemplation, but to a hypothetical dramatic experience. This hypothesis certainly has a great deal of public appeal, however: Karajan in the pose of the unapproachable man, playing out the role of the solitary against the background of the wide and unfathomable Segantini landscape.

It can come as no surprise that the residences of a man whose existence seemed the very incarnation of a hypothesis felt strikingly impersonal and empty. Although they were most exquisitely furnished and decorated, they revealed nothing about Karajan. His houses in Anif, St Moritz and St Tropez had the feel of places uninhabited, dens of loneliness. There was hardly anything personal there, nothing of unmistakable character that would have provided a clue to the man who lived there. Everything personal and private seemed to have been banished from them. Karajan's interiors looked like stage sets. They were sterile and strange, interchangeable, second-hand, as if chosen by someone unknown. They had the stamp neither of personal originality nor of individual uniqueness. They told no stories. They were designed for defence and isolation. The library of his St Moritz villa, designed by the Berlin interior architect Paul Döhler, might just as well have been in the luxury dwelling of any businessman wishing to give the appearance of being well-read. In its order and tidiness it did not give even the impression that anyone had ever opened a book there: it was designed for representation, like all his remarkably pallid interiors, which looked like the reflection of an uninhabited existence.

Karajan's tendency towards self-dramatization and self-stylization, bound up with the loss of any critical vision of reality, penetrated his life and work on every imaginable level. Karajan, or life as staging: a life and a life's work can be brought down to this common denominator if we dig deeply enough beneath the levels of Karajan's concealment and disguise. The core of his being, thus brought to life, then revealed curiously puppet-like traits. It seemed as if it was moved from without, its impulses coming not from inside, but from a force applied externally.

One of Karajan's chief stylized images, the pictures of advertising and wishful thinking, was the touching image of the family, in which Karajan, discussing his role within the family, also included his role as the caring father of his orchestra. The stylization of this role reads as follows:

> . . . we have something here which can only come about over many, many years through a constant and unchanging – and I can really say the word – love, and we have become a family. It is not a matter of people playing under a baton; we are a family, all watching together to see how far we can get in making as much good music as possible. The readiness to make sacrifices, application, untiring application and, of course, human contact. You know, I'm now actually in the third generation among our members. Every time I'm told that a loyal member is leaving the orchestra, it's as if someone is tearing a piece from my heart . . . [10]

These were Karajan's moving words to the Berlin Philharmonic Orchestra on the occasion of his twenty-five-year jubilee.

Karajan was never lost for words when he took the opportunity to describe 'his' Philharmonic and his relationship with them. We might back this up by quoting another declaration of love to the Berlin Philharmonic:

I have made this instrument with a great deal of love and an equal amount of effort. And we have now actually become a single heart, a single soul. We are two partners, facing and respecting one another. This is the only way that this mass experience is possible, a hundred musicians joining together to become a single instrument. If you see an orchestra as being only a mass of so many people who have to do what you tell them, you will never attain the true joy of making music. When the Philharmonic and I rehearse, it's sometimes as though two friends were sitting down together to read a book, and asking each other what they felt about it. Our work is also built on the knowledge of what we have already achieved and experienced together. It is more of a discussion of what is still missing, and how a particular expression might be found. Then we also reach the creative moment – the most beautiful thing we can experience.

Grippingly put, and also genuinely felt from the master's point of view. But does it correspond to the facts? Is it not, rather, a series of invocations, appeals to the philharmonic spirit, so that friendship and human contact might yet arise after decades of partnership, by being magically conjured up? Karajan, beyond a doubt, always took the side of his orchestra, was always concerned with the private interests of his musicians, gave them medical advice and listened to their worries. But these things are quite natural when one has a lifelong commitment to an orchestra. It is also a fact that Karajan always ensured good treatment for the musicians in his employ. He had no hesitation in exchanging friendly words with people, shaking their hands, as long as they were inferior to him and consequently unthreatening, a confirmation of his status. Here he was jovial, revealed all his charm and showed his best side.

In many of my conversations with members of various orchestras, I often encountered a resentment, sometimes expressed openly, sometimes more discreetly, sometimes even quite forcibly, a quiet grudge hidden from Karajan, which contradicts his projected idyll of the intact family. Karajan was frequently accused of treating individual groups of musicians in a schoolmasterly way, leaving them feeling like sheeplike schoolchildren. Orchestra members, let us not forget, who had earned an international reputation and worldwide renown as members of private chamber music associations, as teachers or even as composers. They spoke of the impossibility of settling the differences provoked by this, the frustration caused by harsh rebukes, their displeasure over being drilled and spoon-fed in stick-and-carrot fashion, and with an often inappropriately catty and moody attitude.

It is true: voices were never raised in Karajan's rehearsals. But that did not mean that everything was fine. The occasional liberating and violent word might have been of greater benefit to the mental health of the high-voltage musical community than the apparently non-committal and friendly tone with which Karajan decisively suppressed the merest hints of insurrection. With the result that they sometimes seethed beneath their apparently placid surface. Fault was often also found with the lack of respect with which Karajan sometimes treated the decisions of the autonomous orchestra, as in the case, reported by Wolfgang Stresemann, of a horn-player whom Karajan wanted to force on the orchestra against its will.[11]

A similar event produced open quarrels between December 1982 and March 1983, which, in the Jubilee year celebrating a century of philharmonic harmony, almost brought an end to the orchestra's twenty-eight-year marriage with Karajan. The Berlin Philharmonic Orchestra rejected the twenty-three-year-old clarinettist Sabine Meyer, proposed by Karajan, apparently for artistic reasons, and because no agreement was reached in discussions between Karajan and the orchestra's management committee, Karajan threatened to take action.

'In accordance with my contract I shall carry out my duties in Berlin,' he told his beloved Philharmonic on 3 December, but also announced 'certain reprisals, which could seriously jeopardize the worldwide reputation of the orchestra, and, even worse, its considerable extra earnings: "The orchestra tours, the Salzburg and Lucerne Festivals, the recording of operas and concerts for television and film and the entire complex of audiovisual production are hereby frozen as a result of the given situation." '[12] The Nestor of German music criticism, H. H. Stuckenschmidt, commented as follows on Karajan's unambiguous offer: 'He is exerting heavy pressure. Malicious people are talking of "blackmail methods". The concerns at the centre of this are not so much artistic as

234

financial. If no agreement is reached, the orchestra will lose an income totalling millions.'[13] And beneath the arresting headline 'Dickey-bow thuggery', the magazine *Der Spiegel* contained the following words about the Philharmonic trouble caused by an internal pettiness which had been inflated into a matter of state:

The heady idea of the ideal partnership has lost its attraction. The unifying and inspiring sense of art of which Berlin had been so proud must now be long gone, and the co-operative affection, that much-lauded human 'touch' between Karajan and his collective, has long ceased to exist, or else the petty matter of a vacancy in the woodwind section could not have roused the whole élite apparatus against its father figure, and vice versa.

Now that the fracture has grown into a break, and straight talking has now become the rule in the Philharmonie, these ladies and gentlemen will finally have to abandon the fixed idea that they are inseparable. Their only harmony now is in their vain and excessive self-esteem.

So what kind of supposedly democratically organized orchestra is it that would bow for years to the absolutist allures of its boss, complying with his moods and becoming obedient to the point of self-renunciation, and would then, at the first audible crack, present the autocrat of the podium with the legal definitions of its right to self-determination and want, on top of this, to take the matter to court?

What remained of the touching and total devotion of Karajan the patriarch, if, unaccustomed to any kind of resistance, he peevishly shrugged off his entire life's work, so-called, when confronted with this kind of disagreement, and rubbed their noses in the source of their cash?[14]

The months of argument between the two parties were finally settled, at least as far as the outside world was concerned, with the engagement of the clarinettist for a probationary year, but brought to light a further crisis: that of the orchestra, and not least in the incomplete adaptation of a company of gentlemen to altered social structures. 'A hundred years of democratic process in the admission of new members resulting in the engagement of one single woman: no more need be said about democracy and the orchestra's opinion of women's instrumental abilities,' said the *Frankfurter Allgemeine Zeitung* under the headline 'Battle of the Giants'.[15]

235

Appearances deceive, then, and the image of the harmoniously united family has more gaping holes in it than a glimpse through the rose-tinted spectacles of Karajan's promotional apparatus might tell us. The relationship between the orchestra and its boss was probably rather more matter-of-fact than Karajan described it. This does not mean that the orchestra did not stand loyally behind the conductor, or was unaware of how much it owed him. There is no need to stress its obligation to its head conductor. With every concert, rehearsal and recording the orchestra demonstrated what it thought of Karajan as an artist. Although in the mid-1970s Karajan did tell the then Berlin Senator for Science, Stern, in response to the general inquiry about how things were with the orchestra: 'They are waiting for me to die.'[16]

Where people work, tensions always arise, particularly if the people are highly sensitive artists. The question is only how these tensions can be eased and smoothed over. As I found out from my conversations with certain members of the Philharmonic, there were occasional disagreements, sometimes violent ones, on this matter between Karajan and the orchestra. Karajan's difficulty – or perhaps his incapacity – when it came to seeing relationships in non-hierarchical terms, is apparent in the statements of some of the Philharmonic musicians. They reveal a high level of insularity from his fellow men. What was involved here was a fake sympathy for his subordinates. Being kind and helpful to one's underlings, or to people who have little or nothing to say to one, is an accomplishment that costs nothing. One can become socially involved at this level because it always looks winning and bears out one's reputation of treating one's underlings in a courteous fashion.

So it does not tell us a great deal if Karajan's immediate colleagues describe him as being tenderly and understandingly concerned with his co-workers. It was entirely in the interests of the 'boss' to break through the hierarchy from time to time, thus assuming something like human warmth and appearing to be a helpful man. He weighed up the benefits among people who liked to see the great master descending from his podium from time to time and making himself small, and the advantages which would accrue to him in the process. This corresponds to an attitude that was not unknown even among absolute monarchies, since it has all the trappings of personal strictness. This view is backed up by Karajan's tendency to punish people who seemed less successful

236

or talented than himself with a sense of silent contempt, and to fight off those who could become dangerous to him or disturb his spheres of interest with the full power of his inner defences, which he always kept at the ready.

Karajan was always quick to get rid of people once they had fulfilled their obligations. He seemed to see his fellow men as creatures to be manipulated, failed to perceive them as having their own lives, and perceived them as threats in their claims to independence. The specific type of conduct which led him in his professional life to drop his colleagues, and in private to drop his friends when he felt insulted, must be seen as a consequence of his inability to form lasting relationships. This also partly explains why Karajan found it difficult to make friends. The references to his 'friends', among artists, representatives of the business world and statesmen, which tripped quickly and easily off his tongue, are best ignored. They were barely anything more than phrases from public relations, aimed at stylizing the image of Karajan as the friend and confident of important men, and as the born leader who can keep any kind of worthwhile company. This showed Karajan up as a bad judge of character – as many of his long-standing close colleagues would attest – and 'also insecure in this respect, filled with a profound suspicion, so oppressive at times that one might have thought him suspicious of himself'.[17] In addition, he was 'often cool and dismissive, and also intentionally hurtful to a painful degree'.[18] And then there was also, as manager Stresemann was able to report, 'unfortunately a very angry, hate-filled Karajan if – rightly or wrongly – he thought he had good reason to be so'.[19]

Karajan had to pay for his bad judgement of character on more than one occasion, and punished deception, which was also taken as an insult, with hatred – although he liked to stress that he was unfamiliar with such an emotion. The break with his former general secretary at the Vienna Staatsoper and his later adviser, Emil Jucker, who could not get over this break and died shortly afterwards as a *persona non grata* of the Karajan coterie, falls under this heading. Clearly Karajan had never developed any sensitivity to the finer nuances of interpersonal gestures. The following example might shed some light on this. In Berlin, where I was staying in order to conduct discussions with Karajan, the management of the Berlin Philharmonic Orchestra once gave me a bottle of fine German wine, with the request that I should pass it on to Karajan as a present from the twelve cellists in the orchestra who, as an independent ensemble, had become a first-class musical institution.

237

It was one of the first bottles from a vineyard dedicated to the twelve cellists and named after them, and the intention was that at one of our working sessions Karajan and I should clink glasses to the success of the cellists as a result of Karajan's orchestral work. Unfortunately this was not to be: when I passed the bottle on to Karajan in the Bristol Suite of the Hotel Kempinski, his face froze. The bottle was put to one side. There was other wine to drink. I do not wish to go so far as to claim that it was unconfessed jealousy or injured pride that led Karajan to refuse to taste the wine as planned, because the twelve cellists had been remembered in a vineyard which now bore their name while he was unable to claim anything similar, let alone a Cuvée Karajan, which would have been the only suitable thing for him. But we may be looking in the wrong direction if we try and find the answer here.

Karajan's whole system of fake concern and sympathy always purposefully sought out those people who were unable to damage him, to whom he was superior or at least equal, connected with the primacy of his leadership: people whom he had under his control, or who could be useful to him in one way or another in his project of self-dramatization and the construction and maintenance of his legends and his myth. That was true just as much in the professional as in the private sphere. Karajan had long since ceased to select his employees solely according to the standard of their ability. His more immediate artistic staff was primarily chosen according to criteria which granted absolute loyalty to Karajan and submission to his unimpeachable position of total artistic control. He preferred to forego outstanding artistic quality in favour of a tried and tested standard, rather than have someone outvote him in artistic issues.

Karajan resisted persuasion, and did not accept advice without further ado. It took a great deal of diplomatic skill to persuade him of the impossibility or wrongness of a conception. Employing a great deal of empathy, one had to present him with suggestions and solutions in the most indirect way, so that he thought he had had the idea himself. It was an attitude that derived from a structural insecurity, and which was one of the reasons for his partial failure as a stage and film director. Just as he was not relaxed enough to take good advice which benefited the matter in hand without any fuss or delay, he was equally incapable of trusting others to do anything better than he could do it himself, unless he was unable to match their superiority and yet could not do without it. It may come as a surprise to the uninitiated that as well as directing Karajan did not also design the stage set and the

238

costumes: that would truly have been total artistic control. The only reason he did not do so may be attributed to his lack of talent as a draughtsman, a failing which Karajan himself regretted: he would have liked to draw caricatures. We might regret, for his part, that he could not. Who knows what Karajan's sarcasm might have given us in pictorial form. Karajan was always right. If he praised his employees, he always did it behind their backs, and then they were often 'the greatest'. Chiefly, in all probability, and not least, because they were his employees.

'An artistic career has to be built up laboriously and over a long period of time – it takes half of one's life. Creative work is something exclusive. It sharpens the senses, but distorts the perception of real values, because it feeds on egocentricity,' said Karajan, ennobling, to a certain extent, his uncompromisingly egocentric personality with the unimpeachable insignia of the fine arts, an egocentricity feeding on insularity and the incapacity to make contact with the people around him by any means other than the synthetic methods of dramatization and role-playing. It can come as no surprise that his self-absorption was such that he was unable to form any true partnerships existing for their own sake, and that his interpersonal contacts, however much time was put into them, went no further than pseudo-relationships, whether in the professional or the private sphere. Karajan was clearly incapable of lasting relationships with women. He married three times, and his marriage to Eliette Mouret, for all the trouble that went into maintaining the image of its constancy, merely encouraged the assumption that Karajan was barely capable of true, rather than purely illusory, companionship. We might ask, without false timidity, whether Karajan's marriage to a woman inferior to him both intellectually and musically was what we might, applying critical judgements, term a happy one.

Far be it from me to provide a gossip-hungry public with details from Karajan's private life, as I know them from my own personal dealings with him or via close friends. But I cannot avoid pointing out a few facts and observations from this marriage which are inseparably connected with Karajan the artist. Beyond a doubt the marriage to Eliette contributed to Karajan's self-dramatization and self-stylization in a way that should not be underestimated. Before I go into this in greater depth, it would doubtless be helpful to know Karajan's opinion of what his wife actually meant to him.

For me a wife is the absolute. I have thought about it many times. But neither can you classify it by saying: is she a friend, is she a comrade, is she . . . that gets you nowhere. All you have to know is: she is fulfilment and a complete necessity for a man. So I've never seen it any other way, and I can't imagine it being any other way.

Karajan aimed for the absolute, for his self-image and his image of the world were unrealistically perfectionistic. Thus, his wife too could be nothing less than complete necessity, the absolute. She became the Madonna, Gaea, the great omnipotent Mother Earth from which all things come and to which all things seek to return. She was the image of womanhood, which was not measured against reality, but which drew its deal from the longing for perfection in the unity of security. '*Das Unbeschreibliche./ Hier ist's getan:/ Das Ewigweibliche/ Zieht uns hinan.*'[20] What is this all about? Does it refer to the suppression of women by placing them on too high a pedestal, by restricting and de-realizing them into a principle of imprecise, infinite temptation?[21] Karajan was constantly in search of something absolute. He sought it both in music and in humanity. Thus, along with absolute approval and admiration, he also sought absolute love, which he took as meaning the self-same thing. He sought absolute love in Eliette, too, and thus showed himself unable to accept natural limitations. Their relationship, because of his, and, I believe, their structural deficiencies, never got beyond a *folie à deux*. But that was not enough for Karajan, because he had simply fallen victim to his own illusion about absolute love, and because the relationship finally proved to be less than profound. But it was not without a kind of purpose for Karajan. He, who had often been seen to be in a particular kind of conflict with his own masculine side, cured himself, so to speak, with a wife.

When he met Eliette he was at the zenith both of his musical power and his virility, his empire was at its greatest, in accordance with the biological fact that surface multiplication means greater power. It was the time of unchallenged and unbroken stardom, the glamorous era of Hollywood, which Karajan kept alive in the old world and later preserved in his Easter Festival. Eliette, Dior's star fashion model and a photographic model, the epitome of blonde, youthful attractiveness, corresponding to the ideal of beauty of the late fifties, was, in her sensuality and youth, the outer counterpart to Karajan's lived dream of eternal youth.

In his radical hedonism, part of Karajan's reason for taking

Eliette as his wife was her function as a status symbol, an advertisement, an accessory of success. His possession of her was less one of being than one of having. Woman as an absolute need became the quite concrete need to have her as an accessory, for example, in the running of his festival. Eliette's appearances at the festival were unforgettable in their ritualized convention, when, to the accompaniment of the astonished whispers of the festival audience, she would make her entrance on the arm of some fashionable man or Karajan's private secretary Mattoni, the theatre cavalier, walk through the packed auditorium and with remarkable solemnity take her seat moments before the epiphany of the maestro. It was the contrived entrance of blonde womanhood, the entrance which skilfully and effectively, as an act of applied psychology, prepared for the supreme entrance. When Karajan, in his Salzburg staging of *Parsifal*, had a troupe of long-maned blonde girls dance around the holy fool, this looked like a homage to Eliette on the part of Karajan the director, a homage to the apotheosis of woman as an absolute and a necessity, symbolized in the sensual and seductive round dance of lots of little Eliettes. Was it her resemblance to nymphs and sylphides, the outward purity and faultless beauty of Eliette, barely twenty at the time, that allured and conquered the forty-four-year-old maestro, who could have been her father? But what father would not secretly enjoy being tempted by his daughter, while he, for his part, seduced her?

Was it not this kind of love, based on a confirmation of self-esteem, that finally reduced his relationship with his wife to the level of keeping a household pet? Be that as it may: what a woman is left with in such circumstances is a life on a long leash, restricted to appearance and representation. The world of representation is always a fictional world. It is the phoney world of *Vogue* and *Town and Country*, of glamour, pose, illusion, glitter, wealth, superficiality and vacuousness. Here the only apparent dilemma seems to be whether one should go hunting pheasant or moorhen the following day, whether to drive the blue Rolls-Royce or the green Bentley, or whether to dine at Maxim's, Chez Max or – a chic thing to do every now and again – at McDonald's in Boca Raton. If Eliette was chosen as a 'glamour-girl' in the exclusive Corviglia ski club in St Moritz, this is another expression of her conflation of being and illusion, underscored by the high status bestowed on external matters, which tainted her existence and characterized the Karajans' relationship as the symbol of a glamorous world.

Eliette was a part of that world in which nothing is more

important than appearing in *Town and Country* in the illustrious company of, for example, Princess Caroline of Monaco or film actor Mathieu Carrière. In addition to her function as a mother, social hostess and housekeeper, Eliette's chief claim to existence was as a representative piece of male jewellery. The secret for which she longed and craved was to be found in the realm of male production: money, respect and power through achievement. She could have become a marquise or a duchess by marriage, as she seldom neglected to mention. Her life moved on the level of representation. A level on which 'there is only appearance, being as commodity',[22] but on which nothing is produced. This is not the place to discuss whether Eliette's paintings could truly be called 'production'.

Herbert and Eliette: a partnership based to a large extent, it would appear, on external appearance. It is curious that Karajan should not have chosen, as mother of his children, someone who shared his professional inclinations and interests in some form or other. For Eliette was neither musically trained nor intellectually educated and well-read, nor did she share Karajan's sporting interests. She did not sail, she did nothing in the way of sport, and she was afraid of flying. I remember a flight from Nice to Zurich, when she placed a little carved wooden madonna under her bodice as an amulet next to her heart, and, after lift-off, hysterically frightened by a routine turning manoeuvre, held a copy of *Le Figaro* over her head for protection with one hand, and with the other grabbed my arm in panic.

Elliette loved confirming the Oedipus complex in her male guests. Karajan thought the opposite question was more appropriate – did she perhaps suffer from a father complex? 'One must know who one is and what one is, and then one will be the most modest of all.'[23] That was the judgement of the famous wife of a great artist: Cosima Wagner, who, in the opinion of George Bernard Shaw, 'had no other function than the illegitimate one of being his chief rememberer'.[24] Eliette did not get as far as Cosima's judgement. At the age where one starts politely taking portrait photographs of women with soft-focus lenses, she made her first public artistic appearance as the graphic designer of the record covers of a jubilee edition, called the 'Karajan Edition', of the hundred best-loved orchestral works as performed by her husband. These record covers now bear details of the pictures that she had painted during the previous years in a spirit of cheerful dilletantism. Eliette's stimulus to paint came from her husband's records. 'Sometimes I feel very lonely, so I put on a record, pick up my brush, and I'm miles away for a few hours. It's like a trance. Then I'm like a *courant d'eau*, like flowing water.'[25] Intoxicated by the emotions of Karajan's orgies of sound, she summoned up her inner world to transfer it to the canvas. That associative dreaming, that sentimental and lulling rapture, immersed in the moods of uncomprehended music, stirred up visualizations of sound landscapes from the depths of the unconscious – for which Karajan had nothing but contempt, if that. For what, more than anything else, did he feel he had to destroy in himself? 'Traditions that we've been carting around for ages. A tradition that saw listening to music as a surrogate for the imagination. I would like music to be listened to for music's sake . . . You have to break with these traditions instilled from childhood.'[26] Now, in the Karajan household, they have fallen on the most fertile ground.

Eliette, as *The Times* had it, was trying 'rather against her will to ride to fame on her husband's coat-tails'[27]. Her introduction to the Karajan media package was, from the advertising point of view, a promising one: Herbert conducted, Eliette did the decorating. Together they produced a *Gesamtkunstwerk* from orchestral music and record-cover painting surrounded by the halo of beauty, wholeness and placidity. After all, what did Eliette say about the state of things in our chaotic world? 'Nothing but trouble and disasters everywhere! It doesn't do you any good to be thrown into a panic. Perhaps people should spend more time with art, with positive ideas.'[28] Well – that is easily said by someone who lives a wandering life of luxury, drifting about between the well-cared-for and well-supplied islands of St Moritz, Salzburg and St Tropez, far from reality and its problems; it's easy for them to put the demand for more art before other more imminent and urgent needs.

'Painting is a journey into my inner world,' Eliette confessed.[29] It was a world of idylls, flowers, dream cities, threatening storms and gentle fantasy landscapes disappearing into the distant haze. Eliette captured them in paint with the talent she learned from the master, Antoni Clavé, presenting us with an *œuvre* whose ground has a two-dimensional lack of perspective and depth. Eliette's painterly work might be understood as an attempt to give us a clear idea of what we might understand by the concept of 'women's art'. The outsider often had the impression that it was on this same two-dimensional, poster-like, pretentious, incomplete and vague level of her painting that their partnership was played out. What they had once had might have been ruined a long time ago: but the façade, the illusion of an idyllic family and an idyllic marriage had to be preserved. When the impresario and eccentric Andreas von Bennigsen said of Eliette: 'Saint Eliette – we should change her name to Mary,'[30] with his *bon mot* he captured Karajan's idealistic picture of womanhood just as much as the fall into the 'human, all-too-human' world that lies in between, and which, in accurate or inaccurate but certainly gloating love-stories about a lonely woman, found their way into the gossip columns of the glossies and the tabloids. Hélène Rochas, the perfume queen of Paris and Eliette's friend, once described Eliette's duty and essence as Frau von Karajan in the gentle style of French poetry: 'Herbert is the wall. And Eliette is like a blossoming clematis climbing up that wall and making it more beautiful.'[31] And if this wall is a façade, what does the flower care? It goes on climbing as long as it can find purchase there.

The promotionally effective pairing of the two artists – the conductor Herbert von Karajan and the painter Eliette von Karajan – into the musical and artistic media concern of a surrogate culture, also serves the stylization and mythologization of the whole Karajan world, in which everything is beautiful and noble and perfect. Eliette and Herbert with 'Scenes from a Marriage' in music and painting: a beautiful couple, they acted as the protagonists of this perfect world. But was it actually perfect? Was it not, perhaps, a façade like the Potemkin villages, with the yawning world of existential hollowness behind it? Whatever Eliette's life and Herbert's relationship with her may have been, it did not seem, in any case, either a full existence for a genius, not the unexampled community of life and work, the magnificent symbiosis of two extraordinary people that Richard and Cosima Wagner managed to attain.

Karajan fathered two daughters, Isabel (born 1960) and Arabel (born 1964). It is only strange at first glance that neither daughter enjoyed any profound musical training. In an environment geared to a large extent to the fiction of the theatre, of display and the imaginary, it is doubly difficult to acquire instrumental skills such as playing of the violin or the piano in a systematic, persistent and tenacious way. It can come as no surprise that in a family where the lady of the house saw music as an acoustic stimulus to personal hygiene, painting and daydreaming, and where in consequence the Adagio from Mahler's Fifth Symphony or Richard Strauss's *Don*

Quixote are used as a digestive after a heavy dinner or as an accompaniment to the morning wash, and where a theatrical atmosphere predominates (Eliette, for example, also loves to disguise her voice on the telephone, misleading callers, denying her own presence and claiming to be a visitor or a member of the family retinue), the children are not unaffected by this. Isabel, against the initial resistance of her parents, took the risk of going on the stage.

What Karajan was unable to bring to life in his daughters, a benevolent fortune sent his way in the form of the violinist Anne-Sophie Mutter. He took the prodigy, born in 1963, under his wing, and gave her every imaginable encouragement, making her into a kind of musical foster-child. It almost appeared that Karajan had found, in the precocious artist who first appeared at the Lucerne Festival at the age of thirteen, that pedagogical fulfilment that had been denied him in his own children. The years in which he guided the girl's development with a touching concern and fatherly care, leading her to musical independence and maturity as well as early world fame, may well have been the most beautiful and the happiest of his life. Every time the conversation turned to her, Karajan went into raptures, as he did in the winter of 1981: 'Little Mutter – now she's played her Bruch concert in Berlin. Well, if they'd closed their eyes there, they would definitely have said: That's a man in the prime of his life. That bite that she has now . . . And I assure you, there aren't three people in the world who could play the concerto like that.' And of the performance of Beethoven's Violin Concerto which they gave together, he said: 'You have to be thoroughly capable, and she is . . . I've heard it from Herr Stern now: No two notes in it are the same. You simply can't play it like that any more. That's over. The generation has passed where one kept getting faster towards the end.' Isaac Stern was far from grudging with his praise for the South Swabian prodigy: 'She's unbelievable', was his appraisal, when he heard the young violinist playing this same concerto in Paris.

The training of the younger generation is one of Karajan's favourite themes. It, too, is a major part of his self-dramatization. It is a component in the nurturing of the image of a lifelong programme aimed at posthumous fame, serving to secure that fame for an institution that he himself set up. For how could one's work be better preserved in the long term than by setting up a foundation? Foundations are institutional monuments to successful people,

245

which they hope will ensure their survival. With the Herbert von Karajan Foundation, Karajan created just such a monument in his own lifetime. To it he transferred one important area of his training of the younger generation: the Orchestra Academy of the Berlin Philharmonic and the singing seminars of the Salzburg Festival. Independent of this, more or less from his arrival at a pensionable age, he encouraged young soloists. We might mention, as examples from the nameless horde of Karajan's pupils, the pianists François Duchable and Krystian Zimerman, to whom he gave crucial assistance at the start of their careers.

One special case is the conducting competition held regularly within the context of the foundation. It is an extension of the care for younger conductors to which Karajan had devoted himself in the past. As early as 1955 he ran a conducting course within the context of the Lucerne International Festival – it was a unique exercise, although Karajan's biographies state the opposite. This Lucerne course was continued in one-day sessions that Karajan set up towards the end of the 1950s in Berlin, and ran on a more or less regular basis until the mid-1960s, first at the Hochschule, and finally at the City Conservatory. Most of them were restricted to a few hours of practical orchestral experience, and barely provided any scope for continuous, constructive work. The Berlin conducting courses were finally brought to an end when Karajan began to devote himself to setting up the Easter Festivals. In any case they were rarely more than a demonstration, at which Karajan gave the conducting student a few hints and answered questions. By then Karajan had no time to dedicate weeks at a stretch to young conductors, as he had once done in Lucerne. Instead he gave a selected circle of young adepts the opportunity to sit in at the rehearsals and recordings, and to learn by observation.

The conducting competition first held in 1969 was scarcely more than a façade, because of its administrative and organizational structure, even if Karajan did repeatedly stress, 'Some day they should have an easier time of it than I did.' Karajan left the selection and evaluation of the young conductors to a colourful assembly of judges on whose judgement he was able to rely. At the same time no one was in a better position than he to make the final choice independently and without the assistance of a jury with questionable expert competence. He alone was the man, the undoubted artistic authority capable of saying: 'This is the one, I believe in his talent. I want to encourage him, no matter what happens later on. I shall assume full responsibility for the choice.' But he was not cultivating a potential rival. Karajan was too

246

attached to himself to do that. With the foundation and its praise-worthy institutions he was not cultivating rivals, but a good reputation.

We have established elsewhere why Karajan did not make the jury decision of the prizewinner himself, but made it the result of an apparently incorruptible method of democratic selection: it was the fact that Karajan was unable and afraid to stand by his own opinion. It was the product of his tendency towards withdrawal and evasion, his fear of being tied down and his fear, born of insecurity, of being blamed in the case of an incorrect judgement. 'Karajan liked to avoid unpleasantness and preferred that other people should bear the responsibility, he kept away from decisions, where possible, lest they cause him trouble or embarrassment,' said Stresemann, summing up his experiences with Karajan.[32]

It is extraordinarily suspicious that Karajan had no need of a jury in establishing the talent of an instrumental soloist or singer. He listened to the young musician on his own, and made his own decision, spontaneously and alone. I saw this not least in the case of the French pianist Duchable. But in cases where no one could be more competent at judging than himself he refused to make the final choice and delegated it to a jury, which attempted arithmetically to decide the most gifted and talented young conductors by means of the most unartistic and barbaric process imaginable in the sphere of art, the 'democratic' selection process. If these young conductors, chosen in such a stupid way, failed to make it at all or only after a long period of training, because they represented mediocrity, two things were achieved: the possible rival and presumptive successor was out of the game, and Karajan was able to transfer responsibility for the incorrect judgement to the jury. It was they, not he, who made the choice. It can come as no surprise under such circumstances that no truly outstanding conductors have emerged from Karajan's competition. If certain winners of the Karajan Prize won a public profile in the end, it was only because their musical quality was defined solely by the market value as winners of the Karajan Prize, and compensated for by a music business that spares no expense where public relations is concerned. The competition neither discovered nor trained any original, highly convincing or musical talents. For these truly talented people, who are always outsiders (Karajan should have been aware of this, and a glance at his own biography should have reminded him of it), and who cannot be measured by standardized selection processes, were eliminated in the

247

preliminary rounds, if they ever even took part. It sometimes seemed that the title of the Karajan Prizewinner, a title signifying mediocrity, was, like the Nobel Peace Prize, awarded for reasons that had nothing to do with the matter in hand. That is my personal impression, and neither a declaration nor an insinuation.

The tendency to delegate responsibility where it contains the threat of one's own failure extended to all areas of Karajan's work. It was also apparent in the way he flew. The Falcon 10 jet, a two-engine plane, is flown by two pilots. When Karajan went flying he was naturally the pilot in command, the captain. A professional pilot took the role of co-pilot. Karajan delegated the flight preparations to him, the radio communication, the fusillage check and other time-consuming and responsible tasks. This was not purely for the sake of comfort and the wish to gain time, nor to ensure that everything should be in order and fully prepared when he sat down at the joystick. It also revealed his tendency to delegate responsibility. Thus, in his jet-plane flying, Karajan barely rose beyond the dependent status of a learner flyer (albeit a very experienced one), who was always able to lean on the tried and tested co-pilot in the role of the discreetly observing flying teacher. Here, too, he was unable to break the umbilical cord and assume full responsibility. This is not meant disrespectfully, and is simply said to describe a state of affairs. Just as nothing in this book, concerned solely with facts, is meant disrespectfully. Karajan's way of flying even revealed his awareness of the limits of his abilities. And it does not insult his abilities as a pilot if we mention that – for reasons of safety – he put himself in the hands of a professional pilot with years of experience. I enjoyed flying with Karajan, and got to know him as a careful, reliable and perfectionist pilot. His emergency methods, carried out blamelessly and with a relaxed ease, have my full respect, born of my own experience as a flier, even if, the first and only time I flew as a passenger in his aeroplane, I was sick.

With the skill of a ballet-dancer, Karajan side-stepped any occasions that called for manly action. I have tried to portray this aspect of him in his behaviour in relation to the conducting competition and elsewhere. But if one's decision-making powers are inadequate it is not a bad tactic to give a free hand to the views and opinions of others. These others were to determine the next generation of conductors – he only gave them his blessing. But his delegation of judgement to others reveals an unwillingness to takes risks in his artistic as in his private life: his stagings, based on old and familiar traditions, and his interpretations, which never

248

cover new ground, can be seen entirely from this point of view. 'For the same reason I never play cards. I don't like not being able to predict the result.'[33]

Karajan planned out his life, tried to bring it under the control of perfect organization, constructed himself a safety-net designed to protect the insecure conductor from the ever-possible fall from the familiar into the uncertain. He side-stepped the fear provoked by each unfamiliar situation, taking refuge in the safety of his self-dramatizing and stylized world. And he played off this fear and its consequences – a fear of separation, of breaking loose, assuming responsibility and taking a stand – against his own secure ability to be superior to others. Even such harmless questions as which three works would he take to his desert island remained unanswered, although, in the preface of the book *The Hundred Most Beautiful Concerts*, he himself asked the question. 'It's an old game, yet it's different every time: what books, paintings and scores would you take with you if you were suddenly to be banished to a desert island, and only allowed to take three of your favourite works with you, three and absolutely nothing else?'[34] The answer is very typical of Karajan's way of side-stepping precise questions: 'Look, if I really had to name three records, I would be upset about the many others that I should have included.'[35]

Karajan's tendency to flight, indecision, vagueness, a refusal to be tied down, endless hedging and a fluid indistinctness, which springs from his poor decision-making capacity and reluctance to make decisions, his general fear of commitment, his profoundly irresolute character, were all apparent in his musical affinities. There was barely a single work in operatic literature that preoccupied and fascinated Karajan more thoroughly than Maurice Maeterlinck's drama *Pelléas et Mélisande*, as set to music by Debussy. 'The work is simply as close to me as if it were under my skin . . . Everything's left completely vague . . . I'm not actually one for shadiness in other respects, but this lack of resolution in what is actually stated, in the facts, which are finally all expressed in the music, that is something that fascinates me enormously.'

Karajan or the virtue of presence of mind: no one before or since has had such a sense of how to organize and technologize his musical operations which such a sure sense of what was to come. He was constantly in search of new techniques of musical mass-

249

production. He was a pioneer, and broke new boundaries that go far beyond the musical life of the time and make the musical world of the second half of the twentieth century his own creation to a very large extent. In his absolute artistic rigour he sacrificed everything to his aesthetic dream of the perfect reproduction and performance of symphonic music and operas. Fascinated by the idea of total musical information, which gave him a sense of omnipresence, he exercised a dictator's power, in his irrefutable way, and thus constantly extended the aura of greatness and admiration that surrounded him. His career, a triumph of the will, was also a triumph of contempt. Karajan's sense of purpose, the rigour and unstintingness of his effort, his commitment, his fanatical seriousness, ambition and hard work had their origin in the concept of the ideology of iron will and absolute desire. The voluntaristic trait in his nature brought him where he always wanted to be, and made him what he wanted to be: at the very summit, the best. With the Karajan Foundation, he extended his sphere of influence beyond the immediate world of music. With this institution he staged his own far-sighted flight into immortality. The foundation became the administrator of his estate after his death. It would ensure his survival. It continues his work in the training of the younger generation as he would have wished, caring for and fostering the global distribution and marketing of his musical legacy in countless film and gramophone recordings, in which his genius as a musical stage director was preserved for all time and left as a gift to posterity.

In his own lifetime, the foundation was also a forum for his own self-dramatization. If Karajan invited leading scientists such as Werner Heisenberg or Konrad Lorenz to his scientific symposia, it always had the ring of the emperor calling for the finest scientific minds who would contribute, by researching and teaching, to the further splendour and renown of the court. If Karajan took his seat among the invited experts at the Salzburg symposia as a *primus inter pares*, the peer of a super-élite of musical studies, that too was always a strengthening of his threatened internal equilibrium, as well as his self-enhancement through the borrowed authority of science. Here the academics spoke for Karajan, Karajan's universal spirit emanated through the language of science. Here Karajan listened enthralled to the discourses of his scientific substitutes, who captured for him in clear language and brilliant formulations what he, the musical genius, thought, sensed and, in a higher and more all-encompassing sense, knew. Here he hung fascinated on their every word, in order, finding himself in the ritual of self-dramatization, to nod affirmatively and appreciatively as though to say: 'Yes, that's how it is. That's exactly how it is.'

Karajan himself had the gift of eloquence. When he wished, he was capable of finely honed formulations that placed him among the great rhetoricians. His solid, guttural voice with the timbre of the incomparable Salzburg accent was charming and obliging, his hoarse and sometimes grating baritone could make demands in a pleasantly lovable tone. Although he knew how to formulate and articulate complex experiences like few others, he tended to break off in the middle of his speech, left sentences unfinished and constantly jumped from subject to subject. It was a tried and tested means of evading uncomfortable questions. His answers alternated between prolixity and a concise brevity. Where others would take their time, he often restricted himself to statements of aphoristic sharpness. As, for example, in reply to the question of what had shaped his relationship to Beethoven: 'My boundless admiration for him and because I have attempted to concentrate on it since my youth.' The rhetoric in his interviews was seldom free of stereotypes, being dressed up in clichés and a lack of logic. Wherever something was to be hidden, it sounded like a guarantee against slips of the tongue, a mechanism well practised in the processes of repression and stylization. It was a language that could be striking in its use of obvious or banal yet highly revealing parallels and comparisons, and one concerned with the simulation of authenticity. A language, too, of distraction, leading with skill and refinement beyond gaps in his knowledge and education while never leaving the blank surface of a non-committal stance.

The most important, famous and prominent conductor of our time, Karajan was a much-honoured man. The number of his decorations and honours is legion. He has several honorary doctorates, including those from the universities of Salzburg, Oxford, Pavia and Vaseda in Tokyo. He was a freeman of Salzburg and Berlin, a Grand Officer of the Order of the Italian Republic, Bearer of the Grand Cross of Merit with Star of the German Federal Republic, and the fingers of his famous hands bore numerous rings of honour. The list of his honours was simply endless. And he had deserved these honours. He never turned them down, but he stressed that they meant nothing to him. After the official celebration by the city of Salzburg of his seventieth birthday on Whit Monday 1978, when we were driving the next day, after training flights in the Falcon jet, to his house in Anif for lunch, he declared, as he dashed along the autobahn at the wheel of his sportscar, 'It means nothing to me. No. Whitsun is past and

251

forgotten as far as I'm concerned. After days like that I fly to leave it behind me.' That applies as much to the honour conferred as to his Whitsun Festival. I have my doubts about Karajan's disdain for honours, suspecting that they meant a lot to him. But like all men ambitious for honour he disputed the fact, which is entirely 'normal'. But it would have taken a level of confidence very much higher than Karajan's own to confess this freely. To say: I value honours, I love presents, it makes me happy.

Karajan, who worked away at his legend with unflagging zeal, was constantly hunting for his dream roles. What drove him was the desire to be someone else and yet remain the same. Thus he disguised himself every morning as the Karajan he wished to be. Sometimes it was the conductor, sometimes the director, the husband and paterfamilias, sometimes he became the reciter of his own words, sometimes an entrepreneur. Then again he would be the pilot, the successful sailor, the sportsman. Sometimes he was several of these at the same time, but above all he was the eternal adolescent. His role-playing belonged in a psychological stage play about the life of a mountain-climber who fails in the sweet altitudes of power and splendour to perceive that in his struggle for power, which consists in not being the underdog, and in which he needs other people in order to remain on top, just as up needs down, he derives stability from a false consciousness. I do not wish to claim that Karajan's apparently compulsive urge for confirmation, what the American political commentator Richard Barnet calls the 'hairy-chest syndrome', demonstrates a 'colossal baby ego that has to be constantly fed, a bad case of arrested development.'[36] I only mean that at some point in every man's life there should come a time when experiments in role-playing and the process of self-analysis and self-discovery that these roles, with all the sloughings of skin that they entail, all their transformations, should lead over a period of development to spiritual maturity and security.

Karajan made manliness the theme of his life. He orchestrated his world in terms of this desire. His identification with a clichéed masculine role was made manifest in his first successes, and rose in a crescendo as his musical empire extended. It began with the motor-cycle with which he had dashingly swept up to the stage door in Aachen. After the war, he rapidly became the best male skier in the Tyrol. Soon he was also seen at the wheel of dangerously fast racing cars, circling the course in the rush of speed under the direction of world-class racers. Perhaps it was not a question of speed, but rather an obeisance to the fetish of technical perfection which psychologists might have a go at deciphering? Or might it have been the symbol of a reality which he refused to admit, and which he escaped by high-altitude flight? In any case, Karajan mused on the relationship between flying and speed, an aviatic *sine qua non:* 'The joy of flying has nothing to do with speed. Rather it is the satisfaction of having everything sensibly organized beforehand. You prepare yourself, and then you give your best. Life becomes more orderly in the process.'[37]

The rise from the one-engine training plane to the two-engine luxury jet was a good symbol for Karajan's career as a conductor – a fairytale career, but one based on a quite hard-headed desire for achievement. His craze for ships was the same.[38] If one wished to be extravagant, one might claim that the Greek in him was coming out here: every Greek his own oarsman. Karajan's flotilla grew constantly according to the pattern of his success. Tonnage, length above all and sail surface fulfilled Karajan's dreams in his maxi-sloop *Helisara VI*, bringing a new satisfaction to his mania for things large. Fulfilment? He took his boyish pleasure in breaking new records to its limits with the marine technological masterpiece of his seventy-foot-class maxi-sloop. And at the same time he satisfied his craving for the greatest and the best, as well as his love of monumental things, to which he devoted himself in exactly the same way in the concert hall and the opera house.

With his new ship he found a means of dramatizing himself in its dimensions, paying tribute to his own mania for immensity: 'The mast is thirty metres high. Thirty metres! The upper part of the Salzburg Festspielhaus is thirty metres high. That's half the size of the Café Winkler... The spinnaker has an area of 500 square metres, and the weight on the windlass is 6,000 pounds.' The ship was developed according to the most modern specifications and built with new kinds of material. 'Those are the new techniques, and things like that quite simply fascinate me. Because I know: that's the best that can be produced in the field. It gave work to a lot of people. It gives us pleasure, so everybody's satisfied. But it is a real challenge.' Karajan took up the challenge, and got the very most out of *Helisara VI*, just as he did with his orchestra. And, as with his orchestra, as both owner and skipper and with a perfectly drilled crew, he enjoyed the mass experience of a single unit made up of many different component parts, where the thought of the individual becomes the act of the many: 'Like

253

flights of birds, where we do not know who gives the orders.'[39] Winning the thirtieth Giraglia Regatta from Toulon to San Remo in the summer of 1982, Karajan announced that he was retiring from competitive sailing. He had done what he had set out to prove: that he could be the greatest at sailing as well, if he wanted to be and if he set his mind to it. With his victory in the regatta, the dramatization of Karajan's masculinity celebrated its greatest triumph. And why should Karajan not have done it? After all, there he was, the great, intrepid, eternally young lad whom everyone thought was great, who was appreciated. Thus he won the admiration that he needed as he needed air to breathe. On his boat, too, he could satisfy his desire for eternal youth by projecting it on to the muscle-bound, strong-limbed, youthfully fresh manliness of his crew. There he could regain his lost youth in the cult of youth, by surrounding and adorning himself with youth and its attributes.

Richly endowed with the gift of a great talent, Karajan had to grow accustomed to superlatives early in life. Exclusivity became a rule and a habit for him early in his life. For that reason it can come as no surprise that he always took the finest of everything. For a very long time he was honoured with the title of best-dressed man: the litheness of his supple body always set off the elegance of his fashionable clothes to the best effect. He did not abandon this outward extravagance even in his old age. In Paris he wandered the boulevards in a striking fur-trimmed coat. Anywhere else it might easily have looked ridiculous. For that reason he loved the city, that soft, gentle structure of wide and promisingly elegant boulevards, sun-dappled parks and imposing architecture that sets every woman's heart racing. Could we imagine Karajan in London, that demanding and reticent city of gentlemen? Karajan, for whom exclusivity was simply natural, attained the most exclusive things in every area of his life: from his orchestra, through his boat, aeroplane, wife and festival, to his own persona. That is why he failed in Vienna. Because exclusivity was withheld from him. But exclusivity does not inquire into the relationship between profit and loss. Exclusivity is not governed by that criterion. It is measured according to its own standards. And it is its own justification.

One of the most enduring Karajan dramatizations is the myth of the conductor submitting himself to the spiritual concentration of yoga, believing in karma and the endless chain of reincarnation.

Karajan often told me that he counted on reincarnation, and it came as no surprise. Anyone who still has so many plans during his seventies that everything he has achieved thus far looks like a preliminary exercise, finds it hard to accept the finite nature of his existence. When Karajan said, 'I was actually born ten years too early,' he was referring to the tragedy of his life, which lay in the fact that the technical developments of the media which he would have considered adequate were lagging behind his own life. Hardly had he recorded the standard works of the musical canon on mono LPs than stereo recordings were developed. So he had to begin all over again. Hardly had that happened, than the technologists came up with quadraphonic sound. Another new start. Then, finally, came the decisive innovative breakthrough of digital recording. It meant that Karajan's work could be preserved for all time in its original quality by means of binary codes based on nothings and somethings. By Karajan's seventies that technique was as advanced as it should ideally have been during his thirties.

Karajan, our century's Sisyphus, went to work again. He wanted to leave the perfect legacy, just as he had striven for perfect reproduction. Karajan's mania for production was not only the expression of a restless nature, a striving for admiration and appreciation, it also concealed the myth of timelessness. If there is no possibility of personal immortality, however much one might yearn for it, however intense one's faith, immortality *per se* is perhaps not such a vain hope. With his legacy of massive multi-media production, does Karajan not recall the first Emperor of China, Qin Shihuang Di, who fitted out his monumental mausoleum with a troop of a thousand life-sized clay warriors and horses, an artificial army designed to give the deceased his last escort and security, and which, simply by virtue of the numbers of this larger-than-life escort into death, ensured him art-historical immortality?

But was Karajan not chasing a chimera in his urge for ever more perfect recordings? His concert and opera films will certainly have documentary importance as far as posterity is concerned, I fear. For what he needed Karajan was too early not by ten, but by twenty, thirty or more years. What he needed was a three-dimensional, holographic means of recording. This would have allowed him to realize the only thing consonant with his own standards: the spatial projection of Karajan and the orchestra on to the concert-hall podium, on which, as a perfect illusory presence, he would have appeared to posterity as the prophet of the beautiful – beautiful because it was perfect – preserved in its incorruptibility.

255

We might also imagine a virtual Karajan being projected before a real-life orchestra, three-dimensional and quite tangible, with this orchestra playing for a spatial depiction of a man. It might be called *Historical Concerts with Herbert von Karajan*, and people might spend the next two hundred years laughing at the curiously out-of-date garb in which the conductor appeared before the audience. But these are, perhaps fortunately, visions, and technologists should be ashamed not to have been able to fulfil this dream of Karajan's. Karajan also came too early for medical research. He was probably simply born too early, for by nature he was probably more a man of the coming millennium, both in his desires and in his appearance. The elixir of youth has not yet been discovered, and the possibility of cloning is still a far-off dream. The first cloned frogs already exist as a triumph of research, and soon there will be a thousand cloned frogs. Why not a thousand identical Karajans, too? Karajan or the experience of reincarnation: the medical profession should likewise be ashamed not to have been of service here.

Thus Karajan dreamed the charming dream of immortality and rebirth. But in turning to Eastern religions he was merely side-stepping the reality of the world of Western culture in which he was inescapably trapped, by dint of being a part and product of that very world. Yoga and karma, the technique and doctrine of Eastern philosophy and religion, thus became the main concept behind his flight from himself. Karajan never missed the opportunity to stylize himself as the great mystic and mystagogue of music, his religion. The very outward appearance of Karajan, turned in on himself, meditating in front of the orchestra, contributed to this mystification. The inward gaze helped him to concentrate on the course of the music. But that concentration is one of the essential preconditions of true mysticism.

When Karajan used his arms to row his way through imaginary worlds of sound, it 'may have been an external expression of what was happening within. The communication basically arises from the music. Music leads us into other areas. For me the orchestra is a living being, and we live together. The playing of music is based on true mysticism: you are so concentrated that you forget everything around you.'[40] In order to have mystical experiences, Karajan did not need to escape into Eastern modes of thought. The fact that one always seeks what is most remote was not only a personal problem of Karajan's, but is a problem of Western society in general. We do not look into the roots of our own existence, at Christianity, for example, the religion into which we have been born, but which we do not know and which is entirely foreign to us. Christianity is too close for us to study. But the other one, remote and exotic, karma, reincarnation, Zen and satori as the experience of enlightenment – that is interesting, and it makes one interesting.

It also allows one to say of oneself, in a self-aggrandizing way: 'I think there's something of the Zen Buddhist in me.'[41] Not least, it is the fascination of the exotic and the charm of the highly technical nature of Eastern methods of meditation that leads one to foreign forms of meditation. Apart from the fact that the conception common to the Semitic religions, of sin and guilt, a burden that the West is often no longer willing to bear, can trigger a flight into the East that is felt to be a liberation and a release.[42]

If Karajan wanted to identify with something, it should have been expressed within the field of Western culture. He could and should have declared his adherence to Christianity, for example, rather than to the Eastern religions. When one gives an account of oneself within this culture, one is obliged to be concrete. But here, too, it is often easy for others to say, 'he speaks the right words, but the essence isn't there'. The Far Eastern religions, however, gave him absolute licence, because they became a means of escaping his own responsibilities. Apart from this it is also chic, in an entirely outwardly-directed way, just as it is chic to read our fates in the position of the stars. It is no coincidence that Karajan, like Schiller's Wallenstein, had a court astrologer, after the manner of the traditional princes and generals. For years Karajan had his future read by Francesco Waldner, the astrologer to an exclusive and self-absorbed society of the top five hundred people, whom I consider to be a good judge of character and psychologist. 'He has the gift of clairvoyance . . . But I only ever ask him: Am I in a phase at the moment in which things are easy for me, or am I not?' Did Karajan really need someone to tell him that? 'Yes, I like it, for in many areas in certain periods of my life almost everything's gone wrong. You say you want to do something, and suddenly, for some reason, it doesn't work.'

But looking for reasons outside of oneself, allowing others to decide for one, transferring responsibility for one's actions and inaction to the stars, to fate, is nothing but a flight from oneself and away from the responsibility of personal action and individuality. But personal responsibility and individuality are part of the concept of Western man.

If one really wishes to find oneself, there is no need to escape into astrology and Asiatic religions. If one wishes to take on board and accept these religions of the Orient, which see man's vain ego as an error and all the splendour of this world as an aspect of the great, unfathomable void, one should forsake everything Western. Then one should renounce everything, and one cannot be Karajan. It is, of course, easier to drift off into the East and represent something that one does not understand than to resolve for oneself the tensions and problems that arise from the contradiction of man and machine which shapes Western culture and places it under a high degree of psychological pressure. It is a refusal to bear the truth of one's own existence, and its legacies for good and ill, because one is unwilling to face up to them, that leads one to escape eastwards into remote religions. But one never integrates the implications of changing to out-of-the-way religions because one is not prepared to break the umbilical cord. Oriental things in the West are a mere imitation, mere fakery, flight from occidental reality, escapism from the superficial industrial culture of our soulless age, a romantic longing for inspiration from far-off places.

We should be able to liberate ourselves from the cause of our restlessness by overcoming it. Then that flight would cease to be necessary. We would arrive, here too, at individuation. But did Karajan get that far? Was he not, rather, in search of healing through rebirth, precisely because he did not want to get that far? Karajan, who only ever presented himself to the public as the portrayer of his own image; in whom being and appearance were one, in accordance with the opinion that one is the way one looks; who always lagged behind himself because he allowed himself to be driven on ahead; who was always in search of effect and wondered what effect he was having; who tangled himself up in a thousand dependencies in his desperate staging of independence, who in his demand for the absolute succumbed to the cult of perfection, who, in his wish to be the metaphor of an era, became the metaphor of effort in the sense of Sisyphus the untiring; in his restlessness he was unable to stop wanting the impossible.[43]

Karajan was fundamentally a restless, driven man. Not only driven to music, but a man pursued, racked by fantasies of omnipotence, hunted into self-dramatization and ever greater success. Here his career is revealed as the product of the compulsion to keep achieving more and more in the service of restlessness. His life and work led to an inability to stop. His old age was taken up with the effort to continue his career, which he had already been through and which now lay behind him, on and on without reaching the end. There was no restfulness there, no peaceful existence for one's own sake, no relaxation, and no giving of elbow-room. It was only ever a matter of striving ever-further, ever-higher above one's own zenith.

But the normal course of life describes a ballistic curve. Once thrown into life, man does not shoot straight ahead like a jet plane on a flight-path leading to his destination. Rather he falls, after reaching his zenith, like a missile to its falling-point, where death, his destination, awaits him. The course of his life is not the tubular path of a bullet, with which one's flight into immortality begins. Man's runway and flight path form a harmonic unity. Talent, the circumstances of one's life, one's own achievements are all that define the height of this course, on which there is no lingering. Life is like the course of the sun. It rises from night to the undimmed 'brightness of the meridian',[44] to sink back down again towards night. The same thing happens to man. 'If he is to live, he must fight and sacrifice his longing for the past in order to rise to his own heights. And having reached the noonday heights, he must sacrifice his love for his own achievement,'[45] was how C. G. Jung described the course of life, in an observation that is as mythological as it is beautiful.

When we are feeling on top of the world we find this exceedingly disagreeable; we resist the sunset tendency, especially when we suspect that there is something in ourselves which would like to follow this movement, for behind it we sense nothing good, only an obscure, hateful threat. So, as soon as we feel ourselves slipping, we begin to combat this tendency and erect barriers against the dark, rising flood of the unconscious and its enticements to regression, which all too easily take on the deceptive guise of sacrosanct ideals, principles, beliefs, etc. If we wish to stay on the heights we have reached, we must struggle all the time to consolidate our consciousness and its attitude. But we soon discover that this praiseworthy and apparently unavoidable battle with the years leads to stagnation and desiccation of soul. Our convictions become platitudes ground out on a barrel-organ, our ideals become starchy habits, enthusiasm stiffens into automatic gestures. The source of the water of life seeps away. We ourselves may not notice it, but everybody else does, and that is even more painful. If we should risk a little introspection, coupled perhaps with an energetic attempt to be honest for once with ourselves, we may get a dim idea of all the wants, longings and fears that have accumulated down there – a repulsive and sinister sight. The mind shies away, but life wants to flow down into the depths.[46]

Had Karajan concluded his career at its zenith, taking his leave at the peak of his artistic life, consciously abandoning the heights and descending to earth with the peaceful content of the mountaineer who has, with the most intense pleasure, reached the peak and looked down on the breadth and depth of the world, of life? He wanted to perpetuate his success. He held firmly on to his Easter Festival, which seemed to be losing its meaning and its quality once his life's goal had been attained – the performance of the work of Richard Wagner as both conductor and director. He held firmly on to his orchestra, trying for the God knows how manieth time finally to wring perfection from it. But this probably reveals the tragic aspect of all interpretative, reproductive art: the fact that its truth lies in the attempt and not in perfection. Because, however much effort one puts in, the aim of reaching the imaginary goal of perfection remains an illusion and cannot be attained in a reality that is simply 'this way and no other'.

In clinging rigidly to his past achievements, refusing to accept the limitations of an individual human existence – whose finite nature cannot be abrogated by any theory of reincarnation – Karajan was moved by a wish for eternal youth. With the effort that he put into keeping his success at its peak, he preserved his image of permanent youth, taut dynamism and vigour. It sometimes appeared that he had stylized himself, and allowed himself to be stylized, into the herald of a society of eternal youth, whose compulsive youth culture reduces anyone old to ballast, to uselessness.

Karajan was unable to incorporate death, that uncomfortable foreign body of hedonistic civilization, into the natural order of things as a universal biological phenomenon. He had no wish to see his own fate as lying in mortality. All of his life was geared towards life after death, without any eschatological expectation, because the ultimate goal was only ever Karajan himself. Death even became the greatest possible insult to him: Karajan resisted it by escaping into intimations of immortality and hopes of rebirth. In doing so he provided an example of the secular process of the alienation of death in a culture aimed at hedonism, perfectionism and pragmatism, which had banished death and only allowed it any validity in the perverted form of spectacle, in which people, as heroes of a single day, run a truly fatal risk because it is easy to market.[47]

260

Old age, the tragedy of ageing, came as a great blow to Karajan, the eternal adolescent, the ever immature *puer aeternus*. For the tragedy of old age is not the fact of growing old but, as Oscar Wilde had it, the fact that one remains young. It cannot be evaded by cosmetic plastic surgery. The wrinkles and creases of life, the loss of one's teeth, sight and hearing have to be accepted as a part of this life, however difficult that might be. We must accept it as we accept death. For life is an inexorable process of wear and tear that ends only with death. Karajan and death: an impossible conceptual coupling. While he lived, it was impossible to imagine his death as anything other than a sudden collapse in the midst of musical intoxication. Or as a powerful, deafeningly beautiful explosion: a monstrous crash. It was hard to conceive of it as being anything but a terrible flash like that of a supernova subsiding into eternity through a Black Hole, leaving no trace.

Karajan, the great and lonely synthesist of self-dramatization, one of the last single-minded egocentrics and egomaniacs, the *magico* who never stopped staging his life: he lived out his life according to the roles he played. Thus he confronted his past with the indifference of the actor faced with roles long past. He lived as a man who rejects everything that might trouble him: mourning, responsibility and love, probably also guilt and expiation. Thus the aura of tragedy encircled his life. His chief driving force proved to be a conformist striving for success, a syndrome of the compulsive desire for admiration, recognition and esteem. If we take away everything dramatic and stagey in his nature, Karajan the man is left remarkably pale and inexpressive for long periods of his life. A personality structure in which everything flows into everything else. The fluidity of this personality, on the other hand, was the opposite of what would have come about if Karajan, instead of dramatizing and stylizing himself, had worked away at himself as a sculptor hammers and grinds at the stone until he gets to the permanent form within, unique and unmistakeable. Individual, in contrast to the lack of differentiation that comes from fluidity. If we examine Karajan's life we will find no useless residues – all by-products, everything superfluous, old-fashioned and mediocre is most painstakingly brushed aside and concealed. It is not presented to us among the things of the past, and is simply left out of account. In *L'Etranger*, Albert Camus has his main character say, just before his execution, that he would live each moment again exactly as he had done; and according to the idea of reincarnation, this transitory stage of the phases of existence is not without importance.

If Karajan the director and actor could have been made to take off the make-up that he wore when he was role-playing, we might, who knows, suddenly find ourselves presented with a face in which the blank spots, like the white areas on a map, indicated unexplored regions. We might be able to establish that the experience of his life had left no mark or structure on the empty areas of his face.

And, in certain circumstances, we might have been able to observe that it showed no secret runes or codes, and no traces of his destiny beyond his own entelechy.[48]

For years Karajan worked on a book about himself. He used it as an excuse to remain silent to biographers about his inner world.

But if a person has a complex, the tragedy lies in the fact that he cannot heal himself because he sees everything through the complex. He cannot undertake a process of self-analysis, because that analysis would be filtered through the very complex that he wished to examine. I have my suspicions that it may not be possible to ignore this aspect of his life when it comes to the evaluation of Karajan's book, should it ever appear.

Karajan and the problem of greatness: I referred to this briefly at the beginning. To conclude, we should ask the question: was Karajan great, and where does greatness lie? Did his work express nothing but morbidly exaggerated demands, or extraordinary greatness? Was Karajan one of the great men who have arrived at the philosophy that the Romans called a life *sub specie aeternitatis?* Was he one such man, who does not sink into resignation but draws a quiet pride from the greatness of his existence, and recognizes death as something inherent in life? In contrast to those who fear it, and at whom Goethe directed his lines in *Selige Sehnsucht*, a poem in the *Westöstlicher Diwan:*

> Und so lang du das nicht hast,
> Dieses: Stirb und werde!
> Bist du nur ein trüber Gast
> Auf der dunklen Erde.

(And until you have grasped this – 'Die and be transformed!' – you will be nothing but a sorry guest on the sombre earth.)

Karajan: was he indeed a great man? If great he was, then his

262

greatness lay in the ambivalence of his greatness. In the case of Karajan we must endure the fact that a great man, for the most personal and opportunistic reasons, clearly aware of previously unimagined possibilities and recklessly exploiting all the means and methods available to him – however dubious and contestable they might be – realized the great dream of musical omnipotence and omnipresence. This too was part of his greatness – 'this' being taken to mean a human achievement of universal validity, of something worthy of being handed down, something that leads us further and further from Karajan the individual and either ignores or mystifies him. Perhaps we should leave the question to future generations, who will know the answer simply by virtue of living in the future.

I should like to close this chapter about Karajan's stagings – his methods, intentions and motives – with an example that conveys an impression of what the urge for dramatization and stylization can achieve if it is able to unfold in an environment of consent and admiration. The quotation comes from a television film made, with Herbert von Karajan's consent, by Vojtech Jasny on the occasion of the conductor's seventieth birthday:

The human span is too short for any great talent. Karajan has within him spiritual, active primal power. By means of his creative power in music he awakens and develops the higher essence of mankind. He needs to make himself quite unified and strong by consciously eliminating everything degrading and vulgar. It is thus that he attains his tirelessness, which relies on certain closed areas of activity. He needs to do battle with himself. He is always finishing something, always starting something else. He needs nature and walks as he needs his daily bread. Herbert von Karajan is a person who can guide us through this chaotic world. Happy are those who can learn it from him.

Karajan from start to finish: divine attributes.

5

The Cult of the Beautiful Illusion or Streamline Aesthetics

Greatness has always fascinated mankind. Acceptance and admiration, but also envy and displeasure, are constant companions to extraordinary talents and achievements. This is something that Karajan had to learn: more emphatically, more forcefully than any other interpreter of our time, Karajan the man and his work became the object of exhaustive interest ranging across the whole spectrum from rigorous rejection to extravagant approval, feeding on the unstoppable flow of the conductor's contradictions. It is one of this book's aims to examine and, however sketchily, to demonstrate the content and the roots of these contradictions. Nothing could be more foolish than to play down or even to deny Karajan's achievements. This was never my brief in writing this book: rather I should like to ask what his achievements really were, what they meant, and examine the motivations and conditions that shaped them.

If we add together everything we have already discussed and established we can, having intimately examined Karajan, say the following: In Karajan we are confronted with a personality whose most prominent features were an inability to engage in relationships and clear desires for acceptance and admiration, as well as an evidently unassuageable urge for dramatization. A personality, in addition, that was easily insulted and that reacted excessively to insults. But above all we recognize in Karajan a man with a pronounced tendency towards flight, whether from his own responsibility or his own past, who constantly escaped into self-dramatization and stylization.

Not only did Karajan refuse to admit his actions in the Third Reich; rather he denied them, and in May 1982, through his lawyers, he still rejected the documented facts of his past as 'false' and 'discriminatory claims'. This flight from historical responsibility into the fiction of his subjective truth expressed a strategy of defence based on the motto: 'What is not permitted, cannot be', which, in Karajan's case, made musical 'history' – insofar as Karajan's own testimonies have constructed an alternative world to historical reality, maintained and reinforced with all the means available to his publicity machine, which we may call corrupt because it has been placed at the service of a false history. Karajan sought to smuggle himself through life into immortality with an intentionally forged past.

With the absolutist attitude of a Renaissance prince, Karajan made the hubristic attempt to challenge his own history, in order to conquer it by strength of will. His portrayal of the past recalled the anamorphosis that Renaissance artists developed as an extreme variety of central perspective. The fascinating thing about this process is the fact that the image in the Renaissance sense (perspectively precise), on a flat surface, no longer exists; through anamorphosis, the painting can only be seen on a distorted plane – an image that no longer exists in the 'correct' sense. Karajan treated his past in a similar way. Just as, in the Renaissance, perspective was transformed, using the distorting method of anamorphosis, from a means of reproducing the visible external world into a means of making an invisible truth visible, in Karajan's distortion of his own history the inner truth of his character is revealed. It expresses an absolutist self-image that seems like a throwback to the Renaissance, a self-image that seeks to bring everything under its own domination whatever the cost.

What became apparent in the perspectival images of anamorphosis was basically the same domination of nature and objects as seen, for example, in the art of Renaissance landscape gardening. It is no coincidence that the only landscape gardening that coincided with the age of central perspective was one in which all the vegetation was tamed and clipped into sculpted forms. What the Renaissance artist wished to show was not only knowledge of the world but above all its domination by man. In the Renaissance this need was filled by anamorphosis, just as Karajan, in our own time, satisfied his absolutist tendencies with a cosmetic rewriting of history, and an attempt to bring his own history into line. Might we then call Karajan a Renaissance man?

In this chapter we shall seek to answer the question of whether the escapism apparent in Karajan's treatment of his own history was manifested in the artistic aspects of Karajan's life – and, if this was the case, how it was done. In doing so, we must attempt to examine whether the urge for dramatization and stylization explained in the previous chapter and described with reference to a number of examples, finds a resonance in Karajan's artistic work. Accordingly, we would have to find an answer to the question of whether, behind Karajan's radical idolization of beauty, there lay the same urge as behind his desperate and vain attempts to be the person he imagined he was. With a few observations and allusions I should like to attempt to present material that might help us to find an explanation. There are clear indications that Karajan's private work and artistic work follow and obey a single stimulus. This is the position to which my observations have led me. In what follows I should like to summarize and discuss those signs.

'Anyone who can make music must do it with love and not be influenced by hatred or feelings of revenge. The very great need for music to which mankind is subject proves the extent to which the hunger for beauty and love has been reawakened, and stands up to the destructive forces of doubt and hatred. This knowledge is the joy of my profession, and I shall pursue it with all my powers.'[1] In this rather vague artistic credo Karajan summed up his complete devotion to beauty. When he spoke of the hunger for beauty and love as a general tendency of our time, what he really meant was his own hunger, unassuaged because it was insatiable. Throughout his life Karajan dedicated himself to a cult of beauty, which may, in our barbaric century, seem just as repellent as if he had devoted himself exclusively to an aesthetic of ugliness at the court of the Medici. Karajan found beauty in music, and he sought love in the loyalty and approval of his audience.

In an age that granted truth only to ugliness and evil, Karajan produced a contrary thesis based on the aesthetic utopia of a paradise of beauty. He confronted the desolation and imperfection of our real world with an alternative realm of Apollonian beauty. For Karajan, beauty was a cosmological category, and so it was only logical for him to seek an exotic alternative to industrial civilization with all its blights and inadequacies in a mythical cult of beauty. But that is an obviously escapist undertaking, which

266

confirms our suspicion that Karajan's tendency to flight was not restricted to his private life, but quite significantly determined his artistic work. For Karajan's self-image as an interpreter lay in the celebration of harmonic and unfeigned beauty, towards which he geared his career as an artist. It was his way as an outsider of announcing his refusal, holding up the message of beauty to an age that seemed to be wandering aimlessly through the darkness of destructiveness and barbarism, a world working towards its own self-destruction. Beyond this bad world Karajan set up his own reserve of beauty. In this paradise, in the midst of technology, civilization and their subversive appurtenances he taught the alternative religion of the beauty of sound. For Karajan, art was primarily concerned with beauty. Thus he insisted on the traditional aesthetic that sees music as a pleasure for mankind. 'In symphonic music it is affirmation above all that gives people what they miss in everyday life. Brooding on one's own misery leads nowhere. But involvement with something that gives us an internal lift is truly beneficial.'[2]

Swearing by the bible of aesthetic harmony, Karajan, a missionary in his own way, had, a good generation before Pope John Paul II, given the media in which his future lay a truly conservative image of the world. Where Christ's earthly representative had an unshaken faith, the artist had untainted beauty. In this Karajan and his retinue felt both secure and entirely in tune with the times. But is it at all possible to leave this world, this society, for the utopian simplicity of the illusory world of beauty? Karajan was not in search of the chance beauties of life or art, but rather a transcendental idea of beauty. He used this as a protest against the shortcomings of the real world. He activated his alternative model to substandard reality through the transient emphasis of conducting: the utopia of beauty as the utopia of the moment. Karajan's aesthetic ideal of beauty became the centre of his existence – as the spokes radiate evenly from the axle to the wheelrim, all his apparently unconnected, independent actions, the expressions of his life, led (in the other direction) from the periphery to the midpoint, the vanishing point of his existence: the aesthetic idea of the harmony of beauty which he saw realized in the ideal of the aesthetic beauty of harmony, and which was nothing less than an apologia for illusion. Art and life, illusion in beauty and being in reality became interchangeable in Karajan's life in a confusing and refined way, so that in the end illusion, the highest and most noble form of being, was revealed as a pure mirror of the soul, a mystery. Or might he have succumbed to an ancient idea in Western culture, which had long represented being as beauty in a metaphysical sense?

The aesthetic model that Karajan erected as an alternative to a reality jeopardized by destructive forces was, generally speaking, always at the same time an expression of hope and optimism, the alternative to a threatened real world. But what meaning did this alternative have for Karajan as an individual, what tangible and experienced reality did it aim to counter in Karajan's case? Here we can only speculate, asking for example: did the reality of his family home in Salzburg, which surrounded him throughout his childhood and his youth, drive him into an imaginary world of beauty, in which he discovered music as a kind of autistic space and found the idea of beauty that was absent from his life? Let us remember: Karajan grew up in a house with three medical practices which became a focus for illness. Herbert's father treated and operated on the goitres of the people of the state of Salzburg. It does not take a great deal of imagination to consider that almost daily contact with the pitifully deformed or otherwise ailing patients might have aroused in Karajan a profound antipathy to everything sick and ill, and an equally emphatic demand for whole-ness and beauty. We can only speculate as to whether this was actually the case. But nothing contradicts this thesis, and certain things tend to bear it out. Throughout his life Karajan avoided anything ill, damaged, frail or deformed. On top of this, his life was always a fight against frailty. He prosecuted this campaign on his own body in many different ways, from plastic surgery to the medical revitalization cure that brought him to Romania for special treatment when he was over seventy. And he was no laggard in his avoidance of the reality of the decay of human life: he stayed away from the deathbed of his mother when she was dying of cancer.

Karajan subordinated everything to his aesthetic ideal of beauty which, as I have indicated, might have been the consequence of earlier experiences. He even sacrificed to it the truth of his life story. The corrections made to his reality were so extensive that this retouched reality was experienced as the true one. His corrections were so deep-rooted in his consciousness that Karajan totally failed to perceive the conflict with history that arose from them, believing instead that the real and the true were what he believed to be so. For him, the truth was his own invented reality. Just as he sought beauty in art, he subjected his life to the laborious urge never to be mundane, and to appear as his idealized image demanded he should be. Karajan subjected his outward appearance

268

to the same compulsion. It was the metaphor for a reality that perceives only the depiction as the true image, and makes this the sole valid reality.

For the general public Karajan was the man on the record sleeve. In consequence everyone knew Karajan as a constantly dynamic man in his prime, with the energetic face of the irresistible master. Until he was seventy-one, the image of Karajan the conductor was always adapted to the ideal of eternal youth. What one saw was a tense, slim apparition, rather on the small side, with striking features, generally with cold and unapproachably glittering, grey-blue eyes expressing a certain reticence. This apparition stalked confidently through its aesthetic beauties like a big cat. Its hair, combed imposingly skywards, gave it the aura of extraordinariness. The image of eternal youthfulness, often adorned with the attributes of casual elegance in both dress and accessories, made way in 1979 for timeless old age. Although he had now grown visibly old, Karajan was ageing timelessly, because the image he had always put across was one of active agelessness. His stylization also tended towards the idea of monastic enlightenment and the interpretational wisdom of old age. His faraway look, his inner gaze, had been turned inside out.

An image such as this is only at first glance a refusal of glamour. Karajan was very fussy and deliberate in choosing his photographs. They were entirely at the service of a stylization that sought to conceal being with illusion. Karajan summarily dismissed photographers whom he believed, often quite rightly, to be unwilling to yield to his craving for stylization, seeking instead to capture him the way he looked to them and not the way he wanted to appear to them, who refused to join in his worship at the shrine of beautiful illusion, wanting instead to unmask him with their lenses. Barbara Klemm, for example, the German photographer known for her analytical portraits, experienced this in a very undignified way in 1978, when she was trying to take photographs in the Philharmonie for an article in the *Frankfurter Allgemeine Zeitung* about Karajan's seventieth birthday. Thus Karajan constantly pursued his ideal, never quite reaching it and, where his appearance refused to agree with that ideal, retouching it according to his ideal. For when it came to stylization, Karajan proved to be a master at the art of retouching.

The transformation into the Karajan that he wished posterity to remember was completed during the years before his rise to the

269

highest official positions. At the end of the forties he was still splaying the little fingers of his right hand when he conducted, like an English lady drinking tea, or like Viennese society ladies, itting in the cafés eating cream cakes.

Then, in the fifties, his fist gripping the cork grip of the baton, he entirely altered his conducting pose. The baton became an extension of his arm, a paintbrush colouring in the black-and-white outlines of the score, turning them into tone-paintings. The secret of Karajan's conducting style was quite crucially rooted in this transformation: the closed hand guiding the baton from the wrist as a painter guides his brush across the canvas. It was a movement which gave energetic expression to the music, leading from the musically inspired torso through the shoulder, elbow, wrist and hand to the tip of the baton, leaping thence to the orchestra like a spark of electricity. Like a burst of electric current flowing from the body, along the arm and into the orchestra. With this almost organic motion Karajan ensured that the flow of energy was not short-circuited in his hand. The movement did not stop in his hand, as it almost always does with conductors who use the baton, but continued through to the baton's tip. The procedure was much like that which occurs when one cracks a whip: the movement follows the arm to the wrist and continues through the whip to its tip, where the crack occurs. It was thus that Karajan created the conditions for his visual, gestural expression: meaning and visibility became one and the same thing, and the conducting motions became symbols expressive of the sound they initiated.

These notably mannered gestures were, like the noble school of classical ballet, the product of physical control taken to its highest limit, leaving no room for random movements. Karajan developed a repertoire of motions that he controlled with an ease unmatched by any other conductor. What appeared quite natural, and quite unthinkable any other way, was in fact the result of years of self-discipline and had become a reflex. However much we may argue about the artistic importance of Karajan the conductor, we may say quite unambiguously that no other conductor has come even close to his gestural talent, his unusually fine sense for the movement that was organically and functionally correct and appropriate to the expression and development of the music. It was the true Karajan gift of harmonic motion, entirely in harmony and identical with what it sought to express, finally realized in sound. In the organization of his movement, in his systematization of a body language which had grown to look entirely natural, Karajan was incomparable. And a great deal of his fascination lay in this very

270

fact. There was nothing misdirected, nothing awkward in Karajan's movements as a conductor. There were no twists of the
body, no bent knees, no dislocations, no wriggling or trembling or
trampling about to display the inability to guide the musical
impulses solely through the arms (Leonard Bernstein remains a
special case in this). For Karajan's conducting was a structured
motion, free of wasted gestures and unco-ordinated movements.

When Karajan stepped up on the podium, he remained standing
for the duration of the entire performance. He stood on the same
spot, rooted to the podium, turning towards the different areas of
the orchestra by turning his hips and his torso. His body, which
appeared to be screwed to the spot, seemed to be entirely static,
in a permanent state of internal tension. When Karajan raised his
arms from the elbow and held them out before him at chest level,
he created a natural tension from the very first moment, a tension
that wrought the greatest attention from the orchestra even when
his hands were at rest. But it was this stance that enabled him to
carry out his wide, expansive rotations, and the elegant fanning
and stirring motions that seemed to move quite naturally from his
elbow through his wrist. With the choreography of his arms, born
of an infallible instinct for the elegance of a movement, Karajan
was irresistibly captivating. This choreography was one of the
decisive media employed by Karajan's art, in both staging and
conducting, if not the most decisive. For conducting, for Karajan,
was not simply a matter of controlling the processes at work in a
complex apparatus, but also an aesthetically beautiful and harmonic portrayal and visual expression of the tensions running
throughout the music, and the organization of these processes
into a movement produced by the supreme virtuosity of physical
control. When Karajan prepared to strike, his hand clenched in a
fist, his body apparently stretched to twice its normal size, his
symbolic act – clutching the thunderbolt – was guided by a
thoroughly conscious motion which, when transmitted to the
orchestra, liberated that sonorous crash that so unmistakably typified the Berlin Philharmonic and gave the listener a real shudder
of acoustic shock.

In the course of their many years of collaboration, conductor
and orchestra became an almost inseparable unit: Karajan's repertoire of movements was so familiar to the orchestra that the transposition of an expressive motion into a corresponding tonal
character was just as instinctive as Karajan's own choreographic
gesture had become, emerging quite automatically from the tension of the music. Over decades of use, the range of extremely

271

stylized conducting motions had become second nature to Karajan. He deployed them as naturally as a perfectly trained dancer would, his perfect mastery of expression through movements resting in his being able to create the perfect illusion of naturalness and weightlessness.

Karajan's aesthetic of beautiful motion was not restricted exclusively to conducting. It determined his entire *habitus*. The mannered gestures of his hands with their elegantly outstretched fingers, for example, were just as much a part of his unmistakable image, in the sense of his aestheticization of his whole persona, as his hairdo was to become. Karajan unstintingly engaged in this work on the external aspects of his persona (which replaced the work he might otherwise have applied to the person within) and never abandoned it. It was a part of his compulsion to pursue his own much-circulated image until it reached total concord with the real man. His hair, which satisfactorily grew more and more silvery, was brushed artistically upwards, giving the impression of a shape pointing towards higher realms, a crown-like conclusion to his body. The first hand extended to Karajan after his concerts, by the leader of the Berlin Philharmonic or by Karajan's personal factotum, held his hairbrushes, so that, when he responded to the adulation that awaited him, he could quickly recreate the illusion of effortlessness and become the mythically beautiful figure once more.

It was no coincidence that Karajan paid so much attention to the care of his platinum-blond hair. This piece of artistic finery served not only to enlarge Karajan's little figure, which he felt to be too small, but was unmistakably also a means of stylizing himself into something unapproachable and regal. When Karajan, replying to a question about his physical size, said: 'I've never given it a thought', he was rationalizing the repression of a fact that preoccupied him even as a child, when he was always the 'little one'. To put it more simply, we might say that his career was the expression of the fate of all small people, who must constantly prove that they are really the big ones.

I feel called to pass on traditions to my students, so that the concept of quality is not lost entirely. People are coming to accept mediocrity as something natural, and I have no sympathy for that. The public still demands what is wrongly called 'élitist' and what is in truth simply quality.

272

The person I overwork the most is myself. I make enormous demands on myself, but without effort you can't achieve anything in art. I have done that since the first day, and shall certainly continue to do so until I die. The people who want to work with me simply have to keep up. I have to say that all through my life I have only ever found people who enjoyed doing it. But there is a difference between overworking somebody and making claims on them. Ask a musician whether a harsh word has ever been said at any of my rehearsals, there's always complete agreement. But we agree that we always want to do the best we can, and that's always exhausting.[3]

Karajan placed idealistic demands on his life, both artistically and privately. Early in his life he created a perfectionistic self-image against which he measured himself and others. The obverse of this self-image, however, is the constant worry of falling short of his own ideals. With his cult of perfection, Karajan managed to manoeuvre himself into a myth that could only be sustained by ever greater achievements. Hence, he overworked himself. His catchword was 'no mistakes'. Because mistakes are less likely to be forgiven a myth than a man. Where beauty and perfection are one and the same, as they were for Karajan, the achievement that brings that beauty – beautiful in its perfection – into existence itself becomes a cult. In that context, one can praise oneself for making 'enormous demands' on oneself, and for 'overworking oneself the most'. Karajan fell prey to his cult of achievement. Had he compared the reality of his existence with his idealized norms, and had he not seen those norms as his reality, he would soon have been forced to realize that perfection is unattainable. He was never able to say: 'Now it's good. It can't get any better.' Because the doubts suddenly crept in. His achievement appeared inadequate. And his divergence from his ideal once more forced him to give the works another batch of finishing touches. Even when he came close to his ideal, the sense of happiness was always limited because it was confronted by the infinite imperfection of his achievement. Karajan, a man who had not quite finished creating himself, sought perfection in the things that filled his world: the orchestra and technology.

It's often been held against me that I enjoy driving fast sports cars. But I'm not concerned with speed. I'm fascinated by these perfect things that the human mind produces these days. If I get hold of something like that and drive it to a concert

273

rehearsal, that striving for perfection is communicated to me, and I say to myself: in doing what you do you mustn't be any worse than the man who produced a car that works so fantastically well.[4]

For the work he should have been doing on himself, Karajan substituted the idealized norms of beauty, perfection and maximum achievement, which need no work done on them because perfection is what they represent. The demands for perfection which he made on others were all the more rigid: anyone who wanted to work with him 'simply had to keep up'. Was his urge for perfection perhaps an attempt to reproduce in his work the perfection which he might in the past, as a child, have felt to be an direct attribute of himself? 'Being close to perfection makes people better,'[5] said Karajan, thus declaring his devotion to a 'positive' image of the world that sought salvation in the synthesis of perfectionism and optimism. With his conducting and staging work, which took its bearings from absolute standards, Karajan sought to struggle against our earthly destiny. But do we really have the choice between total perfection and total self-destruction that such an image of the world opens up to us? Is our earthly destiny not, rather, an infinite imperfection? Would it not be better to deal with oppositions, endure them and work them into a compromise, than to break down all differences and make them disappear in a final total synthesis?

Certainly, this urge for perfection also expresses the negativity of Western thought, the eternal discontent, the unassuageable unrest of Western man, who is unable to accept himself and what he has produced and sees this as his strength. But it is also his limitation: the fanatical desire for the absolute expressed in Karajan's craze for perfection also calls to mind the myth of Sisyphus. Albert Camus retold this story to provide a key to the heroic absurdity of Existentialism. In the restless yearning for the realization of his ideals of beauty and perfection, Karajan appeared to be the Sisyphus of music, his career a magically nonsensical parable of uselessness, of art. Karajan or the hope of Sisyphus: it contains within it the vital compulsion to repeat, the need to repeat one's attempts to find satisfaction until it is, perhaps, attained through ever-greater perfection and refinement. It is the illusion of success, always soberingly followed, in the end, by failure. And the only way of ridding oneself of the sense of failure is to try again. The urge to pursue his ideals came to obsess him, and his obsession became an ideal.

274

The cult of productivity objectified in Karajan's immense output of musical reproductions, the whole vast material expansion of his work – do they not express a secular process of alienation in a world led by hedonism and pragmatism? Is Karajan's work a metaphor for our industrialized society of consumption and exploitation, his life a *comédie humaine?*

When we mean perfection we are not talking about orchestral bravura. For Karajan this was only ever a precondition for the attainment of his artistic goal, the perfect reproduction of a work, fully identical with his imagined ideal. In pursuit of this goal he disciplined and drilled his orchestras, and finally, in the Berlin Philharmonic, created an instrument with which he could undertake this idealistic enterprise with an apparent view to success. However: what were the guiding principles behind Karajan's ideas of musical works? Is there such a thing as the authentic reproduction of historical music, or must the original of a symphony by Mozart, Beethoven or Bruckner not remain a utopia? Is there such a thing as an ideal, perfect reproduction in this idealistic sense of being faithful to the work itself, when we can no longer ask the composer, as crown witness, whether it is right or not? No. Such a thing is possible in contemporary music: then it is quite conceivable that a composer could work in close and fruitful collaboration with a conductor on the reproduction of a work, using the best performers imaginable and the most modern recording techniques, with the result that one might say at the end: this is how it must be, this way and no other. All future performances would have to follow this model interpretation, taking it as their standard, and being judged in terms of it.

The twofold tragedy in Karajan's artistic life lay in the fact that he was restricted to reproductive work in his musical life, and rejected the opportunity to work with present-day composers on interpretations which would set standards for posterity. Karajan wasted his opportunity to make musical history by being remembered as the reliable agent of a living composer. Instead, in a form of compulsive perpetuation, he celebrated the constant recurrence of everything unchanging in music, drawing from it a claim to validity despite the fact that this cannot exist, since the composer himself is doomed to silence on the matter. If we consider the facilities that Karajan had at his disposal, we can see just how much he missed, how many opportunities he turned down: here was an orchestra, perhaps the best in the world, and here a conductor who knew how to milk the possibilities of that orchestra to the full, and here too a digital recording process capable of capturing and reproducing the performance in all its original quality for the rest of time. And what did Karajan do with it? He put it at the disposal of a self-sufficient cult of beauty, worshipping at the fetishistic shrine and making it a part of his cultural apparatus, devoted primarily to exploitation, marketing, dealing and co-operation. He thus led a life as a conductor which was highly dubious in the context of musical history, and exhausted in the repetition of a consumer-friendly repertoire; posterity, for whose attention Karajan was angling so intently in producing such a massive volume of work, may well ignore this body of work in a few decades because the spirit of the age, constantly changing as it is, will have gone far beyond his interpretations and turned him into one case among many, using him now and again for comparative purposes when examining the history of interpretation. A future such as this is more likely than any hope of eternal contemporaneity for a legacy so closely attached to the taste of our own time. What opportunities he missed, what possibilities he rejected, when he could have used his talent and his resources in the service of contemporary music, so that future musicians could take their bearings from it rather than fumble about in the darkness of interpretative speculation, as we are obliged to do when dealing with the works of the past.

It was not a lack of insight, not an intellectual deficiency that made Karajan pass up this possibility: the possibility, surely a source of pleasure to any interpreter, of realizing, with the composers of his time, the idea of a score as its author saw it, under the best possible conditions. Rather it was Karajan's ignorance of contemporary music that led him to ignore this course of action. His ego, taking its bearings from an off-centre conception of the world, led him backwards into the past. Karajan always saw his career as a major aesthetic spectacle, an escape from normality, and in the process he ignored the fact that it led nowhere, however hard he toiled and strained, because, quite unaware, like a hamster in a wheel, he never moved from the spot of his own egoism. For the wheel, tirelessly turning, was his ego. Karajan never tried to overcome the illusory character of his dreams – dreams of domination, love and greatness. He put all his efforts into making them come true. He took his bearings from his visions and myths, transformed his dreams into blueprints for a career and tried to transpose them into reality, the reality of his festivals, his multimedia omnipresence, so that he himself would become a myth and his work a mythical act, an event. But what did this 'Karajan event', so often referred to, actually consist of? And what was its significance for Karajan himself?

Conducting is the display of personal power over a musical object. Yet the conductor is not the incarnation of that power but rather the incarnation of everyone's desire – the desire of the audience, orchestra and conductor – for that power. In the 'Karajan event' the power complex inherent to different degrees within all of us, and to which Karajan devoted himself absolutely, was made manifest. In identifying with the conductor, the listener is able with impunity to work off his fantasies of power and greatness. If such identification were acted out in relation to a political leader, that leader would risk legal sanctions. In the context of music, however, it is tolerated. Music offers a pleasant and generally unconscious involvement in the exercise of power on the part of the conductor. The more unconscious this involvement, the more intense the fascination. And Karajan, who really knew how to deal with that power complex, encouraged the highest level of involvement: in the way he devoted himself to the power complex, applying it to his orchestra and his stagings, he gave his audience full scope for the unconscious satisfaction of its own power complexes.

Elias Canetti referred to the image of power that the conductor embodies as a figure visibly elevated above the mass, and in his commanding gestures.

> During a concert, and for the people gathered together in the hall, the conductor is a leader. He stands at their head with his back to them. It is him they follow . . . His hands decree and prohibit. His ears search out profanation. Thus for the orchestra the conductor literally embodies the work they are playing, the simultaneity of sounds as well as their sequence; and since, during the performance, nothing is supposed to exist except this work, for so long is the conductor the ruler of the world.[6]

Thus the conductor, 'if and as long as there are no other leaders available for adulation,' as Theodor W. Adorno established, satisfies the 'sadomasochistic urge' of the audience. For 'while the conductor acts as the tamer of the orchestra, what he actually has in mind is the audience, according to a displacement mechanism with which political demagoguery is quite familiar'.[7]

277

Conducting is revealed here as a formal representation of musical beats, and the listener is shown to be placed in a state of subjection by the fact of the conductor turning away from him. The conductor's fundamental attitude conceals his breast from the audience. The conductor's gaze, his openness, is directed forwards, 'away' from the audience. The relationship is one-sided, totalitarian. Anyone who closed his eyes at a Karajan concert would have had a totalitarian listening experience: another's omnipotence would have resonated in him, and that Other was Karajan. And if the listener opened his eyes, the Karajan concert became a multi-media aesthetic event, a complex of musical and visual messages with a strong symbolic, pseudo-religious and identificatory content. The 'Karajan event' was an event taking place in a busy, bustling, alienated world, but a world short of events. An event is time fulfilled and consequently constant presence, because it brings time to a standstill. Modern man seeks events that fill time. He seeks the event that places him under no obligations. He found this kind of event in Karajan. He was free of all responsibility. At a Karajan concert he was able to surrender voluntarily, for a time, to the ecstatic experience, the mystery of power, as a consumer, following payment of a fee.

Karajan did not only owe his fame to his ability to give a convincing rendering of scores, and of course his suggestive range of gestures was part of the aesthetic business itself; the pantomime with which he made his presence felt was a demonstration of the aesthetic fact that he represented the speaking subject, music, and 'displayed' the abstraction of the 'aesthetic ego', the composer sublimated into an idea.[8] But his conducting was always something else as well. It was the attraction of a dominant personality, geared towards applause. Only here that personality was transposed to the distance of musical space and, instead of a war, it launched a thunderstorm of orchestral music under a compulsion which was not exercised in a dictatorially absolute way, but arrived at by agreement. But the victories won when power is exercised in this way do not demand any fatal sacrifices and can consequently be celebrated all the more openly. For celebration was the chief idea behind this demonstration of power.

Karajan – and herein lies his 'merit' (if any such merit can be demonstrated, which is clearly the case) – revealed this more clearly than any other conductor, because in his case the non-musical phenomena in his work are displayed with a most intense clarity.

278

The conductor bows to the clapping hands; for them he returns to the rostrum again and again, as often as they want him to. To them, and to them alone, he surrenders; it is for them that he really lives. The applause he receives is the ancient salute to the victor, and the magnitude of his victory is measured by its volume. Victory and defeat become the framework within which his spiritual economy is organized. Apart from these nothing counts; everything that the lives of other men contain is for him transformed into victory or defeat.[9]

But defeat is to be avoided. Karajan's entire psychological make-up was, for that reason, nothing but a powerful defence against all kinds of defeat. Defeat in the sense of withheld approval, absent applause, negative criticism as well as his own failure at the head of the orchestra, with the orchestra or in playing to an empty auditorium. For that would have been the worst experience that Karajan could have had to endure: conducting to empty houses. In order to avoid that nightmare, Karajan was prepared to make any necessary concessions to his audience, since he needed cheering ovations, unfettered admiration, unbridled and unbiased approval. Karajan had a voracious appetite for affirmation and praise, and with a bare-faced arrogance he demanded an admiring public, which was to include the critics. This public was primarily important to him when it was invited to participate in his exercise of power – the embodiment, it appeared, of his fantasies of greatness – and thus to confirm it.

The relationship between the conductor and the audience was a symbiotic one. The two fed off one another, so to speak. In its applause, the public satisfied Karajan's hunger for response, his demand for confirmation – in Karajan's case a hunger and demand for love. In return, in the act of submission to the powerful leader-figure of the conductor the public perceived itself as great, following the equation: the greater the leader, the greater his follower.[10] This desire to be subjugated expresses the emotional need of the masses to be connected with a leader-figure, a need that has become the elemental motivating force in the history of this century. In just this way, idolatrous mass projection turned the perfect artist into a miracle-worker, honouring him as a demigod. And Karajan, who depended upon this because he needed it just as urgently as a fish needs water, did nothing to counteract the irrationalism, myth-making and mass hysteria, which must have suited him. Instead, he collected together the yearnings of the age, to fill himself with them and derive strength from them.

The idealization of the star into a fetish for the audience, the fans' fixation on the idol – in the case of Karajan these processes were apparent in an exemplary fashion. Not even his opposite pole, Leonard Bernstein, seemed so exposed to the hysteria of the affirmation of power that comes from the audience's identification with the conductor.

Like racing-car drivers and film-stars, Karajan became a showbusiness figure, a slave to the emotional need of the masses, who sought in him the sensation of perfection and greatness that comes from the power to achieve that perfection. But the obligation to achieve great things, the obligation to greatness, which Karajan had wrested both from himself and from his audience, hampered him in his life. It closed the way to what he sought with such yearning: the human happiness that comes from love. Instead he won admiration and veneration. And the longer he had to do without love, the more intense was his quest for success and approval through achievement, until he finally mistook fame for happiness. This might be seen as the effect of increasing one's strength, but in the wrong direction.

In love and attention Karajan found a panacea for the conflicts he felt in his self-esteem. However: the short-term effect of this miracle-cure meant that he constantly required more confirmation, more admiration and veneration, that he constantly needed new actions, new dramatic stagings.[11] These factors shaped his entire life. Concerts and operatic productions were stagings and actions like his flying and sailing, or his constant preoccupation with opportunities to see himself reflected in newspaper photographs, interviews or the promotional events organized up by his record companies. The side of his character that adored magnificence demanded satisfaction; through unstinting stagework he sought to protect his magnificent internal world against collapse, against the invasion of reality. His concerts and stagings were nothing less than an emergency reaction, to prevent the magnificence of his illusory world collapsing into the reality of his life, which would have amounted to his slipping into depression. By means of constantly new actions – whether in the form of concerts or attempts at self-affirmation in the cockpit – by intensifying the brilliance of his interpretations and perfecting the apparatus of his dramatic productions, he attempted to preserve that magnificent world. For magnificence guaranteed the continued existence of the illusion that he was loved.[12]

But it was a love applied not to him but to his achievements, his qualities and successes. A love for what he had done, not for what he was. Karajan was unable to undo that typical and tragic connection of admiration and love. It drove him compulsively to more and more new actions that assured him of admiration. His conducting, his stage work became a compulsion to repeat, and his career was the product of that compulsion. His sense of self-esteem was not rooted in the reality of his own feelings, but in the possession of certain qualities.[13] Karajan provided proof of these throughout his life. He had always wanted to prove something, be it that he was not too small to do what his brother could do, that he was better than his brother, that he was a more capable conductor than anyone else because he located the work within the music (whatever that might mean), that he was the best sailor in his class of boat, that he could master the technically complex apparatus of a jet, a racing-car or a modern theatre. Insatiably, in his compulsion to repeat he sought the admiration that finally failed to satisfy him precisely because admiration and love are not identical. Thus, in the end, his music became a superficial event in the psychological sense. Playing music did not supply him with the ideal peace of equilibrium between body and soul (although he thought it did), an entirely vital and vivid condition of life. The emergency reaction of his playing and his staging was, rather, a process very close to the biological survival instinct, if not its psychological correlative.[14]

The key reference-point in Karajan's power was his loneliness. It was thence, it seemed, that he escaped into the autistic space of music, a space of preverbal emotionality, in which exhibitionism can be directly satisfied by sensual attraction. I would not wish to go so far as to claim that the essence of conducting is therefore that of sexual energy building up to the rape of music, or that Karajan's loneliness was that of a child finding solitary satisfaction. But we can say that throughout his life Karajan only ever communed with himself, either because he was not given or because he failed to take the opportunity to come into direct contact with his environment. He would always interpose the filter of some theatrical device, be it an escape through denial, a non-committal attitude or evasion through vagueness or generalizations. As a child, Karajan had obviously seen music as an alternative means of communication with his environment. The intensity with which he made use of that means of communication gives us an idea of the magnitude of his lack of love and affection, and the hurt hidden away behind the rigid armour of his inaccessibility, perhaps as the result of profound humiliation. If we bear this in mind, we will understand Karajan's attempt to use conducting as both a

281

means of winning love and a desperate bid to keep that love as all-embracing as possible – global, in fact. For what else was his talk of man's hunger for beauty and love if not the expression of his own hunger for the very same things – a hunger that he satisfied by saturating the world with his mass-produced interpretations, trying to win himself the admiration that he mistook for love?

He called it the 'democratization' of music – bringing his sounds and images to the people. But by means of this 'democratization' of music, did he not succeed in boxing off the image of music in an area of the culture industry in which manner is always destined to appear more important than content? What was the 'democratization' of art, as Karajan practised it, but the commercial aspect of musical stardom, using the vehicle of music, in a monomaniac piece of self-dramatization, as a means of extolling the commodity called 'Karajan'? It is no coincidence that the most successful of his records, compilations and anthologies bore titles such as *Karajan-Express, HiFi Karajan, Stargala Herbert von Karajan* and *Karajan-Edition*. Did Karajan's alliance with big business, the driving force behind that same 'democratization', not encourage the processes of alienation at work in our culture rather than dismantling them? Were the speakers and cabinets, combinations of plastic and electronic components, not the precise reflection of a society in which the increasing egoism and fear of interpersonal contact observed by psychologists have replaced communication and dialogue with the world? This dialogue should also have been found in the musical works that Karajan wanted to communicate to the world. But what was the audience's level of musical training? Democratization without general education is impossible. Democracy is based on everyone's ideas. And it must be admitted that before the democratization of music can take place, universal musical illiteracy would have to be eradicated, and the ability to grasp and understand music as such would have to be developed and trained.

Is it fair to hold Karajan responsible for the desolate reality of the distressing state of his audience's musical education? Perhaps it is, in so far as Karajan did little to counteract the general process of stultification. This he could have done, for example by introducing his audience to the works, as Leonard Bernstein had, or by giving statements to his interviewers, or publishing his own thoughts about the works in his repertoire. The explanation of musical connections, a gloss on the content of a composition at the start of a music film or a record, or written statements in the accompanying texts to the records, giving thorough information – by and large, Karajan left these opportunities for direct communication, influence and education unused. And having every available means of musical communication at his disposal, he could have exploited them to give his life's work a meaning beyond the questionable activity of perpetual production. Did he really believe that all he had to do was simply to make music, and the audience would somehow grasp its meaning?

Thus, I believe, his work largely remained nothing but a contribution to the greed of an excessive society which, in the age of mass-communication, is losing its ability to communicate. How is the musically unskilled listener from our primarily visually-oriented culture to respond to music – a listener, in addition, from a generation which has grown up with the controlled diversity of an abstract reality delivered by television, and which constructs its vision of the world according to that false reality because it seems more authentic than the real world? A listener who, by listening too much but not really listening at all, has forgotten how to listen? This audience, Karajan's mass audience, did not really listen at all because it had no grasp whatsoever of the music it was listening to. Alternatively, because the mental effort demanded by listening to serious music was either refused by his audience, or simply beyond them, all they chose to hear was a pleasant kind of mood-music. They allowed the sounds to transport them to imaginary worlds, sensing something akin to happiness in the epiphany of the famous 'beautiful' passages; they surrendered to an absent-minded longing, and let their imagination play with their dreams; they sat and listened, carried away by the intoxication of the music into an unreal world of hazy emotions; they yielded to the play of free association or simply enjoyed the music without a thought in their heads as people do in the concert-halls and opera houses of the world – a fact which, when we consider the works that are our cultural heritage, is simply scandalous. Not to speak of the complete devaluation of that music into a kind of acoustic backdrop, a background noise to pleasure, work, profit and waste, undifferentiated from the general acoustic wallpaper of consumer society.

This associative and emotional, passive and sentimental way of listening reveals the spirit of the age of self-abuse. This listening, this pleasure, is the expression of an ever-present fear that a moment of silence might be waiting around the next corner, that one might be required to speak or to listen in an active way; in the century of alienation it is also the expression of the age of masturbatory vibrator-sex, in which the work of art has been stripped of its dignity, the reproduced recording has become a disposable acoustic object, and music as a whole has been turned into fodder for the ears – fodder for an audience which, either sitting by the stereo, withdrawn and isolated, or, even more cut off from the world, listening to the music on headphones, surrenders to the musical intoxication of the 'Karajan' drug; in its demand for ever more and ever greater musical stimuli, its addiction to Karajan's overwhelming *Schönklang* – designed to sweeten a life constantly threatened by boredom – it ends up damaging its hearing with over-amplification.[15]

'Beethoven has been interpreted before, but never more successfully,' Deutsche Grammophon proudly announced, talking about Karajan's 1962 recording of the Beethoven Symphonies. It was a success measured by the number of records sold rather than by artistic quality. This does not mean that Karajan's Beethoven interpretations are lacking in quality – the opposite is the case, as we know – but rather that the conflation of success and achievement is the ethic of people incapable of believing in anything but themselves, because their goal is success. But in the process Karajan came to be seen as the metaphor for 'all the pleasure-craving consumption of such holy art',[16] anticipated by the far-sighted Nietzsche, a metaphor for our industrialized consumer society, which he industriously kept supplied with his productions, constantly complemented and rerecorded using the most advanced techniques of the day. In the process, Karajan was destroying the uniqueness of his work – for uniqueness and mass-production are actually mutually exclusive (or did his uniqueness lie in the extent of his mass-production?). On the other hand there were, of course, reasons for this mass-production and marketability, for this no-expense-spared promotion: the fetish needed new disciples, new addicts, new believers to swell its congregation of consumers.

It would be unfair not to point out that people truly interested in music, musically educated people, were able to use the limitless riches of Karajan's interpretations to extend their knowledge; or that those interpretations gave them access to the great works of the music of the world, in a form close to perfection in its orchestral bravura and in artistically valid interpretations. But the brief that was forced on Karajan in the context of musical politics, because of his influence and the unique opportunities presented to him – to have a widespread effect based on profound musical understanding – was finally abandoned in favour of self-worship.

Here it was of no account whether anyone understood the music; on the contrary: understanding would have been an undesirable distraction. Thus the idea of the 'democratization' of music, the idea of an understanding involvement in the great creations of Western music, remained, for all those who never had the good fortune of hearing Karajan in concert, nothing but an empty phrase.

Karajan's Amazing Art only came to fruition in the concert hall or the opera house. His recordings were frequently produced more for commercial than for artistic motives and often recorded on a *prima-vista* basis because Karajan believed that the standard of the orchestra would make this defensible from an artistic point of view – in 1979 alone he supplied the market with twenty-seven recordings. There were exceptions, such as his recording of Schoenberg's Orchestral Variations opus 31, carried out under ideal studio conditions, but otherwise the quite specific fluidity of a Karajan concert was not conveyed by his recordings, any more than they could capture the inner fire and intensity of his performances as they were unleashed in his concerts. The Karajan of the gramophone records was, we might say, the brilliantly depersonalized, level-headed director, while the Karajan of the concert-hall was the musician affected by the musical event, with all the shaman-like and magical aspects that went into creating the aura of his performances.

But what, in fact, was a Karajan concert, what were its meaning and function for the conductor and the audience, apart from its most obvious function of reproducing music? What was the essence of a Karajan concert? As I have already indicated, the concert audience surrendered to the mystery of power, not only the mystery of music. The conductor became a populist, drawing his power from the mass of his listeners, a virtuoso gesticulating from the podium like a circus animal-tamer, but with the aura of a demigod. In his concerts Karajan was exercising his power as the charismatic leader, certain in his ability to create a resonance in his fellow men, without having to come into personal contact with them. His concerts, then, like his operatic productions, were the arena for the powerful, mimic self-dramatization with which Karajan maintained his magnificence. His concerts became the consecration of his greatness, the celebration of the extreme demands he made on himself and his orchestra.

It was into the personal staging of consecrations such as these

285

that Karajan directed all his talents: the air of mystical other-worldliness was just as much a part of the skilful ritual of this self-dramatization as his shaman-like appearance was of the theatrical performances with which he captivated the great collective of listeners in his congregation. Karajan worked with ritualized postures, with an almost religious apparatus and vocabulary ('Music is based on true mysticism') and messianic intentions – the pacification of man through beauty, through perfection. His conducting bore the stamp of an alternative religion: mystery, holiness, radiance, grandiosity, ecstasy, other-worldliness, inwardness. He administered himself to the audience like a drug, replaced level-headedness with the intoxication of the masses, and believed that the audience, which, almost unconsciously, truly claimed him as its own, owed him the applause he craved. But the audience, which projected its yearnings on to him and identified with him, was always applauding itself when it applauded Karajan. In the carefully calculated ritual of his performances the audience formed a backdrop for him. These were stagings like those of the Florence of the Medici: the Großes Festspielhaus was Karajan's royal court theatre, where, in the court ceremonial of dissembling and self-dramatization, Karajan brought to life everything external, the total illusory world of the operatic stage, and exercised his power over the very thing that had him in its thrall.

Yes, the star had a profound human meaning. As the expression of human perfection, he acted as a kind of stand-in to an audience in search of a truly great and strong authority, the epitome of the charismatic leader. In Karajan it found a universal father-figure, an idol that had risen to mythic cult status. In its collective identification with him, the irresistibly attractive superstar Karajan, the audience perceived itself as a part of the celebration, and participated in the intoxicated confidence of the successful man who, with great psychological finesse and a skilfully developed array of psychological stimuli, set the audience to work on the myth of his existence.

The relationship between Karajan and his audience was an illusory coupling in which both partners needed one another, not in order to communicate with one another, but to experience themselves as seen, heightened and intensified, through the eyes of the other partner. It was a relationship based on alienation, and as such it was expressive of our age. Karajan was buoyed up on the spirit of the age, which constantly invents new religions, addictions and gratifications. Music has become a source of euphoria for the age of alienation, and the musical concert, in its dissimulation of a communal experience, has become the institutionalized response to fears of loneliness. The intellectual content of music is no longer perceived, having been degraded into an addictive drug which gives a sick society the opportunity to regress for a while – a last hopeless escape from reality: from the unbearable alienations that occur in human relationships.

If this is so – and the reality of our everyday life constantly gives us reason for believing that it is – we must ask what music meant for Karajan himself, how it was useful to him, what he used it for and what he did with it. His desire for effect was, as I have attempted to show, the same as his yearning for love. The brightly lit action of his stage productions, the spells he cast upon himself, were sentimental symbols of his appeals for love. His stagings and rituals were despair made material. Just as the audience, like the rest of the world we live in, crazed as it is by images and sounds, escapes into music as a surrogate for an alienated reality, Karajan did not withdraw into music in order to do something with it in his own right, as a composer, but in order to satisfy his megalomaniac fantasies and his craving for approval. Since he felt constantly threatened, music and, along with it, his inexhaustable repertoire of stagings, gave him a permanent sense of extravagance, with which he botched together his fragmented, lonely world. Karajan was 'lonely' because he closed himself off, because his ideas were the ones that mattered, the only ones worthy of consideration, and because nobody understood him in one way or another. The loneliness of Herbert von Karajan was illusory. There is a different experience, that of complete loneliness, a total inability to communicate – quite a different matter from the form of loneliness that had become a need for Karajan. The two experiences differ as egoism differs from individuation. It is possible to turn one's immunity, one's isolation, into a cult, and then say: I am lonely. Thus Karajan's concerts and stagings became stations of the Cross, in a sense. In the cult of beautiful illusion he hoped to leave his earthly tribulations behind.

Modern man's outward appearance has come to be a mere illusion; he only ever appears in public as a depiction of himself, and organizes his life in terms of that depiction. Karajan too was always a representative of that mendacious world of show and illusion which, to use a phrase of Nietzsche's, craves dazzlement rather than illumination. But Karajan's concerts and stagings were also always something other than this, something different. In his music and his stagings he devoted himself to his fantasies of power, greatness, beauty and love, and assuaged his yearnings to escape

287

all boundaries, his yearnings for transcendence and unity. This also explains Karajan's comparatively regressive musical programmes, in which works were selected to satisfy those very same needs. Karajan's affinity with the great works of sacred music is plain. They were in perfect accord with his demand for 'mysticism' just as they served his pseudo-cultic depiction of himself. The Requiems of Verdi and Brahms, Beethoven's *Missa Solemnis* and Bach's *B Minor Mass* passed like a thread through an artistic life musically devoted to fantasies of omnipotence, fantasies concerned with the individual's experience of death and the afterlife.

'The older we grow, the easier it becomes to return. The same works accompany us through our lives.'[17] And that was how it was: Karajan never left the unchanging climate of his repertoire. This climate supported his grandiosity which, like the high-heat plasma of a fusion reactor, decomposes in a moment as soon as the magnetic field supporting it is broken, its energy withdrawn. Throughout his life, Karajan constantly returned to the same works, similar in their internal structure. By and large he never broke away from the intoxicating character of his first Salzburg concert: Strauss's tone poem *Don Juan* and Tchaikovsky's Fifth Symphony, with which the twenty-one-year-old Karajan had launched his conducting career, are representative of the continually repeated programmes of his career, always geared towards self-confirmation – programmes which never underwent any true development. All through his life Karajan ran on the spot where his programmes were concerned: if development there was, it was a development towards a higher level of perfection, but barely at all in the sense of expansion and increased profundity.

Karajan, the very opposite of the adventurer, the man who never broke the cord, never went exploring at any point in his career as an interpreter. His excursions into new musical territory were never anything more than the little walks of a child, never straying where his mother, the source of protection and refuge, cannot see or call to him. That mother was tradition. Karajan was a traditionalist, and as such he was a timeless conservative. His interpretations were never adventurous affairs. He never resisted traditions or examined them critically, nor did he, where there were no traditions, establish new ones. In music he sought only stability and conservation. His interpretations always soared into the timeless heavens of an idealist aesthetic, thus avoiding possible critical attacks. As an artist who kept the world at a distance, who worked neither for nor against the contemporary world, but rather alongside it, Karajan never tested his own interpretations against

288

the standards of the present day. He was not a truly creative artist, who does not simply borrow or even accept anything at all, who takes the questionable aspects of traditions seriously because they are worth questioning, and sheds light on them. His interpretations after he took over the Berlin Philharmonic were acoustic choreographies which did not so much as revolt against traditional expectations. Toscanini had anticipated him in this with his tempi, unusually fast for the time, and the cool brilliance of perfect orchestral virtuosity.

The history of Karajan's interpretations has not yet been written. At this point I can only put forward a few brief observations for discussion, as a contribution to that book that still waits to be written. If I have said that Karajan is more of a custodian than an experimenter, this only seems to contradict the modernity often attributed to his work. For that modernity was illusory. To take an example: his interpretation of Beethoven was more traditional than was generally stated. It was in the tradition of Karajan's models, Toscanini and Furtwängler. Karajan's interpretation was an attempt at an exemplary mediation between these two supposed extremes, in the form of a synthesis – unable, certainly, to escape the plagiaristic character of such a mediation.

Karajan did not delve too deeply into the works in his repertoire. His work was untouched by any philological curiosity. His fidelity to the text was often nothing more than fidelity to an unexamined traditional way of listening. And this was too often starkly opposed to the original text. To stay with Beethoven: Karajan's apparently 'original' Beethoven has been retouched in a completely unnecessary way. Interpretatively, too, he often deviated from the path of textual reliability. In the coda to the last movement of Beethoven's Fourth Symphony, for example, he took the semi-quaver figure, already slowed down to a quaver figure, and dragged it out and slowed it down even further, in a way that cannot be justified either musically or philologically. There is nothing in the score to authorize this. Beethoven had already completed his musical joke. But in the traditionally heard version, which is in this case nothing but a manhandling of the text, the surprise effect, the syncopated and attenuated eructations of the motif, a subtle joke on Beethoven's part to conclude the symphony, collapse. Where philological precision might have disclosed the meaning of the score, Karajan often went the comfortably uncritical way of a 'tradition' based on ignorance.

Another example of Karajan's approximative treatment of the great symphonic scores is found in his version of Bruckner's Fifth

289

Symphony. There he shortened the composed pauses between the fortissimo choruses in the introduction of the first movement. When I asked him why he did this, he looked startled, and said he was keeping to the score. Karajan did not justify his abbreviation of the pauses in a musical sense (he was not even aware of it), something that he could not in any case have done, since they are an integral part of the musical idea – a metrical breathing-space between the alternating blocks of sound of brass and tutti. Interpretative criticism is always a criticism of details. I shall content myself with these brief references, but I should also like to point out that in his treatment of this same symphony, Karajan showed himself to be a master in his shaping of the work, when, for example, towards the end of the development of the first movement, with unique interpretative clear-sightedness, he revealed the almost pagan background (if it is impossible to avoid religious references when discussing Bruckner) of ostinato, unison beats (in bars 323–4 and 329–330). In Karajan's version, the closing chorale of that symphony becomes an apotheosis of solidity and strength, a liturgy of power captured in art. In its monumentality, its brilliance and the all-engulfing magnificence of its sound, Karajan felt that his yearnings for greatness, power, admiration and love were true. This closing chorale is exemplary of the type of music in which Karajan found fulfilment, escaping all boundaries and, in an 'oceanic emotion',[18] attaining unity with the world (Beethoven put it similarly in the closing chorus of the Ninth Symphony: *'Seid umschlungen, Millionen'*), and 'consequently found a socially acceptable form of magical omnipotence and a repetition of early, primitive kinaesthetic joys', which sent him soaring through space along with the notes of the music.[19]

It was a state of fusion with the music and the audience, behind which we might suspect the unconscious wish to perish, in an act of sacrifice, in the ecstatic intoxication of the almost painful hugeness of the music, just as people can reach the raptures of supreme ecstasy when being dismembered. He was drunk on beauty, brilliance and monumentality, losing himself in the sea of sound of great symphonic music. It is up to the psychologists to say what these seas of sound may mean. They might tell us whether, in those musical oceans in which he abstractedly submerged himself, he was in search of the limitless vagina of his ideal woman, the 'infinite vagina',[20] whether conducting gave him the state of unity that he sought, whether he sought a pleasurable symbiosis with a non-consuming mother, and whether homosexual tendencies might have played a part in this longing for limitlessness.

'With the orchestra I reach ecstasy in the true sense of the word. I stand outside myself,' Karajan straightforwardly confessed, tellingly describing the state of his rapture.[21] In his ecstatic enjoyment of music, in which he was emotionally united with the music, Karajan extended his internal world into the nonverbal universe of sound.[22] The intoxication of that musical experience was reflected, after his concerts, in a strangely enraptured, glazed expression that might almost have been called religious. An ecstatic, will-o'-the-wisp smile came into his eyes. I always saw this almost divine, ecstatic smile after his concerts, while he was still floating in the euphoria of immediate success, but also when he raved, in the euphoria of memory, about the great successes of his career. It was a strangely boyish, yet timelessly ecstatic smile. The smile of a god, perhaps. The Lord God himself might smile in just that way, if he existed, when gazing upon his universe in the joy of eternity. The photographer Roger Hauert captured a hint of that ecstatic smile on the face of the forty-seven-year-old Karajan in a particularly happy moment, and saved it for posterity.[23] This beaming, silent smile is the same as the smile we see on the face of a Chinese sentenced to the 'torture of one hundred parts', his body dismembered by the knife while still alive, and whose transfigured smile reveals the identity of divine ecstasy and the most extreme terror, the connection of religious ecstasy and eroticism.[24] The ecstatic smile, the complete rapture of the expression that lit up his face for a few moments after his performances – did it perhaps reflect an erotic relationship towards music? Would it be wrong to suppose that Karajan's understanding of music could be reduced to the following formula: music is Eros made sound? And if we added that for Karajan music was emotion made concrete? Music as 'mysterium tremendum'? The fearful effect of the divine?

In any case it is certain that for Karajan music was also always a means of expressing power. He resolutely transferred his absolutist self-image into music and the audience. In his demand for the absolute and his desire for fusion he revealed the spirit of the age, with all its contempt for the measure of man. The gigantism of the twentieth century was reflected in Karajan's style of interpretation and staging, aimed at greatness and monumentality, perfection and the beauty that came from it. This century's colossal architecture found an echo in the elevated raptures of his music, and the gigantism of the age reappeared unexpectedly in his operatic stagings, as well as in his musical performances, which aimed for the most intense explosions of sound and found an aural counterpoint in the cult of inaudibility, the pianissimo of the masses.

Just as Frank Lloyd Wright, the creator of the Guggenheim Museum, in his old age designed a tower to contain a complete city, in his music Karajan constructed a zone that was larger than life, in which he sketched out his visions of omnipresence, omnipotence and perfection. In place of the utopia of the total city, Karajan dreamed of the utopia of perfection. And just as the enormous buildings of the present day, such as the double tower of the World Trade Centre, are, for all their technical impressiveness, primarily gestures of power, the same is true of Karajan's operatic productions on the stage of the Salzburg Festspielhaus, where, with his realization of the *Ring des Nibelungen*, he examined the problem of power: 'I simply wanted to find out what it means to have power.' Karajan consecrated the Berlin Philharmonie and the Großes Festspielhaus as temples dedicated to the aesthetic religion of the pure beauty of sound. They were secularized cathedrals where omnipotence and dignity were reserved for art, and where Karajan presented his own consecrated host to his congregation.

Given the obvious taste for power and the yearnings for fusion apparent in Karajan's musical and theatrical style, in our examination of the history of Karajan's interpretations we should pursue the question of whether Karajan's monumentalism, the expression of human longings, was in fact something that he had kept alive from the time of the Third Reich. We should examine whether Karajan, who always refused to give a clear account of his past, learned from the irresistible art of seduction propagated by National Socialism, in the sense of being able to harness it and use it in the sphere of art. We should try and discern whether the major stylistic trademark of National Socialism, kitsch in all its varieties, became a part of Karajan's dramatic and interpretational style, either directly or transformed in some way. And we should then consider a particular example, analysing one of his operatic stagings: this should explain whether the theatricality and choreography of the NSDAP 'Party Days', the suggestive effect of mass processions, the gestures of strength and solidity overintensified by the 'Triumph of the Will', as well as the rituals of National Socialism as a 'public staging of things forbidden',[25] passed into Karajan's theatrical style, in his private or his artistic life. Whether the mass processions were reduced to the demonstrations of power in his operatic productions and concerts, in which all that had to

292

be won was unthreatening musical battles – and the extent to which the glamour of National Socialism was to be found in Karajan's repertoire of theatrical gestures and stylizations.

For example, with reference to his Easter Festival staging of *Parsifal*, which had the air of being a last will and testament, and which he saw as a summation of his work in music theatre, we might examine whether the static geometry, the symmetrical arrangement of the columns in the Grail Temple, recalling colossal architecture, the precise and rhythmic march-step of the militant masculine order of the Grail Knights, committed to purity, and the dramatic centrepiece, clearly left quite neutral, of the meeting between Kundry and Parsifal, expressed an affinity with the phenomena of National Socialism that Karajan never quite discarded, as well as a deep-rooted relationship to a community structured on latent homosexuality.[26] In this context too we might discuss the question of whether the men's club of the Berlin Philharmonic, the orchestra used in the *Parsifal* production, should be examined with reference to the same issues; and whether the production should or must be seen as an instrument of fascist reality – something that would also cast doubt on Karajan, its producer. The history of his interpretations which still remains to be written, and which would take into account his life and character, would also have to explain whether Karajan's relationship with music, his 'science', was moral or simply real, and whether his work was simply the expression and the result of a perfect self-deception, and his career, in consequence, the story of the decline of a man's character.

Karajan's choice of works and the organization of his programmes was, as we have already established, strongly influenced by non-musical considerations and intentions. But one aspect of this, and one which I consider to be quite important, has still not been considered – the role of the audience in the context of the programmes that Karajan chose. The fact that the audience was invited to take part in Karajan's celebration of himself, to confirm his power, was not the only reason for its importance, after all. The audience was also burdened with the task of granting Karajan the recognition that he demanded: the recognition of his artistic achievement. Thus he became dependent on the taste of his audience, which he himself had shaped to a great extent. It is barely conceivable that an interpreter would constantly win recognition and approval from an audience that did not like the music performed. The recognition that Karajan had in mind was linked to the satisfaction of the audience's desires. If he had not taken these into consideration he would soon have found himself without an audience, and his major fear would have become a reality: he would have played to empty houses. So Karajan did everything he could to win the love of his audience and to keep its good favour. For this was what he needed; the audience lent support to his grandiose self-image, whose conservation was of prime importance. If Karajan had included in his programmes contemporary works alien to the taste of the audience, he would have risked losing his audience and consequently its admiration.

This does a great deal to explain why Karajan did not engage with contemporary music. It would have been an unrewarding goal, because it would probably not have won him the much-needed approval of the people in the auditorium. Another reason may lie in the fact that contemporary music, which often calls for profound sobriety, and which sometimes demands a gestural repertoire restricted to functional coolness and clarity, could not provide the conductor with those kinaesthetic experiences that were a significant motivating force behind his conducting. In his highly ephemeral dealings with contemporary music, Karajan required the established guarantee of applause, however muted it might have been. When he conducted 'the moderns' he almost always chose tried and tested works. A work was not worthy of Karajan's consideration until it had met with at least a friendly reception elsewhere. The fact that performances sometimes failed through Karajan's lack of engagement with and interest in contemporary works supplied him with the satisfactory argument that 'modern' music was no great shakes. The remarkably few occasions on which Karajan gave the première of a work cannot conceal the fact that he used his 'engagement' with contemporary music as a form of alibi. When, for example, in 1973 he performed Carl Orff's melodrama *De Temporum Fine Comoedia* at the Salzburg Festival, he stressed this fact by his method of dealing with the work. He had it rehearsed by Gerhard Lenssen in Cologne, and, since he was preoccupied with the filming of Verdi's *Otello* in Munich, took the work over at the dress rehearsal, with the result that he 'owed Orff everything'.[27]

And why should he have performed contemporary music, when he saw it as an entirely thankless task (and one which others carried out with greater ease) and when in any case he was not primarily concerned with music. Karajan was concerned first and foremost with applause in all its forms. When, at the end of a successful performance, he made a curtain call or returned to the hall to receive the audience's thanks, admiration, recognition and love, he was the happiest man alive. He fed on the surge of applause just as he gave his internal world its life-giving tonic in the euphoria of his musical orgy. When, accepting the adulation of the audience, he took a breath before the applauding auditorium, it was always a long draught of immortality.

How did Karajan justify – or rather rationalize – his reticence towards the work of contemporary composers when his encouragement of them could have brought him the real merits on which he had set his sights throughout his life?

You see, a well-run museum is a very fine thing. If we keep returning to the great masterpieces, it is because they probably have a general, universal value. The human testimony about the values that we hold to be eternal and valid is in the end the only authoritative thing. It has found expression in the great works of art. That is why we always find our way back to them. As far as composers taking new directions are concerned, they must first prove that their work will live, and that their music is capable of addressing a broad range of people. Obviously each of us will do everything we can to bring new directions to the public.

The avant-garde . . . I've seen a few people doing it much better, getting notes out of a garden hose. People ought to go and see that. But there's no audience. Things don't have a value just by virtue of the fact that they're written today. It's hard to say whether the new directions in modern music are the right ones. We shouldn't always be so impatient. Stravinsky and Bartok are already part of the standard repertoire today. Twenty years ago it was quite different. In my opinion, it's a mistake to compare things: it's wrong to play one thing off against another. We can't yet know where these new directions are leading. It would be a mistake to reject the phenomena that are emerging so forcefully today, such as electronic music. Because it comes from a quite different basic tendency. In that sense every new experiment should be welcomed. But we shouldn't set any standards of value – everyone should do what he considers right. And if, for example, a radio station thinks it is using its money in a sensible way by spending it on avant-garde musical productions, it should go right ahead. I'm in favour of everything that opens up new horizons.

The production of new music is, for quite understandable reasons, so complicated and so expensive that an orchestra working with a large repertoire is very pressed for time. And for that reason I say that the audience is better served with new music elsewhere. It should go there and listen to it. I do the things I'm convinced are good. And the works we don't do are played elsewhere. If people come to my concerts they hear the whole repertoire from Bach to Stravinsky, Schoenberg and Bartok. And, I believe, very carefully rehearsed and played.

We have to agree with him there: Karajan left nothing to chance. Everything was always calculated, in the playing of music as elsewhere. This calculation was used and tested in rehearsal. The life of a conductor is a constant re-examination of what is and what should be. In rehearsal, when Karajan had to concentrate on this consideration, when he was surrounded by his peers and not facing an audience, his true singularity as a musician became apparent. For here the magic of his baton and the gift of suggestion were directed entirely towards the object of his work, the music.

In unironed casual trousers, worn out sandals or jogging shoes, and with a cardigan around his armpits or a pullover thrown over his shoulders, Karajan would come to his desk. The feline suppleness of his movements, the mannered air of his physical stance, the upright body and the carefully combed mop of hair were reserved for public appearances. Thoroughly charming, smiling non-committally, he demanded discipline and concentration from his orchestra with the greatest of ease. Winningly endearing in his treatment of his musicians, he was still relentless in his qualitative demands.

The gleaming chrome conductor's chair on which he sat was at once a throne and a couch. He rested on it during his short breaks, leaning his legs against the conductor's desk. Aesthete and magician in one, he followed his movements, circling around and constantly swimming in the flow of the music, as if he wanted to be charmed by his own elegance. Every now and again he would pass the back of his hand over his nose: how much condescension and nonchalant arrogance there was in that symbolic nose-blowing. He was generally preoccupied with trivial points, nuances; it was these that he got his teeth into, and which he fanatically rehearsed and re-rehearsed with the determination of the eternally discontent. In the fortissimo passages he would take his feet away from the desk. Suddenly he was standing there, unambiguously, firmly on his two feet, raising his arms for the strike, losing himself in the intensification of the music and taking the sound to the limits of the bearable. This was music, quite elementally. As his highly trained, suntanned body arched, his belly and navel were freed – the omphalos of the passions.

Anyone listening attentively to Karajan during his concerts would, in passages containing powerful explosions of sound, the break-down of emotional barriers or the tension preceding an instrument's entry, have heard primeval, almost grunting noises emerging from his throat. He explained these grunts, which often had to be laboriously suppressed on his gramophone recordings, as follows: 'I think they are the expression of a level of tension between achievement and intention.' The interpreter's tension before the performance is similar to that which precedes musically important passages. Did Karajan suffer from stage-fright, that feeling of nervous unease and internal apprehension before the concerts, which afflicts many artists? 'No, I never suffer from stage-fright, I don't know that feeling. I only know that I'd like to get started. I want to get on with it!'

I have already tried to show what kind of pleasure Karajan derived from his concerts. Have I explained clearly enough that it might also be the pleasure of self-gratification? The artist as self-portraitist – was Karajan not one of these? So how might Salvador Dali's ideas of the artist as *le grand masturbateur* apply to Karajan? Karajan's relationship to music was, as I have already shown, an erotic one, because it was a relationship with power. But anyone who experiences power as a stimulant acts in an emotional way. Consequently Karajan's understanding of music was emotionally defined.

One should not understand music intellectually so much as feel and experience it. No one can have such a profound feeling for the moments of tension as a conductor who really works from the heart. Those are things that you need to have experienced and suffered as a conductor. It's actually impossible to explain to someone who hasn't experienced it himself what it means to experience the beauty of the work on a good evening, and the gratitude of the one for the other.

Karajan was not an analyst. His analytical understanding of music was not very highly developed. Instead he had an unerring, intuitive sense of the music's nerve-centres. Nevertheless, he was not concerned with the most direct communication in his perform-ances. He also lacked spontaneity. 'Conductors are never genuine,'

297

observed the impresario Andreas von Bennigsen, highly experienced at dealing with eccentric interpreters. 'Nothing is spontaneous. Everything's kept on a tight rein. Everything's always kept tightly under control,' he said of Karajan. 'Control is fine. But you also have to be able to break loose.'[28] Karajan never relaxed his hold, because his goal was perfection, and it was in perfection that he sought fulfilment. Perfection is not only a highly virtuoso orchestral culture, the minimum requirement for halfway decent performances, not only the most flawless, correctly articulated and dynamically balanced performance possible, but also a subtle organization of structures, processes, lines and tonal colour. Precision, then, not only in a superficial technical sense, but also precision in the compositional content. Behind this there lies the visionary and utopian idea, which also seems solipsistic, of making music in accordance with the ideal of that music. And Karajan was in search of thoroughly controlled expression. But did he find it? Did he have within his grasp the strong and genuine feeling that is the basis and starting-point for that kind of control? Before I answer that question, I should like Karajan himself to say something about what he felt when he was conducting.

Gratitude to be able to do it. And joy . . . You know, when you're young, you have a lot of ideas about what (if anything) is hidden in the heart of it. The more I go to the bottom of things now, and the more precisely I do it, the more all I find is music. And I feel – I don't think I'm mistaken – that the youth of today is no longer burdened with the intellectual or symbolic interpretative ideas that beset my father's generation to a great extent, for example, but rather experiences and hears music as music – as the expression of an internal dynamic of the soul and the mind.

Just as I now wonder how I experience music, I also ask my listeners what happens in them when they listen to music, whether they have a purely sensuous way of listening, or whether they combine music, in some way, with other ideas. A concert is a very complex business, because it emerges from an intellectual idea. In between these there is a path about which people generally know very little. First of all it is the transposition by the composer of an intellectual idea into a musical form. The interpreter then faces the difficult task of turning notations into sound.

But the written notes are at best an indication of what the composer means. All the information in a score is relative. How many decibels does a *forte* correspond to, for example? When do you have to start a *stringendo*, how does the dynamic of a *diminuendo* occur? These are all questions to which the score provides only an inadequate answer. For that very reason, you cannot expect to do justice as an interpreter to a composer's intentions. An objective rendering is, for that reason, virtually impossible. And the concept of fidelity to the work is a contradiction in itself. I always demand from a conductor that he should be entirely familiar with the score. But even the most precise familiarity does not replace its transposition into living sound. In music there are also things that a conductor must grasp, in the full sense of the word, just as one must touch a sculpture in order to feel its form. What one experiences in music is, to a large extent, just such a feeling of form.

Karajan's call for the most precise familiarity with the score also reflects the demands which he made on himself for the best possible interpretative conditions. For by familiarity with a work he meant complete mastery of the work itself, and not only its existence as a score. It was a principle of Karajan's to conduct by heart. What this meant in practice could only be measured by comparing the performance with the score. From Bach's choral works to Wagner's lengthy operas, Karajan had all the music in his head. For example, he conducted the entire *Ring des Nibelungen* by heart – over fifteen hours of music. We have only to imagine the workload involved in his Easter Festival to have an idea of his capacity: symphonic pieces, choral works or operas, following one another day by day – Karajan conducted them all without a score. For Karajan, the extraordinary had become self-evident.

Certainly a conductor's powers of memory are often misjudged, because one is unaware of the conditions that attend the learning by heart of such a complex structure as a musical score. The process of learning things by heart, music included, is primarily based on hard work. This would make Karajan, in this respect as in many others, the most hard-working of conductors – for is there anyone to match him?

I take a great deal of time to get to know things that are new to me. Only by repeatedly engaging with a work does one reach the point where one feels that this is actually how it must be – and one knows where one has to intervene and where the work can carry itself. For it has a quite normal life of its own. It resists any outside influence, and erects a barrier if one fails to let it live and breathe as it needs to do. You have to let a work mature in you until it becomes a part of you. And at that point you realize that something you would never have conducted that way before is now something quite natural, without your even thinking about it. That is the beautiful thing about the development of a man, the fact that this maturing process brings him closer and closer to things. And it would actually unsettle me a great deal if I had to use a score to do that. There is a great advantage in conducting a work by heart, because you have to become very involved with the work. It takes hours and hours to incorporate a work entirely within yourself and come into purely spiritual contact with it. Of course there are works that cannot be conducted without a score because they are too complicated, because so many things are happening at the same time that it is actually one's reactions that are being tested. But in general I must say that this is not so much a feat of memory as the reproduction of something entirely within oneself. It rises from within, without one's having to think about it.

For instance, I didn't conduct *Die Meistersinger* for twenty-five years. The work lay dormant in me. And the moment I began the orchestral rehearsals for the recordings, everything was just as fresh as it had been. The price I pay for this is that I forget everything else: names, telephone numbers and so on. That doesn't stay with me. I would call the visual memorization of the score a feat of memory. The Vienna Philharmonic, who are very quick to notice things, could tell from Dmitri Mitropoulos's head when he was turning the pages in his mind, because Mitropoulos visually memorized the score. That isn't the case with me.

And yet Karajan was a thoroughly visual person. He grasped things with his eyes, and from a distance, rather than with his hands. Karajan was always in search of the ideal line. He looked for it in beautiful people, formally perfect machines and in melodies. His ears and eyes compulsively followed that line, to capture in an ideal form what they saw and heard. The ideal sound of Karajan's acoustic world corresponded to ideal space in the concrete world. Karajan's performances derived from the phenomenon of sound. His pronounced sensitivity to impressions and his finely tuned receptivity, normally encountered only among very sensitive artists and sophisticated women, found full expression in his sense of the finest tonal values.

'Tension should be aesthetically beautiful as well.' That is the confession of a radical sensualist. It is also the key to his art as an interpreter. In his performances, Karajan radicalized the principle of art for art's sake. He purged the music of all intellectual, poetic or allegorical content and brought it down to the elements of sound and their effective possibilities. There were no meanings or secrets for Karajan, no laws or stories behind the music. They all lay in the phenomenon of sound, which he stylized in his interpretative art. Karajan was a colourist with the intuitive ability to indulge in the pleasure of sounding out the tiniest nuances, in which his whole wealth of observation and experience were stored. Meaning for him was entirely a matter of the senses, not of the analytically operating intellect. He was an alchemist in sound, he conjured up polyphonic fantasies where they did not seem to occur in the score. He gave even his pauses the allure of beauty. He trained the Berlin Philharmonic up to become a congenial partner in his celebration of sound. He alone knew how to bring out that incomparable orchestra's most characteristic ability to deal most delicately with quiet musical nuances, and turn it into a beguiling aural experience.

Was it a fetishization of *melos* and harmony that came to light here? Was Karajan's fetish, the source of his pleasure and power, one of beautiful sound? Karajan's musical virtues lay in the cult of beauty and purity, the glorification of the aesthetic ideal of the harmony of beauty and the rejection of the intellect as an analytic, reflecting factor. Were these not equally present in fascist structures? If we were to join Hans Heinz Stuckenschmidt in describing 'Nazi culture as the very thing its proponents accused Jewish culture of being: incapable of original achievements, and only capable of reproducing traditional values with a strong sense of external effect',[29] might we then – given that this was the case – along with the virtues mentioned, draw parallels with Karajan's artistic work?

With his cult of beautiful sound, having brought it to its zenith with the Berlin Philharmonic, Karajan repeatedly encountered massive criticism. Whereas his interpretations, in their stainless presence, affected the audience like a drug, bringing about a state of euphoria, they were rejected by a large proportion of music critics. Karajan's luxuriance, his sensualistic playing, his refinement and diversification of tonal colours, his exhaustion of the entire dynamic range, in fact all the qualities that made up

301

Karajan's talent, for years brought him the disapproval of the critics, who take themselves very seriously. They accused him of using his superlative gifts in the service of a cult of beauty which only gave rise to a kind of playing that was two-dimensional, unrounded, sketchy and superficial.

Was this a misunderstanding? And who or what was misunderstood, and by whom? Was Karajan misunderstanding the music, were the critics or the audience misunderstanding Karajan? Or the critics misunderstanding the music? Perhaps we might explain the misunderstanding, if that was indeed what it was, with reference to Karajan's extra-musical activities, and find an answer to the aesthetic dimension of his urge for perfection.[30] Let us once more imagine the type of artist that Karajan represented: Karajan was the twentieth-century artist *par excellence*. That sounds completely banal, and is far from obvious. The twentieth century has been the age of technology, the machine. The *Titanic*, Concorde, Saturn rockets, the Space Shuttle, the television and the computer are metaphors for this century. Karajan, the modernist, was entirely in harmony with his age, the age of technology, the mass media and the ideal of perfection. An ideal which states that the perfect is also beautiful. In his field, Karajan was the uncontested protagonist of the age. He always recognized developments at the very beginning, and was able to use them to his own ends. Western man, as a 'machine-man', is a man needed, limited and hampered by the machine. His spontaneity, which he believed to be his own, belonged to the machine. Karajan tried to resolve the contradiction between man and machine for himself, and to reconcile the two, believing that he could subjugate the machine. For the machine may have arisen from human ideas, but it has grown so independent that technology threatens to dominate man. Here, too, Karajan fell prey to his over-inflated sense of his own greatness, believing that machines were his subordinates; and thus he became the victim of his own machinery, internally and externally. He identified technology with immortality. Karajan's machines were the jet-plane, the ocean-going racing yacht, the experimental motor-car, the whole apparatus of the synthetic production of sounds and images. The latter was of central importance for Karajan's artistic work, and the highly complex apparatus of the jet was the symbol both of his life and his existence. Flying allowed him to experience the meaning of technology to the full – leaving the planet, as Icarus had dreamed of doing.

Karajan used these machines because of his fascination with perfection, and in the pleasure he took simply in the way they worked. As he himself stressed, he was not concerned, whether he was flying, sailing or driving a motor-car, with the experience of speed, but rather with the experience of the perfect operation of the technical apparatus.[31]

Karajan's machines were all streamlined. The aeroplane no less than the sailing-ship and the sportscar. Steamlined objects have the lowest degree of resistance to the elements through which they move. The lower the resistance, the more friction-free the motion – and consequently the higher the speed for a given power – or a lower level of power for a given speed. As Karajan was not concerned with the experience of speed, as far as our considerations are concerned the latter variant is significant: the reduction of resistance to achieve the same motion at a lower level of power. Karajan's fascination, the pleasure of overcoming resistance. In the streamlined design of the aeroplane, the pilot overcomes the resistance of the surrounding medium, air, just as the skipper of a steamlined yacht does with water. For what is the chief interest in flying and sailing, if not that of finding the ideal streamline design to counteract the resistance of the medium? But this occurs through the laminar flow surrounding the body so as to minimize turbulence. The more successful the design of the body in achieving a laminar flow in motion, the lower will be the resistance.

The streamlined body satisfies this aim to the full. To a certain extent it embodies the objective spirit of the present century. It is, as the expression of an aesthetic of civilizing modernity, captured in the smooth form of Jaray's first streamlined motor-car in 1921, as well as in the clear and highly intellectual forms of a supersonic jet. It occurs in the non-wind-resistant, skin-tight, armouring costumes of skiers, ski-jumpers, divers or cresta-riders, as well as those mirror-smooth plastics that present no resistance to the eye in search of soft lines, and which display nothing but the beauty of the material. It also occurs in the timeless, organically rounded industrial forms of futuristic-looking streamline designs such as those of Luigi Colani. And, in the world of music, it is manifested in the perfectionistic interpretations, geared towards the beauty of sound, of Karajan. It is a streamline aesthetic of the least resistance, in which the objective spirit of the technical age seeks artistic expression.[32]

In the technical machines of our time, the automobile and the aeroplane, Karajan not only fulfilled his childhood dream of driving and flying, which is everyone's childhood dream. The freedom of driving and flying not only expresses a resistance to the knowledge of one's own mortality, seeking to escape it through motion. In mastery of the machine modern man also seeks his own identity. It is an absolute machine, a subjugated, devitalized support for identity, in which he hopes to find unity.[33] This machine can be an aeroplane, a ship or a motor-car or, just as easily, the whole organizational complex of a theatre or the 'music-machine' of the orchestra. The possession of powerful weapons such as a high-tech aeroplane or a highly trained, virtuoso orchestra provides security (via the work) and endorses the owner by anticipating the victory that comes through mastery of the machine. The orchestra that Karajan created from his team of one hundred musicians was equivalent to the technical dream-construction that he raved about as a young student of technical science. The functionally perfect ensemble-playing of pistons, valves, connecting rods and gear-wheels was replaced by the perfect harmony of groups of strings, woodwind and brass, percussion and the other orchestral instruments.

Karajan was united with the absolute musical machine, working in it as a creative motivating force. For the machine itself had no creative power. It only worked for as long and as much as its input allowed. It was not a living organism capable of acting as a 'person'. The same applied to Karajan's orchestra: for him it was primarily an apparatus rather than an organism. This was the deeper reason behind the frustration often expressed by the orchestra's musicians, victims of the insoluble contradiction of fulfilling, as an organism, the functional perfection of the machine.

Karajan attained his ideal of perfection when he was most closely connected to the machine: in the cockpit of the jet, surrounded by highly complicated technology, he became a part of the machine at the same time as he controlled it; he was, so to speak, its soul, communicating with the organism of the apparatus by means of the dials on the instrument panel. The machine became the soul's armour against the medium through which it was propelled. The jet-age pilot is cut off from direct contact with his environment, the medium that carries him. The instrument-panel keeps him airborne. He has been rendered more and more dependent on the instruments under his control. The medium that carries him is kept well away from him. It flows, unfelt, past the outer skin of his streamlined armour, in a laminar flow. Only turbulence, stalling or the breaking of the sound barrier bring the element to his attention. Stalling signals the disaster of an impending crash, in breaking the sound-barrier one overtakes the sound of one's own motion. Visibility is restricted by the range of the windscreen.[34] In the new generation of aeroplanes it has been replaced by a digital computer visibility system that gives a synthetic image of the aeroplane's surroundings: the pilot has lost all direct contact with the outside world. He only communicates with it via the indirect signals from the instrument panel and the sensors of the technical electronic apparatus as they appear on the screen.

What has that to do with music? people will ask. The streamline aesthetic, as I have already shown, is not only an aesthetic of technical disciplines. It can also be applied to art, and that is what Karajan did. But what was the musical consequence of this streamline aesthetic, an aesthetic of least resistance? Karajan's interpretative style was the attempt to find the most favourable musical streamline profile to counteract the resistance from the score. For this reason he devoted himself to laminar performances. With his orchestral music-machine he sought to move through the medium of sound with as little resistance as possible, without friction (in the sense of flow without turbulence or stalling). This meant that all edges, roughness, corners and points in the score had to be rubbed smooth. Karajan's performances were a means of moving without resistance, and without breaking any resistance. He slipped the score over himself and the orchestra, moulded, smoothed and beautified it in his interpretations, as a master of adaptability, until it had arrived at the most favourable form from the point of view of flow: this was found once the interpretation, in the smoothness of its contours, had been given its ideal streamlined form. For the smoother the surface, the more laminar the flow. Karajan's orchestra, the music-machine, was rightly seen as a 'unified ensemble, balanced in every sense, very soft in tone, never growing hard even in a tight, concentrated forte, and noble in timbre, radiating, as Karajan himself did, an aura of noble perfection'.[35]

Just as the aeroplane's streamlined body can be seen, from the topological point of view, as diversity in two dimensions, Karajan's laminar performances, as the topography of an emotion, were always two-dimensional. Thus Karajan's interpretative work precisely reflects the dominant characteristics of his age, transferring three-dimensional reality into the intangible, two-dimensional world of the cinema and television screen and, in the synthetic reproduction of sound, omitting the dimension of spontaneity. The shielding of the pilot from the outside world, making contact only through a digital external visibility system, and everything to do with the electronic aeroplane technology, corresponds to

305

the shielding and detachment of the conductor from the audience in the production of records and music films, where the musical product is not judged and corrected with reference to its reality, but rather via the filtered, synthetic reproduction of the recording as influenced by the sound mixer, which is then corrected, where necessary, according to the acoustic handicaps of the sound mixer, the core of the recording sensorium. Just as the digital external visibility system communicates his environment, the load-bearing element, to the pilot, so the recording apparatus, dominated by the sound mixer, communicates to the conductor the acoustic reality of his interpretation.

Because of its emotional two-dimensionality, the streamline aesthetic reduces emotional depth to mere sentimentality. For me, this also answers the question of whether Karajan did have at his disposal the genuine and strong emotion that is the indispensable precondition of thoroughly controlled expression. Because laminar flow is a surface phenomenon, Karajan's interpretations seem, on the one hand, smooth, polished, gleaming and, on occasion, something like a large-scale camouflage, but on the other hand they seem emotionally constricted and unspontaneous rather than controlled, failing to touch the depths of the soul. In short, their effect is superficial. In the end, all criticism of Karajan's interpretative and directing style can be reduced to this. The external, unusually mannered and smooth form, the sentiment and pathos of Karajan's stylized performances and stagings are the basis for a criticism that suspects substance behind every surface, without asking whether the surface might not be the very essence of the matter.

The two-dimensionality of Karajan's streamline aesthetic explains why the conflicts in the work are never delivered, and why there is no engagement with its material in terms of the present day. This is the source of the criticism that perceives shortcomings in the avoidance of conflicts, this escape into vagueness and 'timelessness' in the stage arrangements and the cool dispassion and neutrality of the stagings.[36] Joachim Kaiser wrote of the 1970 Salzburg *Götterdämmerung*:

> In the meantime, Karajan's stagings – despite certain important details, particularly in *Rheingold* – have regressed into the past. Feel like a hangover from Wieland's abstract symbolism. Either explain nothing at all or nothing new. Can't get beyond bright

ideas. Obviously even this brilliant man lacks the time or the strength to realize the demanding principle of the *Gesamtkunstwerk*.[37]

The staging of *Meistersinger* in 1974 led Heinz Josef Herbort to make the following observation:

This year Karajan rediscovered realism, both for himself and for his staging of Wagner. Lest there be, for heaven's sake, any misunderstanding: I do not mean the barren-rock-type of realism, which might be translated as 'stage truth', but a picture-book-illustration realism, a sham reality, an opulent 'show-all-the-details' art, a kind of neo-Meininger-dom which, with every square inch of backdrop or costume, demonstrates the statement: We have survived and vanquished Wieland Wagner . . . Herbert von Karajan's realism has nothing to do with the character on stage. There are no insights into the actual thoughts or the real feelings of anyone involved.[38]

On *Falstaff*, which the seventy-three-year-old Karajan staged in Salzburg in 1981, Wolfgang Schreiber wrote:

The piece is supposed to develop as inconspicuously as possible, not independently or even contrapuntally. If he is lucky, the singers supply the necessary acting abilities themselves, compensating for the weaknesses of Karajan's personal direction, the lack of any personal conception of the play.[39]

Wagner's *Parsifal* in the 1980 Salzburg staging encountered particular resistance from the critics. Peter Wapnewski said of the much-celebrated and musically highly praised staging:

Yet the word 'staging' may be too high-flown, presumably Karajan wanted hardly anything but a theatrically submissive conformity to the music – that music which, thoroughly dominating the evening, he executed brilliantly. If we demand fresh interpretations from the director, if we expect from him what we now call 'innovatory impulses', then we will not easily be satisfied by Karajan the director. What he demanded from his actors was the conventional gestures of traditional productions, a glance to the right and a glance to the left, and a step backwards as a sign of astonishment and two as one of horror; stance and movement are predictable, and no surprising turns or

307

unfamiliar steps ever rewarded the curiosity of anyone hoping to understand something new. Still, this kind of theatrical arrangement has this to be said for it: that the fine old convention (and conventionality) is still preferable to the furious rage with which some directors put themselves and their problems on the stage instead of the work in question, which is thus reduced to a mere pretext.[40]

And Franz Endler, critically particularly favourable to Karajan, said of the direction and stage set of the *Parsifal* production:

It suggested a large number of fashions, especially those of days long past . . . The singers had little problem integrating themselves into this stage concept of a reliable and beautiful rendering, they didn't really have to do anything . . . Karajan on the other hand, dreamed his beautiful gestures, which could be performed equally well by marionettes. There were no conflicts or dialogues.[41]

In his review of *Parsifal*, Peter Cossé summed up Karajan's work as a director in the following words:

Over the years, however, he showed an increasing inability to see further than opulent surface effects, in order to bring the characters into an appropriate relation to one another . . . The *Lohengrin* and the *Meistersinger* suffered from stark dramatic blunders, and even worse, almost, errors were apparent in the long awaited *Parsifal* at this year's Easter Festival . . . Once again, the direction proved to be a cover for the undistanced depiction of disorganized core ideas . . . Karajan suppresses the reaction from person to person, groups are not successfully broken down into individuals . . . The work's descent into a visual panorama with few conflicts, a consecrating play with dancing . . . seems at least to be slowed down by the use of the Berlin Philharmonic . . . The stage lacks depth and height. A broad effect is supposed to stress its monumental character.[42]

Karajan, whose immense life's work was, in its entirety, like one desperate cry for affection and approval, stood in the cross-fire of increasingly violent and increasingly polarized criticism. The artistic approval that he found in his worldwide concert audience and the Salzburg Festival community, he sought in vain in a section of the music critics that was clearly important to him. Karajan, who claimed never to read any criticism, proved to be well informed when asked about criticism that had entered the public eye. When I referred him to the *Spiegel* interview with the music theorist Heinz-Klaus Metzger, who said in 1980: 'Karajan and Böhm are grossly overvalued' and 'I see Karajan as a highly deadly phenomenon',[43] he answered, 'You can't take a man like Herr Metzger, a complete ignoramus in these matters, so that – he's employed for that very reason – so that he will write badly about things because they thrive on negatives. But it's wonderful to be able to write something bad about somebody.'

Karajan's relationship with the critics was ambivalent because it was emotional. His encounter with criticism was far from objective. It was accepted when it backed him up. If it did not, it was disparaged and condemned. A critical review was misunderstood as an attack on his person. His sensitivity to any kind of criticism was a striking trait in him. Behind inflammatory criticism he insanely suspected the existence of conspiratorial groups:

That's some group of people who swore after the war: we must unsettle and destroy this career. It was all planned quite thoroughly . . . These people pick up on all the negative things, or all the things portrayed as being negative, because I made a career without or even in the face of the press . . . Particularly the Viennese press. They encouraged certain people because they said: We want to determine who is good and who makes it. From my own experience I now know that there is only one defensive weapon against conspiracies such as these: the quality of one's work.[44]

Karajan's extreme touchiness meant that he was unable to bear rejection of any kind. For the frustrating reality of 'bad' criticism he substituted the illusion of infallibility. He considered his artistic achievements sacrosanct, and arrogantly rebelled against any outside judgement which he rejected as outrageous and incompetent. His particular brand of touchiness was coupled with a paranoid suspicion that a large-scale conspiracy lurked behind all forms of criticism. His perfectionistic self-image ruled out the very idea that he might be a worthy object of genuine criticism. The fact that he might have merited criticism escaped him through pure navel-gazing. Karajan sometimes gave the impression of conducting simply to prove that he was not as black as he was painted. Because he could not achieve this, he was insulted, unsettled and unhappy. He was wounded that he could not win approval where he particularly craved it, particularly among the Viennese critics. He never got over that, any more than he got over Stravinsky's silence about his performances of the composer's work. Karajan's response to this was enlightening in many respects. Let us therefore quote from our conversation of 17 June 1980, when Karajan was criticizing Maurice Béjart's staging of *Le Sacre du Printemps*.

RCB: Did you ever talk to Stravinsky about that?
Karajan: No, I never met him. Because he studiously avoided it. He hated all conductors. I played *Jeu de cartes* on tour. So I've actually played a lot of pieces by him. And I've recorded *Threni* and his most important works.[45] And all the recordings were sent off to him immediately. He didn't even say thank you. I believe I know why: it was Robert Craft, his secretary, and he seemed to do everything for him. And he was also . . . he said: I will grant as much to a conductor as I do to the bell-ringer in church. He was furious that he couldn't conduct himself. Because he was the clumsiest of conductors. And he couldn't come to terms with that complex. Of course, I thought it was a shame that we never talked. At the time it was easy to say: he's a Nazi, we won't have anything to do with him. Idiotic things like that, you know.
RCB: But that's how it was. You conducted in the Nazi period, and were an advertisement for them.
Karajan: It did me no harm.

We can only agree with Karajan in this. But some critics are unwilling to agree with his extravagant treatment of beautiful sound, the dramatic nature of his stylization, his aestheticism of sound, the soothing aura that surrounds his music. They accuse him of being an 'aestheticizing sound-fetishist'[46] and of indulging in 'tune-fetishism' and 'obscuring the internal musical structures'.[47] A glance at the enormous range of concert and record reviews will hardly be able to avoid such descriptions. They were part of the repertoire of a critical community that fed on Karajan's sensualistic treatment of the phenomenon of sound just as much as it was disturbed by it. Did this sensualistic play with sound run the risk of drifting into an aestheticizing sterility, or was it, for Karajan, the only responsible reaction to the work of art? It may be pointless to argue about this. Let us hear how Karajan answered his critics' accusations in one of our conversations in 1981.

Karajan: Look, what does 'aestheticism of sound' mean, what is it? He's making too beautiful a sound? I know that, I know the other sound, I hear it when I put a record on and I know very well what happens. People aren't capable . . . Music can be dramatic or not dramatic. Nobody's ever told me my music isn't dramatic. But music with burping noises doesn't come into it. We recorded the four records by the Second Viennese School. Some sixty hours of rehearsal time went into each of them.

RCB: You were said to have played them too 'beautifully' as well.

Karajan: Yes, that's what I wanted. That's the beautiful thing, that you can play a kind of music in such a way that dissonance becomes an aesthetic sound impression. But there's a tension in it. And I told the orchestra that over and over again. I know how other people did it, with two or three rehearsals. You can hear that, it's the wrong approach. Even the dissonance has to have a pure intonation. And it didn't get a pure intonation. And so you have these uncultivated performances. Look at all the post-war Mahler, in festivals and Mahler cycles. What orchestras have played him? The Vienna Symphony and the Philharmonic. During that whole time in Germany he wasn't played at all, and of course lots of members of the orchestra went. So a new generation started playing those pieces after the war. And instead of cultivating them, everybody – including myself, at the first Mahler Festival – got two rehearsals . . . That's how things were done in those days, and you only did as best you could. And everybody said I didn't play Mahler because I was a Nazi. In Vienna we were brought up on Mahler in the late twenties. That was our daily bread. I said to myself: I'll wait until the orchestra has come far enough for me to have a palette that corresponds to the music. But simply playing schmaltz: that isn't Mahler. I knew too much to do that. And now, of course, it's entirely different. Now I can demand a particular tone. I have the palette of a painter or a photographer, more or less. They say that photography has twenty-seven different shades between black and white. And Mahler has six. What happened to Mahler: music for serving-girls, just banal and awful. – But I'll play you what I consider to be my most important recording: the Barcarolle from *Tales of Hoffmann*. In this record I think I gave the music its true value. It isn't musical-box music, it's profoundly serious music: it gives you man's passage from life to death. And the waves of the canal go on splashing as if nothing had happened. That contrast is what startles me. But that took a lot of time. I told the

311

musicians: you can never be entirely with me, but we can't be worlds apart. The way it drags – imagine a man pulling a woman behind him by the hair . . .

In rehearsal I make sure to tell the musician how he should play it. But there are also little similes. One-liners. It has to be concise. I said at one point – and the main thing is that an orchestra will understand it if it's funny – when I wanted a tortured, riven chord: imagine you're lying on the floor and someone with stiletto heels climbs on to your chest. Everybody laughed – and I had it, quite exactly. But otherwise I first have to say what I mean. In the case of the Barcarolle I said: First of all it will have to be legato, and secondly every note has to be placed rather than hammered in. You have to explain that to people. And then it works. That over-sentimentality – look what there is left for the audience from Mahler's Fifth: today we go to *Death in Venice*. But it doesn't have to be that way . . .

I make my music. And it will be elevated and a lot of people will certainly like that, and the records that come out later on will be even better. They can write what they want. It's of no importance to me. You can't simply let yourself be influenced by the press, because everyone writes the opposite of everyone else – so what's the point? How does that concern me? But ask one of the people: 'Whistle me the beginning of a symphony, or beat out the right rhythm.' They can't do it. What are you supposed to do with people like that? If Herr Kolodin says to me: 'I object to that', then I'd accept it. Because he's a person who has listened to 40,000 hours of music in his life, and a person who's capable of writing an introduction to a work by Beethoven, as he did for our records. He was with me for three hours, and I wanted to crawl away and hide, and said to myself that I'd have to go back to school . . . If you think about those dreadful exegeses of symphonies in the programmes! I told Dr Girth [manager of the Berlin Philharmonic Orchestra], let's stop all that . . . The musical academics have developed a jargon you wouldn't think possible . . . Nothing but platitudes, all of them: 'And it's like that and it's also the opposite. And then there's this coincidence . . .'

RCB: Did you never have the ambition to write an introductory commentary to your records, like Bernstein?

Karajan: I know his books. What does it tell you? Tell me a single sentence that really. . . it explains things very well for children, and nothing more.

RCB: But didn't you intend to do it for adults?

Karajan: No. I'd like them simply to forget, and stop saying: 'I'd like to understand music.' They should enjoy it!

Karajan, who didn't get what he wanted from criticism, justified his work with reference to its success with his audience. And he was sure of his audience; after all, he had educated it himself over the decades. It never eluded the magic of his art, the charm and appeal of his personality. Karajan's standard for success was a full house, high viewing figures and record sales. He equated saleability with artistic success. The future will show whether Karajan, who was always right during his lifetime, will still be right after his death. There is also a phenomenon called artistic error. Aware of his success, he was therefore able to ask, with a measure of confidence, and rhetorically in that he himself provided the answer: 'Why, in that case, are all my performances sold out, with the others following far behind? Why do all the records I make sell on average between twenty and forty times as many as the others? There must be a reason for it.'

It has been the intention of this book to seek out that reason. Like the portrait photographer who tries to capture the inner truth of the person in his face through the shadow-play of light, I have tried to illuminate Karajan's life and work from various angles, in order, through the various points of view thrown up in the process, to track down the reasons, hidden in the depths of his being, for his work and his success – in short, to track down the Karajan phenomenon. I would not claim that I have managed to do this. But if the attempt has provided any indication of the direction in which research should be carried out, then something has been achieved.

The multivalence of his talent makes any judgement of Karajan almost impossibly difficult. For his talent seems also to have been the gift of dissimulation, deception and mimicry. Karajan withheld everything that might have helped to answer the question of the truth of his life. But what he disclosed unconsciously still tells us a great deal. Anyone who wishes to analyse Karajan has to do a careful reading of the unspoken score, in order to uncover and recognize the falsifications and deceptions that mask his official biography. My book sets out to describe the symptoms. The elucidation of the key events of his life as an individual is a matter for the psychologist.

They might answer the question of whether Karajan managed a secret entelechy, whether he achieved a kind of perfection. Whether he succumbed to a manic musical madness, or whether music was a safeguard against madness. They could tell us something about the causes of his behaviour, which followed the pleasure rather than the reality principle. They might tell us why Karajan, who achieved so many things in his life, always foundered on rejection. They might reveal the roots of his power, the miracle of his potent ability to represent the audience in an elevated form. They might tell us what freedom Karajan had in mind when he said: 'We are not free in the beginning. Freedom only comes in the end as a self-won freedom. Whatever happens had to happen – that is the motto of my working life.'[48] Equipped with all the senses of the menaced animal, Karajan lived a life which, to use a phrase of Nietzsche's, endeavoured 'to derive the most magnificent accomplishments from internal inhibitions or shortcomings'. Where the technical preconditions of his life's work were concerned, he was always a stimulus to further developments. His life described what happens when a man sets out to find his dream.

Karajan represents the magic of this century. But magicians are hermaphrodites. The judgement of the future, with the benefit of hindsight, will show whether Karajan, the gnomon of his age, was an original or a derivative figure in cultural history. The latter of these two possibilities of artistic life would seem more likely if the precondition for his creativity had been mourning rather than its opposite.[49] Karajan had not simply drifted like a piece of flotsam from another era to our own. He was, to answer our earlier question, not the Renaissance man he was claimed to be, and which he sometimes gave the impression of being. His development was as closely bound up with his environment and its historical conditions as it is possible to imagine. These gave rise to a type of man that Karajan represents much more closely than he does the type from an era long past, whose character might well be the universal property of the people of the future – a structure marked by superficial and contingent relationships, with little subjective emotional involvement. It is the expression of changes in identificatory processes in a world increasingly characterized by mobility 'in the socio-economic, technological and geographical schemes of identification'.[50]

Karajan can hardly be seen as an artist with a truly extraordinary imagination. Where did his genius lie? Did he really have a timeless creative genius? Allowing that genius contrasts starkly with the reason of responsible, pragmatic man, that sensibility brought to a psychologically conspicious level is a precondition for true knowledge: might we then call Karajan a genius? Or was his genius merely organizational, restricted to the organization of sounds, the portrayal of his own character and a highly successful promotional structure? Or is there also a genius of mediocrity? Eccentricity is certainly the quality that sparked in him like a hidden electric charge, and which we might see as genius. Is genius like greatness, in that much depends on where one's genius lies? The question of Karajan's genius must remain unanswered. It reminds us that genius itself is finally inexplicable, an enigma.

But Herbert von Karajan's uniqueness, based in the contradictoriness of his personality, left no doubt that music was an extremely sensual matter for him, affecting every fibre of his being. His answer to the question of how he mastered the physical and psychological burdens of his artistic work, a work that demanded his all, and to which he gave everything, is as concise as it is clear: 'A very healthy life.'

And what did he mean by that?

'The principle of *mens sana in corpore sano* – a healthy mind in a healthy body.'

Afterword

Because Robert Bachmann's book is not a biography, the fact that is was published in Germany, after prolonged legal disputes, six years before Karajan's death in 1989, does nothing to render it outdated. Nonetheless, it is interesting, in the light of the facts and arguments that Bachmann adduces, to look briefly at the final years of Karajan's life, and at the range of reactions to his death.

Whatever else one may say about him, Karajan unquestionably demonstrated heroic fortitude in his last years. The greatest drama of his performances during that period was his progress from the artists' entrance to the podium. Understandably, he concealed his extreme physical frailty for as long as possible, but when it could no longer be hidden, his refusal to submit to it became for his audiences, if not for him, a ritual of the will triumphant over the recalcitrant flesh. In this respect, though in no other, he came to resemble Otto Klemperer, whose entrances were similar demonstrations of obduracy and refusal to submit to physical weakness. But even here there was a crucial difference. Klemperer's performances had always, during his last period, seemed continuous with his determination to give them. Effortful and increasingly slow, they seemed the perfect expression of his Beethovenian striving to affirm no matter what. With Karajan, there was a quite contrary impression. Once he had hoisted himself on to the rostrum, and perched on the tiny ledge invisible to the audience, the performances were more sleekly mellifluous than ever before, even if his tempi were often broader than they had been in his prime. Indeed, he seemed to have become so obsessed with 'streamline aesthetics', as Bachmann calls them, that often there was no tension at all in his performances, so that *within* them there were no victories; those were confined to the fact that they were actually occurring.

This provides further evidence of the correctness of Bachmann's thesis concerning the nature of Karajan's conception of the relationship between the conductor, the work and the orchestra. That Karajan was complete master of the Berlin Philharmonic, at least in performance, is no news. Nor, for many listeners, is his mastery of the works he conducted. What remains a matter of bitter contention is the nature of that mastery. In the case of the Berlin Philharmonic, the contention became ever more public as it became more acute, until there were, in the last years, such bitter disagreements that a few months before his death Karajan severed his connection with them altogether and turned to the Vienna Philharmonic exclusively. He frequently stressed in interviews – which also assumed a ritual aspect during this period – that he regarded the orchestra as an extension of himself. He seemed to be unaware of how revealing this image was. But the players in the Berlin Philharmonic clearly weren't. For all the prodigious success he brought them, especially in the sales of records, they became increasingly restive being viewed by him as further limbs of his. One of them, the long-time tympanist Werner Thärichen, who had played in the orchestra as a very young man under Furtwängler, wrote a fascinating book *Paukenschläge: Furtwängler oder Karajan?* (Drumbeats: Furtwängler or Karajan?) in which he analysed the nature of their respective styles, and came down decisively in favour of Furtwängler, partly on the ground that with him the orchestra was making music as if it was a body of chamber musicians, while with Karajan they were subjugated to another man's conception of the work.

Of course it is easy to reply to that by saying that Furtwängler's conception of how music should be was, to put it mildly, at least as strong as Karajan's. But the point is that with Furtwängler it was a matter of communication and the willing eliciting of a shared vision, while with Karajan it was the imposition of a view which they had no choice but to purvey. It is only superficially a paradox to say that the price of the famed 'chamber-music' delicacy that Karajan achieved with the Berlin Philharmonic, especially in the least likely works, such as Wagner and Richard Strauss, was the result of a tyranny such as very few conductors have ever wanted to achieve over a body of a hundred players. Certainly Toscanini and Klemperer were also tyrants, and more evidently terrifying ones, but their demonic qualities were employed, no doubt sometimes mistakenly, in order to realize what they were convinced

317

was the composer's vision. One has, with Karajan, the sense that he increasingly treated the symphonic repertoire as a series of concertos for orchestra, in which above all his demands on his players were exactly met, so that they might even be called concertos for conductor. And if, instead of the grandiose gestures of the earlier years, his conducting style was now minimalist, that only served to emphasize the uncanny degree of control which he still exercised. If anything, his sparse movements seem more closely related to what the orchestra is playing during his last years. Earlier, as Bachmann says, it had seemed as if he was acting out a private drama which was only in contingent relationship to what the players were doing, so was merely a distraction.

At the same time. Karajan is never an interesting conductor to watch. Nothing is added to the listener's appreciation by seeing as well as hearing him at work. That makes all the more frustrating, and in the end offensive, his obsession with preserving himself on CDV. In the highly instructive film *Karajan in Salzburg* which was made in 1987 for his eightieth birthday (and which he is said to have disliked intensely – but can one imagine him permitting its publication if he did?) he can be seen in his cellars at his home in Anif with a wall of television screens in front of him, and an assistant working a computer beside him, as he selects the best of the vast range of images for the performance of Verdi's Requiem that is being reproduced. 'Incredible', he pronounces after José Carreras's singing of the Ingemisco, but all one sees is Karajan's profile on the screens. In fact there are extremely few performances which I want to see, as opposed to hear, repeatedly, whoever the conductor may be. Karajan was famous for conducting with closed eyes. That seems to me to be the obvious way to listen, unless one is following a score, or is present at the actual performance. I find it hard to believe that even Karajan's most frenetic fans will want to watch these forty-odd performances more than once or twice – the extent of the megalomania would be too apparent.

As to that celebrated megalomania: Karajan's most devoted apologists seem to be divided within themselves between admitting it and passionately denying it. What seems most likely is that they are enormously fascinated by it, but that there is some extra *frisson* for them in claiming that it didn't exist. It is so foolish to ignore the glamour of power that one wonders why people go on doing it. No one can sensibly deny the fascination of Karajan as a phenomenon, however sincerely they may deplore it. The question that needs to be asked is what *kind* of phenomenon he was. The smoothness with which people move from his being a conductor to his being *ipso facto* an artistic phenomenon is remarkable, given the highly questionable nature of that profession, which even some of its most distinguished practitioners have admitted. It simply won't do to say, 'Forget about the fast cars, the concern with technology, etc., what counts is that he was a conductor.' For his persona was too much of a unity, and too widely marketed, for such an act of selection to be a genuine possibility. That is, he is a quite different case from Wagner, of whom one can say, 'Forget about the anti-Semitism, the love of luxury, the sponging, etc., and concentrate on the works.' For Karajan was presented, and fully connived in the presentation of himself, as a package. His frequent boast about the number of records sold was an involuntary tribute to advertising as much as anything. An extreme and briefly notorious case of this was a mid-seventies recording of Richard Strauss's *Ein Heldenleben* on the cover of which was an extraordinarily sinister photograph of Karajan in a black leather coat, fixing the viewer with a menacing glare, the very image of frightening power, and a piece of extraordinary audacity on the part of the record company. Anyone who permits such a mode of salesmanship must be very naïve if they are surprised that they acquire a certain kind of reputation. And they must be equally naïve if they don't reflect that such packaging results in a 'product' which is viewed as part of a 'lifestyle' characterized by affluence, consumerism and the viewing of music as luxury.

After a point such methods seem to have backfired on Karajan, and there was a good deal of propaganda to the effect that he was the opposite of what he seemed and of what, in many respects, he clearly was. One began to read a great deal about his essential modesty, his humility, his self-effacingness, when for the longest time he had been presented as the Artist as Superman. When in 1983 Deutsche Grammophon produced a vast book of photographs along with a record to celebrate his seventy-fifth birthday, the blurb emphasized, strangely in the circumstances, that Karajan hated being photographed, 'as is well-known', and that he would only consent to it if he was actually conducting at the time, and definitely didn't permit photographers into his private life. What follows are innumerable photos of him either conducting or in one of the poses, holding a baton or with arms outstretched, which were long employed to portray him as The Conductor, though it is clear that there is no orchestra around. Then, still more at odds with the blurb, by now insolent in its mendacity, there are pictures of the great man relaxing, in one or another of his homes, playing with his daughters, building a wall of logs, piloting his jet, and so

319

forth. Just as, as Bachmann shows in conclusive detail, Karajan had an incapacity to admit some of the most obvious facts about his career, so his propagandists need to negate the truth with sycophancy or blatant falsehood.

The film made at Salzburg during the summer Festival of 1987, to which I have already referred, contains many connoisseurs' items of both these activities. The sycophancy is incessant and overwhelming, and some of the scenes suggest Fellini at his most inspired. The sight of Karajan's closest cronies having dinner in the Goldener Hirsch after a performance of *Don Giovanni* and discussing precisely how they think Karajan is now greater than he has ever been deserves classic status. Michel Glotz, Karajan's 'second pair of ears', explains to Dr Märkle and the rest how Karajan is now less sophisticated 'in the bad sense', how he now conducts from beyond the grave, employing 'the third eye of the philosophers', though I can think of no philosopher who would understand his explanation, and agrees that his performances, though now less precise, are deeper, by which he means more human, than ever before. His companions nod their enthusiastic agreement while eagerly consuming pasta. After what seems an unremarkable rehearsal with the Vienna Philharmonic, Eliette, whom we have seen sitting alone in the auditorium, goes up to him, kisses him and says, 'This is an historic moment', leaving us, if not Karajan, to work out what she might be talking about. Some Japanese visitors shake their heads in disbelief when Karajan tells them that he has a new Porsche which accelerates from zero to one hundred kilometres an hour in three seconds. There are fairly extensive interviews with the maestro in which he tells of his commitment to letting things look after themselves, whether it is a horse one is riding, a yacht one is sailing to victory in, an orchestra one is conducting or a love affair. Once more, the technique seems to be to say something so outrageously false that the listener will have no breath to answer back – a well-tried propaganda technique.

Karajan's death, which occurred suddenly on 16 July 1989, came as a surprise in spite of his long-failing health. Since it was only ten days before the Salzburg Festival was due to open with his new production of Verdi's *Un Ballo in Maschera*, the musical-commercial world's immediate preoccupation was with finding someone to take over. Once that had been settled, the question was who was to inherit Karajan's empire, and it was very soon

320

clear that no one could. It had so many ramifications, and had been so carefully organized round the central figure himself, that the idea of a successor to Karajan, in the sense that he had been a successor to Furtwängler as chief conductor of the Berlin Philharmonic Orchestra, was not even intelligible. That the issue had nothing to do with artistic stature – though there was no superfluity of that – demonstrated the kind of structure that Karajan had erected. He had realized his own fantasies so precisely, his charisma was so completely one of personality rather than function, that disintegration was bound to follow. There is no reason to think he would have wanted it otherwise. He had done nothing to ensure a succession – quite the reverse. His death conclusively proved his indispensability to the kind of organization that he had wanted. Musically it left no gap. In all other respects that he cared about the abyss opened as impressively as he could have wished. Whatever happens to the various festivals that he led or created, they will necessarily be quite different from what they have been. Karajan's relationship to them was very similar to that of Wagner's *works* to the Bayreuth Festival.

The immediate obituaries, at least in England and West Germany, were on the whole surprisingly candid in their coolness. Several journalists who had regularly praised his performances did an abrupt about turn, while those who had been hostile over the years took one more opportunity to explain their lack of enthusiasm. One highly regarded English critic wrote in a weekly that 'he was a bad man, I think, and a bad conductor, and the world will be a better place without him'. Though that was extraordinary in its ferocity, others damned with faint praise or pondered on why, for all his gifts, final greatness as an interpreter had eluded Karajan. It wasn't until a couple of months later that Richard Osborne, his leading English disciple and the author of *Conversations with Karajan*, produced a lengthy article in *The Gramophone*, which appeared in even more extensive form elsewhere, to rebuke and refute Karajan's critics and continue the tone of hagiography which had characterized his writings on this subject over the years. He even announced the imminent publication of documents and explanations which will show that Karajan's relationship with the Nazis was something completely different from the way it is depicted in this book. On that subject we can do no more than wait and see, though clearly any refutation of Bachmann will have to cope with some remarkably impressive evidence.

It isn't surprising that Osborne hit it off with Karajan, since his manner towards him, as revealed in the *Conversations*, is one of obsequious gratitude at being allowed to commune with greatness. The final conversation, held around the time of Karajan's eightieth birthday, concludes:

> *RO*: People say that when you are on the rostrum and making music . . .
> *H v K*: Yes, I know. And it makes me completely happy.

It was a skilfully devised dying fall. The notion of Karajan being completely happy is one that is strange in a quite particular way. If we are to understand why it strikes us as so odd, I don't think we have a better chance at present than that given us by this book.

Michael Tanner

Notes

Abbreviations

Haeusserman: Ernst Haeusserman, *Herbert von Karajan*, Vienna 1978
Löbl: Karl Löbl, *Das Wunder Karajan*, approved, extended and up-to-date paperback edition, Bayreuth 1978
Muck: Peter Muck, *Einhundert Jahre Berliner Philharmonisches Orchester*, 3 vols, Tutzing 1982
Prieberg: Fred K. Prieberg, *Musik im NS-Staat*, Frankfurt 1982
Rathkolb: Oliver Rathkolb, *Politische Propaganda der amerikanischen Besatzungsmacht in Österreich, 1945 bis 1950*. A study of the history of the Cold War as expressed in press, radio and cultural policies. Doctoral dissertation, humanities faculty of Vienna University, Vienna 1981
Stresemann: Wolfgang Stresemann, . . . *und abends in die Philharmonie*, Munich 1981

FAZ: Frankfurter Allgemeine Zeitung
NZZ: Neue Zürcher Zeitung

Introduction

1. Rudolf Bing, *5000 Abende in der Oper*, Munich 1973, p. 287
2. Haeusserman, pp. 45f.
3. Helena Matheopoulos, *Maestro*, London 1982, pp. 251 and 254f.
4. Letter from Karajan to the author, 9 April 1977
5. The task that Legge left unfinished was finally undertaken by his wife, the former singer and Party member, Elisabeth Schwarzkopf. In 1982, under the title *On and Off the Record* (Faber and Faber, 1982), in order to 'do the best thing', assisted by the novelist Gustl Breuer, she brought out a literary conglomerate of posthumous writings which adds further half-truths and asseverations to the stockpile already amassed. Thus we hear, for example, that Karajan travelled to Berlin in 1926 to hear Toscanini (p. 221) – but Toscanini did not visit Berlin until 1928, and Karajan heard him in Vienna. Likewise, Legge is the first to tell us that Karajan was arrested in the Second World War: 'Karajan and his wife were caught in Milan in 1944. But he made his way to Vienna by acting as interpreter and guide for American convoys' (p. 221) – the content of this is very vague. With her book, Schwarzkopf has made a further contribution to the literary genre of widow's necrology, which, good as we may presume the author's intentions to be, has done the greatest disservice to the deceased. 'The volume as a whole is not the greatest accomplishment of the artist Elisabeth Schwarzkopf,' was how the *Neue Zürcher Zeitung* reviewer politely put it (*NZZ*, No. 292, 1982)

1 Beginnings

1. Letter to the author from the Central Bureau for Meteorology and Geodynamics, Vienna, 26 January 1982
2. *Genealogisches Taschenbuch der Ritter- und Adels-Geschlechter*, Brünn 1880, p. 22; and *Wiener Genealogisches Taschenbuch*, Vol. VIII, 1937, p. 89
3. *Genealogisches Taschenbuch der Ritter- und Adels-Geschlechter*, p. 222
4. Franz Herre, *Kaiser Franz Joseph von Österreich*, p. 363
5. Adolf Hitler, *Mein Kampf*, Munich 1934, p. 11
6. Ibid., p. 28
7. Franz Herre, op. cit., p. 372
8. Ibid., pp. 405f.
9. Karl Kraus, *Beim Wort genommen, Werke*, Vol. 3, p. 351
10. See J. C. Fest, 1973, pp. 59f.
11. Adolf Hitler, op. cit., p. 60
12. Interviews between the author and Wolfgang von Karajan, 1980 and 1982
13. Ibid.
14. Ibid.
15. Stresemann, p. 124
16. Interview between the author and Wolfgang von Karajan, 1980
17. Ibid.
18. 'Überall ist Karajan', *Bunte Illustrierte*, No. 40, 1977, p. 49
19. Interview between the author and Wolfgang von Karajan, 1980
20. Ibid.
21. Letter from Karajan to Hofrat Paumgartner, 20 September 1957, copy in the possession of the author
22. 'Die alte Haut ist herunter,' *Stern Magazin*, 20 March 1983, p. 60
23. Letter from Hofstötter to Dr Rehrl, 17 January 1929, copy in the possession of the author
24. 'Außergewöhnliches Symphoniekonzert', *Salzburger Volksblatt*, 23 January 1929, copy in the possession of the author

2 The Career

1. 'Ein Wunder wird siebzig', *Stern Magazin*, No. 15, 1978, p. 52
2. Joseph Wechsberg, *An Stelle eines Interviews*, Salzburg Easter Festival Programme, 1974, pp. 11f.
3. See J. C. Fest, *Hitler* (Trans. Richard and Clara Winston, 1974), p. 586
4. See also Rolf R. Bigler, *Zeitgenossen*, 1980, p. 58; and Haeusserman, p. 49
5. Haeusserman, pp. 103f.
6. In: K. Löbl, *Fernsehporträt Arturo Toscanini*, 1983
7. J. C. Fest, op. cit., p. 269
8. See J. P. Stern, *Hitler, the Führer and the People*, 1975, p. 269
9. J. C. Fest, op. cit., p. 272
10. Ibid., p. 292
11. Ibid., p. 275
12. See Ronald W. Clark, *Albert Einstein*, p. 318
13. J. C. Fest, op. cit., p. 392
14. Ibid., p. 400
15. *Ulmer Sturm*, 9 March 1933, p. 597
16. *Schwäbischer Volksbote*, 21 March 1933, p. 8
17. See Prieberg, p. 207
18. Muck, Vol. 2, p. 99
19. J. C. Fest, op. cit., p. 404
20. *Ulmer Sturm*, 22 March 1933, p. 12, and *Schwäbischer Volksbote*, 22 March 1933, p. 5. Ulm City Archive
21. *Schwäbischer Volksbote*, No. 71, 1933
22. *Ulmer Sturm*, 25 March 1933, p. 741
23. See J. C. Fest, op. cit., p. 422
24. *Ulmer Sturm*, 13 March 1933, p. 627
25. Letter from Prieberg to the author, 23 October 1982
26. *Illustrierte Stadtzeitung*, Berlin, VII/8, 1983, p. 59
27. Communiqué from Ortsgruppe V, 'Neustadt'-Salzburg, to the Gau treasurer of Salzburg NSDAP, 15 May 1939 (see p. 349)
28. *Illustrierte Stadtzeitung*, op. cit., p. 59

29. Thomas Bernhard, *Die Ursache, Eine Andeutung*, p. 73
30. Leopold Spira, *Attentate, die Österreich erschütterten*, 1981, p. 107
31. Thomas Bernhard, op. cit., p. 75
32. Klaus Mann, *Mephisto*
33. A. and M. Mitscherlich, *Die Unfähigkeit zu trauern*, p. 31
34. Haeusserman, p. 51
35. Memorandum from Otto de Pasetti to Captain Epstein, Headquarters of US Forces in Austria, copy in the possession of the author
36. 'Die Lehrstätte in den Schmutz gezogen', *Südwestpresse*, No. 63, 1968, p. 18. Ulm City Archive – G2 Karajan
37. Haeusserman, p. 48
38. Letter from Otto Schulmann to the author, 6 May 1983
39. Communiqué from the Führer's representative to the NSDAP in Austria to the Reich Treasurer of the NSDAP in Munich, 4 February 1939
40. *Ulmer Sturm*, 2 May 1933, p. 5
41. *Evangelische Kirchenzeitung*, Düsseldorf, 1963, pp. 127f.; see also A. and M. Mitscherlich, op. cit., 1977, p. 58
42. 'Der Mann, der Hitlers Baumeister was', *FAZ*, No. 67, 1980, p. 5
43. 'Einer, der alles wagte', *FAZ*, No. 206, 1980, p. 5
44. Löbl, pp. 70f.
45. Prieberg, p. 19
46. Löbl, p. 88
47. J. Lorcey, *Herbert von Karajan*, 1978, pp. 57f.
48. Paul Robinson, *Herbert von Karajan*, 1981, pp. 17f. The German edition of Robinson's book is in many respects considerably different from the English publication
49. Paul Robinson, *The Art of the Conductor Karajan*, 1975, p. 12
50. Paul Robinson, *Herbert von Karajan*
51. Another accomplice in Karajan's beautification of history is Walter Legge, without whom Karajan's post-war career would have been very different, and much less successful and stormy. With the support of his wife, Legge circulated the following version of Karajan's Party membership: 'Aachen's advantages were almost beyond his dreams. But there was a price. He had to join the National Socialist Party. Politics as such never interested Karajan – only musical politics of which he was later to become the supreme master. He made no secret of his affiliation.' This passage occurs in Elisabeth Schwarzkopf's collection of posthumous writings by her husband (*On and Off the Record, A Memoir of Walter Legge*, Faber and Faber, 1982, pp. 220–1). Regrettably, she neglects to mention that she hushed up her own dedication to the cause of National Socialism after the war, and did not shy away from making false statements. Understandably enough: Elisabeth Schwarzkopf joined the NSDAP in 1940, by which time there was no longer any doubt about the aims of the regime
52. Haeusserman, p. 79

53. Prieberg, pp. 19 and 22

54. *Ulmer Sturm*, 27 April 1933, p. 5

55. See Ronald W. Clark, op. cit., p. 337

56. *Ulmer Tagblatt*, 31 March 1934. Ulm City Archive

57. Source as 36, as well as telephone conversation with Kaiser, May 1983

58. Haeusserman, p. 51

59. Ibid., p. 53

60. Ibid., p. 54

61. Willy Wesemann, 'Acht Jahre habe ich zu ihm aufgeschaut', *Fono Forum*, No. 4, 1978, p. 368

62. 'Ein Wunder wird siebzig', *Stern Magazin*, No. 15, 1978, p. 161

63. Communiqué from the President of the Reich Theatre Chamber to the Propaganda Ministry, 9 August 1934. Bundesarchiv – B55/1184–61

64. *Illustrierte Stadtzeitung*, op. cit., p. 59

65. Source as 63

66. *Westdeutscher Beobachter*, 10 December 1934. Source: Aachen City Archive

67. *Westdeutscher Beobachter*, 13 April 1935

68. Ibid.

69. 'Theaterbesuch ist Ehresache', *Westdeutscher Beobachter*, 15 September 1934

70. See Prieberg, p. 110

71. Ibid., p. 173

72. J. C. Fest, op. cit., p. 425

73. *Westdeutscher Beobachter*, 1 July 1935

74. See Haeusserman, p. 275

75. Interview between the author and Irmgaard Seefried, 1978

76. Stresemann, p. 165

77. During the examination of Furtwängler before the Berlin De-Nazification Commission, the former dramaturge and press secretary of the Staatsoper, Dr Julius Kapp, said: 'I listened to him [Karajan] a year previously in Aachen, on the orders of the manager [Tietjen], to whom he had been recommended as a young conductor. The first thing he conducted was *Fidelio*. Since nobody knew him, the house was half empty. He got good reviews, but nothing special. Then, a week later, he conducted *Tristan*, after three orchestral rehearsals, and it was after this performance that the review "Das Wunder Karajan" came out, and the public became aware of a sensation, and the third production, *Fidelio* again, caused a complete hubbub, and nowhere near as many people could get in as wanted to. That was true success, and from that day forward Herr Karajan was a sensation as far as the Berlin audience was concerned.' From the files of the Berlin De-Nazification Commission for Artists, second hearing of Dr Wilhelm Furtwängler, Tuesday, 17 December 1946, copy in the possession of the author

78. Communiqué from the NSDAP-Reichsleitung, Reich Treasurer, to the Finance and Party Authorities in Austria, 5 January 1939

79. Communiqué from the NSDAP-Reichsleitung, Membership Office, to Arthur Lehmann, Gau Treasurer of Cologne-Aachen, 5 January 1939

80. Communiqué from the NSDAP-Reichsleitung, Membership Office, to Arthur Lehmann, Gau Treasurer of Cologne-Aachen, 7 July 1939

81. *Westdeutscher Beobachter*, 7 June 1937. Institut für Zeitungsforschung der Stadt Dortmund

82. *Westdeutscher Beobachter*, 19 and 20 April 1938. Aachen City Archive

83. Muck, p. 330. In attempting to answer the question of whether van der Nüll's 'Wunder' review was the result of a directive from above, from the Propaganda Ministry and Göring, with the intention of creating an anti-Furtwängler mood, Furtwängler tried to discredit this very positive review: 'He gave concerts in the Philharmonie before, a long time ago, and then the press response wasn't anything special: it was objective.' (From the files of the Berlin De-Nazification Commission on Artists, second hearing of the trial of Dr Wilhelm Furtwängler, Tuesday, 17 December 1946, copy in the possession of the author)

84. The procedures leading up to Karajan's invitation from the Berlin Staatsoper, following which he quickly became State Kapellmeister, are unclear. In Haeusserman (pp. 68–71) Karajan gives an account that is highly anecdotal but short on facts. The record producer Walter Legge claimed in his posthumous memoirs that he had recommended the young Karajan to General Manager Tietjen: 'On my advice he invited Karajan to conduct guest performances of *Fidelio* and *Tristan*' (Elisabeth Schwarzkopf, *On and Off the Record*, p. 221). In the Third Reich Legge produced records for Elektrola and others in Berlin. He was often economical with the truth on this matter. Passages of the highly praised recording of the *Magic Flute* for example, were not recorded, contrary to the published information, with the Berlin Philharmonic under Beecham, but with the orchestra of the Berlin Staatsoper under Bruno Seidler, because Beecham and the Philharmonic were not available for the recording when the studio was free; a manipulation that amounts to a deception of the listener, and which tells us something about Legge's conception of truth and authenticity (see also Schwarzkopf, p. 158)

85. 'Die alte Haut ist herunter', *Stern Magazin*, 30 March 1983

86. Prieberg, p. 330

87. See S. Haffner, *Anmerkungen zu Hitler*, 1981, p. 134

88. J. P. Stern, *Hitler*, 1981, p. 80

89. Max Domarus, *Hitler, Reden und Proklamationen 1932–1945*, 1965, p. 1058

90. *Kunst im 3. Reich, Dokumente der Unterwerfung*, 1979, p. 69

91. Muck, Vol. II, p. 146

92. Is Karajan making a mistake here? Strauss celebrated his birthday in Vienna. The evening before his birthday he attended a festival

329

performance of *Friedentag* at the Staatsoper, conducted by Clemens Krauss, in the presence of the Führer and senior Party officials.

93. H. W. Mueller, Karajan interview, *Fono Forum*, No. 4, 1978, p. 376

94. *Westdeutscher Beobachter*, No. 272, 1939, source as 81

95. *Westdeutscher Beobachter*, 7 June 1937, source as 81

96. Goebbels, Diaries. Source: Bundesarchiv – NL 117, with acknowledgement to François Genoud, owner of the rights to the literary estate

97. J. C. Fest, op. cit., p. 635

98. See Hanns Grösel, 'Die meisten blieben – und schrieben', *FAZ*, No. 186, 1982

99. Promotional pamphlet, City Concerts 1941–2. Source: Aachen City Archive

100. *Westdeutscher Beobachter*, 29 August 1942. Source as 99

101. Haeusserman, p. 72

102. Goebbels, op. cit., NL 118. Furtwängler had already complained in high places, immediately after the publication of van der Nüll's review describing 'Das Wunder Karajan', which Furtwängler took as a personal attack. As he said to the De-Nazification Commission: 'If Goebbels had represented my interests as the interests of his institute, or I might put it this way: my interests and the interests of the Berlin Philharmonic as a single unit, Goebbels would have put a stop to that. Goebbels was the man with the greatest official control of the press, and even if it was in Göring's interest to highlight Herr von Karajan, Goebbels could have ensured that it didn't happen so much to my disadvantage.' Van der Nüll, a writer for the *Berliner Zeitung* since 1933, was finally removed from his influential post by being called up to the Wehrmacht. (From the files of the Berlin De-Nazification Commission on Artists, second hearing of the trial of Dr Wilhelm Furtwängler, Tuesday, 17 December 1946. Copy in the possession of the author)

103. Rathkolb, p. 358. Rathkolb was the first to study the documents from Karajan's de-Nazification trial in the USA. The quotations published here are based on Rathkolb's valuable work, and backed up by the material that he has kindly shown to the author.

104. Stresemann, p. 132

105. From the statement of the freelance *Berliner Zeitung* employee, Annalise Theiler, to the Berlin De-Nazification Commission: 'It was undeniable that Dr van der Nüll was actually convinced that von Karajan the conductor deserved the spirited encouragement that he bestowed on him. He was actually enthusiastic beyond measure about Karajan's achievements ... He took a boyish pleasure in talking about what good terms he was on with Hermann Göring's Ministry. He always called it the "Hermann Ministry" ... Dr van der Nüll often told me that this "battle for Karajan" or "battle against Furtwängler" – the two were inseparable – had the *support* of Hermann Göring's immediate circle, and that he, Nüll, was not only egged on in this "battle" by that circle, but that playing Karajan off against Furtwängler was the "Hermann

Ministry's" own project, so to speak! . . . Extravagant praise, I would like to emphasize, was only possible when it was especially sanctioned or directly demanded by a "high authority". (From the files of the Berlin De-Nazification Commission on Artists, second hearing of the trial of Dr Wilhelm Furtwängler, Tuesday, 17 December 1946, copy in the possession of the author)

106. See Löbl, p. 6

107. Rathkolb, p. 358. According to the former production manager of Telefunken, Lucas (at the Berlin De-Nazification Commission's second hearing on Furtwängler), Karajan worked with Rudolf Vedder in 1936–7. Vedder 'immediately went great guns in favour of Karajan. Vedder was not overly selective in the means he used, and I know precisely that he particularly made use of his connection with the SS, above all with Herr von Alvensleben who, I think, was Himmler's personal adjutant at the time, and who spent a great deal of time in his company, often attending concerts with him; I often saw him with Alvensleben, trying to win his influence in Karajan's favour . . . Vedder had got himself into a very strong position with the help of the SS . . . Thanks to his lack of scruples, Vedder finally managed to worm his way into every little corner of the Third Reich.' Furtwängler had the following to say about Vedder to the Commission: 'Herr Vedder is one of the central issues in the whole business. He is completely inseparable from the van der Nüll case and the case of the 'Wunder' review. He was Karajan's agent, he was at the Staatsoper – *persona gratissima* – and his fight with me was partly a private one, whose origins I can explain to you if you want; but he formed a major part of this whole clique against me as a National Socialist.' And after the presentation of a letter containing references to Vedder, Furtwängler added: 'In saying that I only wanted to indicate that there were many people in musical life who had been fighting for years against Herr Vedder's terrorism, his dictatorship. This dictatorship was bigger and stronger than any other dictatorship in this field has ever been.' (From the files of the Berlin De-Nazification Commission of Artists, second hearing of the trial of Dr Wilhelm Furtwängler, Tuesday, 17 December 1946, copy in the possession of the author)

108. Memorandum from Otto de Pasetti to Captain Epstein, Head-quarters of US Forces in Austria, copy in the possession of the author

109. Muck, Vol. II, pp. 153f.

110. Ibid., pp. 154f.

111. Ibid., pp. 154f.

112. Goebbels, op. cit., NL 118.

113. In December 1934, in connection with his advocacy of Hindemith, Furtwängler resigned all his offices. In a conversation with Goebbels, however, he declared himself prepared to continue to make himself available as a conductor of the Berlin Philharmonic Orchestra. In the second hearing before the De-Nazification Commission, Furtwängler described the content of this conversation, on the basis of which he

placed himself at the service of the Nazi regime's cultural political struggle, in the following terms: 'At that time I conceded to Herr Goebbels that I would stay in Germany as a non-political artist, and he gave me the assurance that that was possible. I was protected, and believed I was protected, to the extent that I could do this.' (From the files of the Berlin De-Nazification Commission on Artists, second hearing of the trial of Dr Wilhelm Furtwängler, Tuesday, 17 December 1946, copy in the possession of the author)

114. Haeusserman, p. 74
115. Goebbels, op. cit., NL 118
116. Hauesserman, p. 73
117. Walter Hofer, *Der Nationalsozialismus, Dokumente 1933 bis 1945*, p. 297
118. Ibid., p. 298
119. Ibid., p. 297
120. Ibid., p. 289
121. Letter from Dr Oliver Rathkolb to the author, 12 November 1982
122. Memorandum from Otto de Pasetti to Captain Epstein, Headquarters of the US Forces in Austria, copy in the possession of the author
123. Vote by the commission of experts at the Federal Ministry of Education, Vienna, 25 March 1946. Authenticated copy in the possession of the author
124. We might also recall the escapades of Gustaf Gründgens and Göring's protection. See also Klaus Mann's novel, *Mephisto*
125. Letter from Fred K. Prieburg to the author, 14 November 1982
126. Letter from the Chancellery of the Führer of the NSDAP to the NSDAP Reich Treasurer, 19 November 1942. 'For the reason quoted I request you to inform me whether the above named is still listed as a member in the Reich files, and, if so, in which Ortsgruppe.' The reply to the Chancellery of the Führer of the NSDAP, 14 December 1942, confirms 'that the above named is listed as a member according to the entries in the Reich file with effect from 1 May 1933. Please note that a membership card was made out for the person named, on 13 July 1939.'
127. Letter from Karajan to a state secretary in the Propaganda Ministry, 14 August 1944. Source: Bundesarchiv – R 55/558–59
128. Letter from the President of the Reichskulturkammer to the Reichsleitung of the NSDAP, 4 April 1944. 'Re Staatskapellmeister Herbert von Karajan . . . The wife of the above named, Anna Marie Sauest, *née* Gütermann, born Cologne, 2.10.1917, is *one quarter Jewish*. As we now know, Karajan is said to be a member of the NSDAP. We request information as to whether this accords with the facts. By order: von Loebell.' The letter of 12 May 1944 contains a reminder of this correspondence 'since no answer has as yet been received.'
129. Letter from Oberbereichsleiter Schneider to the President of the Reichskulturkammer, 25 May 1944

130. Paul Moor, 'The Operator', *High Fidelity*, VII/10, October 1957. Source: UB Hannover Z 331, thanks to F. K. Prieberg

131. Haeusserman, p. 74

132. Stresemann, p. 134

133. Muck, Vol II, p. 180

134. Prieberg, pp. 20, 27 and 257

135. Interview between the author and Carl Gustav Rommenhöller, 1978

136. Goebbels, op. cit., NL 118

137. Source as 127

138. Muck, Vol II, pp. 177f.

139. Ibid., p. 176

140. See also: Berlin De-Nazification Commission, second Furtwängler hearing, 17 December 1946

141. Muck, Vol II, p. 180

142. See *Ibid.*, p. 181. The date has been established from these data.

143. Prieberg, p. 13

144. Ibid., p. 341

145. Ibid., p. 34

146. Ibid., pp. 175f.

147. Ibid., p. 203

148. F. Schmidt, 'Die Menschheit hungert nach Schönheit und Liebe', Karajan interview, *Welt am Sonntag*, No. 42, 1977

149. Prieberg, p. 261

150. Ibid., p. 397

151. Unfortunately, we must add. The role of intellectuals in the Third Reich is a whole subject in its own right. George Steiner tried to describe it with reference to Heidegger. In his essay he probes into Heidegger's intellectual responsibility as a philosopher in the Third Reich and his relationship with National Socialism beyond the level of superficial affinities of political opportunism, namely on the level of an essential affinity, which he seeks to prove with some linguistic examples. Steiner sees Heidegger's 'calculated silence' after 1945 as significantly more reprehensible than his behaviour in 1933–4. With this silence, according to Steiner, Heidegger's intellectual betrayal began. (See also Jürg Altwegg, *Der neue Verrat der Intellektuellen. Ein Gespräch mit George Steiner*, FAZ, No. 216, 1982.) In Stanislaw Lem's holocaust theory, which he puts into the mouth of his fictional author Horst Aspernicus in *Provocation*, he does not say 'that Heidegger or any of his kind was obliged to make a public stand for the victims of persecution . . . Rather the important thing is simply that Heidegger was a philosopher. Anyone dealing with the nature of human beings could not pass in silence over the crimes of the Nazis . . . The fact that a man called Heidegger was judged for the support that he personally gave the doctrines of the Nazis, but that this accusation was not directed against his works, reveals [. . .] a tacit agreement between guilty people. Everyone who agrees in granting this crime the lowest possible status in the scale of human existence is guilty.'

(S. Lem, *Provocation*, 1981, pp. 20–3.) An analysis of Karajan's interpretative history might tell us whether Karajan's membership of the Nazi Party was a matter of affinity or merely of political opportunism

3 The Empire

1. A. and M. Mitscherlich, *Die Unfähigkeit zu trauern*, 1982, p. 32
2. Ibid., p. 37
3. Ibid., p. 65
4. Ibid., p. 39
5. Haeusserman, p. 77
6. Ibid., p. 77
7. See; 'Ein Wunder wird siebzig', *Stern Magazin*, No. 15, 1978, p. 161
8. On this point, see also Freud's observations: 'For it seems very evident that another person's narcissism has a great attraction for those who have renounced part of their own narcissism and are in search of object-love. The charm of a child lies to a great extent in his narcissism, his self-contentment and inaccessibility, just as does the charm of certain animals which seem not to concern themselves about us, such as cats and the large beasts of prey.' (Freud, 'On Narcissism: An Introduction', Penguin Freud Library, Vol 11, pp. 82–3)
9. Haeusserman, p. 77
10. F. Schmidt, 'Die Menschheit hungert nach Schönheit und Liebe', Karajan interview, *Welt am Sonntag*, No. 42, 1977
11. Karajan was by no means alone in this. When questioned about her political past, Elisabeth Schwarzkopf remained silent about any relationship she might have had with the NSDAP, although she had joined the Party on 1 March 1940, with membership number 7548960. Because of the intentional forgery of three forms, the performance permit granted her by the Salzburg De-Nazification Commission was withdrawn again. Egon Hilbert had brought Schwarzkopf to the Vienna Staatsoper in the autumn of 1945, where she performed despite the fact that the first information about her Party membership had been released in Berlin. On 14 October 1946 Elisabeth Schwarzkopf finally received her performance permit, and set about building up her global career with Karajan, as the wife of the record producer Walter Legge. With the establishment of a singing seminar at the Herbert von Karajan Foundation in the summer of 1982, the artistic collaboration of the two former Party members was

completed: Karajan invited Elisabeth Schwarzkopf to foster and train a new generation of singers in Salzburg (see Rathkolb, pp. 390–4)

12. Rathkolb, p. 359
13. Ibid.: letter from Otto de Pasetti to Wolfgang Thomas, 18 December 1945, copy in the possession of the author
14. Memorandum from Otto de Pasetti to Captain Epstein, Headquarters of the US Forces in Austria, p. 3, copy in the possession of the author
15. See Rathkolb, p. 360: communiqué from Pasetti to US Headquarters, 13 January 1946, copy in the possession of the author
16. Ibid: memorandum fom Pasetti: Meeting with Captain Epstein, 13 January 1946, copy in the possession of the author
17. Ibid., pp. 363–4
18. Ibid., p. 263, documents of the Allied De-Nazification Bureau, 22 and 30 January 1946, copies in the possession of the author
19. See Haeusserman, pp. 276f.
20. *Bausteine zum deutschen Nationaltheater I/3*, December 1933, p. 67
21. Friedrich Nietzsche, *Kröner Taschenausgabe*, Vol 74, p. 245
22. Haeusserman, pp. 79f
23. 'Die alte Haut ist herunter', *Stern Magazin*, 30 March 1983, p. 63
24. See Rathkolb, p. 360f., memorandum from Pasetti: Meeting with Captain Epstein, copy in the possession of the author
25. Rathkolb, p. 365
26. The explanation for Hilbert's defence of politically incriminated artists lies not least in his desire to make his dream of a star-studded theatre a reality as soon as possible after the war. As Rathkolb reveals, a few weeks after his appointment as manager of the Landestheater in Salzburg, Hilbert defended politically dubious artists such as Böhm, Werner Kraus, Emil Jannings, Elisabeth Schwarzkopf and Karajan. 'The only known example of an "artist" who was persecuted by the National Socialists and subsequently received particular encouragement once he had regained his freedom, was that of a "music-lover" in the narrower sense of the word rather than a practising artist – Egon Hilbert. Before being imprisoned in Dachau concentration camp he had been a press attaché in Prague, and received a great deal of support from Pasetti. In a short time Hilbert, who was collecting news information for the D-Section of the ISB, rose from his position of temporary manager of the Salzburg Landestheater in September 1945 to the post of chief administrator of the Bundestheater in Vienna.' (Rathkolb, p. 331)
27. Rathkolb, p. 366: vote of the expert commission, 25 March 1946, copy in the possession of the author
28. Ibid., p. 366
29. Ibid., p. 368: letter from the four-part Division for Internal Affairs to the Federal Chancellor, 21 June 1946, copy in the possession of the author
30. Ibid., p. 379: letter from Chancellor Figl to the chairmen of the

four-part Division for Internal Affairs, 29 June 1946, copy in the possession of the author
31. Ibid., p. 370
32. Haeusserman, p. 83
33. Rathkolb, p. 369: letter from Dr Ernst Lothar to Baron Puthon, 6 April 1946, copy in the possession of the author
34. Ibid.: letter from Puthon to Lothar, 6 August 1946, copy in the possession of the author
35. Ibid., p. 376: letter from Colonel Norcross to Chancellor Figl, 17 September 1946, copy in the possession of the author
36. Ibid., p. 371: letter from Figl to the Allied Commission, 4 November 1946, copy in the possession of the author
37. Ibid., p. 371
38. Prieberg, pp. 30f.
39. See Haeusserman, p. 85
40. Dr Hajas, 'Karajan und die "Neunte" ', *Österreichische Zeitung*, 24 December 1947, p. 3
41. See Haeusserman, p. 93
42. 'That's why I couldn't get on with Wieland Wagner either. He rejected everything that had been done before, the wound was very deep, and in the process he simply left out everything that actually belonged there.' Interview with Karajan, *Der Spiegel*, No. 23, 1979
43. Muck, Vol. II, p. 235
44. Ibid., p. 232
45. Ibid., p. 240
46. Ibid., p. 232
47. Ibid., p. 240
48. Ibid., p. 247
49. Ibid., p. 265
50. Ibid., p. 266
51. Ibid., p. 269
52. Ibid., p. 269
53. Haeusserman, p. 96
54. Ibid., p. 96
55. Muck, vol. II, p. 256
56. Ibid., p. 269
57. Ibid., p. 272
58. Interview between the author and André Mattoni, 1980
59. See Haeusserman, p. 96
60. Stresemann, p. 137
61. Muck, Vol. II, p. 282
62. Ibid., p. 281
63. Ibid., pp. 280f.
64. Stresemann, pp. 138f.
65. Ibid., pp. 147f.
66. Muck, Vol. II, p. 290

67. Ibid., p. 292
68. Ibid., p. 293
69. F. Schmidt, 'Die Menschheit hungert nach Schönheit und Liebe', Karajan interview, *Welt am Sonntag*, No. 42, 1977
70. Interview between the author and Irmgard Seefried, 1978
71. See Rolf R. Bigler, *Zeitgenossen*, p. 58
72. Interview between the author and Carl Gustav Rommenhöller, 1978
73. Ibid.
74. Letter from Wolfgang von Karajan to the author, 1982
75. Paul Robinson, *Herbert von Karajan*, 1981, p. 127
76. Haeusserman, p. 287
77. Ibid., p. 188
78. Löbl, p. 115
79. *Neue Zeit*, Graz, 21 July 1964
80. Telegram from Lechner to Karajan, 24 July 1965, copy in the possession of the author
81. Letter from Professor Paumgartner to Landeshauptmann Lechner, 5 August 1964, copy in the possession of the author
82. Vienna, 1966, Schumann's Fourth Symphony, Mozart's Violin Concerto K. 219, with Menuhin
83. Herbert von Karajan in Salzburg, exhibition catalogue 1978, p. 39
84. Letter from Winifred Wagner to Karajan, 19 March 1967, copy in the possession of the author
85. Letter from Karajan to Clemens Holzmeister, 26 November 1965, copy in the possession of the author
86. Interview between the author and Professor Holzmeister, 1978
87. Will Quadflieg, *Wir spielen immer*, 1976, pp. 176f.
88. 'Journal', *Die Welt*, 17 April 1982, p. 15
89. See Löbl, p. 149
90. Reinhard Beuth, 'Bankrott einer Idee', *AT München*, 23 March 1978
91. Franz Endler, 'Nur Karajan kann da noch helfen', *Die Presse*, 25 March 1978
92. Horst Reischenböck, 'Karajan arbeitet gegen Troubadour-Sänger', *Salzburger Tagblatt*, 23 March 1978
93. Joachim Kaiser, 'Fidelio als symphonisches Melodram', *Süddeutsche Zeitung*, 27 March 1978. The Berlin Philharmonic 'had actually ceased to provide any human dimensions . . . but played in a broad, grandiose and even megalomaniac way that might well have been in the spirit of the Salzburg Festspielhaus, but which was unsuited to the mood of *Fidelio*, a hot-house mood yet one produced by human beings'.
94. Official programme, Salzburg Easter Festival 1968
95. Thomas Bernhard, *Die Ursache*, 1977, pp. 73f.
96. H.H. Stuckenschmidt, 'Zwischen Elite-Ästhetik und Manager-Konzeption', *FAZ*, 17 April 1976
97. Ibid.
98. See Haeusserman, p. 265

99. *Der Spiegel*, No. 18, 1980, p. 254
100. Monopol-Kultur, *FAZ*, 23 April 1980
101. Dieter Schnebel, *Das Schöne an Mahler*, programme of the concert on 30 September 1982, Berlin Philharmonic Orchestra, p. 113
102. Muck, Vol. II, pp. 473f.

4 On Staging

1. Peter Cossé, 'Karajan's *Parsifal* – ein Nachgeschmack von Langeweile', *Stereo*, No. 5, 1980, Munich, p. 9
2. Karlheinz Roschitz, 'Nur Marionettenoper', *Kronenzeitung*, Vienna, 23 March 1978
3. Joachim Neander, 'Karajans Hände . . .', *Die Welt*, No. 270, 1977
4. Interview between the author and Andreas von Bennigsen, 1980
5. 'Karajan-Kränkung', *FAZ*, No. 105, 1977; and 'Tief der Wiener Hochkultur', *Die Welt*, No. 98, 1977
6. Rudolf Bing, *5000 Abende in der Oper*, Munich 1973, pp. 292f.
7. Ibid., p. 292
8. 'Ganz hoch hinaus bei sibirischer Kälte', *FAZ*, 30 October 1982
9. 'Die alte Haut ist herunter', *Stern Magazin*, 30 March 1983, p. 60
10. Muck, Vol II, p. 474
11. Stresemann, pp. 246f.
12. 'Schlag ins Konto', *Der Spiegel*, 10 January 1983, pp. 114f.
13. 'Berliner Musikstreit', *FAZ*, No. 6, 1983
14. 'Knüppel aus dem Frack', *Der Spiegel*, No. 4, 1983, p. 173
15. Wolfgang Sandner, 'Kampf der Giganten', *FAZ*, No. 13, 1983
16. Stresemann, p. 259
17. Ibid., p. 150
18. Ibid., p. 150
19. Ibid., p. 156
20. Goethe, *Faust*, Part II, Act 5, Conclusion
21. Klaus Theweleit, *Männerphantasien*, Vol. I, 1977/1980, p. 293
22. Ibid., p. 394
23. Dietrich Mack, *Cosima Wagner, Briefe und Aufzeichnungen 1883–1930*, 26.3.1930
24. 'Ein Buch über Cosima Wagner', *NZZ*, No. 252, 1982
25. Peter Sager, 'Die Zeit', *Zeitmagazin*, No. 17, 1982, p. 39
26. *Der Spiegel*, No. 21, 1968, p. 152
27. Peter Sager, op. cit., No. 17, 1982, p. 39
28. Ibid., p. 39

29. Vojtech Jasny, *Fernsehfilm Karajan*, 1978
30. Interview between the author and Andreas von Bennigsen, 1980
31. Peter Sager, op. cit., p. 39
32. Stresemann, p. 261
33. William Bender, *Karajan – Künstler und Mensch*, Polydor International, 1977, pp. 22f.
34. Walter Panofsky, *Die 100 schönsten Konzerte*, 1977, p. 5
35. H.W. Müller, Karajan interview, *Fono Forum*, No. 4, 1978, p. 379
36. 'Rutsch rüber, hier kommt dein Präsident', *Der Spiegel*, No. 43, 1982, p. 22
37. William Bender, *Karajan – Künstler und Mensch*, Polydor International, 1977, p. 22
38. Interview between the author and Wolfgang von Karajan, 1980
39. Ursula Klein, *Herbert von Karajan, Festival 72*, Deutsche Grammaphon, p. 26
40. William Bender, op. cit., p. 22
41. *Der Spiegel*, No. 21, 1968, p. 148
42. Alois M. Haas, 'Aktualität der Mystik', *NZZ*, No. 43, 1981
43. Interview between the author and Wolfgang von Karajan, 1980
44. C.G. Jung, *Symbols of Transformation*, trans R.F.C. Hull, RKP 1956, pp. 356–7
45. Ibid.
46. Ibid.
47. Stanislaw Lem, *Provocation*, 1981, pp. 75 and 78
48. Will Quadflieg, op. cit., p. 250. Quadflieg describes the opposite experience in the case of his last encounter with the dead actor Albert Bassermann in the mortuary: 'There was something entirely sexless about his old corpse's face, it had both female and male features. It contained a thousand secret signs and runes, and was run through with the richness of a suffered destiny, beyond his own entelechy.'
49. Vojtech Jasny, op. cit.

5 The Cult of
Beautiful Illusion or
Streamline Aesthetics

1. H. v. Karajan, 'Die Menschheit hungert nach Schönheit und Liebe',
Magazin Welt am Sonntag, 22 June 1980, p. 4
2. 'Mein Nachfolger muß sich von selbst hervortun', Karajan interview,
Der Spiegel, No. 23, 1979, p. 188
3. H. v. Karajan, op. cit., p. 4
4. 'Ich mußte vieles in mir zerstören', Karajan interview, *Der Spiegel*,
No. 21, 1968
5. Rolf R. Bigler, op. cit., p. 64
6. Elias Canetti, *Crowds and Power*, 1973, pp. 458f.
7. T. W. Adorno, 'Einleitung in die Musiksoziologie', 1968, p. 117. For
the listener, as his audience, 'the maestro is both, a substitute for a
leader figure and a religion, and an expression of the victory of
technology and administration over music; in him they feel, now that
they too are musically subject to his administration, safe and secure'.
(Adorno, *Gesammelte Schriften*, Vol. 16, p. 66)
8. Carl Dahlhaus, *Der Dirigent als Statthalter*, Melos, No. 5, 1976, p.
371
9. Elias Canetti, op. cit., p. 459
10. Erich Fromm, *Die Seele des Menschen*, 1979, p. 88. 'Personalities
who are particularly narcissistic as individuals are best suited to this
function. The narcissism of the leader convinced of his own greatness
and free of doubts is precisely what attracts the narcissism of those who
subordinate themselves to him.' On the relationship between the leader
and the crowd, also seen in the relationship between the conductor and
the orchestra/audience, A. and M. Mitscherlich have the following to
say: 'There is a relationship of obedience to the leader, a relatioship
based on a severe lack of freedom. False consciousness, however,
experiences it as a sense of self, a feeling of liberation. Then something
paradoxical occurs: in their state of obedience crowds humble
themselves before leader-figures, in order to attain a new sense of self
[. . .] Their acute infatuation with the leader intensifies their
masochistic readiness for pleasure as well as their tendency to take action

against the enemies of the leader.' (A. and M. Mitscherlich, *Die Unfähigkeit zu trauern*, p. 74)

11. Alice Miller, *The Drama of the Gifted Child*, 1981, p. 58. 'It is thus impossible for the grandiose person to cut the tragic link between admiration and love. In this compulsion to repeat he seeks insatiably for admiration, of which he never gets enough because admiration is not the same thing as love, it is only a substitute gratification of the primary needs for respect, understanding, and being taken seriously – needs that have remained unconscious.'

12. Ibid., p. 62. 'Continuous performance of outstanding achievements may sometimes enable an individual to maintain the illusion of constant attention and availability of his self-object (whose absence, in his early childhood, he must now deny just as much as his own emotional reactions). Such a person is usually able to ward off threatening depression with increased displays of brilliance, thereby deceiving both himself and those around him.'

13. Ibid., p. 60. 'The grandiose person is never really free, first, because he is excessively dependent on admiration from the object, and second, because his self-respect is dependent on qualities, functions and achievements that can suddenly fail.'

14. Cf. A. and M. Mitscherlich, op. cit., p. 35

15. Cf. Heinz Kohut, 'Uber den Muskgenuß', in: *Introspektion, Empathie und Psychoanalyse*, 1977, pp. 195ff.

16. Friedrich Nietzsche, *Richard Wagner in Bayreuth*, Universalbibliothek, 1973, p. 33

17. Deutsche Grammophon bulletin on the *Matthew Passion*, 1973

18. Sigmund Freud, *Civilization and its Discontents*

19. Heinz Kohut, op. cit., pp. 213–15. 'There is hardly anything in music more affirmative than the end of a Beethoven symphony [. . .] The fact that the discharging of energy in the pleasure of true musicality occurs through largely musical means can be demonstrated with reference to Beethoven's symphonies. The triumphant intensity of the conclusion is the solution of the musical task that coincides with the composition's return to consonance, whose mastery is finally assured. This is the point when the greatest amount of energy is liberated, and the summit of pleasure reached. The fact that the musical composition reaches its victorious peak at this particular moment can only mean that the listener and the music have become emotionally as one – that the music now expresses and discharges the liberated energies of the listener. In identifying with the music, the listener has managed an external task. Through regression he has taken it to an earlier stage of his ego, which allows an ecstatic enjoyment of music. Part of this ego-stage is the most primitive form of coping, through incorporation and identification. At this point the ecstatic listener no longer makes a sharp distinction between himself and the external

world; he perceives the notes as emerging from himself, or even as a part of himself, because they are emotionally what he feels.'

20. See Klaus Theweleit, *Männerphantasien*, Vol. I, 1980, p. 437
21. 'Die alte Haut ist herunter', *Stern Magazin*, 30 March 1983, p. 56
22. H. Kohut, op. cit., pp. 215–16. 'After he has overcome the original menace of music, and after he has recognized, during the ludic repetition of the task of coping with it, that the feelings expressed in the music are his own, the listener finally attains a condition of fusion with the music; this extends his self so that it encompasses a whole primitive, non-verbal universe of notes. The ability to regress to this early ego state, while at the same time retaining the complicated ego functions required for the recognition and mastery of the ingress of organized notes, is the precondition for the enjoyment of music.'
23. In: B. Gavoty and R. Hauert, *Herbert von Karajan*, 1956, p. 5
24. In: Georges Bataille, *Les larmes d'Éros*
25. Klaus Theweleit, op. cit., Vol I, p. 447
26. When, in his discussion of the *Walküre*, on the occasion of the opening of the 1967 Easter Festival, Franz Endler indicates that parts of the stage set 'were embarrassingly reminiscent of the Nuremberg Rally' (*Die Press*, 21 March, 1967) and Jochen Schmidt speaks of 'neo-Salzburg kitsch' and the 'spirit of Speer's architecture for the Party rallies' in the stage sets of Schneider-Siemssen (*FAZ*, No. 100, 30 April 1983), both have raised a set of problems that had previously been conspicuously avoided.
27. H. Lesch, *Abendzeitung*, Munich, 22 August 1973
28. Interview between the author and Andreas von Bennigsen, 1980
29. H. H. Stuckenschmidt, 'Die Musen und die Macht', *FAZ*, No. 284, 1980
30. The compulsion to perfection clearly has the intensity of a craving, comparable to the fetishist's fixation on the fetish, as Kohut shows. 'Creative artists and scientists are also chained to their work with the intensity of the addict, and try to master and shape it with the powers and towards the purposes that are part of a narcissistically experienced world. They then attempt to recreate a perfection in their work which they previously experienced as a direct attribute of themselves.' (H. Kohut, *Die Zukunft der Psychoanalyse*, 1975, p. 158)
31. See also Adorno's observation about Toscanini: 'Like all pleasure in the mere functioning of things, his perfectionism was allied with something regressive.' (T. W. Adorno, op. cit., 'Die Meisterschaft des Maestro', p. 62)
32. Cf. Ibid., pp. 52f. In his essay on the history of Toscanini's interpretations, Adorno uses the concept of 'streamlining'. 'His performances sparked and glittered as if coated in chrome; the wheels of the apparatus meshed seamlessly, and their whirring conjured the illusion of inevitable necessity. Any resistance from the material, any threat of anything contingent or unforeseen seemed to be overcome

[. . .] To a degree, he brought the style of musical rendering to the level of rationalization, the "streamlining" that began to make its presence felt in Europe around the beginning of the thirties in technical utilities as well as the organization of economic and social institutions.'
33. Klaus Theweleit, op. cit., Vol. 2, p. 223. 'All the totality machines in which they function assume their ego-functions, and likewise mechanical machineries to which they "connect" themselves [. . .] It might almost be said that he uses them as a part of his body armour. This "ego" is always dependent on one of these supports; when they fail, it collapses and escapes the overwhelming influx and outbreak of life by means of its "containment mechanisms", de-differentiation, devitalization.' Theweleit is talking about male soldiers and their unstinting work for the good of the 'whole'.
34. The study of Karajan's interpretative history, still to be written, would be enriched by a closer examination of the question of whether, and, if so, to what extent, Paul Virilio's outlined philosophy of the windscreen, which attempts to describe the changes in perception of our mobile way of life, is applicable to Karajan's interpretative style. (Paul Virilio, 'Die Dromoskopie oder das Licht der Geschwindigkeit', in: *Konkursbuch*, No. 5, 1980)
35. Muck, Vol. II, p. 291
36. 'Where Karajan is, there is nonchalance as regards the dramatic moment, there is cold fascination, false perfection', says Franz Endler in a discussion of the *Walküre*. He describes Karajan's style as 'synthetic, clever-clever, no longer felt'. He also mentions the 'passion of deep-frozen people'. (*Die Presse*, 21 March 1967)
37. J. Kaiser, 'Wagner von morgen und gestern', *Die Zeit*, No. 13, 1970
38. H. J. Herbort, 'Aus Karajans Bilderbuch', *Die Zeit*, No. 16, 1974
39. W. Schreiber, *Süddeutsche Zeitung*, 28 July 1981
40. P. Wapnewski, 'Oper als ein Stück sakralen Kultes', *Die Zeit*, No. 15, 1980
41. F. Endler, 'Träumen zwischen Einmaligkeit und Mittelmaß', *Die Presse*, 1 April 1980
42. P. Cossé, 'Karajans Parsifal – ein Nachgeschmack von Langeweile', *Stereo*, No. 5, 1980, pp. 8f.
43. 'Karajan und Böhm sind maßlos überwertet', *Spiegel* interview, *Der Spiegel*, No. 47, 1980, pp. 224ff.
44. 'Mein Nachfolger muß sich von selbst hervortun', Karajan, interview, *Der Spiegel*, No. 23, 1979, p. 182
45. Karajan did not record *Threni* (Michael Tanner's note)
46. Alfred Beaujean, *HiFi Stereophonie*, No. 12, 1981. Beaujean sometimes reveals himself as a resolute champion of an aesthetic position directly opposed to Karajan's. On Karajan's recording of *Pelléas et Mélisande* (EMI 1C 165–03–650/52), he said (*HiFi Stereophonie*, No. 5, 1980, p. 604): 'Here neither darkness, vagueness nor aimless mellifluousness predominate; the unity of tension in

Pelléas, as described by Boulez, between static drama and the theatre of cruelty, are lost here in favour of a luxurious sensualism. As this production is a saleable commodity, from the point of view not only of the result but also of the preconditions of the production, I imagine Karajan's state of industrial consciousness as that of someone making jam, sometimes doing so as if he wanted to create a seething poison, but instead producing nothing but artificial honey. [...] If we compare Karajan's interpretation with Debussy's notes in the score, it is actually time to forbid this maestro to organize conducting competitions. What he allows himself in the form of caprice or thoughtlessness (it is difficult to say which predominates) borders on cultural permissiveness. This lack of concern – to put it mildly – with regard to what we can quite pragmatically identify as the desire of the composer, leads to the familiar Karajan "Blow-Up".'

47. A. Beaujean, *HiFi Stereophonie*, No. 8, 1979
48. 'Ein Wunder wird siebzig', Karajan interview, *Stern Magazin*, No. 14, 1978, p. 52
49. Cf. A. Miller, *The Drama of the Gifted Child*, p. 140. 'The inner necessity constantly to build up new illusions and denials, in order to avoid the experience of our own reality, disappears once this reality has been faced and experienced. [...] The situation is similar in regard to creativity. Here the prerequisite is the work of mourning and not a neurosis, although people often think it is the latter [...].'
50. Cf. H. Argelander, *Der Flieger*, 1980, p. 9. 'Some authors suppose that the narcissistic character includes the personality structures of the future. Bellak, for example: "I believe that a character structure will increasingly develop which we are used to considering a character disorder. It is marked by superficial and transitory object-relationships with a low level of subjective emotional involvement." '

Documents

1. Membership card of Party member and Generalmusikdirektor Herbert von Karajan from the NSDAP Reich Files. No mention is made of Karajan's claimed resignation from the Party in 1942.

2. Communiqué from the NSDAP-Reichsleitung, 5 January 1939, to the Finance and Party Authorities in Austria, 5 January 1939

3. Communiqué from Ortsgruppe V 'Neustadt'-Salzburg to the Gau treasurer of Salzburg NSDAP, 15 May 1939. 1 Schwarzstraße, the Party recruitment office according to this document, is the same address as Karajan's home; the Karajan family lived on the first floor of 1 Schwarzstraße, which contained three separate properties.

4. Letter from the Chancellery of the Führer of the NSDAP, Hauptamt für Gnadensachen [Head Office for the granting of pardons], Berlin, 19 November 1942, to the Reich treasurer of the NSDAP, Munich

5. Letter from the President of the Reichskulturkammer, 12 May 1944, to the Reichsleitung of the NSDAP, Munich, with the reply, 25 May 1944

6. *Westdeutscher Beobachter*, No. 272, 3 June 1939. *Manifestation of German Art*. From the Institut für Zeitungsforschung, Dortmund

7. Kreistag of the NSDAP, Aachen, City and District, 1939. Programme of the open-air performance of *Meistersinger (Festwiese)* in the Katschhof, 7 June 1939, conducted by Karajan. Source: W. Wesemann Archive, Aachen

8. Letter from Karajan to a state secretary in the Propaganda Ministry,

14 August 1944. Source: Bundesarchiv – R 55/558–59. With thanks to the Bundesarchiv, Koblenz

Translations of Documents

2.

From the Membership Office, NSDAP Reichsleitung, 5 January 1939
To the Finance and Party authorities in Austria

Re: Membership card application for Party Member Herbert von *Karajan*, Kapellmeister, b. 5.4.08, address: Aachen-Burtscheid, Eupenerstrasse
Membership No.   3 430 914
                 1 607 525

In letter ref 10 318, 6 July 1938, the Cologne-Aachen Gauleitung requests a membership card for Party Member Herbert von Karajan.
Before this request can be granted, von Karajan's membership must be clarified.
The entries in the Reich File concerning the membership of Party Member Herbert von Karajan read as follows:

8.4.1933 – joined with Party number 1 607 525 in Salzburg, Austria, address: Salzburg, Schwarzstr. 1
1.5.1933 – without any interim cancellation, joined once more with Party number 3 430 914 in Ortsgruppe Ulm (Gau Württemberg), address: Ulm, Stadttheater.

After various transfers, Herr von Karajan is currently registered in the Reich Files with Ortsgruppe Aachen (Gau Cologne-Aachen), address: Aachen-Burtscheid, Eupenerstrasse.

We request confirmation as to whether the membership effective as of 8 April 1933 came into effect with the delivery of Temporary Membership Card No. 1 607 525, and whether, and if so, for how long after this, membership contributions were paid. We request a prompt reply.

Heil Hitler!

3.

Ortsgruppe V, 'Neustadt'/Salzburg
To the Gau Treasurer of the NSDAP, Salzburg

Re: Herbert von Karajan, b. 5.4.08, address: Aachen-Burtscheid, Eupenerstrasse
Membership Number: 1 607 525

The inquiries of Ortsgruppe Neustadt with the purpose of examining the membership of the abovenamed produced the following:
Party Member Herbert *Klein*, Salzburg, Sigmunds Haffnergasse 16, confirms that in April 1933 he recruited Herbert von Karajan in Salzburg as a member for the NSDAP, and received from him 5 schillings as a recruitment fee, and also sent him the relevant certified registration form. Party Member Klein later handed in the registration form at the recruitment office in Salzburg, Schwarzstrasse 1
Shortly after the Party ban, Karajan left Salzburg and moved to the old Reich.
Party Member Klein never heard anything more from him, and thinks it possible that Karajan did not pay any Membership contributions in Austria. In order to refute this suspicion, Karajan would have to provide further information so that this could be examined.

Heil Hitler.

4.

Hauptamt für Gnadensachen
To: Reich Treasurer of the NSDAP, Membership Office
24.11.42

Re: Herbert von Carajan [sic], b. 5 April 1908, Membership No: 3 430 914, previously Berlin-Schöneberg, Rosenheimerstrasse.

For the reason quoted I request you to inform me whether the abovenamed is still listed as a member in the Reich files, and, if so, in which Ortsgruppe.

Heil Hitler!

5.

President of the Reichskulturkammer
To the Reichsleitung der NSDAP, Munich, 'Braunes Haus'
12 May 1944

Re: State Kapellmeister Herbert von Karajan, b. 5.4.1908, in Salzburg
address: Aachen, Salier-Allee 41 (?)
Ref: Letter of 4.4.44
You were asked for information as to whether Karajan, who is married
to the quarter-Jewess Anna, Marie Sauest, née Güterman, is a member
of the NSDAP.

As we have not yet received an answer, we repeat our request for the
matter to be carried out.

To the President of the Reichskulturkammer
25 May 1944

In response to your enquiry of 4.4.1944, I should like to give you
the following information re: the membership of Herbert von Karajan.
According to the notes in the Reich File, Herr von Karajan joined the
Party with membership number 3 430 914 in Ortsgruppe Salzburg. Party
Member Herbert von Karajan is currently enrolled as a member in
the Reich Files, in Ortsgruppe Aachen/Gau Cologne-Aachen, with the
address: Eupenerstrasse

8.

Sanatorium Dr von Dapper
Bad Kissingen
14 May 44

Dear Herr Staatssekretär! Further to my suggestion with regard to Feldpost number 00080: I should like to request that the Reichsminister
authorize the Reichs-Brucknerorchester to make recordings with me for
the 'Immortal Music' series. I have conducted the orchestra recently and
can absolutely vouch for its quality. My reasons: the increased possibility
of the use of the orchestra and the lessening likelihood of recordings
being threatened or jeopardized by air raids. I also believe it is in your
interest to allow me involvement in the recordings more than once during
the run of the broadcasts, which will soon have gone on for a year. The
orchestra still has dates free. If your decision is positive I shall get in
touch immediately. With my very best regards to the Reichsminister and
best wishes to yourself

– Heil Hitler – Herbert von Karajan

Name _von Kerssen_ _Herbert_

G. D. _5. 4. 00_ Ort _S._

Stand _Jan. Musikdirektor_ _Kapellmeister_

Mitgl.-Nr. _1607575_ Eingetr. _7. 4. 33_

Aufnahme ungültig lt. R.L./Oe. vom 21. 7. 39.

Ausgetr. _____

Wieder-Eingetr. _1. 5. 33._ **— 3 430 914**

Wohnung _S._ _Schrangstr. 1_

O.-Gr. _Salzburg_ Gau **Oesterreich**
1. 5. 33.

Wohnung _U._

O.-Gr. _Ulm_ Gau _Württbg._
Württbg. 3. 35. 123 u. ausw. 7. 35 / 33 / m.

Wohnung _B._

O.-Gr. _Berlin_ Gau _Berlin_

Nationalsozialistische Deutsche Arbeiterpartei
Reichsleitung

Verwaltungsbau der NSDAP.
München, Arcisstraße 10
Briefanschrift: München 33
Fernruf: Ortsverkehr 5708 - Fernverkehr 51031
Postscheckkonto München 23310

Zentralorgan der Partei:
„Völkischer Beobachter"
Verlag: München, Thierschstr. 11, J 221 31
Berlin, Zimmerstr. 88, J A 1 Jäger 0022
Schriftleitung: München, Schellingstr. 30, J 20801
Berlin, Zimmerstr. 88, J A 1 Jäger 0022

Reichsschatzmeister
An: Mitgliedschaftsamt

Unser Zeichen und Geschäfts-
ist bei Antwort stets anzugeben: K Va Dr.H/Bs/Rö.
1.39

Ihr Zeichen:

Gegenstand:
Buchantrag für den Pg. Herbert von Karajan, Kapellmeister, geb. 5.4.08, wohnhaft: Aachen-Burtscheid, Eupenerstrasse
Mitglieds-Nummer 3 430 914
1 607 525

München, den 5. Januar 1939.

An die

Finanz- und Parteiverwaltung
in Österreich

- Mitgliedschaftswesen -

W i e n XIX

Mit Laufschreiben Nummer 10 318 vom 6. Juli 1938 stellt die Gauleitung Köln-Aachen für den Parteigenossen Herbert v o n K a r a j a n Antrag auf Ausstellung des Mitgliedsbuches.

Bevor dem Buchantrag stattgegeben werden kann, ist die Mitgliedschaft des Genannten zu klären.

Die Eintragungen in der Reichskartei über die Mitgliedschaft des Parteigenossen Herbert von Karajan lauten wie folgt:

8.4.1933   aufgenommen unter der M.Nr. 1 607 525 bei der ehem. Ogr. Salzburg/Österreich mit der Anschrift: Salzburg, Schwarzstr. 1

1.5.1933   ohne zwischenzeitliche Abmeldung wiederaufgenommen unter der M.Nr. 3 430 914 bei der Ortsgruppe Ulm (Gau Württemberg) mit der Anschrift: Ulm, Stadttheater.

Nach verschiedenen Ummeldungen wird der Genannte zur Zeit bei der Ortsgruppe Aachen (Gau Köln-Aachen) mit der Anschrift: Aachen-Burtscheid, Eupenerstrasse in der Reichskartei geführt.

Keine Karteikartei

Registratur kein Vorgang

.../.

Es wird um Feststellung gebeten, ob die
Aufnahme mit Wirkung vom 8. April 1933 durch Aushändi-
gung der Provisorischen Mitgliedskarte Nr. 1.607.525
in Kraft getreten ist, ferner ob und gegebenenfalls für
welche Zeit nach dieser Aufnahme Mitgliedsbeiträge ent-
richtet wurden.

Einer baldigen Rückäusserung wird entge-
gengesehen.

H e i l   H i t l e r !
i.A.

NSDAP

Gau Salzburg

Ortsgruppe V „Neustadt' / Salzburg

Rainerstraße Nr. 4/I links

Ruf Nr. 13-22

Salzburg, am 15.Mai 1939.

Betrifft: Ihr Zeichen: Unser Zeichen:

Herbert v.Karajan   P Vark./Dre./ We.II.39.   735/39

An den

Gauschatzmeister der NSDAP

S a l z b u r g .

Gegenstand: Herbert v.K a r a j a n.geb.5.4.08 wohnhaft :
            Aachen-Burtscheid.Eupenerstrasse
            Mitgliedsnummer :1 607 525

Die Erhebungen der Ortsgruppe Neustadt zwecks Mitglied-
schaftsnachweisung des Obgenannten haben zu folgenden
Ergebnis geführt:

Pg.K l e i n Herbert,Salzburg.Sigmunds Haffnergasse 16
bestätigt,dass er im April 1933 den Herbert v.Karajan
in Salzburg als Mitglied für die NSDAP geworben hat und
von ihm S 5.- als Werbebetrag erhalten und ihm auch den
dafür bescheinigten Anmeldzettel ausgefolgt hat.Pg.Klein
hat den Anmeldeschein nachher bei der Werbestelle in
Salzburg,Schwarzstrasse 1 abgegeben.

Kurz nach dem Parteiverbot hat Karajan Salzburg verlassen
und ist in das Altreich übersiedelt.

Pg.Klein hat von ihm nie mehr etwas gehört und ist die
Vermutung nicht von der Hand zu weisen,dass Karajan in
Österreich keine Mitgliedsbeiträge bezahlte.Zur Entkräft-
igung dieser Vermutung,müsste K.nähere Angaben machen,um
diese nachprüfen zu können.

Heil Hitler

Der Ortsgruppenleiter.

Kanzlei des Führers
der NSDAP.

Haupt- Amt für Gnadensachen

Aktenzeichen: III r - 201 055 ay/

Eingegangen
20. NOV. 1942 KA
Netzeichme ... NSD... Berlin W8, den 19. November 42
Nummer ...-44 Voßstraße 4
24. II. 42 Fernruf: Ortsverkehr 12 00 54
Fernverkehr 12 66 21

An den
Reichsschatzmeister der NSDAP.
Amt für Mitgliedschaftswesen
M ü n c h e n 33.

SIEHE
HINWEIS

Betr.: Herbert von C a r a j a n, geb. 5. April 1908, Mitgliedsnummer: 3 430 914, früher Berlin-Schöneberg,
Rosenheimerstrasse.

Aus gegebener Veranlassung bitte ich Sie, mir mitzuteilen,
ob der Obengenannte noch als Mitglied in der Reichskartei,
gegebenenfalls bei welcher Ortsgruppe, geführt wird.

Heil Hitler!
I. V.

Oberbereichsleiter.

Der Präsident
der Reichskulturkammer

Geschäftszeichen: RKK - K 50

(In der Antwort anzugeben)

15. MAI 1944

Berlin, den 12. Mai 1944
W 15, Schlüterstrasse 45
Fernspr. 92 8011

An die

Reichsleitung der NSDAP.,

M ü n c h e n
"Braunes Haus"

Betrifft: Staatskapellmeister Herbert von K a r a j a n ,
geb. 5. 4. 1908 in Salzburg
wohnh.: Aachen, Salier-Allee 41(?)

Bezug: Hiesiges Schreiben vom 4. 4. 44

Sie wurden um Mitteilung gebeten, ob Karajan, der mit der
Vierteljüdin Anna, Marie Sauest geborene Gütermann verhei-
ratet ist, Mitglied der NSDAP. ist.

Da bisher eine Antwort nicht eingegangen ist, wird an die Erledigung der Angelegenheit erinnert.

Im Auftrage:

gez. von Loebell

beglaubigt:

C/LMS

X Va Schn/Wa.

RKK - K5o

Mitgliedschaft des Pg.
Herbert von K a r a j a n,
geb.5.4.1908, ~~wohn.:~~
Aachen, Salier Allee 41;
Mitglieds-Nummer: 3 430 914.

25.Mai 1944

30. 5 44

An den
Präsidenten der
Reichskulturkammer

B e r l i n W 15

Schlüterstrasse 45

In Erledigung Ihrer Anfrage vom 4.4.1944
teile ich Ihnen bezüglich der Mitgliedschaft des Herbert
von K a r a j a n nachstehendes mit:

Gemäß den Aufzeichnungen in der Reichskartei
ist der Genannte am 1.5.1933 unter der Mitgliedsnummer
3 430 914 bei der Ortsgruppe Salzburg in die NSDAP aufgenommen worden. Z.Zt. wird der Parteigenosse Herbert
von K a r a j a n bei der Ortsgruppe Aachen/Gau Köln-Aachen
mit der Anschrift: Eupenerstrasse als Mitglied in der
Reichskartei geführt.

(Schneider)
Oberbereichsleiter.

Westdeutscher Beobachter

Köln-Stadt V

Amtliches Organ der NSDAP. und sämtlicher Behörden / Ausgabe Köln (Stadt)

Nr. 272 / Jahrgang 15   Morgen-Ausgabe, Samstag, 3. Juni 1939   Preis 10 Pf.

Festaufführung in der Staatsoper

Manifestation deutscher Kunst

Der Führer mit seinen Gästen bei der Festvorstellung der „Meistersinger"

Berlin, 3. Juni

Eine Infanterieabteilung beim Vorbeimarsch

Heute Besuch in Potsdam

Kranzniederlegung am Grabe Friedrichs des Großen

Berlin, 3. Juni

Für Samstag, den 3. Juni 1939, hat in Rahmen des jugoslawischen Staatsbesuches folgende Veranstaltungen festgelegt:

Um 10.30 Uhr empfängt Prinzregent Paul von Jugoslawien den Oberbürgermeister von

(Fortsetzung siehe 2. Seite)

Noch 85 Mann in der „Thetis" eingeschlossen

Die englische Admiralität schweigt – Luftvorrat noch bis Samstag – Hilfsschiffe unterwegs

(Drahtbericht unseres eigenen Vertreters)

W. J. London, 3. Juni

Die große Truppenparade zu Ehren des jugoslawischen Staatsbesuches. Der Führer und sein hoher Gast nehmen den Vorbeimarsch ab. Rechts: Eine Abteilung der Fallschirmtruppen vor der Ehrentribüne

Freilichtaufführung auf dem Katschhof

Die Meistersinger von Nürnberg
(III. Akt: Festwiese)

von Richard Wagner

Musikalische Leitung: Herbert von Karajan — Szenische Leitung: Anton Ludwig — Dekorative Gestaltung: Paul Pilov
Chorleitung: Wilhelm Pitz

P E R S O N E N :

Hans Sachs, Schuster	Arthur Bard
Veit Pogner, Goldschmied	Emmerich Marbod
Kunz Vogelsang, Kürschner	Hermann Schmid-Berikoven
Konrad Nachtigall, Spengler	Wilhelm Graf
Sixtus Beckmesser, Stadtschreiber	Frodewin Illert
Fritz Kothner, Bäcker	Willi Schmitz
Balthasar Zorn, Zinngießer	Alois Orth
Ulrich Eislinger, Würzkrämer	Hubert Kutsch
Augustin Moser, Schneider	Carl Schmitz
Hermann Ortel, Seifensieder	Kurt Joussen
Hans Schwarz, Strumpfwirker	Heinz Roslowski
Hans Foltz, Kupferschmied	Otto Mundhenk
Walter von Stolzing, Ritter aus Franken	Bernd Alderhoff
	vom Opernhaus Düsseldorf a. G.
David, Sachsens Lehrbube	Christoph Reuland
Eva, Pogners Tochter	Ria Beckhaus a. G.

Bürger und Frauen aller Zünfte, Gesellen, Lehrbuben, Mädchen und Volk

Ort: Nürnberg — Zeit: Mitte des 16. Jahrhunderts

Der Chor des Stadttheaters ist durch die Extra-Chöre des Stadttheaters, den Männergesangvereinen Harmonia,
Aachen-Forst, Schubert-Chor, sowie durch die Damen des städtischen Gesangvereins verstärkt.

Technische Einrichtung: Peter Kreutz — Ausführung der Kostüme: Anneliese Moeller und Matthieu Görtzen

Sitzplatz: RM 2,—, Stehplatz RM 1,—,
Stehplatz für Jugendliche RM 0,25.

Anfang 18 Uhr   Ende gegen 18.45 L

HERBERT v. KARAJAN

Sanatorium Dr. v. Dapper
Bad Kissingen   14. Aug. 44.

59

Sehr verehrter Herr Staatssekretär!

<u>Anbei</u> mein Vorschlag zu Feldpostnummer 00080 :
Der Herr Reichsminister möchte seine Genehmigung dazu geben dass das <u>Reichs-Brucknerorchester</u>

mit mir Aufnahmen für die „Unsterbliche Musik" macht. Ich habe das Orchester kürzlich dirigiert und kann es qualitativ absolut vertreten.

<u>Gründe</u>. Die grössere Möglichkeit des Einsatzes und der Wegfall der Gefährdung oder Infragestellung der Aufnahmen durch Fliegeralarm

Ausserdem glaube ich ist es in Ihrem Sinne
wenn ich bei ,der nun bald einjährigen Dauer
,der Sendung öfter als ein einziges Mal zu Wort
komme.

Orchester hat noch Daten frei . Bei positiver
Entscheidung setze ich mich sofort ins Benehmen

Mit verbindlichen Empfehlungen an den Herrn
Reichsminister und besten Grüssen an Sie

Aur Hitler

[Unterschrift]

Index

362

363

368

369